A strong vocabulary—your key to

- a more challenging and rewarding job
- greater self-confidence in speaking and writing
- improved comprehension in all your reading
- success in your studies

Convinced that memorizing lists of words was both difficult and unrewarding, Ida Ehrlich developed a direct and successful method of vocabulary building, based on the keys to the English language.

- Each key is clearly defined and discussed.
- Examples are provided showing the role of the key in a variety of words.
- Selected words are analyzed showing how keys combine within words, preparing you to integrate your knowledge of a variety of keys.
- Practical exercises—with answers—allow you to test your comprehension and to delight in your progress.

By using your knowledge of familiar words you will soon master the secret of vocabulary building—starting with the thousands of words in this book.

Instant Vocabulary

Ida L. Ehrlich

PUBLISHED BY POCKET BOOKS NEW YORK

Another *Original* publication of POCKET BOOKS

POCKET BOOKS, a Simon & Schuster division of
GULF & WESTERN CORPORATION
1230 Avenue of the Americas, New York, N.Y. 10020

Copyright © 1968 by Simon & Schuster,
a division of Gulf & Western Corporation

ISBN: 0-671-83042-2

First Pocket Books printing March, 1968

16   15   14   13   12

POCKET and colophon are trademarks of Simon & Schuster.

Printed in the U.S.A.

To Peter

CONTENTS

PREFACE

The origin of this book lies in an experience which I had when I began to teach in junior high school nineteen years ago.

My eighth-grade class had an excellent reader full of literary gems, one of which was Henry Wadsworth Longfellow's *Evangeline*. I looked forward to glorious days of leading young people into the many byways of good literature. Consequently, I was shocked to find that the students refused to tackle the poem. They argued that the vocabulary was so far beyond them that they would have to use the dictionary all the time.

The poverty of their language was appalling! They had been reading digests and simplifications. They had had no meaningful contact with the beauty of great writing. They wanted to read poems like *Evangeline*, but they were also practical. I had to admit that in the struggle for comprehension much of the grace and beauty would be lost.

The English of great literature was a foreign language to them. What to do about this problem?

We devised a plan: four boys volunteered to look up the words needed for the daily assignment in reading, each one responsible for one fourth of the list. We called these boys Dictionary Dicks.

I read the poem aloud while the class silently followed the text in their readers. When a word was not understood, it was asked for by a raised hand, and the boy who had that word on his list supplied the meaning.

Each day, as the poem unfolded, the enjoyment of the reading increased. I shall never forget the emotion of this class when I read the end of *Evangeline*. It was a memorable experience for all. Of course they wanted more of the same. But I refused. I assured them that their enjoyment would have been many times greater if they had done the reading themselves. They believed me and were eager to learn how to read fine literature. We discussed the problem and, as usual, the solution turned out to be very simple:

Build a strong vocabulary!

It was then that I began my system of KEY building: the system you will find in this book. The method is simple, interesting, and always rewarding. It is an infallible method of vocabulary building.

One KEY a day opens the door to mastery of the English language. I guarantee that if you learn only the KEYS you will know the words. Every KEY has many words. *Do not try* to memorize them! Merely read and understand. Then use them in the practical exercises on the facing pages. Soon your vocabulary will expand greatly and you will begin to understand new words instantly. . . . You will possess an *instant vocabulary*.

You will find the proof of this statement on page 521. There you will find a test to give yourself and readings. You will see that you know the meaning of the longest word in the *Webster's New International Dictionary of the English Language*—a word of forty-five letters. When you read the passages you will understand them.

I am convinced. *You* try it and convince yourself.

You will immediately get into the habit of looking for KEYS to word meaning. You will recognize the KEYS. You will be amazed at the speed of your vocabulary enrichment, at the ease with which you will be able to understand the most difficult words in the language.

PROCEDURE

Look at the Key.
Close your eyes and visualize it.
Look over the list of words.
Read the brief introductory paragraph.
Study the list of words:
>   Pronounce each word carefully.
>   Read the meaning of each word.
Look at the word analysis. It is the model for your own analysis.
Work out the practical exercises.
Check your answers.

Take another look at the key.

The only thing you need remember is the key.

REMEMBER THE KEY AND YOU WILL RECOGNIZE IT THE INSTANT YOU SEE IT AGAIN.

Ida Ehrlich
Brooklyn, N. Y.

PUBLISHER'S NOTE

While you work with this book you will become aware of many words that do not seem usable. Why are they included? They are present to reinforce your ability to recognize keys. Often the long technical words offer a perfect opportunity to show many keys in combination. Some of the words are now obsolete or rare, but when you read old books you encounter them. Therefore it has been necessary to combine the practical everyday words with words that are of interest primarily because they demonstrate the diversity and richness of the language. The words you encounter frequently are given a pronunciation based on those listed for them in *Webster's Seventh New Collegiate Dictionary*. This is a wonderful desk dictionary. The words not found in this volume have been based upon the pronunciations and meanings presented in *Webster's New International Dictionary of the English Language*, Second Edition—the dictionary that has been the authoritative dictionary for many years.

INSTANT
VOCABULARY

KEY NO. *1*

0—⚷

Y.

**inclined to
tend to**

is the Suffix *Y* which means IN-
CLINED TO; TEND TO. It is a very
valuable KEY because it shows its
effectiveness so clearly. That single
letter added to a root word has an
immediate and powerful effect. It
characterizes, not the root word, but
the person to whom the adjective is
applied. Example: *smart* is a compli-
mentary word, of genuine praise;
smarty shows up a fake. Being shown
this difference has changed many a
smart-aleck into a genuinely smart
person.

1. cheery   cheer Y (cheer′ ee) adj.
       Tends to see the bright side; cheerful.

2. catty   catt Y (kat′ ee) adj.
       Tends to be stealthy; spiteful.

3. arty   art Y (art′ ee) adj.
       Inclined to be artistic but not really so.

4. crafty   craft Y (kraf′ tee) adj.
       Inclined to be sly; tricky.

5. furry   furr Y (fur′ ee) adj.
       Tends to be covered with fur.

6. dreary   drear Y (dreer′ ee) adj.
       Tends to be dull; as, a dreary day.

7. faulty   fault Y (faul′ tee) adj.
       Inclined to be at fault.

8. dirty   dirt Y (dirt′ ee) adj.
       Tends to be unclean; soiled.

9. smarty   smart Y (smar′ tee) adj.
       Inclined to be tricky; smart-alecky.

10. foxy   fox Y (fok′ see) adj.
       Tends to be a bit sly, like a fox.

11. hairy   hair Y (hair′ ee) adj.
       Tends to have more hair than needed.

12. itchy   itch Y (ich′ ee) adj.
       Inclined to itch; bothersome.

13. misty   mist Y (mis′ tee) adj.
       Tends to be obscured by a slight mist.

14. pretty   prett Y (prit′ ee) adj.
       Tends to beauty but has not quite reached it.

15. rosy   ros Y (roze′ ee) adj.
       Tends to be pinkish, like a rose.

16. salty	salt Y (sal' tee) adj.
	Tends to taste of salt.
17. sleepy	sleep Y (sleep' ee) adj.
	Inclined to sleep; not wide awake.
18. slinky	slink Y (slink' ee) adj.
	Inclined to slither, like a snake.
19. wary	war Y (ware' ee) adj.
	Tends to be watchful; on guard.

word analysis

SMARTY—No. 9
    SMART—Root = bright; clever
    Y—Suffix = inclined to; tend to

practical exercises

1. Supply the missing words:
    It is praiseworthy to be artistic, but to be ....
    is mere pretense. He who is .... of dirt will
    not, himself, become ....

2. Analyze No. 4.

3. Supply one word to express the phrase:
    Example: bright and cheerful   ....sunny....
    a. like a snake   ....
    b. with many errors   ....
    c. remarks that are spiteful   ....
    d. pink like a rose   ....

KEY NO. 2

AR · ER · OR

one who
that which

is the Suffix which has three spellings, *AR—ER—OR*, meaning ONE WHO or THAT WHICH. This is one of the simplest keys to remember and you will see a great deal of it. It is listed so that you will become accustomed to seeing words, not as one lump to be swallowed whole, but as a combination of keys which are to be recognized separately.

1. doctor   doct OR (dok' tor) n.
   One who is learned, especially in medicine.

2. baker   bak ER (bake' er) n.
   One who bakes.

3. actor   act OR (ak' tor) n.
   One who acts a part in a play or in an event.

4. fighter   fight ER (fite' er) n.
   One who fights.

5. beggar   begg AR (beg' ar) n.
   One who begs.

6. dancer   danc ER (dan' ser) n.
   One who dances.

7. jester   jest ER (jes' ter) n.
   One who tells jokes.

8. killer   kill ER (kil' er) n.
   One who kills.

9. liar   li AR (lie' er) n.
   One who tells lies.

10. miser   mis ER (mize' er) n.
    One who lives miserably in order to hoard money.

11. toiler   toil ER (toil' er) n.
    One who works hard.

12. tractor   tract OR (trak' tor) n.
    A machine used on the farm for drawing a plow.

13. barber   barb ER (bar' ber) n.
    One whose work is to give shaves and haircuts.

14. wrecker   wreck ER (rek' er) n.
    Machinery used to break down buildings and remove the wreckage.

15. painter   paint ER (pane' ter) n.
    One who paints.

4

16. sufferer   suffer ER (suf' er er) n.
One who suffers, especially from a disease.
17. exhibitor   exhibit OR (eg zib' it or) n.
One who shows things to the public, as art.
18. racer   rac ER (rase' er) n.
One who races in a sport event.
19. amplifier   amplifi ER (am' pli fie er) n.
That which magnifies sound, a loud speaker.
20. pacifier   pacifi ER (pas' i fie er) n.
That which quiets, like a ring for babies to suck or bite on.

word analysis

PACIFIER—No. 20
    PAC (*pacis*)—Latin Root =peace
    FI (*fy*) (facere)—Latin Suffix =make
    ER—Suffix =one who; that which

practical exercises

1. Supply the missing words:
    The .... and the .... soon had the land cleared of the old tenements. The .... gave the .... a sedative.

2. Analyze No. 15.

3. Choose the number which best expresses the italicized word:
    Example: *tractor*   (1) doctor   (2) farm machinery
            (3) toil   (4) dancer   (5) baker   ....2....
    a. *jester*   (1) sings   (2) fights   (3) paints
         (4) tells jokes   (5) is a barber   ....
    b. *crafty*   (1) gay   (2) jolly   (3) silly
         (4) easy   (5) tricky   ....
    c. *rosy*   (1) pale   (2) fat   (3) sly
         (4) pinkish   (5) showy   ....

KEY NO. *3*

RE

**back
again**

is the Prefix *RE* which means BACK;
AGAIN. It is a very simple key and
here it is used with simple root words.
The only word in the list which is a
bit difficult is No. 8 and that is analyzed for complete understanding.
You will meet *RE* again later with
more difficult words. Just now, remember that *RE* means BACK;
AGAIN.

1. rebuild	RE build (re bild′) v.	
	Build again.	
2. recall	RE call (re kal′) v.	
	To bring back to mind; remember.	
3. recede	RE cede (re sede′) v.	
	Go back, as the tide will recede at 4 P.M.	
4. redye	RE dye (re die′) v.	
	Color again.	
5. reflect	RE flect (re flekt′) v.	
	Throw back, as a mirror will reflect *an image.*	
6. refold	RE fold (re fold′) v.	
	Fold again, as refold *a letter.*	
7. regain	RE gain (re gane′) v.	
	Get back, as regain *health.*	
8. reiterate	RE iterate (re it′ er ate) v.	
	Say again; repeat.	
9. rejoin	RE join (re join′) v.	
	Come together again, as rejoin *the company.*	
10. relate	RE late (re late′) v.	
	Tell again, as relate *a story.*	
11. relive	RE live (re liv′) v.	
	Live over again, as relive *a happy moment.*	
12. remarry	RE marry (re ma′ ree) v.	
	Marry again.	
13. remind	RE mind (re minde′) v.	
	Mention again, as remind *me to buy bread.*	
14. repay	RE pay (re pay′) v.	
	Pay back, as repay *a loan.*	
15. repeat	RE peat (re pete′) v.	
	Say again; reiterate (see No. 8).	
16. resell	RE sell (re sel′) v.	
	Sell again, as buy a house and resell *it.*	
17. return	RE turn (re turn′) v.	
	Come back, as return *home.*	

18. reverse   RE verse (re vers') v.
                Turn about; make a complete change, as,
                reverse *judgment.*

19. rewarm   RE warm (re warm') v.
                Heat again, as rewarm *supper.*

20. rewrite   RE write (re rite') v.
                Write again, as rewrite *a story.*

word analysis

REITERATE—No. 8
     RE—Latin Prefix =again; back
     ITER (*iterum*)—Latin Root =a second time
     ATE—Suffix =cause; make

practical exercises

1. Supply the missing words:
     I shall .... my family when I ....
from Paris.

2. Analyze No. 2.

3. Look at the following list and recognize the keys you have
had so far and underline them:
     pretty   scanty   repay
     dancer   peculiar   reside
     tractor   mover   motor

KEY NO. 4

UN

not

is the Prefix *UN* which means NOT. It is the first of the negative keys which you will meet. It is a very satisfactory negative. It says NO! and it means just that and nothing else.

1. unable   UN able (un ay' b'l) adj.
   Not having the skill to do something.
2. unabridged   UN abridged (un a brijd') adj.
   Not shortened.
3. unclothed   UN clothed (un klothd') adj.
   Not dressed; naked.
4. unadvanced   UN advanced (un ad vansd') adj.
   Not having gone forward.
5. unalloyed   UN alloyed (un a loid') adj.
   Not mixed; pure.
6. unadorned   UN adorned (un a dornd') adj.
   Not fancy; simple.
7. unambitious   UN ambitious (un am bish' us) adj.
   Not eager to get ahead.
8. unaffected   UN affected (un a fek' ted) adj.
   Not touched; unconcerned.
9. unaltered   UN altered (un al' terd) adj.
   Not changed.
10. uneducated   UN educated (un ed' yu kate ed) adj.
    Not learned.
11. unfinished   UN finished (un fin' ishd) adj.
    Not ended, as an unfinished *story.*
12. unhurried   UN hurried (un hur' eed) adj.
    Not in a rush; slow.
13. unknown   UN known (un none') adj.
    Not recognized; strange.
14. unloved   UN loved (un luvd') adj.
    Not cherished.
15. unread   UN read (un red') adj.
    Not read.
16. unspoken   UN spoken (un spoe' ken) adj.
    Not stated orally; not said.
17. untouched   UN touched (un tuchd') adj.
    Not touched.
18. untouchable   UN touchable (un tuch' a b'l) adj.
    Cannot be touched.

19. unwelcome   UN welcome (un wel' kum) adj.
      Not received graciously; unwanted.

word analysis

UNTOUCHABLE—No 18
  UN—Prefix =not
  TOUCH—Latin Root =contact
  ABLE—Suffix =can do; able

practical exercises

1. Supply the missing words:
      "Of the .... word thou art master.
   The spoken word is master of thee."
      One who leaves books .... is as one who is
   .... and cannot read.
2. Analyze No. 19.
3. Match the key with its meaning:
   a. un   1. one who   ....
   b. y   2. not   ....
   c. ar   3. back   ....
   d. re   4. tend to   ....

9

KEY NO. 5

LESS

without

is the Suffix *LESS* which means WITHOUT. It is a very simple key and much in use. It is added to nouns and makes adjectives of them. On the next two pages you will have another simple key added to LESS and almost the same list of words. Let's see what happens!

1. baseless   base LESS (base′ les) adj.
      Without a base; groundless.
2. artless   art LESS (art′ les) adj.
      Without art; natural.
3. careless   care LESS (kare′ les) adj.
      Without care; slovenly.
4. effortless   effort LESS (ef′ ert les) adj.
      Without effort; easily.
5. friendless   friend LESS (frend′ les) adj.
      Without friends; alone.
6. graceless   grace LESS (grase′ les) adj.
      Without grace; clumsy.
7. fearless   fear LESS (feer′ les) adj.
      Without fear; unafraid.
8. helpless   help LESS (help′ les) adj.
      Without help; defenseless.
9. homeless   home LESS (home′ les) adj.
      Without a home.
10. hopeless   hope LESS (hope′ les) adj.
      Without expectation.
11. listless   list LESS (list′ les) adj.
      Without spirit.
12. noiseless   noise LESS (noiz′ les) adj.
      Without noise; quiet.
13. powerless   power LESS (pow′ er les) adj.
      Without power; lacking strength.
14. sleepless   sleep LESS (sleep′ les) adj.
      Without sleep; always awake.
15. restless   rest LESS (rest′ les) adj.
      Without rest; uneasy.
16. tireless   tire LESS (tire′ les) adj.
      Without getting tired; never weary.
17. tasteless   taste LESS (taste′ les) adj.
      Without taste; flat taste.
18. voiceless   voice LESS (voi′ sles) adj.
      Without voice; soundless.

19. trackless   track LESS (trak' les) adj.
                   Without a track; pathless.
20. weightless   weight LESS (wate' les) adj.
                   Without weight, light as a feather.

word analysis

WEIGHTLESS—No. 20
     WEIGHT (vehere)—Latin Root =weight
     LESS—Suffix =without

practical exercises

1. Supply the missing words:
     Toward morning the fever dropped, and after a ....
night the patient fell asleep. It must be a strange sensation
to feel oneself ....

2. Analyze No. 2.

3. Syllabicate and indicate the placement of the accent mark ('):
     tireless   rewrite   weightless
     unhurried   voiceless   exhibitor
     useless   untouchable   hairy

KEY NO. 6

LY

like manner of

is *LY*. It is a Suffix and means LIKE; in the MANNER OF. You will notice that the Root words are nearly all the same as in the previous lesson in which the Suffix *LESS* was added to them. *LESS* made adjectives out of the nouns. *LY* added to the adjectives makes adverbs out of them.

1. carelessly — careless LY (kare′ les lee) adv.
   In a careless manner.
2. baselessly — baseless LY (base′ les lee) adv.
   Groundlessly.
3. artlessly — artless LY (art′ les lee) adv.
   Naturally.
4. effortlessly — effortless LY (ef′ ert les lee) adv.
   Easily.
5. fearlessly — fearless LY (feer′ les lee) adv.
   Like one who is unafraid.
6. gracelessly — graceless LY (grase′ les lee) adv.
   Clumsily.
7. restlessly — restless LY (rest′ les lee) adv.
   Like one who is unable to rest.
8. hopelessly — hopeless LY (hope′ les lee) adv.
   Like one who is without expectation.
9. listlessly — listless LY (list′ les lee) adv.
   Like one who is without spirit.
10. noiselessly — noiseless LY (noiz′ les lee) adv.
    Soundlessly.
11. powerlessly — powerless LY (pow′ er les lee) adv.
    Like one who is without strength.
12. helplessly — helpless LY (help′ les lee) adv.
    Like one who is defenseless.
13. sleeplessly — sleepless LY (sleep′ les lee) adv.
    Like one who cannot sleep.
14. tirelessly — tireless LY (tire′ les lee) adv.
    Like one who never gets weary.
15. weightlessly — weightless LY (wate′ les lee) adv.
    Like one who is without weight.
16. shamelessly — shameless LY (shame′ les lee) adv.
    Like one who is unable to be embarrassed.
17. breathlessly — breathless LY (breth′ les lee) adv.
    Like one who is without breath.
18. lifelessly — lifeless LY (life′ les lee) adv.
    Like one who is dead.

19. voicelessly   voiceless LY (voi′ sles lee) adv.
      Like one who has no voice.

word analysis

SHAMELESSLY—No. 16
    SHAME—Root =shame
    LESS—Suffix =without
    LY—Suffix =in the manner of, like

practical exercises

1. Supply the missing words:
   He went into the haunted house .... but soon
ran out .... when he heard a strange sound.
.... the detective followed the suspect up the
stairs.

2. Analyze No. 19.

3. In the following sentences change the adverb into an adjective:

Example: He worked
            tirelessly.   He was a ....tireless.... worker.

a. He performed fault-
      lessly.   He was a .... performer.

b. He danced grace-
      lessly.   He was a .... dancer.

c. He kept on trying
      hopelessly.   It was a .... effort.

d. The work proceeded
      noiselessly.   They worked in a .... room.

KEY NO. 7

O—

NESS

state of

is the Suffix *NESS* which means the STATE OF. *NESS* is added to the Suffix *LESS* and makes the adjective back into a noun again. Just as *LY* makes adverbs, so *NESS* is the sure sign of a noun. Keeping the same Root words and adding the different keys show how important it is to know what the keys mean.

1. effortlessness   effortless NESS (ef′ ort les nes) n.
     The state of not trying.

2. baselessness   baseless NESS (base′ les nes) n.
     The state of being baseless.

3. carelessness   careless NESS (kare′ les nes) n.
     The state of being careless.

4. artlessness   artless NESS (art′ les nes) n.
     The state of being natural.

5. friendlessness   friendless NESS (frend′ les nes) n.
     The state of being friendless.

6. fearlessness   fearless NESS (feer′ les nes) n.
     The state of being fearless.

7. gracelessness   graceless NESS (grase′ les nes) n.
     The state of being clumsy.

8. restlessness   restless NESS (rest′ les nes) n.
     The state of being restless.

9. hopelessness   hopeless NESS (hope′ les nes) n.
     State of being hopeless.

10. listlessness   listless NESS (list′ les nes) n.
     State of being listless.

11. noiselessness   noiseless NESS (noiz′ les nes) n.
     State of being soundless.

12. helplessness   helpless NESS (help′ les nes) n.
     The state of being helpless.

13. sleeplessness   sleepless NESS (sleep′ les nes) n.
     The state of being sleepless.

14. tirelessness   tireless NESS (tire′ les nes) n.
     The state of not being weary.

15. tastelessness   tasteless NESS (taste′ les nes) n.
     The state of being tasteless.

16. voicelessness   voiceless NESS (voi′ sles ness) n.
     The state of being voiceless.

17. weightlessness   weightless NESS (wate′ les nes) n.
     The state of having no weight.

18. shamelessness shameless NESS (shame′ les nes) n.
               The state of being without shame.
19. breathlessness breathless NESS (breth′ les nes) n.
               State of being without breath.
20. lifelessness   lifeless NESS (life′ les nes) n.
               State of being lifeless.

word analysis

TIRELESSNESS—No. 14
    TIRE—Root =tire
    LESS—Suffix =without
    NESS—Suffix =state of

practical exercises

1. Supply the missing words:
          .... is the condition of the astronaut in space.
       The utter .... of his situation caused him
       many sleepless nights.

2. Analyze No. 3.

3. Change adjectives back to nouns by adding *NESS:*
    a. They were helpless. Their .... was pitiful.
    b. The situation was hopeless. The .... of the
       situation was evident.
    c. She seemed lifeless. Her .... had the appear-
       ance of death.
    d. It was a joyless occasion. The .... was de-
       pressing.
    e. It was a careless piece of work. There was no excuse for
       such ....

KEY NO. *8*

0—⚷

FUL

full of

is the Suffix *FUL* which means FULL OF. Notice the spelling of this key. The suffix has only one "l" whereas the word "full" has two. Notice Nos. 7, 8 and 14. In adding *FUL* the y in *beauty* is changed to *i;* the same change occurs with *pity* and *duty. LY* can be added to each one of these words, except Nos. 5 and 13.

1. frightful   fright FUL (frite' ful) adj.
Able to make one full of terror.
2. careful   care FUL (kare' ful) adj.
Taking care; watchful.
3. doubtful   doubt FUL (dout' ful) adj.
Having doubts; uncertain.
4. grateful   grate FUL (grate' ful) adj.
Full of thanks; glad to give thanks.
5. earful   ear FUL (eer' ful) n.
An ear full of news or gossip.
6. fearful   fear FUL (feer' ful) adj.
Full of fear; frightened.
7. beautiful   beauti FUL (byue' ti ful) adj.
Full of beauty.
8. dutiful   duti FUL (due' ti ful) adj.
Fulfilling all duties.
9. helpful   help FUL (help' ful) adj.
Willing to help; able to help.
10. graceful   grace FUL (grase' ful) adj.
Full of grace; tactful.
11. hopeful   hope FUL (hope' ful) adj.
Full of hope; expectant.
12. joyful   joy FUL (joy' ful) adj.
Full of joy; happy.
13. mouthful   mouth FUL (mouth' ful) n.
As much as the mouth will hold.
14. pitiful   piti FUL (pi' ti ful) adj.
Able to fill with pity; pathetic.
15. restful   rest FUL (rest' ful) adj.
Bringing rest, as a restful sleep.
16. shameful   shame FUL (shame' ful) adj.
Full of shame; disgraceful.
17. tearful   tear FUL (teer' ful) adj.
Full of tears; weeping.

16

18. vengeful   venge FUL (venj' ful) adj.
                   Full of plans to repay evil for evil.

19. tactful   tact FUL (takt' ful) adj.
                   Having a nicety of feeling so as not to hurt others; poised.

20. worshipful   worship FUL (wor' ship ful) adj.
                   Worthy of respect, of honor.

word analysis

UNTACTFULLY—No. 19+UN+LY
    UN—Prefix =not
    TACT (tactum)—Latin Root =touch
    FUL—Suffix =full of
    LY—Suffix =like; manner of

practical exercises

1. Supply the missing words:
     (Un) .... (ly) the hostess placed two enemies side by side at the table. She was .... to both of them for being .... not to anger each other.

2. Analyze No. 14.

3. Choose the number which best expresses the italicized word:
    Example: *untactful*   (1) tactless   (2) careful
            (3) charming   (4) gracious   (5) bitter   ....1....
    a. *frightened*   (1) happy   (2) fearful   (3) hopeless
           (4) grateful   (5) bitter   ....
    b. *unwelcome*   (1) invited   (2) excused
           (3) shameless   (4) not wanted   (5) lost   ....
    c. *return*   (1) sell   (2) repay   (3) come back
           (4) undo   (5) change   ....

KEY NO. 9

O—⚷

AN · IAN

**native of
relating to**

is *AN—IAN* a Suffix meaning NATIVE OF; RELATING TO. *AN* makes an adjective out of the noun it is added to. It is a very important key these days. It opens the door to knowledge of the peoples of the world and to the members who participate in the United Nations.

1. Czechoslovakian — Czechoslovak IAN
   (chek o sloe va' ki an) adj.
   A native of Czechoslovakia, a Czechoslovakian.

2. Cuban — Cub AN (kyu' ban) adj.
   A native of Cuba, a Cuban.

3. Colombian — Colombi AN (ko lum' bi an) adj.
   A native of Colombia, a Colombian.

4. African — Afric AN (af' ri kan) adj.
   A native of Africa, an African.

5. Dominican — Dominic AN (do min' i kan) adj.
   A native of the Dominican Republic, a Dominican.

6. Ethiopian — Ethiop IAN (ee thi oe' pee an) adj.
   A native of Ethiopia, an Ethiopian.

7. Italian — Ital IAN (i tal' yan) adj.
   A native of Italy, an Italian.

8. Jamaican — Jamaic AN (ja mae' kan) adj.
   A native of Jamaica, a Jamaican.

9. Somalian — Somal IAN (soe ma' li an) adj.
   A native of Somaliland, a Somalian.

10. Libyan — Liby AN (lib' i an) adj.
    A native of Libya, a Libyan.

11. Mongolian — Mongol IAN (mon goe' li an) adj.
    A native of Mongolia, a Mongolian.

12. Nicaraguan — Nicaragu AN (ni ka ra' gwan) adj.
    A native of Nicaragua, a Nicaraguan.

13. Liberian — Liber IAN (lie beer' i an) adj.
    A native of Liberia, a Liberian.

14. Syrian — Syr IAN (sir' ee an) adj.
    A native of Syria, a Syrian.

15. Tanzanian — Tanzan IAN (tan zae' ni an) adj.
    A native of Tanzania, a Tanzanian.

16. Tunisian — Tunisi AN (tu ni' zi an) adj.
    A native of Tunisia, a Tunisian.

17. Ugandian	Ugand IAN (u gan' di an) adj.
	A native of Uganda, a Ugandian.
18. Venezuelan	Venezuel AN (ve ne zuay' lan) adj.
	A native of Venezuela, a Venezuelan.
19. Yugoslavian	Yugoslav IAN (yu goe slav' i an) adj.
	A native of Yugoslavia, a Yugoslavian.
20. Australian	Austral IAN (aws trale' yan) adj.
	A native of Australia, an Australian.

word analysis

ETHIOPIAN—No. 6
    ETHI (aithein)—Greek Root =to burn
    OP (ōps)—Greek Root =face
    IAN—Suffix =native of

practical exercises

1. Supply the missing words:
    Many .... exiles wish to return to Cuba. A spokesman for Australia said, "Australia is for ...."

2. Analyze American.

3. Add the missing KEY which completes the word of which the meaning is given:
    Example: not related— ....related   ....unrelated....
    a. doing his duty— duti..........
    b. inclined to want to sleep— sleep..........
    c. state of not seeing— blind..........
    d. in a dainty manner— dainti..........
    e. without mercy— merci..........

KEY NO. *10*

ABLE · IBLE

able
can do

is the Suffix *ABLE—IBLE*. It means just what it says: ABLE; CAN DO. A very useful key it is. Remember the difference between Suffix and Prefix: a prefix comes at the beginning of a word, and a suffix at the end.

1. capable   cap ABLE (cape′ a b′l) adj.
   Able to do things well.

2. bearable   bear ABLE (bear′ a b′l) adj.
   Able to be endured.

3. agreeable   agree ABLE (a gree′ a b′l) adj.
   Able to please; as, agreeable *manners.*

4. acceptable   accept ABLE (ak sept′ a b′l) adj.
   Able to be accepted; welcome.

5. comfortable   comfort ABLE (com′ fert a b′l) adj.
   Able to give ease, strength.

6. enjoyable   enjoy ABLE (en joy′ a b′l) adj.
   Able to be enjoyed; able to give satisfaction.

7. transferable   transfer ABLE (trans fer′ a b′l) adj.
   Can be carried across.

8. forcible   forc IBLE (fors′ i b′l) adj.
   Can be powerful; as, a forcible *writer.*

9. horrible   horr IBLE (hor′ i b′l) adj.
   Able to shock.

10. laughable   laugh ABLE (laf′ a b′l) adj.
    Can be laughed at; as, a joke.

11. manageable   manage ABLE (man′ ij a b′l) adj.
    Can be managed.

12. portable   port ABLE (port′ a b′l) adj.
    Can be carried; as, a portable *typewriter.*

13. reliable   reli ABLE (re lie′ a b′l) adj.
    Can be depended on; trustworthy.

14. sociable   soci ABLE (so′ sha b′l) adj.
    Friendly; can get along with people.

15. tenable   ten ABLE (ten′ a b′l) adj.
    Can be held or defended; sensible.

16. terrible   terr IBLE (ter′ i b′l) adj.
    Can excite terror.

17. edible   ed IBLE (ed′ i b′l) adj.
    Can be eaten.

18. transmissible transmiss IBLE (trans mis′ i b′l) adj.
> *Can be sent across; can be imparted hereditarily.*

19. transportable transport ABLE (trans port′ a b′l) adj.
> *Can be carried across.*

20. visible   vis IBLE (viz′ i b′l) adj.
> *Can be seen; perceptible.*

word analysis

COMFORTABLE—No. 5
    COM—Prefix =with
    FORT (fortis)—Latin Root =strength
    ABLE—Suffix =can do

practical exercises

1. Supply the missing words:
> If you remember the KEYS you will acquire a .... vocabulary. You will be .... of expressing yourself in ...., convincing and .... language.

2. Analyze No. 2.

3. Add the missing keys to express the following phrases:
    a. accept ....   can be accepted
    b. hope ....   complete despair
    c. tact ....   in the manner of all tact
    d. beauty ....   in a lovely manner
    e. .... mark ....   not worth noticing again
    f. .... accept ....   cannot be accepted

KEY NO. 11

🔑

TRA · TRANS

**across
through
over**

is the Prefix *TRA, TRANS* meaning ACROSS; THROUGH; OVER. Every word in the list contains this Prefix and tells you that much about the word. When you learn more keys you will know what every part of the word means and then the word will be entirely yours. All you need to do is REMEMBER THE KEYS!

1. transatlantic TRANS atlantic (trans at lant' ic) adj.
   Across or beyond the Atlantic Ocean.

2. transcontinental TRANS continental (trans cont in ent' al) adj.
   Across the continent.

3. transact TRANS act (trans akt') v.
   Put a business deal through.

4. transaction TRANS action (trans ak' shun) n.
   Putting through of a business deal.

5. transfer TRANS fer (trans fer') v.
   To bring from one place to another.

6. transferable TRANS ferable (trans fer' a b'l) adj.
   Can be transferred.

7. transmit TRANS mit (trans mit') v.
   Send from person to person or place to place.

8. transmitter TRANS mitter (trans mit' er) n.
   One who or that which sends across.

9. translate TRANS late (trans late') v.
   To change from one form to another; as, to translate a book into another language.

10. translator TRANS lator (trans late' or) n.
    One who translates from one language to another.

11. transport TRANS port (trans port') v.
    To carry from place to place.

12. transportation TRANS portation (trans por tay' shun) n.
    The act of carrying something from place to place.

13. transform TRANS form (trans form') v.
    Change one form or structure to another.

14. transfusion TRANS fusion (trans fyue' zhun) n.
    Passing from one to another; as, a blood transfusion.

15. transcend TRANS cend (trans end') v.
    Cross to a higher level.

16. transit	TRANS it (trans' it) n.
	The way from one place to another.
17. transitive	TRANS itive (trans' it iv) n. (Gram.)
	A verb that has a direct object.
18. transplant	TRANS plant (trans plant') v.
	Plant in another place.
19. traverse	TRA verse (tra' vers) adj.
	Lying across; as, a bridge over a stream.
20. traduce	TRA duce (tra dyuse') v.
	To disgrace; lower the good name of.

word analysis

TRANSPORTATION—No. 12
    TRANS—Prefix =across; over
    PORT (portare)—Latin Root =carry
    TION—Suffix =act of

practical exercises

1. Supply the missing words:
    The variety of ways of .... is a miracle of
    our times. I.R.T. stands for Interborough Rapid ....
    You cannot get a .... on this bus.

2. Analyze No. 5.

3. Write the number of the word or expression which most nearly
    expresses the italicized word:
    Example: *transit*   (1) station   (2) beauty parlor
        (3) store   (4) going across   (5) costume   ....4....
    a. *translate*   (1) purchase   (2) sell   (3) read
        (4) unite   (5) bring into another language   ....
    b. *transplant*   (1) plant in another place   (2) unload
        (3) chop   (4) serve   (5) embrace   ....
    c. *wearable*   (1) tastes good   (2) explainable
        (3) can be worn   (4) expensive   (5) cheap   ....
    d. *skill*   (1) leisure   (2) ability   (3) taste
        (4) friendship   (5) carelessness   ....

KEY NO. 12

o—🔑

PORT

carry

is the Root *PORT* which means CARRY. All the words on the list have something to do with carrying in one way or another. Look at No. 11. The two *e's* at the end of the word have a special meaning—the deportee is the one who receives the action, the one who is deported, carried away, banished.

1. port
   PORT (port) n.
   Place ships may wait in, or bring or take cargo to or from.

2. porter
   PORT er (port' er) n.
   One who carries things, as baggage.

3. portable
   PORT able (port' a b'l) adj.
   Can be carried.

4. export
   ex PORT (ek sport') v.
   Carry out; bring or send elsewhere.

5. exporter
   ex PORT er (ex sport' er) n.
   One who sells goods to other countries.

6. exportation
   ex PORT ation (ek spor tay' shun) n.
   The act of carrying goods out of the country.

7. import
   im PORT (im port') v.
   To bring in goods; as, from a foreign country.

8. importer
   im PORT er (im port' er) n.
   One who brings in goods from a foreign country.

9. importation
   im PORT ation (im por tay' shun) n.
   The act of bringing in goods from a foreign country.

10. deport
    de PORT (de port') v.
    To send a person away; to banish.

11. deportee
    de PORT ee (de por tee') n.
    One who is sent away.

12. deportment
    de PORT ment (de port' ment) n.
    Manner of behaving oneself; conduct.

13. report
    re PORT (re port') n.
    An account of something which happened.

14. reporter
    re PORT er (re port' er) n.
    One who brings news; as, for a newspaper.

15. reporting
    re PORT ing (re port' ing) verbal noun
    The bringing in of news.

16. support
    sup PORT (su port') v.
    To carry along with help.

17. transport	trans PORT (trans' port) n.
	Act or means of carrying from place to place; as, an airship to carry soldiers.
18. transport	trans PORT (trans port') v.
	To carry from place to place.

word analysis

DEPORTEE—No. 11
  DE—Prefix =away; from
  PORT (portare)—Latin Root =carry
  EE—Suffix =the one who receives the action

practical exercises

1. Supply the missing words:
  Every .... tries to be the first to reach his paper with news. Many of the needy citizens are .... by government welfare until they find jobs and are able to .... themselves.

2. Analyze No. 14.

3. Key review. Match keys with their meanings:

a. port	1. one who	....
b. trans	2. not	....
c. able, ible	3. native of	....
d. un	4. can do	....
e. re	5. inclined to	....
f. y	6. across	....
g. an	7. again	....
h. or, er, ar	8. carry	....

KEY NO. 13

O—x

IN · IM

not

is the Prefix *IN* which means NOT. The words from 1 to 9 show this. All the other words change that Prefix to *IM* because the root word which follows the Prefix begins with a *b*, *m*, or *p*. These are called lip letters, or labials, because they are made with the lips. Before these labials *IM* sounds better than *IN*. Try it and see for yourself. It is also easier to pronounce. When a change is made because the sound is better or easier to make, we say the change is made for the sake of EUPHONY—pleasant sound. You will meet this word again.

1. inability IN ability (in a bil' it ee) n.
State of not being able.

2. inadequate IN adequate (in ad' e kwat) adj.
Not enough; insufficient.

3. inaccessible IN accessible (in ak ses' i b'l) adj.
Not able to be reached.

4. inarticulate IN articulate (in ar tik' yu lat) adj.
Not able to express oneself.

5. inclement IN clement (in klem' ent) adj.
Not mild, often said of the weather.

6. inhospitable IN hospitable (in hos pit' a b'l) adj.
Unwilling to be host to others.

7. intolerable IN tolerable (in tol' e ra b'l) adj.
Not to be endured.

8. insatiable IN satiable (in say' shi b'l) adj.
Can never be satisfied; always wanting more.

9. invisible IN visible (in vis' i b'l) adj.
Cannot be seen.

10. imperfect IM perfect (im per' fekt) adj.
Having errors; flawed.

11. impossible IM possible (im pos' i b'l) adj.
Incapable of being or happening.

12. improbable IM probable (im prob' a b'l) adj.
Not likely to occur or be true.

13. implacable IM placable (im plak' a b'l) adj.
Cannot be appeased; cannot forgive.

14. immature IM mature (im a tyure') adj.
Not full grown; still unripe.

26

15. immoral   IM moral (im mor' al) adj.
                      Not of good character.
16. immobilize   IM mobilize (im o' bi lize) v.
                      To make immovable; like a stroke that makes a person incapable of movement.
17. immoderate   IM moderate (im mod' e rat) adj.
                      Inclined to go beyond bounds.
18. imbalance   IM balance (im bal' ans) n.
                      A lack of balance; more weight on one side than on the other.
19. impassable   IM passable (im pas' a b'l) adj.
                      Cannot be passed; blocked.
20. immortal   IM mortal (im ort' al) adj.
                      Not subject to death; like Shakespeare's immortal poetry.

word analysis

INACCESSIBLE—No. 3
    IN—Prefix =not
    AC—Prefix =to
    CESS (cessus)—Latin Root =go
    IBLE—Suffix =can do

practical exercises

1. Supply the missing words:
     Of all his enemies the king was the most ....
     Only time can cure ....ity.

2. Analyze No. 15.

3. Syllabicate and indicate which syllable is most strongly accented by placing the accent mark ('):

     inability   inarticulate   immature
     inadequate   inaccessible   immortal
     implacable   imperfect   immoderate

KEY NO. 14

O—⚷

EN · EM

into
in

is the Prefix *EN* which means INTO, IN. Before *b*, *m*, and *p* *EN* becomes *EM*. That's right! They are the lip letters, the labials, and it is easier to pronounce an *m* before them than an *n*.

1. encamp — EN camp (en kamp') v.
   Set up camp; as, on maneuvers.

2. encourage — EN courage (en kur' ij) v.
   Put heart into one; encourage with hope, spirit.

3. endanger — EN danger (en dane' jer) v.
   Put into danger.

4. enroll — EN roll (en rol') v.
   To enter; register.

5. enslave — EN slave (en slave') v.
   Put into slavery; make a slave of.

6. entrap — EN trap (en trap') v.
   To catch in a trap.

7. envenom — EN venom (en ven' om) v.
   To poison; as, by a snake bite.

8. environ — EN viron (en vie' ron) v.
   To put a ring around; to encircle.

9. environment — EN vironment (en vie' ron ment) n.
   The life that surrounds one; as, a neighborhood.

10. embark — EM bark (em bark') v.
    Get into a train or a ship for a journey.

11. embrace — EM brace (em brase') v.
    To take into one's arms.

12. embitter — EM bitter (em bit' er) v.
    To make bitter.

13. employ — EM ploy (em ploy') v.
    To find a use for.

14. embody — EM body (em bod' ee) v.
    To give a body to something; as, a law must embody freedom.

15. employee — EM ployee (em ploy ee') n.
    One who works for wages from an employer.

16. employer — EM ployer (em ploy' er) n.
    One who hires others to work for him for wages.

17. employable   EM ployable (em ploy' a b'l) adj.
                  Able to hold a job.
18. unemployable un EM ployable (un em ploy' a b'l) adj.
                  Not able to hold a job.
19. embroider   EM broider (em broid' er) v.
                  To make fancy with stitching.
20. embellish   EM bellish (em bel' ish) v.
                  To decorate; to make beautiful.

word analysis

UNEMPLOYABLE—No. 18
      UN—Prefix =not
      EM—Prefix =in; into
      PLOY—Root =action; doing
      ABLE—Suffix =can do; able

practical exercises

1. Supply the missing words:
      Some scientists believe that the most important factor in
      a child's development is .... The soldiers
      reached the port and .... for France and the
      war.

2. Analyze No. 3.

3. Use one word for each of the following phrases:
      a. give one courage   ....
      b. take into one's arms   ....
      c. take on for a job   ....
      d. cannot be made to forgive   ....
      e. not able to express oneself   ....

KEY NO. 15

0—⚷

AD

to
toward

is the Prefix *AD* which means TO; TOWARD. This key is a bit difficult. Please look at No. 15 on the list. The *AD* has become *AC*. In No. 16 the *AD* has become *AF;* in No. 17 *AD* has become *AG*. In No. 18 it is *AL*. In No. 19 it is *AN*. The *d* in all these words has assimilated with the letter of the root. Before *r* the *d* becomes *AR;* as in ARrange; before *s* we have ASsure; before *t* we have ATtract; before *p* we have APproach. But they still all mean TO; TOWARD.

1. adaptable   AD aptable (a dap′ ta b'l) adj.
Is able to fit in; pliable.

2. addict   AD dict (ad′ ikt) n.
One who is given over to a habit, often drugs.

3. adequate   AD equate (ad′ e kwat) adj.
Equal to the need; sufficient.

4. adhere   AD here (ad here′) v.
Stick to; be faithful.

5. adjacent   AD jacent (a jase′ ent) adj.
Lying near; side by side.

6. adjunct   AD junct (aj′ unkt) n.
One thing joined to another.

7. admire   AD mire (ad mire′) v.
Wonder at with pleasure.

8. adulterate   AD ulterate (a dul′ te rate) v.
To change to an impure quality; as to put sand in the cement.

9. advance   AD vance (ad vans′) v.
To go forward.

10. advantage   AD vantage (ad vant′ ij) n.
A favorable condition.

11. advertise   AD vertise (ad′ ver tize) v.
To notify about; bring to public attention.

12. advocate   AD vocate (ad′ vo kate) v.
To speak out for a worthy cause.

13. advise   AD vise (ad vize′) v.
To give guidance, advice; to caution.

14. administer   AD minister (ad min′ i ster) v.
To take charge of; to manage.

15. accept   AC cept (ak sept′) v.
To receive; to take to oneself.

16. affiance   AF fiance (a fie' ans) v.
                   To promise to wed; to engage for marriage.
17. aggressive   AG gressive (a gres' iv) adj.
                   Inclined to attack; drive forward.
18. allege   AL lege (a lej') v.
                   To declare.
19. announce   AN nounce (a nouns') v.
                   Make known to the public.
20. assert   AS sert (a sert') v.
                   To declare, state positively.

word analysis

ADVOCATE—No. 12
     AD—Prefix =to; toward
     VOC (vocare)—Latin Root =call; speak
     ATE—Suffix =make; cause

practical exercises

1. Supply the missing words:
     His .... manner made him unpopular. They
     are ....d and will be married shortly. Do not
     .... any further; if you continue in that direc-
     tion you will encounter danger.

2. Analyze No. 4.

3. Choose the number which best expresses the italicized word:
     Example: *embrace*   (1) shut out   (2) lead   (3) call
            (4) take into one's arms   (5) scold   ....4....
     a. *advance*   (1) succeed   (2) trail behind
            (3) delay   (4) go forward   (5) ignore   ....
     b. *impossible*   (1) easy   (2) hungry   (3) unable
            (4) sold   (5) caught   ....
     c. *euphony*   (1) discord   (2) concert
            (3) interference   (4) pleasant sound
            (5) racket   ....

KEY NO. 16

O━━

IL · IR

not

is the Prefix *IL* and its partner *IR*, meaning NOT. It seems that the Prefix *IN* is also assimilated with certain consonants. Before a root word beginning with *l*, *IN* becomes *IL*. Before *r*, *IN* becomes *IR*. All this is to make it pleasant to say and pleasant to hear.

1. illegal
   IL legal (il ee' gal) adj.
   Not according to law.

2. illegible
   IL legible (il lej' i b'l) adj.
   Not able to be read.

3. illiterate
   IL literate (il it' e rat) adj.
   Having little education; cannot read or write.

4. illiteracy
   IL literacy (il it' e ra see) n.
   The state of being uneducated; inability to read or write.

5. illusion
   IL lusion (il ue' zhun) n.
   An unreal image.

6. illogical
   IL logical (il oj' i kal) adj.
   Not having sense.

7. illiberal
   IL liberal (il ib' e ral) adj.
   Not open minded; being a bigot.

8. illicit
   IL licit (il is' it) adj.
   Not allowed; not lawful.

9. irreclaimable
   IR reclaimable (ir e klay' ma b'l) adj.
   Cannot be claimed again.

10. irregular
    IR regular (ir eg' yu lar) adj.
    Not as it should be.

11. irreligious
    IR religious (ir e lij' us) adj.
    Lacking religious feelings.

12. irreverent
    IR reverent (ir ev' rent) adj.
    Showing a lack of respect about holy matters.

13. irreparable
    IR reparable (ir ep' e ra b'l) adj.
    Cannot be repaired.

14. irresolute
    IR resolute (ir ez' o lute) adj.
    Cannot make up his mind.

15. irreproachable
    IR reproachable (ir e proche' a b'l) adj.
    Cannot be blamed in any way.

16. irresponsible
    IR responsible (ir e spon' si b'l) adj.
    Not having a sense of duty.

17. irrevocable
    IR revocable (ir ev' o ka b'l) adj.
    Cannot be recalled.

18. irresistible   IR resistible (ir e zis' ti b'l) adj.
                          Not able to be withstood.

19. irrational   IR rational (ir ash' u nal) adj.
                          Unreasonable; illogical.

20. irrelevant   IR relevant (ir el' e vant) adj.
                          Has nothing to do with the case; unrelated.

word analysis

ILLOGICAL—No. 6
    IL (in)—Prefix =not
    LOG (logos)—Greek Root =word
    IC—Suffix =like
    AL—Suffix =relating to

practical exercises

1. Supply the missing words:
    The spoken word is .... and the harm it may
    do is .... Her manners were ....
    and her charm was ....

2. Analyze No. 1.

3. Indicate the correct pronunciation by placing the accent
    mark ('):

illegible	illiterate	irreverent
illegal	irresponsible	irresolute
illusion	irrational	irrevocable

KEY NO. *17*

ITE

**native of
quality of
mineral product**

is the Suffix *ITE*. It means NATIVE OF; QUALITY OF; MINERAL; PRODUCT. When ITE is used, there is always the quality of belonging. As you read the list you will learn words describing nationality, science, chemistry, geology, and zoology. *ITE* is a convenient little Suffix to make names with.

1. appetite   appet ITE (ap' e tite) n.
   Craving; desire.
2. exquisite   exquis ITE (ek skwiz' it) adj.
   Having the quality of great beauty.
3. expedite   exped ITE (ek' spe dite) v.
   To hasten; to quicken.
4. anti-semite   anti-sem ITE (ant i sem' ite) n.
   One against the semitic race, especially against Jews.
5. anthracite   anthrac ITE (an' thra site) n.
   A hard, natural coal.
6. dynamite   dynam ITE (die' na mite) n.
   A powerful explosive.
7. granite   gran ITE (gran' it) n.
   A firm, grainy rock.
8. Israelite   Israel ITE (iz' ree e lite) n.
   A native of Israel.
9. graphite   graph ITE (graf' ite) n.
   A pure carbon used in lead pencils.
10. meteorite   meteor ITE (meet' ee o rite) n.
    A stony metallic body falling from outer space.
11. suburbanite   suburban ITE (su bur' ba nite) n.
    One who lives in a suburb.
12. stalactite   stalact ITE (sta lak' tite) n.
    A rock formation which hangs like an icicle from the ceiling of a cave; a product of dripping.
13. stalagmite   stalagm ITE (sta lag' mite) n.
    A rock formation which rises from the floor of a cave.
14. favorite   favor ITE (fave' o rit) n.
    One who is regarded above others.
15. dolomite   dolom ITE (do' lo mite) n.
    A mineral composed of carbonates of calcium and magnesium.

16. sulfite   sulf ITE (sul' fite) n.
                    A salt of sulphurous acid.

17. pyrite   pyr ITE (pire' ite) n.
                    A common mineral of yellow brass color; sometimes called "fool's gold."

word analysis

FAVORITE—No. 14
    Favor (favere)—Latin Root =favor
    Ite—Suffix =quality of

practical exercises

1. Supply the missing words:
    Alfred Nobel invented ....
    .... and .... are found in caves.

2. Analyze No. 8.

3. Complete the following sentences:
    a. A popular vote is called a   ....
    b. One who is preferred is called a   ....
    c. If you are not logical you will be called   ....
    d. If you are not patient you will be called ....
    e. If one house is right beside another, the
       houses are said to be   ....

KEY NO. *18*

O—🗝

AL

relating to

is the Suffix *AL* which means RE-LATING TO. It is one of the most useful keys. *AL* can be attached to a vast number of words and brings to all of them the simple and all-important message of RELATIONSHIP. This is the basic idea of this system of vocabulary building. Words are not isolated symbols. They are related to each other by their prefixes, suffixes, and roots.

1. sensual   sensu AL (sensh' u al) adj.
   Relating to the senses.
2. autumnal   autumn AL (au tum' nal) adj.
   Relating to the autumn of the year.
3. animal   anim AL (an' i mal) n.
   Relating to creatures which live and breathe.
4. aural   aur AL (aur' al) adj.
   Relating to the ear; heard.
5. cerebral   cerebr AL (se ree' bral) adj.
   Relating to the brain.
6. decimal   decim AL (dec' i mal) adj.
   Relating to the system of counting based on ten.
7. gradual   gradu AL (graj' u wal) adj.
   Relating to movement by steps or degrees.
8. intellectual   intellectu AL (int el ek' chu wal) adj.
   Relating to the power to think.
9. infernal   infern AL (in fern' al) adj.
   Relating to hell.
10. internal   intern AL (in tern' al) adj.
    Relating to the inside part of.
11. manual   manu AL (man' yu al) adj.
    Relating to the hand.
12. mental   ment AL (ment' al) adj.
    Relating to the mind.
13. natural   natur AL (nach' u ral) adj.
    Relating to nature; unforced.
14. optional   option AL (op' shun al) adj.
    Relating to a matter of choice.
15. oral   or AL (or' al) adj.
    Relating to the mouth; spoken.
16. reprisal   repris AL (re prie' zal) n.
    Related to the paying back of evil for evil.

36

17. spiritual   spiritu AL (spir' ich u al) adj.

                   Relating to the spirit as opposed to the body.

18. technical   technic AL (tek' ni kal) adj.

                   Relating to mechanical arts.

19. usual   usu AL (yuzh' u al) adj.

                   Relating to the common things; normal; ordinary.

20. phenomenal   phenomen AL (fe nom' in al) adj.

                   Relating to what is unusual among its kind.

word analysis

SUPERNATURAL
     SUPER—Prefix =beyond
     NATUR—Root =nature
     AL—Suffix =relating to

practical exercises

1. Supply the missing words:

     George Washington said, "It is .... whether the United States will be respected and prosperous, or contemptible and miserable."

     .... and .... values are part of our religious training.

2. Analyze No. 17.

3. Key Review. Match key and meaning, letter and number.

a. ite	1. (ad) to	....
b. il	2. relating to	....
c. port	3. native of	....
d. al	4. across	....
e. ac	5. (before L) not	....
f. an (suffix)	6. carry	....
g. trans	7. again; back	....
h. re	8. native of; quality of	....

KEY NO. *19*

DI

two
double
separate

is the Prefix *DI* which means TWO; DOUBLE; SEPARATE. Notice the SEPARATE idea of DIvide, DIvorce, and DIvulsion. It is a difficult key.

1. dicephalous   DI cephalous (die sef′ a lus) adj.
       Having two heads.

2. didactyl   DI dactyl (die dak′ til) n.
       An organism with only two digits on each extremity.

3. diota   DI ota (die o′ ta) n.
       A vessel with two handles.

4. dicellate   DI cellate (die sel′ ate) n.
       Having two prongs; as, a fork.

5. dicotyledon   DI cotyledon (di kot el eed′ on) n.
       A plant that has two seed leaves.

6. dicotyledonous   DI cotyledonous (di kot el eed′ on us) adj.
       Having two seed leaves.

7. dichromatic   DI chromatic (die kroe mat′ ik) adj.
       Having two colors.

8. dichotomy   DI chotomy (die kot′ o me) n.
       A separation into two parts.

9. diclinic   DI clinic (die klin′ ik) adj.
       Having two oblique intersections behind three of the axes of a crystal.

10. diacid   DI acid (die as′ id) n.
       An acid having two hydrogen atoms.

11. dimeter   DI meter (dim′ et er) n.
       A line of verse with two metrical feet.

12. dilemma   DI lemma (di lem′ a) n.
       A situation which poses two or more difficult choices.

13. dilogy   DI logy (dil′ o jee) n.
       Speech that has two or more meanings.

14. diphthong   DI phthong (dif′ thong) n.
       A sound made by joining two vowels; as, OU in hOUse.

15. dioxide   DI oxide (die ok′ side) n.
       A compound containing two atoms of oxygen.

16. digraph   DI graph (die' graf) n.
                Two vowels written together and making
                one sound; as, Æ in Æsop.

17. divide   DI vide (di vide') v.
                To separate into two or more parts.

18. divorce   DI vorce (di vors') n.
                Separation, one from the other.

19. divulsion   DI vulsion (die vul' shun) n.
                A tearing apart.

word analysis

DICHROMATIC—No. 7
    DI—Prefix =two
    CHROMAT (chromato)—Greek Root =color
    IC—Suffix =like

practical exercises

1. Supply the missing words:
    "A strong .... in a desperate case,—
    To act with infamy or quit the place." (Swift)
    In the name AEsop the AE is a .... pro-
nounced as a very long E.

2. Analyze porter.

3. Choose the number which best expresses the italicized word:
    a. *dichromatic*   (1) black   (2) white
       (3) two-color   (4) three-color   (5) four-color   ....
    b. *portable*   (1) heavy   (2) can be carried
       (3) straight   (4) circular   (5) unknown   ....
    c. *dilemma*   (1) contract   (2) pleasure
       (3) satisfaction   (4) 2 hard choices   (5) puzzle   ....
    d. *desperate*   (1) happy   (2) frantic   (3) rejoicing
       (4) hopeless   (5) sincere   ....
    e. *grateful*   (1) jealous   (2) bitter   (3) sorry
       (4) hateful   (5) thankful   ....

KEY NO. 20

O—x

FER

**bring
bear
yield**

is the Root *FER* which means BRING; BEAR; YIELD. It comes from the Latin *ferre*, to bring. The simplest word with this meaning is FERtile and not alone of the earth, but of the body and the mind. In your list you will find as many psychological inFERences as physical ones. It's a good key and yields a great deal.

1. coniferous   coni FER ous (koe nif′ e rus) adj.
     Bearing cones; as, pine trees.

2. circumference   circum FER ence (sir kum′ fe rens) n.
     The line that goes around a circular plane.

3. deference   de FER ence (def′ e rens) n.
     Respect for; courtesy.

4. fertile   FER tile (fer′ til) adj.
     Bearing good fruit; yielding much.

5. fertilization   FER tilization (fert il i zay′ shun) n.
     The act of causing to bear richly.

6. cross-fertilization   cross FER tilization (kros′ fert il i zay′ shun) n.
     Fertilization from one type to another.

7. conference   con FER ence (kon′ fe rens) n.
     A bringing together; a meeting.

8. reference   re FER ence (ref′ e rens) n.
     A thought relating to a subject.

9. inference   in FER ence (in′ fe rens) n.
     Carrying over a truth from one point to another.

10. odoriferous   odori FER ous (ode e rif′ e rus) adj.
     Bearing an odor, usually pleasant.

11. preference   pre FER ence (pref′ e rens) n.
     Bringing forward; as, the first choice.

12. suffer   suf FER (suf′ er) v.
     To bear sorrow or pain.

13. transfer   trans FER (trans fer′) v.
     To bring from one place to another.

14. proffer   prof FER (prof′ er) v.
     To bring forward; to offer.

word analysis

FERTILIZATION—No. 5
    FER—Root =bear
    IL (ile)—Suffix =capable of
    IZ (ize)—Suffix =make; cause
    TION—Suffix =act of; state of

practical exercises

1. Supply the missing words:
    Pines are .... evergreens. The boys resented
    any .... in their game. Some people have a
    .... for short, amusing plays.

2. Analyze No. 13.

3. Use one word to express each of the following phrases:
    a. a meeting of executives   ....
    b. a favored choice   ....
    c. a situation of two hard choices   ....
    d. manner of carrying oneself   ....
    e. to carry out a piece of business ....

KEY NO. 21

EN

**made of
make**

is the Suffix *EN* which means MADE
OF; MAKE. *EN* is a simple key and
the roots to which *EN* is added are
all simple words. When the word is
an adjective *EN* means MADE OF;
when it is a verb, *EN* means MAKE.

1. silken   silk EN (sil′ ken) adj.
      Made of silk.
2. brazen   braz EN (braze′ en) adj.
      Made of brass.
3. frozen   froz EN (froze′ en) adj.
      Made icy; as, frozen foods.
4. hempen   hemp EN (hem′ pen) adj.
      Made of hemp; as, rope.
5. molten   molt EN (molt′ en) adj.
      Made by melting.
6. oaken   oak EN (o′ ken) adj.
      Made of oak.
7. woolen   wool EN (wool′ en) adj.
      Made of wool.
8. wooden   wood EN (wood′ en) adj.
      Made of wood.
9. golden   gold EN (gol′ den) adj.
      Made of gold.
10. broaden   broad EN (broad′ en) v.
      Make broad; widen.
11. brighten   bright EN (brite′ en) v.
      Make bright.
12. hasten   hast EN (hase′ en) v.
      Make haste; put on speed.
13. heighten   height EN (hite′ en) v.
      Make high; increase.
14. lighten   light EN (lite′ en) v.
      Make light; reduce.
15. roughen   rough EN (ruf′ en) v.
      Make rough.
16. toughen   tough EN (tuf′ en) v.
      Make tough; strengthen.
17. soften   soft EN (sof′ en) v.
      Make soft.

18. smoothen   smooth EN (smue' then) **v.**
                  Make smooth.
19. whiten   whit EN (hwite' en) **v.**
                  Make white.
20. frighten   fright EN (frite' en) **v.**
                  Make fearful.

word analysis

TOUGHEN—No. 16
    TOUGH—Root =hard; strong
    EN—Suffix =to make

practical exercises

1. Supply the missing words:
    How dear to the heart is the old .... bucket.
    A good dentifrice will .... your teeth,
    .... your smile and .... your
    charms.

2. Analyze No. 14.

3. Use one word for each of the following phrases:
    a. make tough   ....
    b. pleasing sound   ....
    c. right next to   ....
    d. make it known to the public   ....
    e. cannot be claimed again   ....

KEY NO. 22

O—x

IN · IM

in
into

is the Prefix *IN, IM,* meaning IN; IN-TO. I know on a previous page I said *IN, IM* means NOT. And now the very same thing means IN; INTO. Well, that's life! And the keys are just as contrary. No help for it. When you see *IN* or *IM* you'll have to stop and think. Is it NOT or IN? One good thing, though: the rules for labials remain the same. *IN* becomes *IM* before *b, m,* and *p.*

1. interior   IN terior (in ter' ee or) n.
    The inside; the inner part.

2. influx   IN flux (in' fluks) n.
    An inward flow.

3. ingress   IN gress (in' gres) n.
    Act of entering; coming in.

4. inhale   IN hale (in hale') v.
    To breathe in.

5. imbue   IM bue (im byue') v.
    To inspire; as, to imbue with a love for books.

6. imbibe   IM bibe (im bibe') v.
    To drink in; to take into the mind; as, to imbibe wisdom.

7. immure   IM mure (im yure') v.
    To wall in; build a wall around.

8. immigrate   IM migrate (im' i grate) v.
    To come into a country in order to settle.

9. immigrant   IM migrant (im' i grant) n.
    One who comes into a country as a settler.

10. imminent   IM minent (im' i nent) adj.
    About to occur.

11. immingle   IM mingle (im ming' g'l) v.
    Mix with; join; blend.

12. important   IM portant (im port' ant) adj.
    Having significance.

13. impress   IM press (im pres') v.
    To leave a mark or an image on.

14. impression   IM pression (im presh' un) n.
    The mark or image one leaves.

15. impressionable   IM pressionable (im presh' u na b'l) adj.
    Easily impressed.

16. imprison   IM prison (im priz' on) **v.**
                 Put into jail.

17. implosion   IM plosion (im ploe' zhun) **n.**
                 A bursting inward.

18. impinge   IM pinge (im pinj') **v.**
                 To dash, strike; to come into close contact with something.

19. imperil   IM peril (im per' il) **v.**
                 To put into danger.

20. impulsive   IM pulsive (im puls' iv) **adj.**
                 To act suddenly; to cause to be.

word analysis

IMPULSIVE—No. 20
    IM—Prefix =in; into
    PULS (pello)—Latin Root =to push
    IVE—Suffix =causing

practical exercises

1. Supply the missing words:
    Emigrant and .... are one and the same person, leaving one country and entering another. The children were ....(d) with love for the .... values in life.

2. Analyze Implant.

3. Recognize, in the following words found in the news of the day, keys which you have learned, and underline them:

1. attack	4. division	7. cordially
2. immune	5. unnecessary	8. translate
3. immunity	6. proper	9. interfere

KEY NO. 23

O—⚡

EX

out
from

is the Prefix *EX* which means OUT; FROM. It is a very common key. You meet it daily, many times, with a red light to show the way OUT. If you notice the pronunciation carefully you will see that *EX* is not always "eks" but sometimes "egs" (eggs).

1. exact
EX act (eg zakt') v.
To demand; to make give out.

2. excel
EX cel (ek sel') v.
To surpass; outdo others.

3. excellence
EX cellence (ek' se lens) n.
The highest quality.

4. excite
EX cite (ek site') v.
To rouse; to stir up.

5. excitable
EX citable (ek site' a b'l) adj.
Can be easily roused.

6. excitement
EX citement (ek site' ment) n.
State of being excited.

7. exclude
EX clude (eks klude') v.
Shut out.

8. exclaim
EX claim (eks klame') v.
Cry out; shout out.

9. exclamation
EX clamation (eks kla may' shun) n.
An outcry.

10. exit
EX it (eg' zit) n.
A way out of a building.

11. exit
EX it (eg' zit) v.
To leave; go out of.

12. expect
EX pect (ek spekt') v.
To look out for; await.

13. expelled
EX pelled (ek speld') v.
Thrown out; as, expelled from school.

14. express
EX press (ek spres') v.
To speak out.

15. expression
EX pression (ek spresh' un) n.
The act of stating something.

16. excavate
EX cavate (ek' ska vate) v.
To hollow out; make a hole in.

17. exception
EX ception (ek sep' shun) n.
Something left out of general use; as, an exception to a rule.

46

18. extend   EX tend (ek stend') v.
              To stretch out; to lay out at full length.

word analysis

EXCLAMATION—No. 9
  EX—Prefix =out
  CLAM (clamare)—Latin Root =cry out
  TION—Suffix =act of; state of

practical exercises

1. Supply the missing words:
     Charles Dickens wrote a book called "Great ...."
     Respect for .... is one of the moral and spir-
   itual values inherent in our Democracy.

2. Analyze No. 8.

3. Use one word for each of the following phrases:
   a. plant in another place   ....
   b. can be agreed upon   ....
   c. can be endured   ....
   d. cannot be approached   ....
   e. a situation which presents two or more
      disagreeable choices   ....

47

KEY NO. 24

0—x

E · EC · EF

out

is a three-fold change of the Prefix *EX*. The first change was to drop the *X* which is an awkward letter to use, so we have *E* standing alone. Then the *X* was changed to *C* making the key *EC*. The last change I'm sure you guessed—assimilation of *X* with *F* so we have *EF*. *E, EC, EF*=OUT.

1. eject	E ject (e jekt') v. *To throw out.*
2. ejaculate	E jaculate (e jak' yu late) v. *To call out; exclaim.*
3. elaborate	E laborate (e lab' o rate) v. *To work out carefully.*
4. emanate	E manate (em' a nate) v. *To flow out; as, fragrance from roses.*
5. eccentric	EC centric (ek sen' trik) adj. *Having a different center; odd ways.*
6. eclipse	EC lipse (e klips') v. *Darken; to hide; as, an eclipse of the sun.*
7. ecstasy	EC stasy (ek' sta see) n. *Joy out of control; overwhelming emotion.*
8. eczema	EC zema (ek zee' ma) n. *A breaking out of the skin.*
9. effect	EF fect (e fekt') n. *The outcome; result.*
10. effete	EF fete (e fete') adj. *Lacking fertility; worn out; tired.*
11. effort	EF fort (ef' fort) n. *Exertion of strength; an attempt.*
12. effulgent	EF fulgent (e ful' jent) adj. *Shining out; brilliant; as, effulgent rays of the sun.*
13. efflux	EF flux (ef' luks) n. *A flowing out.*
14. effusion	EF fusion (e fyue' zhun) n. *A pouring out; an escape of fluids.*
15. effusive	EF fusive (e fyue' siv) adj. *Pouring forth freely; gushing.*
16. effervesce	EF fervesce (ef er ves') v. *To bubble; display liveliness.*
17. effervescent	EF fervescent (ef er ves' ent) adj. *Bubbling; lively.*

18. effeminate   EF feminate (e fem′ i nat) adj.
Wanting in manliness; having qualities that are feminine.

19. efficient   EF ficient (e fish′ ent) adj.
Very capable; produces results.

word analysis

EMANATE—No. 4
    E (ex)—Prefix =out
    MAN (manare)—Latin Root =to flow out
    ATE—Suffix =cause; make

practical exercises

1. Supply the missing words:
    Although he was .... in many ways he was, really, a lovable old man. She was so .... that the .... of her welcome was a bit embarrassing.

2. Analyze Express.

3. All the incomplete words begin with an assimilated form of AD =TO. Give the prefix the correct form:
    Example: plead to   ....*ap*...peal
    a. make sure to   ....sure
    b. come near to   ....proach
    c. plan to   ....range
    d. draw to   ....tract
    e. make known to   ....nounce

KEY NO. 25

O—⚷

ION · SION
TION

**act of
state of
result of**

is the Suffix *ION, SION, TION* meaning ACT OF, STATE OF, RESULT OF. It is very much in use. The most common of the forms are *TION* and *SION*. It is a noun ending.

1. diction   dic TION (dik′ shun) n.
     The choice of words.
2. celebration   celebra TION (sel e bray′ shun) n.
     The act of honoring some special event.
3. action   ac TION (ak′ shun) n.
     Something done; way of performing.
4. dominion   domin ION (do min′ yun) n.
     Authority over; absolute power over.
5. injection   injec TION (in jek′ shun) n.
     Act of throwing in; forcing something in.
6. formation   forma TION (for may′ shun) n.
     Act of giving form or shape.
7. infection   infec TION (in fek′ shun) n.
     Result of contamination.
8. function   func TION (funk′ shun) n.
     Occupation; purpose.
9. junction   junc TION (junk′ shun) n.
     A state of being connected, joined.
10. limitation   limita TION (lim i tay′ shun) n.
     State of being confined within a limited space; a set boundary.
11. location   loca TION (loe kay′ shun) n.
     A place; a locality.
12. option   op TION (op′ shun) n.
     The act of choosing; the choice.
13. partition   parti TION (par tish′ un) n.
     The act of separating; division into elements.
14. purification   purifica TION (pyur i fi kay′ shun) n.
     The act of making pure.
15. question   ques TION (kwes′ chun) n.
     The act of inquiring; that which is asked.
16. reflection   reflec TION (re flek′ shun) n.
     An image thrown back; as a reflection in a mirror.

17. suspension   suspen SION (sus pen' shun) n.
                 State of being stopped temporarily.
18. verification   verifica TION (ver i fi kay' shun) n.
                 Act of giving proof; proven truth.
19. versification   versifica TION (ver si fi kay' shun) n.
                 The act of expressing thought in verse form;
                 poetic form.
20. vitrification   vitrifica TION (vi tri fi kay' shun) n.
                 The act of being made into glass.

word analysis

VITRIFICATION—No. 20
     VITRI (vitrum)—Latin Root =glass
     FIC (facere)—Latin Root =to make
     A—Suffix =causing
     TION—Suffix =act of

practical exercises

1. Supply the missing words:
     Narcissus fell in love with his .... in the
     lake. His failure to obey the .... imposed by
     the school resulted in his ....

2. Analyze Enslave.

3. Syllabicate and indicate which syllable is most greatly stressed
   by placing the accent mark ('):
       vitrification   versification   verification
       suspension   purification   celebration

KEY NO. 26

o—➤

NASC • NAT

to be born
to spring forth

is the Root *NASC, NAT* meaning TO BE BORN; TO SPRING FORTH. It comes from the Latin *nascor*. There are so many words with this key that one list will not accommodate them all.

1. natal   NAT al (nate' al) adj.
Relating to birth.

2. native   NAT ive (nate' iv) adj.
Belonging to by birth.

3. naive   NA ive (na eve') adj.
Acting as one born yesterday; artless.

4. naiveté   NA iveté (na ee ve tay') n.
Quality of being childishly simple.

5. nature   NAT ure (nay' chur) n.
The essence of a person or a thing.

6. natural   NAT ural (nach' u ral) adj.
Relating to nature.

7. nativity   NAT ivity (na tiv' it ee) n.
The process of being born; a coming into the world.

8. nativism   NAT ivism (nate' iv iz um) n.
A policy favoring the native born.

9. naturalize   NAT uralize (nach' u ra lize) v.
To give citizenship to one foreign born.

10. naturalization   NAT uralization (nach u ra li zay' shun) n.
The process by which one can become naturalized.

11. naturopathy   NAT uropathy (na chu rop' a thee) n.
A system of treating disease by assisting nature.

12. natuary   NAT uary (nat' u ar i) n.
A ward in a hospital for women during childbirth.

13. innate   in NAT e (in ate') adj.
Inborn; inherent in.

14. renascent   re NASC ent (re nas' ent) adj.
Reborn.

15. renascence   re NASC ence (re nas' ens) n.
A rebirth; a revival.

16. nation   NAT ion (nay' shun) n.
A people with a common origin.

17. national   NAT ional (nash' un al) adj.
                 Relating to a nation.
18. nationalism   NAT ionalism (nash' un al iz um) n.
                 The belief that to support the nation is the
                 highest duty.
19. nationality   NAT ionality (nash u nal' it ee) n.
                 Country of origin.
20. international   inter NAT ional (int er nash' un al) adj.
                 Between or among nations.

word analysis

NATURALIZATION—No. 10
     NAT (natus)—Latin Root =born
     URE—Suffix =state of
     AL—Suffix =relating to
     IZE—Suffix =make
     TION—Suffix =state of

practical exercises

1. Supply the missing words:
     The American policy of democracy does not approve of
     .... President John Tyler invited all refugees to
     come to America and become ....(d).

2. Analyze No. 17.

3. Write a word on the line which expresses the meaning of the
     word or phrase in parenthesis below the line:
     a. His talent is ....
                   (inborn)
     b. She answered with ....
                   (childish simplicity)
     c. No one knew the man's ....
                   (country of origin)
     d. Luther Burbank was a .... (ist).
                   (one versed in natural science)
     e. Washington's Birthday is a .... holiday.
                   (relating to the nation)

KEY NO. 27

IC

nature of
like

is the Suffix *IC* which means NA-TURE OF; LIKE. Now, just to check, are you sure that you are saying *IC* and not just having a hiccough? In the word *hiccough* the *IC* is not at the end and has no value at all. Since *IC* is so simple, I'll add the Suffixes *AL* and *LY*. You will now have a compound Suffix, *ICALLY*. It can be added to pract*ICALLY* every adjective and then it becomes an adverb as: acid*ICALLY*, caust*ICALLY*, barbar*ICALLY*, strateg*ICALLY*, geolog-*ICALLY*, hero*ICALLY*, majest*ICAL-LY*, etc.

1. endemic   endem IC (en dem′ ik) adj.
   Native to a particular people or country.
2. barbaric   barbar IC (bar bar′ ik) adj.
   Like a barbarian.
3. caustic   caust IC (kaw′ stik) adj.
   Characterized by burning, sharpness.
4. acidic   acid IC (a sid′ ik) adj.
   Like an acid.
5. geologic   geolog IC (jee o loj′ ik) adj.
   Relating to geology.
6. metallic   metall IC (me tal′ ik) adj.
   Like metal.
7. drastic   drast IC (dras′ tik) adj.
   Relating to rapid action.
8. heroic   hero IC (he roe′ ik) adj.
   Like a hero.
9. majestic   majest IC (ma jes′ tik) adj.
   Like royalty.
10. galactic   galact IC (ga lak′ tik) adj.
    Relating to the galaxy.
11. metaphoric   metaphor IC (met a for′ ik) adj.
    Like a metaphor, a figure of speech.
12. prosaic   prosa IC (pro zay′ ik) adj.
    Related to the prose form; commonplace; dull.
13. poetic   poet IC (poe et′ ik) adj.
    Relating to poets or poetry.
14. patriotic   patriot IC (pay tree ot′ ik) adj.
    Characterized by love of one's country.

15. Semitic   Semit IC (se mit' ik) adj.
                 Relating to the Semites.

16. strategic   strateg IC (stra tee' jik) adj.
                 Relating to planning for defense.

17. satanic   satan IC (sa tan' ik) adj.
                 Like Satan; devilish.

18. tragic   trag IC (traj' ik) adj.
                 Like a tragedy; calamity.

19. emphatic   emphat IC (em fat' ik) adj.
                 Characterized by strong expression.

20. realistic   realist IC (ree a lis' tik) adj.
                 Like reality; like life as it is.

word analysis

GEOLOGICALLY—No. 5+ALLY
    GEO—Root =earth
    LOG (logos)—Greek Root =word
    IC—Suffix =nature of
    AL—Suffix =relating to
    LY—Suffix =in the manner of

practical exercises

1. Supply the missing words:
    For .... reasons he assumed the role of a
spy, but actually he was a .... soldier of his
country and a .... one.

2. Analyze No. 13.

3. Where possible use the compound Suffix ICALLY:
Example: instead of saying "to use a metaphor," I can
      say "metaphorically speaking."
    a. like a poet   ....
    b. like a hero   ....
    c. in a violent manner   ....
    d. like a patriot   ....
    e. the play ended in tragedy   ....
    f. she spoke with emphasis   ....

is the Root *AUD, AUS* (which comes from the Latin *audire*) meaning HEAR; LISTEN. All the words with *AUD* are simple words which you have heard many times. The three words with *AUS*, Nos. 18–20, are probably new. Besides, they have a special significance. The listening in those words is to sounds within the body, very small sounds, in*AUD*ible except with an *AUS*cultoscope.

1. audible   AUD ible (aud' i b'l) adj.
              Can be heard.
2. auditor   AUD itor (aud' it er) n.
              One who listens, hears.
3. audience   AUD ience (aud' ee ens) n.
              An assembly of listeners.
4. audit   AUD it (aud' it) n.
              A formal examination of accounts made by an accountant.
5. audition   AUD ition (au dish' un) n.
              A hearing; as, the singer was given an audition.
6. auditorium AUD itorium (aud i tore' ee um) n.
              A part of a building used for audience assembly.
7. audio   AUD io (aud' ee o) adj.
              Relating to sound by electric currents in the air.
8. audiogram   AUD iogram (au' di o gram) n.
              A graph that shows the relation of audibility to frequency.
9. audiometer AUD iometer (aud ee om' et er) n.
              An instrument by which hearing can be measured.
10. audiphone AUD iphone (au' di fone) n.
              A plate which carries sound vibrations; a hearing-aid.
11. auditory   AUD itory (aud' i tore ee) adj.
              Relating to hearing; as, auditory nerves.
12. audile   AUD ile (au' dile) adj.
              Having mental images that are auditory.
13. audivision AUD ivision (au' di vizh un) n.
              Sound accompanying pictures.

14. audivise   AUD ivise (au' di vize) v.
         To receive or transmit, by audivision.
15. audient   AUD ient (au' di ent) adj.
         Listening; paying attention.
16. inaudible   in AUD ible (in aud' i b'l) adj.
         Cannot be heard.
17. audibility   AUD ibility (aud i bil' it ee) n.
         Intensity of a received signal.
18. auscultate   AUS cultate (aw' skul tate) v.
         To listen to sounds within such cavities of the
         body as the chest and abdomen.
19. auscultation AUS cultation (aw skul tay' shun) n.
         The act of listening to sounds within the body.
20. auscultator   AUS cultator (aw' skul tay tor) n.
         A practitioner of auscultation.

word analysis

AUDIVISION—No. 13
    AUDI (audire)—Latin Root = to hear
    VIS (visus)—Root = see
    SION—Suffix = act of

practical exercises

1. Supply the missing words:
    At the .... the singer was so nervous that
she did not do herself justice. Every word he said was
.... throughout the large ....

2. Analyze No. 16.

3. Choose the number of the word which best expresses the italicized word:
    Example: *auditorium* (1) pantry (2) workshop
       (3) laundry (4) assembly room (5) hallway   ....4....
   a. *audient* (1) observant (2) impatient
      (3) subservient (4) obedient
      (5) listening attentively   ....
   b. *auditor* (1) singer (2) listener (3) radio
      (4) computer (5) telescope   ....
   c. *emphatic* (1) majestic (2) tragic (3) comic
      (4) basic (5) forceful   ....
   d. *announce* (1) plead (2) praise (3) evade
      (4) make known (5) deny   ....

KEY NO. 29

VIS · VID

see

is the Root *VIS, VID* which means SEE. It comes from the Latin verb *video, visus,* which means to SEE. The two spellings you have in words with this key come from the two spellings in the Latin verb it comes from. That is why, while most of the words on the list are spelled *VIS*, Nos. 17, 18, 20 have *VID*. You will notice that the two spellings are even found in different forms of the same word. ProVIDe, No. 18, becomes proVISion, No. 19. Julius Caesar wrote, "Veni, *vidi*, vici"—"I came, I saw, I conquered."

1. visa
    VIS a (vee′ za) n.
    An endorsement on a passport giving the bearer the right to proceed.

2. vis-à-vis
    VIS-à-VIS (vee za vee′) n.
    One who is face to face with another.

3. visage
    VIS age (viz′ ij) n.
    The face or look of a person.

4. visible
    VIS ible (viz′ a b′l) adj.
    Can be seen.

5. visile
    VIS ile (viz′ al) adj.
    Relating to vision; recalls visual impressions.

6. vision
    VIS ion (vizh′ un) n.
    Something seen; the ability to see; eyesight.

7. visionary
    VIS ionary (vizh′ un ar ee) n.
    One who sees visions; a dreamer.

8. envision
    en VIS ion (en vizh′ un) v.
    To see in one's mind.

9. visit
    VIS it (viz′ it) n.
    The act of visiting; as, an official visit.

10. visitor
    VIS itor (viz′ it or) n.
    One who makes a visit; a guest.

11. visitation
    VIS itation (viz i tay′ shun) n.
    An official visit; something that visits; as, an affliction.

12. visor
    VIS or (vie′ zor) n.
    A mask for the face; a brim on a cap to protect the eyes.

13. vista
    VIS ta (vis′ ta) n.
    A view from a distance.

14. visual   VIS ual (vizh' yu al) adj.
                Relating to sight.

15. visualize   VIS ualize (vizh' yu wa lize) v.
                *To make visible; to bring into the mind the
                face of one not present.*

16. invisible   in VIS ible (in viz' i b'l) adj.
                Cannot be seen.

17. evident   e VID ent (ev' id ent) adj.
                Can easily be seen.

18. provide   pro VID e (pro vide') v.
                To see what will be needed and supply it.

19. provision   pro VIS ion (pro vizh' un) n.
                That which was provided beforehand.

20. providential   pro VID ential (prov i den' chal) adj.
                Provided by divine guidance; opportune; lucky.

word analysis

VISUALIZE—No. 15
    VISU (visus)—Latin Root =to see
    AL—Suffix =relating to
    IZE—Suffix =make

practical exercises

1. Supply the missing words:
    She was .... and was able to ....
    what the author of the book intended his readers to see. He
    was an excellent ....(r). He stocked up ....
    for the journey.

2. Analyze No. 6.

3. Syllabicate and indicate which syllable is most strongly ac-
    cented by placing the accent mark ('):
       auscultation   strategically   practically
       drastically   pathetically   visitant
       auditorium   television

KEY NO. 30

AGE

act of
state of
function
result of
collection of

is the Suffix *AGE* which means ACT OF; STATE OF; FUNCTION; RESULT OF; COLLECTION OF. It is an easy key to recognize. Other words you will meet with this key are dot-*AGE*, mir*AGE*, sabot*AGE* and many others.

1. carriage   carri AGE (kar' ij) n.
   The act or manner of carrying oneself.

2. courage   cour AGE (kur' ij) n.
   Strength of mind and heart.

3. courageous   cour AGE ous (ku ray' jus) adj.
   Having strength; lacking fear; being brave.

4. outrageous   outr AGE ous (out ray' jus) adj.
   Full of wild misdoing; abusive.

5. marriage   marri AGE (mar' ij) n.
   State of wedlock.

6. marriageable   marri AGE able (mar' ij a b'l) adj.
   Can be married.

7. envisage   envis AGE (en viz' ij) v.
   To see with the mind's eye.

8. outrage   outr AGE (out' raje) n.
   Wild wrong doing; abuse.

9. damage   dam AGE (dam' ij) n.
   Loss due to injury; harm.

10. outrageously   outr AGE ously (out ray' jus lee) adv.
    Wildly; abusively.

11. salvage   salv AGE (sal' vij) v.
    Save; make fit for use; as, salvage a ship.

12. salvageable   salv AGE able (sal' vij a b'l) adj.
    Worth saving.

13. forage   for AGE (for' ij) n.
    Food for horses and cattle.

14. forage   for AGE (for' ij) v.
    Search for food; as, to secure food by stripping a farm.

15. storage   stor AGE (stor' ij) n.
    Act of storing; as, for safe-keeping.

16. pillage   pill AGE (pil' ij) n.
    Act of robbery; plunder in war.

17. visage   vis AGE (viz′ ij) n.
Face; appearance.

word analysis

COURAGEOUS—No. 3
    COUR (cor)—Latin Root =heart; spirit
    AGE—Suffix =state of
    OUS—Suffix =having; full of

practical exercises

1. Supply the missing words:
    Four soldiers were detailed to .... for the
horses. The farmer said that what they were doing was
.... He had forgotten the old ....
and did not count ten before speaking.

2. Analyze No. 2.

3. Key review. Match keys with their meanings:
    a. vis   1. like   ....
    b. aud   2. out   ....
    c. ic   3. hear   ....
    d. age   4. born   ....
    e. nat   5. act of, function   ....
    f. ec   6. see   ....

KEY NO. *31*

0—⚷

DIS

**take away
not
deprive of**

is the Prefix *DIS* which means TAKE
AWAY; NOT (Negative); DEPRIVE
OF. It is different from other keys
which have similar meanings. *DIS*
carries with it a sense of failure; you
had something and lost it. A soldier
who played the violin and lost a
couple of fingers was *DIS*abled. A
man who cheated and lost his credit
became *DIS*credited. See?

1. disarm   DIS arm (dis arm') v.
   To take away a weapon; leave defenseless.

2. disagree   DIS agree (dis a gree') v.
   Not to have the same opinion.

3. disaster   DIS aster (diz as' ter) n.
   A mishap; absence of your lucky star.

4. disabled   DIS abled (dis ay' b'ld) adj.
   To be deprived of use, as by an injury.

5. disadvantage DIS advantage (dis ad vant' ij) n.
   A loss; a detriment; a handicap.

6. disbar   DIS bar (dis bar') v.
   To keep away; as, to disbar a lawyer.

7. discourage   DIS courage (dis kur' ij) v.
   To take away hope; to cause to lose heart.

8. disease   DIS ease (dis eze') n.
   Not in normal state of health; sickness.

9. dishonor   DIS honor (dis on' er) v.
   To take away honor.

10. disgrace   DIS grace (dis grase') n.
    Shame; loss of the good opinion of others.

11. disgusting   DIS gusting (dis gus' ting) adj.
    Away from good taste; sickening.

12. discredit   DIS credit (dis kred' it) v.
    To refuse to accept; disbelieve.

13. disloyal   DIS loyal (dis loy' al) adj.
    Unfaithful.

14. distrust   DIS trust (dis trust') n.
    Lack of trust; doubt.

15. disconcerted DIS concerted (dis kon sert' ed) adj.
    Deprived of control; upset; disturbed.

16. dissolved   DIS solved (diz olvd') adj.
    Melted away; broken up.

17. disregard   DIS regard (dis re gard') v.
    To pay no attention to.

18. dispose   DIS pose (dis poze') v.
               To be inclined to; to throw away.
19. disapprove   DIS approve (dis a pruv') v.
               To regard as wrong.
20. disinherit   DIS inherit (dis in her' it) v.
               To deprive of an inheritance.

word analysis

DISCREDITABLE—No. 12+ABLE
    DIS—Prefix =away; from
    CRED (credere)—Latin Root =believe
    IT (itus)—Latin Root =go
    ABLE—Suffix =can do

practical exercises

1. Supply the missing words:
    The lawyer ....(d) of the will because it
    .... the younger son. Because he was ....
    he was repaid by .... and he was ....(ed)
    at the bank.

2. Analyze No. 6.

3. Fill in keys needed to complete words or phrases:
    a. He could not be thought well of; the man was
       ....reput...........
    b. After so many lies he was completely ....credited.
    c. He could not bear the thought of ....inheriting his son.
    d. He scorned their ideas and he sat with a ....dain..........
       look on his face.

KEY NO. 32

MENT

**act of
state of
result of an action**

is the Suffix *MENT*, meaning ACT OF; STATE OF; RESULT OF AN ACTION. *MENT* makes nouns out of verbs when added to them. If you look down the list, you will see that nearly every word without the Suffix *MENT* is a verb. With the Suffix *MENT* the word becomes a noun. Nos. 12 and 14 are the only ones on the list which do not fall into that pattern. *MENT* is another one of those duplicating keys. It means ACT OF; STATE OF; QUALITY.

1. contentment   content MENT (kon tent' ment) n.
   A state of being satisfied with one's lot.
2. aggrandizement   aggrandize MENT (a gran' diz ment) n.
   State of becoming greater.
3. alignment   align MENT (a line' ment) n.
   Result of setting in line.
4. amendment   amend MENT (a mend' ment) n.
   Result of adding to a law.
5. apartment   apart MENT (a part' ment) n.
   A set of rooms to live in.
6. appeasement   appease MENT (a peze' ment) n.
   Act of quieting anger.
7. compliment   compli MENT (kom' pli ment) n.
   Praise given as a result of an action.
8. attainment   attain MENT (a tane' ment) n.
   The state of having reached a goal.
9. achievement   achieve MENT (a cheve' ment) n.
   A thing accomplished with effort.
10. appointment   appoint MENT (a point' ment) n.
    The result of an arrangement for a meeting.
11. excitement   excite MENT (ek site' ment) n.
    A state of being aroused.
12. ferment   fer MENT (fer' ment) n.
    A state of unrest; excitement.
13. indictment   indict MENT (in dite' ment) n.
    The result of an action in writing charging one with an offense
14. instrument   instru MENT (in' stru ment) n.
    A means to get a result; a tool.
15. nourishment   nourish MENT (nur' ish ment) n.
    Food for the body.

16. postponement   postpone MENT (post pone' ment) n.
> *The result of putting a thing off for later; a delay.*

17. presentiment   presenti MENT (pre sent' i ment) n.
> *A forewarning of evil to come.*

18. resentment   resent MENT (re zent' ment) n.
> *Result of anger against another for cause.*

19. statement   state MENT (state' ment) n.
> *An expression of fact or opinion.*

20. testament   testa MENT (tes' ta ment) n.
> *Result of an expression of tribute; credo.*

word analysis

POSTPONEMENT—No. 16
   POST—Prefix =after
   PONE (ponere)—Latin Root =place
   MENT—Suffix =act of

practical exercises

1. Supply the missing words:
   This .... marks the .... of his ambition. There was .... among the press because in the .... the winner left without making a ....

2. Analyze Disgraceful.

3. Use one word for each of the following phrases:
   Example: a forewarning of trouble   ....presentiment....
   a. food for the body   ....
   b. accomplishment of purpose   ....
   c. an act of delay   ....
   d. words of praise   ....
   e. known to be unworthy   ....

KEY NO. 33

O—⚷

FAC · FACT

make

is the Root *FAC, FACT*, meaning MAKE. It comes from the Latin *facere, factus,* to make; to construct. Word No. 13 is a gem of a word. Many people murder FACTS and insist that they are innocent. However, the word *facticide* is so funny that in the general laughter, the fact can be restored to life without ill feelings roused. Try it!

1. fact   FACT (fakt) n.
              A thing done; a deed.

2. faction   FAC tion (fak' shun) n.
              A small group usually of dissent; a party in government.

3. factious   FAC tious (fak' shus) adj.
              Inclined to dissent.

4. factor   FAC tor (fak' tor) n.
              One who transacts business.

5. factor   FAC tor (fak' tor) v.
              To resolve into factors.

6. factory   FAC tory (fak' to ree) n.
              The place where workmen are employed in making goods of various kinds.

7. faculty   FAC ulty (fak' ul tee) n.
              Ability to act or do.

8. factotum   FAC totum (fak tote' um) n.
              One who can do many things.

9. factitious FAC titious (fak tish' us) adj.
              Made by art, not produced by nature.

10. factive   FAC tive (fak' tiv) adj.
              Making; causing.

11. putrefactive putre FAC tive (pyu tre fak' tiv) adj.
              Causing decay; making a thing rotten.

12. satisfaction satis FAC tion (sat is fak' shun) n.
              The state in which everything is right.

13. facticide FAC ticide (fak' ti side) n.
              The act of killing a fact.

14. facile   FAC ile (fas' il) adj.
              Easily achieved.

15. facility   FAC ility (fa sil' it ee) n.
              The quality of being easy to do.

16. facilitate FAC ilitate (fa sil' i tate) v.
              To make easy to do.

66

17. facient   FAC ient (fay′ shent) n.
                      One who does things; a doer; an agent.
18. facsimile   FAC simile (fak sim′ i lee) n.
                      A copy that is exact in every detail.
19. manufacturer manu FAC turer (man yu fak′ chur er) n.
                      The owner of a factory.
20. dissatisfaction dissatis FAC tion (dis at is fak′ shun) n.
                      The state of being made unhappy; discontent.

word analysis

FACSIMILE—No. 18
    FAC (facere)—Latin Root =to make
    SIMILE (similis)—Latin Root =like; same

practical exercises

1. Supply the missing words:
    Practice makes for .... "The ....
    gates of hell, too slightly barred." (Milton) The company
    enjoyed the host's .... remarks.

2. Analyze No. 4.

3. Choose the number which best expresses the italicized word:
    Example: *fact* (1) aspect (2) party
          (3) nameplate (4) deed   ....4....
    a. *facsimile* (1) indignation (2) poverty
          (3) faculty (4) copy (5) despair   ....
    b. *faction* (1) health (2) type of architecture
          (3) clique (4) truth (5) judgment   ....
    c. *postponement* (1) management (2) statement
          (3) faith (4) delay (5) factory   ....
    d. *compliment* (1) praise (2) opportunity
          (3) choice (4) phantom (5) pleasure   ....
    e. *visage* (1) appearance (2) face (3) basement
          (4) contentment (5) industry   ....

KEY NO. 34

O—➤

FIC · FECT

make

is the Root *FIC, FECT* meaning MAKE. Your list contains only 20 words with this Root, but there are many, many more which you will recognize. You may meet the word *artifice* and you will recognize the root *FIC* and know that something was made. Or you may meet *artificial* and you will recognize two keys— *FIC* and *AL*, and you will know that the word *relates* to something that was made.

1. beneficiary   bene FIC iary (ben e fish′ ee er ee) n.
One who receives a benefit.

2. deification   dei FIC ation (dee if i kay′ shun) n.
Making a god out of something; as of money.

3. amplification   ampli FIC ation (am pli fi kay′ shun) n.
An enlargement.

4. acidification   acidi FIC ation (a sid i fi kay′ shun) n.
Act or process of making into acid.

5. calorific   calori FIC (cal o rif′ ik) adj.
Making heat.

6. certificate   certi FIC ate (ser tif′ i kat) n.
A written proof of a fact.

7. confection   con FECT ion (kon fek′ shun) n.
The act or process of making something; a dainty dish made of sugar and fruits; preserves.

8. affect   af FECT (a fekt′) v.
Make an impression upon.

9. defective   de FECT ive (de fek′ tiv) adj.
Wanting in something; faulty.

10. deficiency   de FIC iency (de fish′ en see) n.
Something lacking.

11. disinfect   dis in FECT (dis in fekt′) v.
To make free from disease germs.

12. effectual   ef FECT ual (e fek′ chu al) adj.
Having results.

13. efficacious   ef FIC acious (ef i kay′ shus) adj.
Producing the wanted effect.

14. efficacy   ef FIC acy (ef′ i ka see) n.
The ability to produce the wanted result.

68

15. magnificent   magni FIC ent (mag nif' i sent) adj.
                    Made grandly; strikingly attractive.
16. personification   personi FIC ation (per son i fi kay' shun) n.
                    Making an object resemble a person.
17. proficient   pro FIC ient (pro fish' ent) adj.
                    Able to do things well.
18. versification   versi FIC ation (ver si fi kay' shun) n.
                    Making lines in poetic form.

word analysis

DEIFICATION—No. 2
     DEI (deus)—Latin Root =god
     FIC (facere)—Latin Root =make
     TION—Suffix =act of

practical exercises

1. Supply the missing words:
     The cancer fund was the .... of the theater
     party.
     The teacher tried to correct my .... speech.

2. Analyze No. 15.

3. Syllabicate and indicate which syllable is most strongly accented by placing the accent mark ('):
     acidification   certificate   efficacy
     beneficiary   effectual   disinfect

KEY NO. 35

O—x

NON

not

is the Prefix *NON* which means NOT in practically all languages in some similar form. You have already had *IN* and *IM* meaning NOT and *UN* meaning NOT. You will see that *NON* is not as emphatic as *IN*, *IM* and *UN*. For example: "He is a non-American" simply means that he is not an American citizen, he is a citizen of another country. "He is un-American" means he's engaged in activities which are contrary to the American way of life; he violates the ideals of American Democracy.

1. nonage
   NON age (non' ij) n.
   State of not being of legal age.

2. nonaggression
   NON aggression (non a gre' shun) n.
   State of not being aggressive.

3. noncommissioned
   NON commissioned (non ko mish' und) adj.
   An officer of minor rank.

4. nondescript
   NON descript (non' de skript) adj.
   Not easily described.

5. nonconformist
   NON conformist (non kon form' ist) n.
   One who does not always adapt himself to set rules.

6. noncontemporary
   NON contemporary
   (non kon tem' po rar ee) adj.
   Not living at the present time.

7. nondelegable
   NON delegable (non del' e ga b'l) adj.
   Not able to be delegated.

8. nonevil
   NON evil (non e' vil) n.
   Not an evil thing.

9. non compos mentis
   NON compos mentis
   (non kom pu sment' us) adj.
   (Latin) Of unsound mind.

10. nonsense
    NON sense (non' sens) n.
    Something which does not make sense.

11. nonsensical
    NON sensical (non sen' si kal) adj.
    Not making sense.

12. nonprofit
    NON profit (non prof' it) adj.
    Not for making money.

13. nontaxable
    NON taxable (non taks' a b'l) adj.
    Not able to be taxed.

14. nontoxic   NON toxic (non tok' sik) adj.
Having no poisonous effects.

15. nonpartisan   NON partisan (non part' i zan) adj.
Not belonging to any party.

16. nonstop   NON stop (non stop') adj.
Without stopping.

17. nonphenomenal   NON phenomenal
(non' fe nom e nal) adj.
Existing as a reality.

18. nonplus   NON plus (non plus') n.
A state of uncertainty, perplexity.

19. nonquota   NON quota (non kwote' a) adj.
Not part of a quota.

20. nonsequitur   NON sequitur (non sek' wi tur) n.
In logic something that does not follow.

word analysis

NONCONTEMPORARY—No. 6
     NON—Prefix =not
     CON—Prefix =with
     TEMPOR (tempus)—Latin Root =time
     ARY—Suffix =one who

practical exercises

1. Supply the missing words:
     The jury acquitted him on the grounds that he was
.... In all questions of social justice he had
a .... attitude.

2. Analyze No. 10.

3. Choose the number which most nearly expresses the italicized
word:
Example: *nonsense* (1) foolishness (2) labor
     (3) science (4) philosophy (5) literature   ....1....
a. *nondescript* (1) stunning (2) glorious
     (3) glamorous (4) not easily described
     (5) fancy   ....
b. *nonage* (1) maturity (2) seniority (3) senility
     (4) under legal age (5) infancy   ....
c. *proficient* (1) capable (2) sufficient
     (3) deficient (4) unable (5) confection   ....
d. *fiction* (1) fact (2) artifice (3) truth
     (4) history (5) biography   ....

is the Suffix *ARY, ERY, ORY*. All are pretty much alike in meaning. They make nouns and adjectives. In adjectives they mean RELATING TO. In nouns they show a certain QUALITY and show PLACE WHERE.

relating to
quality
place where

1. burglary   burgl ARY (bur' gla ree) n.
   The act of breaking into a place for theft.
2. dictionary   diction ARY (dik' shu nar ee) n.
   A book of words and their meanings.
3. dietary   diet ARY (die' e tar ee) adj.
   Relating to diet; as, dietary laws.
4. necessary   necess ARY (nes' e ser ee) adj.
   Relating to need; as, necessary food.
5. primary   prim ARY (prie' mar ee) adj.
   Relating to first things; important things.
6. voluntary   volunt ARY (vol' un tar ee) adj.
   Relating to free will; as, a voluntary service.
7. bakery   bak ERY (bay' ke ree) n.
   A place where foods are baked or sold.
8. bindery   bind ERY (bine' de ree) n.
   A place where books are bound.
9. bravery   brav ERY (brave' e ree) n.
   The quality of courage.
10. bribery   brib ERY (brie' be ree) n.
    The act of influencing the act of another by a gift of money; as, bribery of a judge.
11. reformatory   reformat ORY (re for' ma tore ee) n.
    A place where the young wrongdoer is helped to reform.
12. repertory   repert ORY (rep' er tore ee) n.
    A place where something may be located; the plays presented in turn by a drama group.
13. witchery   witch ERY (wich' e ree) n.
    The quality of witchcraft; charm.
14. depository   deposit ORY (de poz' i tore ee) n.
    A place where valuable things are placed.
15. dormitory   dormit ORY (dor' mi tore ee) n.
    A place where people sleep; as, a college or school dormitory.

16. factory   fact ORY (fak' to ree) n.
                    *A place where workers are employed to make
                    goods.*

17. memory   mem ORY (mem' o ree) n.
                    The process of recalling.

18. obligatory   obligat ORY (o blig' a tore ee) adj.
                    Relating to a duty.

19. stationary   station ARY (stay' shu ner ee) adj.
                    Fixed in one place.

word analysis

REFORMATORY—No. 11
     RE—Prefix =again
     FORMAT (formatus)—Latin Root =form
     ORY—Suffix =place where

practical exercises

1. Supply the missing words:
     It is foolish not to observe the simple ....
     rules for good health. .... hurts the one who
     gives as well as the one who takes. A good ....
     is much to be desired for recalling facts.

2. Analyze No. 16.

3. Use one word to express the phrase:
   a. a list of works which a group can perform ....
   b. a place where valuables can be deposited ....
   c. a building in a college where students sleep ....
   d. document showing the truth of a fact ....
   e. the lack of a vital ingredient ....

KEY NO. 37

0—⚡

ATE

cause
make

is the Suffix *ATE* which means to CAUSE, MAKE. In the following list all the words are verbs. In other places you will find *ATE* as an ending for nouns, as in No. 2, which can also be a noun meaning a defender. No. 7 can be a noun, too, meaning one who deviates. The meaning is practically the same—*ATE* =CAUSES, MAKES.

1. dedicate   dedic ATE (ded' i kate) v.
     To set apart for a purpose.

2. advocate   advoc ATE (ad' vo kate) v.
     To speak for; to defend.

3. arrogate   arrog ATE (ar' o gate) v.
     To claim as one's own without right.

4. educate   educ ATE (ej' u kate) v.
     To provide with schooling; to lead to knowledge.

5. consecrate   consecr ATE (kon' se krate) v.
     To put into religious office by a rite; to make sacred; as to consecrate an altar.

6. abbreviate   abbrevi ATE (a bree' vee ate) v.
     Make short.

7. deviate   devi ATE (dee' vee ate) v.
     To turn aside from the right way; cause to stray.

8. attenuate   attenu ATE (a ten' yu wate) v.
     To make thin; to weaken.

9. enumerate   enumer ATE (e nu' mer ate) v.
     To count; list one after the other.

10. emanate   eman ATE (em' a nate) v.
     To come from; to flow forth.

11. exaggerate   exagger ATE (eg zaj' e rate) v.
     To cause to appear larger than reality.

12. fascinate   fascin ATE (fas' in ate) v.
     To put under a spell; charm.

13. integrate   integr ATE (int' e grate) v.
     To cause to become a whole.

14. infiltrate   infiltr ATE (in fil' trate) v.
     To cause to slip through; as through enemy lines or a filter.

15. liquidate   liquid ATE (lik' wi date) v.
     To end a debt by payment; to eliminate.

16. segregate   segreg ATE (seg' re gate) v.
               To keep apart; separate.

17. permeate   perme ATE (per' mee ate) v.
               To go through and through.

18. enervate   enerv ATE (en' er vate) v.
               To take away strength; enfeeble.

19. emancipate   emancip ATE (e man' si pate) v.
               To set free from control; release from slavery.

20. decimate   decim ATE (des' i mate) v.
               To kill every tenth man in a group; destroy large numbers.

word analysis

SEGREGATE—No. 16
    SE—Prefix =apart; separate
    GREG (gress)—Root =come together
    ATE—Suffix =cause; make

practical exercises

1. Supply the missing words:
    "We cannot ...., we cannot ....
    it is rather for us to be ....(d) here. . . ."
    (Abraham Lincoln) Spies, knowing many languages,
    .... the enemy lines.

2. Analyze No. 15.

3. Key review. Match keys with their meanings.
    a. ate   1. place where   ....
    b. ory, ary, ery   2. hear   ....
    c. fict, fic, fect   3. state   ....
    d. ic   4. deprive of   ....
    e. ment   5. like   ....
    f. dis   6. function   ....
    g. age   7. make   ....
    h. aud   8. cause   ....

KEY NO. 38

ITY · TY

state of
quality

is the Suffix *ITY* which means
STATE OF; QUALITY. This key
makes nouns from adjectives, as *pure
—purITY*. Sometimes only *TY* is used,
as in *liberTY, HumpTY DumpTY*,
and others. Both forms mean the
same thing—STATE; QUALITY.

1. celerity
 celer ITY (se ler' it ee) n.
  The quality of quickness; speed.

2. absurdity
 absurd ITY (ab surd' it ee) n.
  The state of being ridiculous.

3. acerbity
 acerb ITY (a ser' bit ee) n.
  The quality of bitterness.

4. acuity
 acu ITY (a kyue' it ee) n.
  The quality of sharpness, as a needle.

5. debility
 debil ITY (de bil' it ee) n.
  A state of weakness.

6. ambiguity
 ambigu ITY (am bi gyue' it ee) n.
  The quality of uncertainty in meaning.

7. authority
 author ITY (au thor' it ee) n.
  The state of having power to act.

8. amenity
 amen ITY (a men' it ee) n.
  The quality of pleasantness.

9. captivity
 captiv ITY (cap tiv' it ee) n.
  State of being held captive.

10. ability
 abil ITY (a bil' it ee) n.
  The quality of being able to do things.

11. charity
 char ITY (char' it ee) n.
  Kindness to the poor.

12. chastity
 chast ITY (chas' tit ee) n.
  The state of sexual purity.

13. clarity
 clar ITY (clar' it ee) n.
  Quality of clearness.

14. complexity
 complex ITY (kom plek' sit ee) n.
  The quality of being complicated.

15. adversity
 advers ITY (ad ver' sit ee) n.
  The state of bad fortune, suffering.

16. dignity
 dign ITY (dig' nit ee) n.
  The state of being worthy; self respect.

17. eternity
 etern ITY (e ter' nit ee) n.
  State of timelessness; time without end.

18. fraternity
 fratern ITY (fra ter' nit ee) n.
  The quality of being brothers.

19. garrulity   garrul ITY (ga ru' lit ee) n.
                        The quality of talkativeness.
20. luminosity   luminos ITY (lu mi nos' it ee) n.
                        The state of having a great deal of light; brilliance.

word analysis

ACUITY—No. 4
     ACU (acus)—Root =sharp
     ITY—Suffix =quality

practical exercises

1. Supply the missing words:
     The French ideal is ...., ...,
     .... "Almost all .... of conduct
arises from the imitation of those whom we cannot resemble." (Samuel Johnson)

2. Analyze Acidity.

3. Syllabicate and indicate the syllable that is most strongly accented by placing the accent mark ('):

chastity	debility	luminosity
eternity	acuity	acerbity
ambiguity	garrulity	authority

77

KEY NO. 39

O—⚷

OUS

**full of
having**

is the Suffix *OUS* which means FULL OF; HAVING. This key has a positive personality and the words which contain it are positive and strong. For good or for evil, they are powerful in thought, feeling and action.

1. opprobrious   opprobri OUS (o pro' bree us) adj.
     Disgraceful; reproachful.

2. delicious   delici OUS (de lish' us) adj.
     Having a delightful taste.

3. gracious   graci OUS (gray' shus) adj.
     Full of kindness; as, a gracious hostess.

4. homogeneous   homogene OUS (hoe moe jee' nee us) adj.
     Having the same quality throughout.

5. luscious   lusci OUS (lush' us) adj.
     Having a taste and smell that is delicious.

6. mysterious   mysteri OUS (mis ter' ee us) adj.
     Full of obscurity; mystery.

7. nervous   nerv OUS (ner' vus) adj.
     Full of spirit; not calm; excited easily.

8. oblivious   oblivi OUS (o bliv' ee us) adj.
     Forgetful; mindless; unaware.

9. obnoxious   obnoxi OUS (ob nok' shus) adj.
     Hateful; objectionable.

10. obsequious   obsequi OUS (ob se' kwi us) adj.
     Slavishly flattering.

11. obvious   obvi OUS (ob' vee us) adj.
     Easily seen or understood; having a clear meaning; plain.

12. pugnacious   pugnaci OUS (pug nay' shus) adj.
     Having an inclination to fight; quarrelsome.

13. rapacious   rapaci OUS (ra pay' shus) adj.
     Having a grasping nature; greedy.

14. serious   seri OUS (ser' ee us) adj.
     Full of earnestness; thoughtful.

15. tremendous   tremend OUS (tre men' dus) adj.
     Dreadful; powerful; awful.

16. vivacious   vivaci OUS (vi vay' shus) adj.
     Full of life; spirited; merry.

17. voracious   voraci OUS (vo ray' shus) adj.
     Always eating; gluttonous.

18. spacious   spaci OUS (spay′ shus) adj.
                  Having much space; roomy.
19. malicious   malici OUS (ma lish′ us) adj.
                  Full of malice; ill-willed.
20. covetous   covet OUS (kov′ et us) adj.
                  Full of envy; wanting what others have.

word analysis

OBLOQUIOUS
     OB—Prefix =against
     LOQUI (loquor)—Latin Root =to speak
     OUS—Suffix =full of

practical exercises

1. Supply the missing words:
     The customer was .... to the fawning of the
     .... clerk. The estate was known for its
     .... lawns and the hostess for her ....
     hospitality.

2. Analyze No. 7.

3. Supply the word which expresses the phrase:
     a. full of mystery   ....
     b. full of life   ....
     c. full of disapproval   ....
     d. having plenty of space   ....
     e. full of malice   ....

KEY NO. *40*

O—x

AB · ABS

away
from
separation

is the Prefix *AB*, *ABS* meaning AWAY; FROM; SEPARATION. Please note the two ways of spelling this key. The *s* is added to *AB* before the letter *t*. It is easier to say *AB-stain* than *ABtain*. The meaning of the key remains the same. Learn to recognize this key, and be sure it is at the beginning of the word and not at the end. In the middle of a word or at the end it is not the prefix meaning AWAY, FROM, SEPARATION.

1. abbreviate   AB breviate (a bree' vee ate) v.
     To shorten; make brief.

2. abdicate   AB dicate (ab' di kate) v.
     To give up; as, abdicate a throne.

3. abduct   AB duct (ab dukt') v.
     To lead away by force; kidnap.

4. aberration   AB erration (ab e ray' shun) n.
     Act of wandering away; unsoundness of mind.

5. abhor   AB hor (ab hor') v.
     To turn away from; loathe; shudder at.

6. abjure   AB jure (ab jure') v.
     To swear away; renounce.

7. ablate   AB late (a' blate) v.
     To remove; to cut away.

8. ablution   AB lution (a blue' shun) n.
     The act of washing away; often in a rite.

9. abnegate   AB negate (ab' ne gate) v.
     To relinquish; give up forever.

10. abnormal   AB normal (ab nor' mal) adj.
     Away from the normal; aberrant.

11. abolish   AB olish (a bol' ish) v.
     Do away with; completely destroy.

12. abortion   AB ortion (a bor' shun) n.
     Failure to attain full development.

13. abrasion   AB rasion (a bray' zhun) n.
     A rubbing or scraping away.

14. abrogate   AB rogate (ab' ro gate) v.
     To repeal; to do away with.

15. abscond   AB scond (ab skond') v.
     To steal away and hide; to decamp.

16. absolve   AB solve (ab zolv´) v.
                   To free from blame; exonerate.
17. abstain   AB stain (ab stane´) v.
                   Hold off from; as, abstain *from voting.*
18. abstergent   ABS tergent (ab ster´ jent) n.
                   A cleanser; something to remove dirt.
19. abstract   ABS tract (ab strakt´) v.
                   Draw away; separate from association.
20. absorb   AB sorb (ab sorb´) v.
                   Suck in; drink in; as, a sponge will absorb
                   water.

word analysis

ABSTERGENT—No. 18
     ABS—Prefix =away
     TERG (tergere)—Latin Root =wipe
     ENT—Suffix =that which; one who

practical exercises

1. Supply the missing words:
     The Belgians forced the king to .... in favor
of his son. The jury agreed to .... the prisoner
of all blame. Before the treasurer could ....
with the money, he was arrested.

2. Analyze No. 10.

3. Supply the KEY which enables one word to express the
phrase:
     a. the quality of violence   rapac..........
     b. the quality of light   luminos..........
     c. the quality of a needle's sharpness   acu..........
     d. the quality of clearness   clar..........
     e. the quality of worth   dign..........

KEY NO. *41*

O—🗝

SHIP

office
state
dignity
skill
quality
profession

is the Suffix *SHIP* which can mean OFFICE; STATE; DIGNITY; SKILL; QUALITY; PROFESSION. You can add it to practically anything you wish to praise or honor as being skilled, dignified, on top in a profession, or expert.

1. hardship   hard SHIP (hard' ship) n.
   Suffering.
2. friendship   friend SHIP (frend' ship) n.
   Good personal relationships.
3. apprenticeship   apprentice SHIP (a prent' is ship) n.
   The time in a profession when one is learning his trade.
4. authorship   author SHIP (au' thor ship) n.
   The profession of writing.
5. horsemanship   horseman SHIP (hor' sman ship) n.
   Skill in handling horses.
6. marksmanship   marksman SHIP (mark' sman ship) n.
   Skill in hitting the mark.
7. scholarship   scholar SHIP (skol' ar ship) n.
   The qualities of an advanced student.
8. fellowship   fellow SHIP (fel' o ship) n.
   The quality of being companions.
9. courtship   court SHIP (kort' ship) n.
   The act of wooing.
10. lordship   lord SHIP (lord' ship) n.
    A title indicating the dignity of a peer.
11. ladyship   lady SHIP (lade' ee ship) n.
    A title indicating the dignity of a peeress.
12. championship   champion SHIP (cham' pee on ship) n.
    The office of a defender of rights.
13. citizenship   citizen SHIP (sit' i zen ship) n.
    The quality of membership in a community; the status of being a citizen.
14. chancellorship   chancellor SHIP (chan' se lor ship) n.
    The office of the head of a university.
15. professorship   professor SHIP (pro fes' or ship) n.
    The office of a teacher.

16. dictatorship dictator SHIP (dik tate' or ship) n.
   The office of the head of a totalitarian state.
17. craftsmanship craftsman SHIP (kraft' sman ship) n.
   High quality of skill in a craft.
18. sportsmanship sportsman SHIP (sport' sman ship) n.
   Skill in the world of sports.
19. shipmanship shipman SHIP (ship' man ship) n.
   Science of navigation; seamanship.
20. showmanship showman SHIP (sho' man ship) n.
   Skill in display.

word analysis

DICTATORSHIP—No. 16
   DICTAT (dictatus)—Latin Root =dictate
   OR—Suffix =one who
   SHIP—Suffix =office; position

practical exercises

1. Supply the missing words:
   Not all voters accept their responsibility of ....
   toward keeping the government free from ....
   Not all .... shows the .... of a
   Hemingway or the .... of a Conan Doyle.

2. Analyze No. 11.

3. Choose the number of the word which best expresses the
   italicized word:
   Example: *abnormal* (1) happy (2) dignified
      (3) satisfactory (4) unnatural (5) safe   ....4....
   a. *abstract* (1) continue (2) reach (3) command
      (4) draw away (5) return   ....
   b. *abdicate* (1) supply (2) execute (3) renounce
      (4) object (5) entertain   ....
   c. *abhor* (1) adore (2) loathe (3) please
      (4) purchase (5) sell   ....
   d. *obnoxious* (1) beautiful (2) merited
      (3) different (4) tasty (5) disgusting   ....
   e. *opportunity* (1) meeting (2) privilege
      (3) chance (4) adolescence (5) thoughtfulness   ....

O━ⵒ

ANCE · ANCY

action
process
quality
state
degree

is the Suffix *ANCE, ANCY,* meaning ACTION; PROCESS; QUALITY; STATE and DEGREE. It is surprising and pleasing to see how much of the strangeness of a word disappears as soon as you know the Prefixes and the Suffixes.

1. accountancy   account ANCY (a kount' an see) n.
    The job of record keeping.
2. assistance   assist ANCE (a sis' tans) n.
    The act of giving help to one in need of it.
3. attendance   attend ANCE (a ten' dans) n.
    The act of waiting upon; service.
4. allowance   allow ANCE (a low' ans) n.
    The amount granted, often for expenses.
5. alliance   alli ANCE (a lie' ans) n.
    The state of being joined together.
6. defiance   defi ANCE (de fie' ans) n.
    The act of defying; state of being against.
7. endurance   endur ANCE (en dur' ans) n.
    The ability to withstand hardship.
8. elegance   eleg ANCE (el' e gans) n.
    The qualities of tastefulness and gracefulness.
9. reluctance   reluct ANCE (re luk' tans) n.
    Unwillingness.
10. tolerance   toler ANCE (tol' e rans) n.
    An act of courteous forbearance to differences.
11. intolerance   intoler ANCE (in tol' e rans) n.
    Opposite of No. 10.
12. militancy   milit ANCY (mil' i tan see) n.
    A fighting spirit.
13. dominance   domin ANCE (dom' i nans) n.
    State of authority.
14. relevance   relev ANCE (rel' e vans) n.
    Quality of being related to something.
15. vigilance   vigil ANCE (vij' i lans) n.
    Watchfulness; alertness.
16. resistance   resist ANCE (re zis' tans) n.
    The process of standing against something.

word analysis

INTOLERANCE—No. 11
　IN—Prefix =not
　TOLER (tolero)—Latin Root =endure
　ANCE—Suffix =quality of

practical exercises

1. Supply the missing words:
　　"Eternal .... is the price of safety." After
　　the attack the .... disappeared. As if in ....
　　of the storm, a throng of people swelled the ....
　　at the lecture.

2. Analyze No. 16.

3. Key Review. Match keys with their meaning:
　　a. ate　　　1. native of　　　..........
　　b. re　　　 2. across　　　　..........
　　c. an　　　 3. out　　　　　..........
　　d. ible　　 4. separate into two　..........
　　e. trans　　5. bear　　　　　..........
　　f. port　　 6. back; again　　..........
　　g. ex　　　 7. carry　　　　..........
　　h. di　　　 8. to, toward　　..........
　　i. fer　　　9. able　　　　　..........
　　j. ad　　　10. cause　　　　..........

KEY NO. 43

O—x

ENCE · ENCY

action
state
quality

is the Suffix *ENCE, ENCY,* meaning ACTION, STATE, QUALITY. This key means the same as the previous one (No. 42) and, except for a slight change in spelling, they look just the same, too.

1. difference   differ ENCE (dif' e rens) n.
   State, quality, or measure of being unlike.

2. competence   compet ENCE (kom' pet ens) n.
   Quality of fitness; ability.

3. complacency complac ENCY (kom plase' en see) n.
   State of smugness; self-satisfaction.

4. conference   confer ENCE (kon' fe rens) n.
   The act of meeting within a group for exchange of opinions.

5. deficiency   defici ENCY (de fish' en see) n.
   The state or quality of having a lack.

6. existence   exist ENCE (eg zis' tens) n.
   The quality of being.

7. influence   influ ENCE (in' flue ens) n.
   The act of creating an impression; power.

8. obedience   obedi ENCE (o bede' ee ens) n.
   Act of obeying; as, obedience to the law

9. patience   pati ENCE (pay' shens) n.
   The ability to wait.

10. opulence   opul ENCE (op' yu lens) n.
    The quality of plenty; wealth; affluence.

11. proficiency profici ENCY (pro fish' en see) n.
    The state or quality of being skilled; expert.

12. efficiency   effici ENCY (e fish' en see) n.
    The ability to get results.

13. fluency   flu ENCY (flue' en see) n.
    A flow of language; as, fluency in French.

14. urgency   urg ENCY (ur' jen see) n.
    The need for instant action.

15. belligerency belliger ENCY (be lij' e ren see) n.
    The quality of having a fighting spirit.

word analysis

BELLIGERENCY—No. 15
  BELLI (bellum)—Root =war
  GER (gero)—Latin Root =bear; bring
  ENCY—Suffix =act of

practical exercises

1. Supply the missing words:
    She showed .... and .... in the
    language she taught. The .... between ....
    and sufficiency was shown at the ....

2. Analyze No. 13.

3. Use one word to express the phrase:
    a. satisfaction with oneself and the world   ....
    b. that which causes people to go along with her   ....
    c. so far as politics is concerned   ....
    d. great progress in one's subject   ....
    e. the ability to do things well   ....

KEY NO. 44

O—🗝

COR · COUR
CORD

heart

COURT

court

is a double key. Although the words on the list look as if they come from the same root they do not. One is from the Latin COR—COUR—CORD and means of the HEART; the other is from the French COURT and means of the COURT. You will note that the first nine are from the Latin; the list then gives you the words from the French. Be careful!

1. core — COR e (kore) n.
   The heart; central part; as the core of the apple.

2. cordial — CORD ial (kor' jal) adj.
   Cheerful; with warmth; with heart.

3. cordially — CORD ially (korj' a lee) adv.
   In a hearty manner.

4. courage — COUR age (kur' ij) n.
   Bravery; fearlessness.

5. courageous — COUR ageous (ku ray' jus) adj.
   Full of bravery.

6. cordiality — CORD iality (kor jee al' it ee) n.
   Warmth of feeling; heartiness.

7. discouraged — dis COUR aged (dis kur' ijd) adj.
   Deprived of courage; disheartened.

8. undiscouraged — undis COUR aged (un dis kur' ijd) adj.
   Not disheartened.

9. encouraged — en COUR aged (en kur' ijd) adj.
   Given courage; heart; made hopeful.

10. court — COURT (kort) n.
    A king's assembly; also a house of justice.

11. courtesy — COURT esy (kurt' e see) n.
    Courtly behavior; politeness.

12. courteously — COURT eously (kurt' ee us lee) adv.
    Behaving with courtly politeness.

13. courtier — COURT ier (kort' ee er) n.
    A member of the king's court.

14. courtliness — COURT liness (kort' lee nes) n.
    The quality of elegant behavior at the king's court.

15. courthouse — COURT house (kort' hows) n.
    The building where trials are held.

88

16. court-martial   COURT martial (kort mar' shal) n.
    A military trial for a military offense.
17. courtship   COURT ship (kort' ship) n.
    The period of time when the gentleman woos the lady.
18. discourtesy   dis COURT esy (dis kurt' e see) n.
    Rudeness; lack of proper behavior.
19. discourteously dis COURT eously (dis kurt' ee us lee) adv.
    Rudely.
20. courtling   COURT ling (kort' ling) n.
    A courtier; one who courts the favor of the powerful.

word analysis

COURTEOUSLY—No. 12
    COURT—Root =court
    OUS—Suffix =full of
    LY—Suffix =manner

practical exercises

1. Supply the missing words:
    Henry Wadsworth Longfellow wrote a long poem called "The .... of Miles Standish." In the poem a middle-aged general sent a young officer to woo a young lady for him. Priscilla smiled and .... young John Alden to speak for himself.

2. Analyze No. 6.

3. E—EC—EF—EX are all keys which mean OUT. Use them where suitable to complete the following words:

    a. ....istence   h. ....plain
    b. ....fluent   i. ....amine
    c. ....centric   j. ....ducation
    d. ....fect   k. ....manate
    e. ....clipse   l. ....aggerate
    f. ....cellent   m. ....nervate
    g. ....it

KEY NO. 45

0→x

BE

intensive

is the Prefix *BE*. It is a word that has less meaning than it has personality. It does not change the meaning of a word, but it makes the word richer, stronger, fuller than the Root's own meaning. No. 6 means to blockade. No. 9 means to be covered with complete darkness, no light of a star. No. 15 means to make filthy all over. *BE* makes everything INTENSE.

1. bedeck   BE deck (be dek') v.
   To cover up; dress with finery.

2. bedight   BE dight (be dite') v.
   To adorn; as, Spenser's line: "With woody moss bedight."

3. beguile   BE guile (be gile') v.
   To bewitch; to deceive.

4. behavior   BE havior (be hay' vyer) n.
   One's manner; one's conduct.

5. belabor   BE labor (be lay' bor) v.
   To beat soundly; to thwack.

6. beleaguer   BE leaguer (be lee' ger) v.
   To blockade; to surround; as, with an army.

7. beloved   BE loved (be luvd') adj.
   Loved with great intensity.

8. bemused   BE mused (be myuzd') adj.
   Carried away in a dream state.

9. benighted   BE nighted (be nite' ed) adj.
   Overtaken by night or darkness.

10. bewail   BE wail (be wale') v.
    To weep for; express great sorrow; mourn.

11. behoove   BE hoove (be huve') v.
    To be necessary or proper; as, it behooves us to help others.

12. bequest   BE quest (be kwest') n.
    A gift; a legacy.

13. berate   BE rate (be rate') v.
    To scold loudly; harshly.

14. bestow   BE stow (be stoe') v.
    To give; to grant; as, to bestow blessings.

15. besmirch   BE smirch (be smirch') v.
    To make filthy; bespatter; befoul.

16. bereave   BE reave (be reve') v.
    To rob; deprive cruelly.

17. bestride   BE stride (be stride') v.
                    To stride across; as, "He doth bestride *the world. . . ."*

18. betroth   BE troth (be troth') v.
                    To become engaged; affiance.

19. betoken   BE token (be toe' ken) v.
                    To forewarn; as, a dark cloud may betoken *a storm.*

word analysis

BESTOWAL—No. 14+AL
     BE—Prefix =intensely; largely
     STOW—Root =place
     AL—Suffix =relating to

practical exercises

1. Supply the missing words:
    "He doth .... the world like a Colossus. . . ."
    (Shakespeare) Eve said, "The serpent .... me and I did eat." It .... the strong to help the weak.

2. Analyze No. 15.

3. Choose the number of the word which best expresses the italicized word:
    Example: *encourage*   (1) offend   (2) bedim
           (3) enrage   (4) put heart into   (5) maintain   ....4....
    a. *bewail*   (1) dismay   (2) enjoy   (3) perplex
         (4) dominate   (5) mourn intensely   ....
    b. *cordially*   (1) basically   (2) really   (3) violently
         (4) gladly   (5) warmly   ....
    c. *smugness*   (1) stupidity   (2) complacency
         (3) disappointment   (4) benightedness
         (5) foolishness   ....
    d. *endurance*   (1) brilliance   (2) patience
         (3) temperance   (4) perseverance
         (5) entrance   ....
    e. *celebrity*   (1) famous person   (2) reader
         (3) worker   (4) adventurer   (5) visitor   ....

KEY NO. 46

O—➤

IZE

make

is the Suffix *IZE* which means to MAKE. There are hundreds of words in the language with this suffix. It is very satisfying to take a word and change it into a verb by adding *IZE*. Here's something interesting! You can take most verbs on the list and change them to nouns by adding *TION*—act of—to *IZE*, and have *IZATION*, a compound Suffix; acclimat*IZATION*; cauter*IZATION*; familiar*IZATION*; glamor*IZATION*; liberal*IZATION*; mesmer*IZATION*, etc. And here's a long one: senti-mental*IZATION*!

1. acclimatize   acclimat IZE (a klie′ ma tize) v.
   To adapt to new conditions, as of soil.

2. cauterize   cauter IZE (kaut′ e rize) v.
   To sear with a hot iron.

3. emphasize   emphas IZE (em′ fa size) v.
   To make important by putting stress upon.

4. familiarize   familiar IZE (fam mil′ ye rize) v.
   To make well-known.

5. pasteurize   pasteur IZE (pas′ che rize) v.
   To treat foods by Pasteur's method.

6. liberalize   liberal IZE (lib′ e ra lize) v.
   To make free from narrow-mindedness.

7. mesmerize   mesmer IZE (mez′ me rize) v.
   To subject to hypnosis.

8. notarize   notar IZE (note′ a rize) v.
   To make legal by signing before a notary.

9. idolize   idol IZE (ide′ ol ize) v.
   To treat like an idol.

10. ostracize   ostrac IZE (os′ tra size) v.
    To banish from society; to shun.

11. pauperize   pauper IZE (pau′ pe rize) v.
    To make very poor.

12. penalize   penal IZE (peen′ al ize) v.
    To subject to punishment.

13. publicize   public IZE (pub′ li size) v.
    To make the public aware of.

14. scrutinize   scrutin IZE (skrute′ in ize) v.
    To subject to close examination.

15. fertilize   fertil IZE (fert' il ize) v.
> To treat with enriching chemicals; to make fruitful.

16. centralize   central IZE (sen' tra lize) v.
> To make into one system, under one control.

17. decentralize   decentral IZE (dee sen' tra lize) v.
> To cause to withdraw from the center; to divide authority.

18. slenderize   slender IZE (slen' de rize) v.
> To make slender; to make thinner.

19. memorize   memor IZE (mem' o rize) v.
> To make firm in the mind.

word analysis

SECTIONALIZE
> SEC (secare)—Latin Root = cut
> TION—Suffix = act of
> AL—Suffix = relating to
> IZE—Suffix = make

practical exercises

1. Supply the missing words:

Many laws today have been ....(d) in the last fifty years. They ....(d) the photograph carefully to find some resemblance to the murdered man.

2. Analyze No. 18.

3. Use one word for the phrase:
   a. make to suffer punishment for a crime   ....
   b. to banish from society   ....
   c. to make poor   ....
   d. to lay stress upon   ....
   e. to examine most carefully   ....

O━☞

CON

with
together

is the Prefix *CON*. It has various forms as you see in the list. The *n* is left out as in Nos. 6–9; *n* changes to *l* in Nos. 10, 11, 12; *n* changes to *m* as in Nos. 13–18; *n* changes to *r* in Nos. 19, 20. It is one of those assimilated prefixes, but every form means WITH, TOGETHER.

1. connect   CON nect (ko nekt') v.
To link together; create a relationship.

2. connection   CON nection (ko nek' shun) n.
The state of being connected; union.

3. congress   CON gress (kon' gres) n.
The act of coming together; a meeting.

4. congregate   CON gregate (kon' gre gate) v.
To gather with others in one place.

5. congregation   CON gregation (kon gre gay' shun) n.
A gathering of persons.

6. cohere   CO here (ko here') v.
To stick together.

7. coherence   CO herence (ko here' ens) n.
A sticking together; a union of parts.

8. cooperate   CO operate (ko op' e rate) v.
To work together for a common cause.

9. cooperation   CO operation (ko op e ray' shun) n.
A joint effort or labor.

10. collect   COL lect (ko lekt') v.
To gather into one place; to assemble.

11. collide   COL lide (ko lide') v.
To clash; as, many interests collide.

12. collision   COL lision (ko lizh' un) n.
A clash; a violent coming together.

13. combine   COM bine (kom bine') v.
To mix together.

14. combat   COM bat (kom' bat) n.
A fight; a battle; conflict.

15. combatant   COM batant (kom bat' ant) n.
One who engages in battle.

16. commend   COM mend (ko mend') v.
To entrust with; to mention with praise.

17. commendation   COM mendation (kom en day' shun) n.
An act of mentioning with praise.

18. compound   COM pound (kom' pound) n.
Something made of several parts.

19. correct   COR rect (ko rekt') v.
                      To remove faults or errors.

20. correlate   COR relate (kor' e late) v.
                      To establish a relationship with.

word analysis

COOPERATION—No. 9
    CO (com)—Prefix =with
    OPERA (opus)—Latin Root =work
    TION—Suffix =act of

practical exercises

1. Supply the missing words:
      English and Social Studies are .... subjects.
.... is a necessity in a large family. ....
has a big legislative job to do.

2. Analyze No. 3.

3. Select the form of the Prefix *CON* which is suitable to the roots of the following words:
   a. ....nection   f. ....relate
   b. ....mand   g. ....rect
   c. .... plaint   h. ....pound
   d. ....operate   i. ....pany
   e. ....lect   j. ....lide

KEY NO. 48

PRO

**forward
forth**

is the Prefix *PRO* which means FOR-WARD; FORTH. It is a very simple key to learn and most convenient to use. It opens doors to a variety of things from the PROfessional who is today called a PRO, all the way back to ancient days in Rome when the meanest work was done by the lowest class citizen called a PROletarian.

1. proceed   PRO ceed (pro sede') v.
        To go forward; advance.

2. procedure   PRO cedure (pro see' jur) n.
        Method of going toward a goal.

3. proclaim   PRO claim (pro klame') v.
        To bring before the public.

4. proclamation PRO clamation (prok la may' shun) n.
        A notice officially declared.

5. procure   PRO cure (pro kyur') v.
        To get; to gain.

6. produce   PRO duce (pro duse') v.
        To lead forward; as, produce *a play.*

7. production   PRO duction (pro duk' shun) n.
        The act of bringing forth.

8. profess   PRO fess (pro fes') v.
        To take vows; to openly admit.

9. professor   PRO fessor (pro fes' or) n.
        One who professes; a teacher of high rank in an institution of higher education.

10. profession   PRO fession (pro fesh' un) n.
        Art or skill which is the result of study and experience.

11. progress   PRO gress (prog' res) n.
        The act of going forward to a goal.

12. progressive   PRO gressive (pro gres' iv) adj.
        Causing the going forward.

13. progression   PRO gression (pro gresh' un) n.
        The orderly going forward.

14. project   PRO ject (pro jekt') v.
        To throw forward; to create a plan.

15. proliferate   PRO liferate (pro lif' e rate) v.
        To bring forth by rapid production.

16. prolific   PRO lific (pro lif' ik) adj.
        Bringing forth young or fruit.

17. promote   PRO mote (pro mote') v.
                To move forward; to advance in station.
18. prolix   PRO lix (pro liks') adj.
                Drawn out; needlessly prolonged.
19. proficient PRO ficient (pro fish' ent) adj.
                Showing skill; adept.
20. profluent   PRO fluent (prof' lue ent) adj.
                Flowing smoothly.

word analysis

PRODUCTION—No. 7
    PRO—Prefix =forward
    DUC (ducere)—Latin Root =to lead
    TION—Suffix =act of

practical exercises

1. Supply the missing words:
    The Emancipation .... was a ....
    step in civilization. A wise .... will ....
    himself with understudies so that no mishap will wreck
    his ....

2. Analyze No. 6.

3. Supply the words which most nearly express the phrase:
    a. go forward   ....
    b. a move forward toward a higher grade   ....
    c. the manner of going forward to a goal   ....
    d. one who has reached certain skill or
       knowledge   ....
    e. put before the public   ....

KEY NO. 49

𝗼━➤

**ANNI · ANNU
ENNI**

year

is the Root *ANNI, ANNU, ENNI* meaning YEAR. It comes from the Latin word *annus*. You have often heard or used the phrase PER ANNUM: He earns $5,000 per annum; or $5,000 a year. Do not confuse this key with other keys which look similar. For example, *annular* comes from *annulus* which means a *ring*—nothing to do with year. There is also *annul* which comes from *AD—TO*; and *nullus*—nothing, to make void, as annul a marriage.

1. per annum   per ANNU m (per an' um) adv.
  Latin. For a year; as, $5,000 per annum.

2. annuity   ANNU ity (a nyue' it ee) n.
  An amount of money paid annually.

3. annuitant   ANNU itant (a nyue' it ant) n.
  One to whom an annuity is paid.

4. anniversary   ANNI versary (an i vers' a ree) n.
  The annual return of a day or event.

5. biennial   bi ENNI al (bie en' ee al) adj.
  Occurring once in two years; or, lasting two years.

6. triennial   tri ENNI al (trie en' ee al) adj.
  Occurring once in three years; or, lasting three years.

7. quadrennial   quadr ENNI al (kwa dren' ee al) adj.
  Occurring once in four years; or, lasting four years.

8. quadrennium   quadr ENNI um (kwa dren' ee um) n.
  A four-year period.

9. annual   ANNU al (an' yu al) adj.
  Relating to a year; every year.

10. annually   ANNU ally (an' yu al ee) adv.
  Yearly; as, dues collected annually.

11. quinquennial   quinqu ENNI al (kwin kwen' ee al) adj.
  Occurring once in five years; or, lasting five years.

12. sexennial   sex ENNI al (seks en' ee al) adj.
  Occurring once in six years; or, lasting six years.

98

13. **septennial** sept ENNI al (sep ten' ee al) adj.
   Occurring once in seven years; or, lasting seven years.

14. **octennial** oct ENNI al (ok ten' ee al) adj.
   Occurring once in eight years; or, lasting eight years.

15. **decennial** dec ENNI al (de sen' ee al) adj.
   Occurring once in ten years; or, lasting ten years.

16. **centennial** cent ENNI al (sen ten' ee al) adj.
   Occurring once in 100 years.

17. **sesquicentennial** sesquicent ENNI al (ses kwi sen ten' ee al) adj.
   Occurring once in 150 years.

18. **bicentennial** bicent ENNI al (bie sen ten' ee al) adj.
   Occurring once in 200 years.

19. **tricentennial** tricent ENNI al (trie sen ten' ee al) adj.
   Occurring once in 300 years.

word analysis

ANNIVERSARY—No. 4
   ANNI (annus)—Latin Root =year
   VERS (verso)—Latin Root =turn
   ARY—Suffix =that which

practical exercises

1. Supply the missing words:
   We celebrate the .... of Lincoln's birth. The year 1876 was the .... of the Declaration of Independence. The year 1926 was the .... anniversary of the same.

2. Analyze No. 10.

3. Choose the number which best expresses the italicized word:
   a. *sesquicentennial* (1) 100 years (2) 150 years
      (3) 200 years (4) 300 years (5) 125 years ....
   b. *progressive* (1) going forward (2) regressive
      (3) assuming (4) dangerous (5) possessive ....
   c. *congregate* (1) return (2) assemble (3) delay
      (4) fallout (5) scatter ....
   d. *promotion* (1) defeat (2) loss of time
      (3) advancement (4) knowledge
      (5) obedience ....

KEY NO. 50

O—x

ANTE

before

is the Prefix *ANTE* which means BE-FORE. Many of the words in this list are pure Latin phrases, but they have become a part of our language and we consider them English. Do not confuse *ANTE* with *ANTI*, against.

1. antebellum — ANTE bellum (ant e bel' um) adj.
   Existing before the war.

2. antebrachium — ANTE brachium (an tee bray' ki um) n.
   The forearm.

3. antecede — ANTE cede (ant e sede') v.
   To go before.

4. antecedent — ANTE cedent (ant e sede' ent) n.
   The word preceding the pronoun to which the pronoun refers.

5. anteroom — ANTE room (ant' e rum) n.
   A room before another; as, a waiting room.

6. antedate — ANTE date (ant' e date) v.
   To precede in time; to date something earlier than its creation.

7. antediluvian — ANTE diluvian (ant e di lue' vee an) adj.
   Belonging to the time before the flood.

8. anteflexed — ANTE flexed (an tee fleksd') adj.
   Bent forward; as, a displaced organ.

9. antepast — ANTE past (an' tee past) n.
   A foretaste; as, an appetizer.

10. antelucan — ANTE lucan (an tee lue' kan) adj.
    Before dawn; as, meetings of the early Christians.

11. antenuptial — ANTE nuptial (an tee nup' shal) adj.
    Coming before marriage.

12. anterior — ANTE rior (an ter' ee or) adj.
    Preceding in time or place.

13. antennae — ANTE nnae (an ten' a) n.
    The feelers on the head of an insect; used as organs of touch.

14. antepenult — ANTE penult (ant e pee' nult) n.
    The third syllable before the end of the word.

15. antelude — ANTE lude (an' tee lude) n.
    A play before the main play; a curtain-raiser.

16. antescript — ANTE script (an' tee skript) n.
    A note added before something; as, a prefix to a letter.

17. ante meridiem ANTE meridiem (ant e me rid' ee em) adj.
                   Coming before noon.
18. antemortem   ANTE mortem (ant e mort' em) adj.
                   Coming before death.
19. antevocalic   ANTE vocalic (an tee vo kal' ic) adj.
                   A letter before a vowel; as, k *in* kind.
20. antetype   ANTE type (an' tee tipe) n.
                   An earlier type of something.

word analysis

ANTECEDENT—No. 4
    ANTE—Prefix =before
    CED (cedere)—Latin Root =to go
    ENT—Suffix =that which; one who

practical exercise

Read the following excerpt underlining all those words that contain keys you have already learned.

In space flights of extremely long distance and duration future astronauts will probably be propelled by ions, electrically charged particles from so-called ion rocket engines. Although these engines provide very little thrust, they are much more efficient than chemical rocket engines in use today, because they pack more push per pound of fuel. . . . All of this looked good on paper and in the laboratory, but no one knew until last Monday whether an ion rocket would work in space. A National Aeronautics and Space Administration flight answered that question in the affirmative. The test engine is said to have worked extremely well.
                   (From *The New York Times,* July 26, 1964.)

KEY NO. 51

AD · ADE
ATA · ADA

is the Suffix *AD*. The French spell it *ADE*, the Italian is *ATA*, the Spanish is *ADA*. It means ACTION or the RESULT OF ACTION. This Suffix is used as an ending for many different kinds of words.

result of action

1. brigade   brig ADE (brig ade') n.
Troops consisting of two regiments and head-quarters.

2. parade   par ADE (pa rade') n.
A march for show; as, a circus parade.

3. cavalcade   cavalc ADE (kav al kade') n.
A parade of horsemen on the march.

4. chiliad   chili AD (kil' ee ad) n.
A thousand; a period of a thousand years.

5. dryad   dry AD (drie' ad) n.
A wood nymph.

6. decade   dec ADE (dek' ade) n.
A period of ten years.

7. blockade   block ADE (blo kade') n.
The act of isolating an enemy during war.

8. fusillade   fusill ADE (fyu si lade') n.
Rapid discharges of many firearms at the same time.

9. limeade   lime ADE (lime ade') n.
A beverage produced by mixing lime, sugar, and water.

10. hebdomad   hebdom AD (heb' do mad) n.
The number seven; as, seven days a week.

11. lemonade   lemon ADE (lem o nade') n.
A beverage produced by mixing lemon, sugar, and water.

12. monad   mon AD (moe' nad) n.
A unit; an individual; an atom.

13. myriad   myri AD (myr' ee ad) n.
A collective number; ten thousand.

14. promenade   promen ADE (prom e nade') n.
A public place for a leisurely walk.

15. serenade   seren ADE (ser' e nade) n.
A love song in the evening.

word analysis

BLOCKADE—No. 7
    BLOCK—Root =block
    ADE—Suffix =the act of

practical exercises

1. Supply the missing words:
    "The Charge of the Light ...." is a famous poem written by Alfred Tennyson. There are ....(s) of stars in the heavens. Franz Schubert wrote a lovely ....

2. Analyze No. 11.

3. Use one word to express the phrase:
    a. a period of ten years   ....
    b. the number seven   ....
    c. a single organized unit   ....
    d. beautiful evening love song   ....

KEY NO. 52

CLAIM · CLAM

declare
call out
cry out

is the Root *CLAIM, CLAM* which comes from the Latin *clamare*—DE-CLARE; CALL OUT; CRY OUT. Notice the different pronunciation and spelling of the two forms. This key, CLAIM, which is a complete word in its own right, has other keys attached to it, making new words, but they are all related.

1. claim   CLAIM (klame) v.
To call one's own; to ask for; to maintain.

2. reclaim   re CLAIM (re klame') v.
Make an effort to regain; demand the return of.

3. claimable   CLAIM able (klay' ma b'l) adj.
Can be claimed.

4. clamor   CLAM or (klam' or) n.
A shouting; a racket.

5. clamorous   CLAM orous (klam' o rus) adj.
Full of noise.

6. acclaim   ac CLAIM (a klame') v.
To give praise to; to applaud.

7. declaim   de CLAIM (de klame') v.
To make a formal speech.

8. declamation   de CLAM ation (dek la may' shun) n.
A recitation; an oration.

9. disclaim   dis CLAIM (dis klame') v.
Cast off; deny; disown.

10. exclaim   ex CLAIM (eks klame') v.
Cry out; as, with pain.

11. exclamation   ex CLAM ation (eks kla may' shun) n.
A cry; an outcry.

12. claimant   CLAIM ant (klay' mant) n.
One who makes a claim.

13. reclaimable   re CLAIM able (re klay' ma b'l) adj.
Can be restored; can be salvaged.

14. irreclaimable   irre CLAIM able (ir e klay' ma b'l) adj.
Cannot be restored; is not salvageable.

15. irreclaimability   irre CLAIM ability (ir e klame a bil' i ti) n.
The quality of not being able to be restored.

16. proclaim   pro CLAIM (pro klame') v.
Make known to the public.

17. proclamation   pro CLAM ation (prok la may' shun) n.
A notice to the public.

18. proclamatory   pro CLAM atory (pro klam' a toe ri) adj.
                   Related to proclaiming; as, a proclamatory
                   style.

19. unclaimed   un CLAIM ed (un klamed') adj.
                   Not called for; as, many lost things are un-
                   claimed.

20. exclamatory   ex CLAM atory (eks clam' a toe ri) adj.
                   Relating to an exclamation; as, an exclama-
                   tory *remark.*

word analysis

EXCLAMATION—No. 11
     EX—Prefix =out; out of
     CLAM (clamare)—Latin Root =call out
     TION—Suffix =state of; act of

practical exercises

1. Supply the missing words:
     He was chosen to .... the ....
because he had a .... voice and style of speaking. After an .... sentence we place an ....
point.

2. Analyze No. 10.

3. Key review. Match keys with their meanings:
     a. ous   1. (ad) to   ....
     b. ac   2. act of   ....
     c. dis   3. that which   ....
     d. ex   4. full of   ....
     e. tion   5. bear   ....
     f. ory   6. not   ....
     g. fer   7. away   ....
     h. ir   8. forward   ....
     i. pro   9. out of   ....

KEY NO. 53

O—x

DE

away
from

is the Prefix *DE* which means
AWAY; FROM. If you learn the keys
you will not be DEpendent upon a
dictionary; you will be inDEpendent!

1. debark   DE bark (de bark′) v.
              *To get off a ship; as, the soldiers must debark
              at night.*

2. debus   DE bus (de bus′) v.
              To get off a bus.

3. deplane   DE plane (dee plane′) v.
              To get off an airplane.

4. debunk ′   DE bunk (dee bunk′) v.
              To expose as false; talk truth.

5. decay   DE cay (de kay′) v.
              To fall into ruin; rot; spoil; as, fruit will decay.

6. decadence DE cadence (dek′ ad ens) n.
              The state of falling into low conduct.

7. deform   DE form (de form′) v.
              To ruin the form of; to cripple.

8. deformed   DE formed (de formd′) adj.
              Misshapen; as, he was deformed from birth.

9. denude   DE nude (de nude′) v.
              To strip bare; as, winter will denude the trees.

10. depend   DE pend (de pend′) v.
              *To rely upon; to place trust in; as, depend on
              me.*

11. dependent DE pendent (de pen′ dent) adj.
              Relying upon; as, dependent on welfare.

12. independent in DE pendent (in de pen′ dent) adj.
              Relying only on one's self.

13. deprive   DE prive (de prive′) v.
              To take away; as, deprive of one's rights.

14. depose   DE pose (de poze′) v.
              To remove from a position; as, depose the king.

15. deride   DE ride (de ride′) v.
              To make fun of; laugh at.

16. delude   DE lude (de lude′) v.
              To cheat; as, delude with false promises.

17. delouse   DE louse (dee lous′) v.
              To get rid of lice.

18. defend   DE fend (de fend') v.
                 To keep the enemy away; to protect.
19. defender   DE fender (de fend' er) n.
                 One who keeps the enemy away; protector.
20. defenseless   DE fenseless (de fens' les) adj.
                 Without protection; without a defender.

word analysis

DEFENSELESS—No. 20
     DE—Prefix = away; from
     FENSE (fendere)—Latin Root = keep off
     LESS—Suffix = without

practical exercises

1. Supply the missing words:
     "Ill fares the land, to hastening ills a prey,
     Where wealth accumulates and men ...."
                                         (Oliver Goldsmith)
     When we wish to believe something, we often ....
     ourselves.

2. Analyze No. 7.

3. Syllabicate and indicate which syllable is most greatly stressed
    by placing the accent mark ('):
          dependent   transportation   deprive
          decadence   delusion   derision
          deform   reformatory

KEY NO. 54

O——►

MEM

remember

is the Root *MEM* which comes from *meminisse:* to REMEMBER. This is a very easy key to reMEMber. The very sight of it makes for reMEMbrance. It is imbedded in MEMory and, very pleasant to relate, it has only one meaning—reMEMber!

1. memento   MEM ento (me ment' o) n.
   Something to make one remember.

2. memoir   MEM oir (mem' war) n.
   A report; a record of a thing to remember.

3. memorandum   MEM orandum (mem o ran' dum) n.
   A note; a reminder.

4. memo   MEM o (mem' o) n.
   Short form of memorandum; a note.

5. memoirist   MEM oirist (mem' war ist) n.
   One who writes memoirs.

6. memorable   MEM orable (mem' o ra b'l) adj.
   Worth remembering; as a memorable *act.*

7. memorabilia   MEM orabilia (mem o ra bil' ee a) n.
   Things worth remembering.

8. memorandize   MEM orandize (mem o ran' dize) v.
   Jot down a memo; make a note of.

9. memory   MEM ory (mem' o ry) n.
   The ability to recall; as, a memory for dates.

10. memoriter   MEM oriter (me mor' i ter) adv.
    By heart; from memory.

11. memorial   MEM orial (me mor' ee al) n.
    A reminder of a great event; as, Memorial Day.

12. memorialize   MEM orialize (me mor' ee a lize) v.
    To commemorate; to present a memorial.

13. immemorial   im MEM orial (im e mor' ee al) adj.
    Having occurred so long ago that it cannot be remembered.

14. commemorate   com MEM orate (ko mem' o rate) v.
    To observe; as, commemorate *Washington's Birthday.*

15. commemoration   com MEM oration (ko mem o ray' shun) n.
    The act of observing by a memorial or ceremony.

16. remember   re MEM ber (re mem' ber) v.
    Bring to mind again.

17. remembrance   re MEM brance (re mem' brans) n.
                   The act of bringing to mind again.
18. unremembered   unre MEM bered (un re mem' berd) adj.
                   Not remembered.
19. In Memoriam   In MEM oriam (in me mor' ee um) prep.
                   (Latin Phrase) In memory of; as, the name
                   of a poem by Tennyson is In Memoriam.

word analysis

COMMEMORATION—No. 15
     COM—Prefix =with; together
     MEMOR (meminisse)—Latin Root =to remember
     TION—Suffix =state of

practical exercises

1. Supply the missing words:
     From time .... statues have been erected in
.... of heroes. Tennyson wrote a beautiful poem
called "In ...." He delivered the address from
....

2. Analyze No. 6.

3. Group the following words according to key similarity, underline keys and give their meanings. (A word may appear on
lists of more than one key):
     untold; regard; remember; crafty; relate; wary; commem-
orate; retard; memorial; deprive; commit; derision; despair;
connection; lumpy; unsold; desperate; immemorial; delude;
suffer

KEY NO. 55

O—⚡

TEN · TENT
TAIN · TINU

hold together
hold

is the Root *TEN—TENT—TAIN—TINU*. All come from the Latin *teneo*, which means HOLD TOGETHER; HOLD. Looking down the word list I am certain that you are beginning to realize that the more than half-hundred keys which you have accumulated have begun to pay dividends.

1. tenant   TEN ant (ten' ant) n.
               One who holds a lease on a house or apartment; occupant.

2. untenanted un TEN anted (un ten' ant ed) adj.
               Not lived in; not having tenants.

3. tenable   TEN able (ten' a b'l) adj.
               Able to be held, defended; as, a tenable argument.

4. untenable un TEN able (un ten' a b'l) adj.
               Cannot be held; not tenable.

5. tenacity   TEN acity (te nas' it ee) n.
               The quality of holding together; as, tenacity of purpose.

6. tenacious   TEN acious (te nay' shus) adj.
               Tending to hold together firmly.

7. contents   con TENT s (kon' tents) n.
               What is held together; contained; as, the contents of a room.

8. contented   con TENT ed (kon tent' ed) adj.
               Easy in mind; as, contented with one's lot.

9. discontented discon TENT ed (dis kon tent' ed) adj.
               Not contented.

10. contentment con TENT ment (kon tent' ment) n.
               Satisfaction with one's lot.

11. intent   in TENT (in tent') adj.
               Holding one's mind on the matter at hand; engrossed; as, intent on the work.

12. intention   in TENT ion (in ten' chun) n.
               Aim; resolve; as, it is my intention to study medicine.

13. maintain   main TAIN (mane tane') v.
               To keep up; uphold firmly.

14. maintenance main TEN ance (mante' en ans) n.
               Support; as, maintenance of a family.

110

15. retain   re TAIN (re tane') v.
                    To keep; to hold secure; as, retain *control of.*

16. retentive   re tent ive (re tent' iv) adj.
                    Tending to hold; as, a retentive *memory.*

17. continue   con TIN ue (kon tin' yue) v.
                    To carry on; to keep on; as, continue *to beg.*

18. continual   con TIN ual (kon tin' yu al) adj.
                    Often repeated; as continual *ringing of the phone.*

19. continually con TIN ually (kon tin' yu al ee) adv.
                    Without stopping.

word analysis

RETENTIVE—No. 16.
    RE—Prefix =back; again
    TENT (teneo)—Latin Root =hold
    IVE—Suffix =cause; make

practical exercises

1. Supply the missing words:
    The blessing of the house is .... Working .... toward her goal helped her to achieve it. Many windows were broken in the .... house.

2. Analyze No. 4.

3. Choose the number which best expresses the italicized word:
    a. *deride* (1) enjoy (2) entertain (3) mock
        (4) display (5) tell   ....
    b. *continually* (1) often (2) sometimes
        (3) lazily (4) downward (5) keeping on ....
    c. *desperate* (1) cheerful (2) growing (3) large
        (4) hopeless (5) salty   ....
    d. *memento* (1) remembrance (2) story (3) fear
        (4) history (5) banner   ....
    e. *tenacious* (1) sorry (2) holding on
        (3) frightened (4) pretty (5) talkative ....

KEY NO. 56

O━ᵏ

CLUD · CLUS

shut

is the Root *CLUD-CLUS* meaning SHUT. It comes from the Latin *claudo, clausus.* The double spelling in English follows, as you see, the double spelling in Latin. *CLUD-CLUS* mean nothing by themselves. With the Prefixes and Suffixes added to them, however, they are meaningful and useful.

1. recluse
re CLUSE (rek' luse) n.
One who shuts himself away from others; as, a hermit.

2. conclusion
con CLUS ion (kon klue' zhun) n.
The end; as, the conclusion of the course.

3. conclusive
con CLUS ive (kon klue' siv) adj.
Final; as, a conclusive statement.

4. exclude
ex CLUD e (eks klude') v.
To shut out; as, exclude from a club.

5. exclusion
ex CLUS ion (eks klue' zhun) n.
The act of shutting out; as, he resented his exclusion.

6. exclusive
ex CLUS ive (eks klue' siv) adj.
Tending to keep others out; as, exclusive power.

7. include
in CLUD e (in klude') v.
To take in; to count; as, include in the group.

8. inclusion
in CLUS ion (in klue' zhun) n.
The act of taking in; as inclusion of algebra in the program.

9. inclusive
in CLUS ive (in klue' siv) adj.
Counting everything in.

10. preclude
pre CLUD e (pre klude') v.
To close beforehand; to hinder.

11. preclusion
pre CLUS ion (pre klue' zhun) n.
State of hindering; preventing.

12. conclude
con CLUD e (kon klude') v.
To close; as, to conclude a trial.

13. reclusive
re CLUS ive (re klue' siv) adj.
Favoring retirement from society.

14. seclude
se CLUD e (se klude') v.
To shut away; to confine; as, seclude oneself in the woods.

15. seclusion se CLUS ion (se klue′ zhun) n.
    The act of shutting oneself up; as, Emily Dickinson lived in seclusion.

16. occlude oc CLUD e (o klude′) v.
    To shut the way; to bar a passage; as, to occlude *light.*

17. occlusion oc CLUS ion (o klue′ zhun) n.
    The shutting up; as, the occlusion *of an opening.*

18. occlusal oc CLUS al (o klue′ zal) adj.
    Relating to the surface of the tooth used in biting or grinding.

19. occludent oc CLUD ent (o klude′ ent) adj.
    Serving to shut away.

20. occlusor oc CLUS or (o klue′ zor) n.
    An organ which closes.

word analysis

OCCLUSION—No. 17
    OC (ob)—Prefix =against
    CLUS (claudere)—Latin Root =to shut
    ION—Suffix =state of

practical exercises

1. Supply the missing words:
    The witness proved .... that the defendant was innocent. The joker said, "........................... of a bad knee, a weak heart, and a touch of lumbago, I feel just fine."

2. Analyze No. 4.

3. One word will express the phrase if you supply the missing KEY:
    Example: having a tight hold on ....acious   ....TEN....
    a. keeping on without stopping con..........ally   ....
    b. the act of shutting in ....clusion   ....
    c. in the manner of closing up con..........ively   ....
    d. hope all fled away ....spair   ....
    e. come back to mind re..........ber   ....
    f. the act of keeping on con..........ation   ....
    g. the closing of the matter con..........ion   ....
    h. bear pain or sorrow suf..........   ....

113

KEY NO. 57

O—⚷

CIRC · CIRCUM

around

is the Prefix *CIRC, CIRCUM* which means AROUND. There are now three ways of traveling around the world so you can choose from Nos. 1, 2, or 3. Going *CIRCUM* means no short cuts, the long way around. That is all right for travel but not for speech. Use straight talk, not the methods in Nos. 6, 15, or 20.

1. circumambulate CIRCUM ambulate (sir ku mam' byu late) v.
   To walk around.

2. circumnavigate CIRCUM navigate (sir kum nav' i gate) v.
   To go around, especially in a ship.

3. circumaviate CIRCUM aviate (sir kum ay' vi ate) v.
   To fly around in an airplane.

4. circumcise CIRCUM cise (sir' kum size) v.
   To cut around.

5. circumspect CIRCUM spect (sir kum spekt') adj.
   Looking around carefully; watchfully.

6. circumdiction CIRCUM diction (sir kum dik' shun) n.
   Talk that is roundabout; not to the point.

7. circumference CIRCUM ference (sir kum' fe rens) n.
   The line around the plane surface of a circle.

8. circumfluous CIRCUM fluous (sir kum' flue us) adj.
   Flowing around; as the circumfluous *ocean.*

9. circumfulgent CIRCUM fulgent (sir kum ful' jent) adj.
   Shining all around; as the circumfulgent *sun.*

10. circumvolve CIRCUM volve (sir kum volv') v.
    To wind about; to turn around.

11. circumstance CIRCUM stance (sir' kum stans) n.
    A condition of a fact; a situation.

12. circummured CIRCUM mured (sir kum murd') adj.
    Walled around; as, in a dungeon.

13. circumscribe CIRCUM scribe (sir' kum skribe) v.
    To draw a line around; to encircle.

14. circumvallation CIRCUM vallation (sir kum val ay' shun) n.
    Trenches to protect a besieged army.

15. circumlocution CIRCUM locution (sir kum lo kyu' shun) n.
    Circumdiction (see No. 6).

16. circummigration CIRCUM migration (sir kum mie gray' shun) n.
    Wandering around from place to place.

17. circumneutral   CIRCUM neutral (sir kum nue' tral) adj.
    Said of soil that is neither acid nor alkaline.

18. circumvent   CIRCUM vent (sir kum vent') v.
    To encircle; prevent; foil.

19. circuit   CIRC uit (sir' kut) n.
    The distance around an area or a space.

20. circuitous   CIRC uitous (sir kyu' it us) adj.
    Having roundabout ways; sly.

word analysis

CIRCUMVENTION—No. 18+tion
    CIRCUM—Prefix =around
    VEN (venire)—Latin Root =to go
    TION—Suffix =act of

practical exercise

Read the following excerpt underlining all those words that contain keys you have already learned.

I do not know if I was what you call afraid; but my heart beat like a bird's, both quick and little; and there was a dimness came before my eyes which I continually rubbed away, and which continually returned. As for hope, I had none; but only a darkness of despair and a sort of anger against all the world that made me long to sell my life as dear as I was able. I tried to pray, I remember, but that same hurry of my mind would not suffer me to think upon the words; and my chief wish was to have the thing begin and be done with it.

It came all of a sudden when it did, with a rush of feet and a roar, and then a shout from Alan, and a sound of blows, and someone crying out as if hurt. I looked back over my shoulder, and saw Mr. Shuan in the doorway, crossing blades with Alan.

"That's him that killed the boy!" I cried.

"Look to your window!" said Alan; and as I returned back to my place I saw him pass his sword through the mate's body.

(From *Kidnapped* by Robert Louis Stevenson.)

KEY NO. 58

O—x

TUDE

**state of
condition of**

is the Suffix *TUDE* which means
STATE OF: CONDITION OF. It
makes nouns and often, in giving the
meaning, one likes to end the word
with *NESS*, a Suffix which also means
STATE OF. *TUDE* is used to form
abstract nouns from adjectives. No. 1
is a most important word. Your atti-
TUDE to the keys in this book is the
most important single factor in your
success or failure with vocabulary
building.

1. attitude   atti TUDE (at' i tude) n.
         Manner; feeling toward; as, attitude to a job.

2. latitudinarian   lati TUD inarian (lat' i tude in ar' ee an) n.
         One opposed to strict discipline.

3. similitude   simili TUDE (si mil' i tude) n.
         Condition of likeness; resemblance.

4. verisimilitude   verisimili TUDE (ver i si mil' i tude) n.
         Having the appearance of truth.

5. gratitude   grati TUDE (grat' i tude) n.
         State of being grateful; thankfulness.

6. lassitude   lassi TUDE (las' i tude) n.
         State of being limp; weariness.

7. multitude   multi TUDE (mul' ti tude) n.
         Great numbers; as, a multitude of people.

8. pulchritude   pulchri TUDE (pul' kri tude) n.
         State of beauty; loveliness.

9. rectitude   recti TUDE (rek' ti tude) n.
         State of righteousness.

10. latitude   lati TUDE (lat' i tude) n.
         Degree of distance from side to side; width.

11. plenitude   pleni TUDE (plen' i tude) n.
         Abundance; state of fullness.

12. aptitude   apti TUDE (ap' ti tude) n.
         Ability for; state of being capable.

13. beatitude   beati TUDE (be at' i tude) n.
         State of heavenly bliss.

14. solitude   soli TUDE (sol' i tude) n.
         *State of being alone; loneliness; as, living in
         solitude.*

15. solicitude   solici TUDE (so lis' i tude) n.
         *State of great concern for another; as solici-
         tude for the poor.*

16. fortitude	forti TUDE (fort' i tude) n. *State of bravery and strength; endurance.*
17. servitude	servi TUDE (ser' vi tude) n. *State of being subject to another; as, a servant or slave.*
18. turpitude	turpi TUDE (tur' pi tude) n. *Baseness; depravity; as, moral turpitude.*
19. longitude	longi TUDE (lon' ji tude) n. *Length; extent measured in length.*
20. vicissitude	vicissi TUDE (vi sis' i tude) n. *The ups and downs of fortune and fate.*

word analysis

VICISSITUDE—No. 20
    VICIS—Root =change; turn
    TUDE—Suffix =state of; condition

practical exercises

1. Supply the missing words:
    The ....(s) of life are many and varied.
    Her .... for the welfare of the refugees was
    so great that their .... was unbounded.

2. Analyze No. 17.

3. Indicate the correct pronunciation by placing the accent mark ('):

disconcerted	recover	invincible
attitude	triumph	battering
rectitude	verisimilitude	solicitude
vicissitude	turpitude	servitude

KEY NO. 59

o—x

BI · BIN · BIS

two
twice

is the Prefix *BI, BIN* meaning TWO. There is a word *BIS* meaning TWICE, but it is not often used. It is heard at the opera sometimes when an aria is so beautifully sung that the audience gets excited and demands hearing it again. *BI* is used more often than *BIN* but both are commonly used.

1. biceps   BI ceps (bie′ seps) n.
   Large muscle fastened in two places.

2. bicuspid   BI cuspid (bie kus′ pid) n.
   A double-pointed tooth.

3. bicycle   BI cycle (bie′ sik el) n.
   A two-wheeled vehicle for travel by foot-power.

4. biennial   BI ennial (bie en′ ee al) adj.
   Something that occurs at two-year intervals, or lasts two years.

5. bimonthly   BI monthly (bie month′ lee) adj.
   Something that occurs every two months; as, a bimonthly magazine.

6. biweekly   BI weekly (bie wee′ klee) adj.
   Something that occurs every two weeks.

7. bifocal   BI focal (bie foe′ kal) adj.
   Having two lenses; as, bifocal glasses.

8. bigamy   BI gamy (big′ a me) n.
   The act of marrying one person when already married to another.

9. biparental   BI parental (bie pa ren′ tal) adj.
   Born of two parents.

10. bivalve   BI valve (bie′ valv) n.
    An animal with a shell of two parts which open and shut; as, clams.

11. bipedal   BI pedal (bie ped′ al) adj.
    Having two feet; as man.

12. bimanual   BI manual (bie man′ yu al) adj.
    Done with both hands.

13. bidentate   BI dentate (bie den′ tate) adj.
    Having two teeth.

14. bilabial   BI labial (bie lay′ bee al) adj.
    Using both lips, as in pronouncing the letters b, m, and p.

15. binomial   BI nomial (bie no' mee al) n.
                *An expression in mathematics consisting of
                two terms connected by a plus or a minus; as,*
                $a+b$; 7-3.
16. bilingual   BI lingual (bie lin' gwal) adj.
                Using two languages.
17. biracial   BI racial (bie ray' shal) adj.
                Concerning two races.
18. bipartisan BI partisan (bie part' i zan) adj.
                Representing two parties.
19. bisect   BI sect (bie sekt') v.
                Cut into two parts.
20. binocular   BI nocular (bi nok' yu lar) n.
                *An instrument with two eyes, as an opera
                glass.*

word analysis

BINOCULAR—No. 20
    BIN—Prefix = two
    OCUL (oculus)—Root = eye
    AR—Suffix = one who; that which

practical exercises

1. Supply the missing words:
        Some people have difficulty with .... glasses.
    Laws which get .... support are truly the will
    of the people. The .... letters are called labials.

2. Analyze No. 4.

3. Key review. Match keys with their meanings:
    a. en, em   1. remember   ....
    b. mem   2. heart   ....
    c. dis   3. in, into   ....
    d. tude   4. across   ....
    e. circum   5. together   ....
    f. cour   6. away   ....
    g. con   7. hold; grasp   ....
    h. de   8. state of   ....
    i. tent   9. from; away   ....
    j. trans   10. around   ....

KEY NO. *60*

O—➤

VINC · VICT

conquer

is the Root *VINC, VICT* which comes from the Latin *vincere, victus,* and means CONQUER. Please note that in Nos. 13–17 the letter *c* sounds like an *s.* In Nos. 18 and 19 a different spelling and pronunciation comes in because this Root is from the French *vaincre,* a descendant of the Latin, which leads to *VANQU*ish.

1. victim
   VICT im (vik′ tim) n.
   One who is conquered and sacrificed.

2. victimize
   VICT imize (vik′ tim ize) v.
   To make a victim of; use as a sacrifice.

3. victimizer
   VICT imizer (vik′ tim ize er) n.
   One who makes a victim of another.

4. victor
   VICT or (vik′ tor) n.
   One who wins; a conqueror.

5. victory
   VICT ory (vik′ to ree) n.
   The winning; the conquest; triumph.

6. victorious
   VICT orious (vik tore′ ee us) adj.
   Full of victory; triumphant.

7. victoriously
   VICT oriously (vik tore′ ee us lee) adv.
   Triumphantly.

8. Invictus
   in VICT us (in vik′ tus)
   The title of a poem by William Ernest Henley; meaning unconquered; undefeated.

9. evict
   e VICT (e vikt′) v.
   Throw out; as, evict a tenant who does not pay the rent.

10. eviction
    e VICT ion (e vik′ shun) n.
    Throwing out of house and home.

11. convict
    con VICT (kon vikt′) v.
    To prove guilty.

12. conviction
    con VICT ion (kon vik′ shun) n.
    The act of proving someone guilty of a crime.

13. convince
    con VINC e (kon vins′) v.
    Win over; as, convince another in an argument.

14. vincible
    VINC ible (vin′ si b'l) adj.
    Can be defeated; conquerable.

15. vincibility
    VINC ibility (vin si bil′ i ti) n.
    The quality of being able to be defeated.

16. invincible
    in VINC ible (in vin′ si b'l) adj.
    Cannot be defeated.

120

17. invincibly   in VINC ibly (in vin′ si blee) adv.
                  In the manner of one who cannot be de-
                  feated; as, invincibly *courageous.*
18. vanquish   VANQU ish (van′ kwish) v.
                  To conquer; overcome.
19. unvanquished un VANQU ished (un van′ kwishd) adj.
                  Unconquered; not able to be overcome.

word analysis

INVINCIBILITY—In+No. 15
     IN—Prefix =not
     VINC (vincere)—Latin Root =conquer
     IBL (ible)—Suffix =can do
     ITY—Suffix =quality

practical exercises

1. Supply the missing words:
     They argued for a long time before he could ....
     the group that he had a right to the money. They fought
     bitterly, and the .... suffered as much as the
     ....(ed).

2. Analyze No. 9.

3. Choose the number of the word which best expresses the
   italicized word:
   a. *recover* (1) attempt (2) regain (3) declare
        (4) refuse (5) explain   ....
   b. *invincible* (1) defeated (2) learned
        (3) unloved (4) spoken
        (5) cannot be conquered   ....
   c. *attitude* (1) power (2) respect (3) ability
        (4) manner (5) truth   ....
   d. *triumph* (1) victory (2) goal (3) power
        (4) labor (5) authority   ....
   e. *disconcerted* (1) expelled (2) awakened
        (3) rebuffed (4) confused (5) asked   ....

KEY NO. 61

O—x

DENT · DONT

tooth

is the Latin Root DENT, DONT which means TOOTH. All people have teeth and talk constantly about their teeth and their dentist, but they rarely acquire the dentist's vocabulary. A dentist is pleased when a patient talks about DENTin, DENTifrice, and baby's DENTition. Surprise your dentist.

1. dental   DENT al (dent′ al) adj.
Relating to teeth; as, a dental appointment.

2. dentality   DENT ality (den tal′ i ti) n.
Dental quality in speaking.

3. dentilated   DENT ilated (den′ ti late ed) adj.
Toothed; as, a dentilated edge.

4. dentilation   DENT ilation (den ti lay′ shun) n.
The formation of teeth.

5. dentimeter   DENT imeter (den tim′ e ter) n.
An instrument for measuring teeth.

6. dentin   DENT in (den′ tin) n.
An ivory-like substance that is the major part of the teeth.

7. dentification   DENT ification (den ti fi kay′ shun) n.
The formation of the teeth.

8. dentiloquy   DENT iloquy (den til′ o kwi) n.
The practice of talking through the teeth.

9. dentiphone   DENT iphone (den′ ti fone) n.
A plate set against teeth which helps the deaf to hear.

10. dentist   DENT ist (dent′ ist) n.
One who cares for the teeth.

11. dentistry   DENT istry (dent′ i stree) n.
The profession of the dentist.

12. dentition   DENT ition (den tish′ un) n.
The development of the teeth; teething.

13. dentoid   DENT oid (den′ toid) adj.
Resembling a tooth.

14. denture   DENT ure (den′ chur) n.
Artificial teeth.

15. dentiscalp   DENT iscalp (den′ ti skalp) n.
An instrument used in scraping the teeth.

16. denticate   DENT icate (den′ ti kate) v.
To bite; chew; masticate.

17. dentifrice   DENT ifrice (dent' i fris) n.
                  Powder or paste for cleansing teeth.
18. orthodontia   ortho DONT ia (or tho don' chee a) n.
                  The straightening of irregular teeth.
19. orthodontist ortho DONT ist (or tho dont' ist) n.
                  A dentist who practices orthodontia.
20. dentigerous   DENT igerous (den tij' e rus) adj.
                  Bearing teeth; having teeth.

word analysis

ORTHODONTIST—No. 19
    ORTHO (orthos, right)—Greek Prefix =correct
    DONT (dentis)—Root =tooth
    IST—Suffix =one who

practical exercises

1. Supply the missing words:
    Man is a .... creature. A good ....
    and the habit to .... properly will keep the
    teeth healthy and beautiful. Without proper care the
    .... in teeth decays.

2. Analyze No. 1.

3. Supply the missing keys in the incomplete words:
    a. Care must be taken of the tooth's ....in.
    b. The scientific name for teething is ....ition.
    c. The scientific name for a tooth-cleanser is ....ifrice.
    d. A teeth-specialist is called a ....ist.
    e. Many people are ....ims of their own carelessness.
    f. One who conquers his faults is truly in.......... ....
    g. In.......... ....ity begins with oneself.
    h. When one loses his inner calmness he is like a concert
        which has lost its harmony, and we say he is dis..........ed.

KEY NO. 62

o—➤

INTER

between
among

is the Prefix *INTER*, which means BETWEEN; AMONG. It is a very much needed key, very social-minded, and minding other people's business; it always comes *INTER*, BETWEEN, this thing and that, this person and that. Watch the spelling and the pronunciation. Don't say it carelessly because there are two other keys which are similar in spelling and pronunciation, but have different meanings. You must be prepared to understand the distinction between them.

1. interaction   INTER action (int e rak' shun) n.
     Action for mutual advantage.

2. interaxillary   INTER axillary (in ter ak' si lar i) adj.
     Coming between two axils of leaves.

3. interborough   INTER borough (in' ter bur o) adj.
     Operating between boroughs.

4. intercede   INTER cede (int er sede') v.
     To act between two parties in order to restore friendship.

5. interdependent   INTER dependent (in ter de pen' dent) adj.
     Dependent, each one upon the other.

6. interdict   INTER dict (in' ter dikt) v.
     To forbid; as, to interdict trade with certain nations.

7. intercept   INTER cept (in ter sept') v.
     To take between sending and delivery; as, intercept a letter.

8. interciliary   INTER ciliary (in ter sil' i ar i) adj.
     Between the eyebrows.

9. intercostal   INTER costal (int er kost' al) adj.
     Between the ribs.

10. intercourse   INTER course (int' er kors) n.
     Correspondence or trade between or among people.

11. interfaith   INTER faith (int' er fathe) n.
     Involving persons of various religions.

12. interfere   INTER fere (int er fere') v.
     To enter into the concerns of others; to clash; to meddle.

13. interfoliate   INTER foliate (in ter foe' li ate) v.
     Put leaves between pages in a book.

14. interject   INTER ject (int er jekt') v.
                   Throw between or among; as, interject *humorous remarks.*

15. interlude   INTER lude (int' er lude) n.
                   A period between; as, a short play between the acts of a long one.

16. interpose   INTER pose (int er poze') v.
                   To place between; to intrude.

17. interpolate INTER polate (in ter' po late) v.
                   To insert; as, to put into a book matter which changes the purpose of the author.

18. interstate   INTER state (int er state') adj.
                   Between states; as, interstate *commerce.*

19. intervene   INTER vene (int er vene') v.
                   Come between; interfere.

20. intervention INTER vention (in ter ven' chun) n.
                   The act of coming between; interference.

word analysis

INTERVENTION—No. 20
    INTER—Prefix =between; among
    VEN (venire)—Latin Root =to come
    TION—Suffix =act of

practical exercise

Read the following excerpt underlining all those words that contain keys you have already learned.

It was none too soon for me to look to my own part; for my head was scarce back at the window before five men carrying a square yard for a battering ram ran past me and took post to drive the nail in. I had never fired with a pistol in my life, and not often with a gun; far less against a fellow-creature. But it was now or never; and just as they swung the yard I cried out, "Take that!" and shot into their midst.

I must have hit one of them, for he sang out and gave back a step, and the rest stopped as if a little disconcerted. Before they had time to recover, I sent another ball over their heads; and at my third shot (which went as wide as the second) the whole party threw down the yard and ran for it.

(From *Kidnapped,* by Robert Louis Stevenson.)

KEY NO. 63

0——→

AN

not
absence of

is the Prefix *AN* which means NOT; ABSENCE OF. Sometimes, but rarely, the *n* is omitted, as in AByss—bottomless depth. Do not confuse *AN* =NOT with the suffix *AN* which you have had in *AmericAN*—NATIVE OF. It makes all the difference in the world whether the key in question is a Prefix or a Suffix.

1. anecdote   AN ecdote (an' ek dote) n.
   A story or personal item not generally known.

2. anecdotage   AN ecdotage (an' ek dote ij) n.
   A collection of anecdotes.

3. anecdotal   AN ecdotal (an ek dote' al) adj.
   Interesting; lively in conversation.

4. anecdotist   AN ecdotist (an' ek dote ist) n.
   One who tells anecdotes.

5. anemia   AN emia (a nee' mee a) n.
   A condition in which there are not enough red blood cells.

6. anemic   AN emic (a nee' mik) adj.
   Deficient in red blood cells.

7. anesthesia   AN esthesia (an es the' zha) n.
   Absence of feeling; numbness.

8. anesthetic   AN esthetic (an es thet' ik) n.
   An agent to produce anesthesia, such as ether.

9. anesthetize   AN esthetize (a nes' the tize) v.
   To induce anesthesia.

10. anesthetist   AN esthetist (a nes' thet ist) n.
    The physician who administers the anesthetic.

11. anodyne   AN odyne (an' o dine) n.
    Creating an absence of pain; a narcotic.

12. anomaly   AN omaly (a nom' a lee) n.
    A difference from the common rule; an irregularity; as, a bird that does not fly.

13. anomalous   AN omalous (a nom' a lus) adj.
    Irregular; uncomfortable.

14. anonym   AN onym (an' o nim) n.
    A person or a writer who keeps his name unknown.

15. anonymous   AN onymous (a non' i mus) adj.
    Without a name; as, an anonymous *donation.*

16. anonymity   AN onymity (an o nim' it ee) n.
    The state of being nameless.

17. anelectric   AN electric (an e lek' trik) adj.
                  Not electrified by friction.
18. anopia   AN opia (an o' pi a) n.
                  Absence of the eye; vision that is defective.
19. anorganism   AN organism (an or' gan iz um) n.
                  An inorganic body; as, a crystal.
20. anomy   AN omy (an' o me) n.
                  State of absence of law and order.

word analysis

ANESTHESIA—No. 7
    AN—Prefix =not
    ESTHESIA (aisthesis)—Greek Root =feeling

practical exercises

1. Supply the missing words:
    His conversation is vivacious because he usually has a
    good .... to relate. The penguin, a flightless
    bird, is an .... She has been ....
    for years but does nothing about it.

2. Analyze No. 16.

3. All the following keys mean NOT. Use the proper key for
   each of the following words, thus forming the negative of
   the word:
   keys meaning NOT: il, ir, in, im, un, non, an.

a. legal	..........legal	not legal
b. rational	..........rational	not rational
c. perfect	..........perfect	not perfect
d. esthetic	..........esthetic	not feeling
e. seen	..........seen	not seen
f. sense	..........sense	not sense
g. adequate	..........adequate	not adequate
h. emia (Hemia, blood)	..........emic	not having healthy blood
i. reasonable	..........reasonable	not reasonable
j. regular	..........regular	not regular

KEY NO. 64

○━━▻

MAN · MANU

by hand

is the Root *MAN, MANU* which means BY HAND. The words Nos. 6, 7 and 8 are really misnomers. *MAN*Ufactured goods are no longer *made by hand* in a *MANU*factory by a *MANU*facturer with his own hands. In the march of automation we shall soon be obliged to find another name for machine-made goods. Someday, a person who knows the keys well will invent a new word to take the place of the old. You, maybe?

1. manual   MANU al (man' yu al) adj.
     Relating to the hand; as, manual *labor.*

2. manucaption   MANU caption (man yu kap' shun) n.
     A document that was once used to obtain the presence in court of an alleged felon.

3. manuduction   MANU duction (man yu duk' shun) n.
     Leading by the hand; guidance.

4. manacles   MAN acles (man' a k'ls) n.
     Handcuffs; chains.

5. manicure   MAN icure (man' i kyur) n.
     The care of the hands and nails.

6. manufacture   MANU facture (man yu fak' chur) n.
     The act of making by machinery or hand.

7. manufacturer MANU facturer (man yu fak' chur er) n.
     One who hires others to make things in quantity by hand or by machine.

8. manufactory   MANU factory (man yu fak' to ree) n.
     A place where merchandise is made.

9. manifest   MAN ifest (man' i fest) adj.
     Seen at hand; obvious; apparent.

10. manumit   MANU mit (man yu mit') v.
     To release from contract; set free; as, manumit *a slave.*

11. manumission MANU mission (man yu mish' un) n.
     The act of liberating a slave.

12. manumotive   MANU motive (man yu mo' tiv) adj.
     Moved by hand.

13. maneuver   MAN euver (ma nu' ver) v.
     To bring about by skill; to guide; manipulate.

14. manuscript   MANU script (man' yu skript) n.
     A document or literary work not yet printed.

15. manipulate   MAN ipulate (ma nip' yu late) v.
        To work out by hand; to manage.
16. manipulation MAN ipulation (ma nip yu lay' shun) n.
        Skillful handling; as, the manipulation *of puppets.*
17. emancipate   e MAN cipate (e man' si pate) v.
        Release; set free.
18. emancipation e MAN cipation (e man si pay' shun) n.
        The act of liberation; as, the Emancipation *Proclamation.*
19. legerdemain   legerde MAIN (lej erd e mane') n.
        Light-handed magic tricks; sleight of hand.

word analysis

EMANCIPATION—No. 18
    E (ex)—Prefix =out
    MAN (manu)—Root =hand
    CIP (capere)—Root =take
    TION—Suffix =act of

practical exercises

1. Supply the missing words:
        Today the writer sends out a typescript instead of a
        .... The .... of the slaves was difficult for the South to accept.

2. Analyze No. 1.

3. Continue the collection of COMPOUND SUFFIXES: AL+
   ITY =ALITY. You will find many words ending in that compound suffix and it means exactly what the KEYS say—relating to (AL) and quality of (ITY).
   Example: brutALITY—relating to the quality of a brute.
        Many adjectives ending in AL can be changed to nouns by adding this compound suffix—ALITY. And see what a huge piece of the word you have!

   a. animal   quality of an animal   ....
   b. criminal   quality of a criminal   ....
   c. mental   relating to the mind   ....
   d. fatal   relating to death   ....
   e. abnormal   relating to the unnatural ....
   f. total   relating to the sum   ....

129

KEY NO. 65

○━➤

CRED

believe

is the Root *CRED* which means BE-LIEVE. It is easy to see that our key ring is filling up with keys. Many of the words on the list are made with review keys. That is proof that the vocabulary is growing richer and that you know, at sight, the meanings of new words.

1. credo   CRED o (kreed' o) n.
A set of opinions; a creed.

2. creed   CREED (kreed) n.
A formula of faith; a set of principles.

3. credit   CRED it (kred' it) n.
Value; worth.

4. creditable   CRED itable (kred' it a b'l) adj.
Can be believed.

5. creditably   CRED itably (kred' it a blee) adv.
In such a manner that something is believed.

6. discreditable   dis CRED itable (dis kred' it a b'l) adj.
Not worthy of belief.

7. discreditably   dis CRED itably (dis kred' it a blee) adv.
Not believably.

8. creditor   CRED itor (kred' it or) n.
One who loans money to another.

9. credulity   CRED ulity (kre dyu' lit ee) n.
A willingness to believe easily.

10. incredulity   in CRED ulity (in kre dyu' lit ee) n.
A lack of willingness to believe easily.

11. credulous   CRED ulous (krej' u lus) adj.
Inclined to believe readily.

12. incredulous   in CRED ulous (in krej' u lus) adj.
Not inclined to believe.

13. incredulously   in CRED ulously (in krej' u lus lee) adv.
Distrustingly.

14. credulously   CRED ulously (krej' u lus lee) adv.
Trustingly.

15. accredit   ac CRED it (a kred' it) v.
To recognize as acceptable for approval; as, to accredit a school.

16. accreditation   ac CRED itation (a kred i tay' shun) n.
A certificate of acceptance.

17. credence   CRED ence (kreed' ens) n.
Belief; as, he earned the credence of his creditors.

18. credibly   CRED ibly (kred' i blee) adv.
                  Believably; plausibly.
19. incredibly   in CRED ibly (in kred' i blee) adv.
                  Unbelievably; implausibly.

word analysis

ACCREDITATION—No. 16
    AC (ad)—Prefix =to
    CRED (credere)—Latin Root =to believe
    IT (itus)—Latin Root =it goes
    TION—Suffix =act of

practical exercises

1. Supply the missing words:
    No one can afford to lose .... as a person
of .... character. She was ....
........................, and like a child, she listened ....
to every word he spoke.

2. Analyze No. 8.

3. Choose the number of the word or phrase which best expresses the italicized word:
    a. *anecdote*   (1) novel   (2) poem
         (3) illustration   (4) a personal incident
         (5) accident   ....
    b. *credit*   (1) trust   (2) power   (3) rascal
         (4) improvement   (5) energy   ....
    c. *antipathy*   (1) silence   (2) ecstasy
         (3) friendship   (4) order   (5) intense dislike   ....
    d. *manufacturer*   (1) doctor   (2) veterinary
         (3) dentist   (4) maker of goods   (5) professor   ....

KEY NO. 66

ANTI · ANT

against

is *ANTI, ANT,* a Prefix which means AGAINST. In the first six words on the list the *i* is dropped from *ANTI* to avoid using two vowels together. In No. 8, the *h* is joined with the *t*. Others have the full *ANTI* before a consonant. Don't confuse *ANTI* with *ANTE,* which means something entirely different, as you well know.

1. antacid   ANT acid (ant as′ id) n.
                     A remedy for acidity of the stomach; a counteracting agent.

2. antagonism   ANT agonism (an tag′ o niz um) n.
                     A strong feeling against a person or an idea.

3. antalkaline   ANT alkaline (ant al′ ka line) adj.
                     An agent against alkalinity.

4. antapology   ANT apology (ant a pol′ o ji) n.
                     A reply to an apology.

5. antarchism   ANT archism (ant′ ar kiz um) n.
                     Antagonism to government.

6. antarctic   ANT arctic (ant ark′ tik) n.
                     The opposite of the north pole; the south pole.

7. antephialtic   ANT ephialtic (ant ef i al′ tik) adj.
                     Preventing nightmares.

8. anthelmintic   ANT helmintic (ant hel mint′ ik) adj.
                     Expelling worms from the system.

9. antibiosis   ANTI biosis (ant i bi o′ sis) n.
                     Antagonism between organisms in the body.

10. antibody   ANTI body (ant′ i bod ee) n.
                     A substance in the body which opposes foreign substances.

11. antibromic   ANTI bromic (an ti bro′ mik) adj.
                     Deodorant.

12. anticlimax   ANTI climax (ant i klie′ maks) n.
                     The movement from a great event to one of lesser importance; a let down.

13. anticoagulant   ANTI coagulant (ant i ko ag′ yu lant) adj.
                     Hindering the coagulation of the blood.

14. antidote   ANTI dote (ant′ i dote) n.
                     A remedy against a poison.

15. antifreeze   ANTI freeze (ant i freze′) n.
                     A substance which slows up the freezing process.

16. antisepsis   ANTI sepsis (ant i sep' sis) n.
                    Prevention of infection; acting like an anti-
                    septic.

17. antitoxin   ANTI toxin (ant i tok' sin) n.
                    An agent which counteracts poison in the
                    body.

18. antipathy   ANTI pathy (an tip' a thee) n.
                    A strong feeling of dislike.

19. antipodes   ANTI podes (an tip' o deze) n.
                    Parts of the world which are opposite to each
                    other.

20. antithesis   ANTI thesis (an tith' e sis) n.
                    A contrast of ideas.

word analysis

ANTHELMINTIC—No. 8
    ANT (anti)—Prefix =against
    HELMIN (helmins)—Root =worm
    IC—Suffix =like; nature of

practical exercises

1. Supply the missing words:
    "They are .... of each other in temper and endowment." (Lowell) Oliver Wendell Holmes wrote a book called "A Mortal .... Children are given .... to prevent some diseases.

2. Analyze No. 10.

3. Syllabicate and indicate which syllable is most greatly stressed by placing the accent mark ('):

clamor	admirable	facile
biennial	interpolate	antipodes
antiquity	antitoxin	alkaline
discreditable	incredibility	certitude

KEY NO. 67

UNI

one

is the Root *UNI*. It comes from the Latin word meaning ONE. Smallest in number, it is greatest in idea, expressing itself in the ideal of UNIversality, ONENESS of the whole world.

1. unicorn — UNI corn (yu' ni korn) n.
    A legendary creature with one horn.

2. uniface — UNI face (yu' ni fase) n.
    A design that appears only on one side.

3. unify — UNI fy (yu' ni fie) v.
    Make into one.

4. unification — UNI fication (yu ni fi kay' shun) n.
    The act of making into one.

5. unifoliate — UNI foliate (yu ni foe' lee at) adj.
    Bearing one leaf.

6. unilateral — UNI lateral (yu ni lat' e ral) adj.
    One-sided.

7. unique — UNI que (yu neke') adj.
    One of a kind; having no equal; as, unique *in excellence.*

8. unimanual — UNI manual (yu ni man' yue al) adj.
    Done with one hand.

9. union — UNI on (yu' nyun) n.
    The joining of many into one; as, a trade union.

10. uniparous — UNI parous (yu nip' a rus) adj.
    Producing one child or egg at a time.

11. unison — UNI son (yu' ni son) n.
    Singing all the parts in one pitch; the chorus sang in unison.

12. unitarianism — UNI tarianism (yu ni tar' ee a niz um) n.
    A belief in one god.

13. unity — UNI ty (yu' nit ee) n.
    Oneness; togetherness; harmony.

14. unanimous — UN animous (yu nan' i mus) adj.
    Having one opinion held by all; as, a unanimous *vote.*

15. universe — UNI verse (yu' ni vers) n.
    All parts of the world as one; the Cosmos.

16. universal — UNI versal (yu ni ver' sal) adj.
    Relating to the whole world.

17. **universality** UNI versality (yu ni ver sal′ it ee) n.
     The quality of appealing to all the world.
18. **university** UNI versity (yu ni ver′ sit ee) n.
     An institution of learning whose program includes all branches of knowledge.
19. **unanimity** UN animity (yu na nim′ it ee) n.
     The state or quality of agreement.
20. **reunification** re UNI fication (re yu ni fi kay′ shun) n.
     The state of being one again.

word analysis

UNIVERSALITY—No. 17
    UNI—Root =one
    VERS—(versum)—Latin Root =to turn
    AL—Suffix =relating to
    ITY—Suffix =quality of

practical exercises

1. Supply the missing words:
    Part singing is more interesting than singing in ....
    "In .... there is strength" is a ....
    truth.

2. Analyze No. 8.

3. Read the following excerpt underlining all those words that contain keys you have already learned.
    Nebraska's unicameral legislature, the only one in the nation, is receiving renewed attention in states from coast to coast. Inquiries have reached officials here this week from legislators, newspapers, civic groups and ordinary citizens.
    The flurry began following the recent decision of the United States Supreme Court that both houses of a state legislature must be apportioned on the basis of population. In the past, area has traditionally been a consideration.
    (From *The New York Times,* July 18, 1964.)

KEY NO. 68

**FEDER · FIDE
FID · FEAL**

**trust
faith**

is the Root *FEDER, FIDE, FID, FEAL* which comes from the Latin *fidere*, to TRUST, have FAITH. The various spellings are interesting, and due, no doubt, to the various languages in which this Root is used. No. 12 when used for the feminine is spelled with an *e*—confidante (French).

1. federacy   FEDER acy (fed' er a si) n.
   An alliance or confederacy.
2. federal   FEDER al (fed' e ral) adj.
   In the nature of an alliance; united.
3. federation   FEDER ation (fed e ray' shun) n.
   A union; alliance through agreement.
4. federalism   FEDER alism (fed' e ra liz um) n.
   The principle of national organization.
5. federalist   FEDER alist (fed' e ra list) n.
   One who believes in federalism.
6. federate   FEDER ate (fed' e rate) v.
   To unite in mutual loyalty and faith.
7. confederacy   con FEDER acy (kon fed' e ra see) n.
   A union for mutual support and common action.
8. confederate   con FEDER ate (kon fed' e rat) n.
   One of a band united for a purpose; an accomplice.
9. bona fide   bona FIDE (boe' na fide) adj.
   In good faith; genuine.
10. confide   con FIDE (kon fide') v.
    To have trust in someone; as, to confide in a friend.
11. confident   con FID ent (kon' fid ent) adj.
    Self-reliant.
12. confidant   con FID ant (kon' fi dant) n.
    The person in whom one can confide.
13. confidence   con FID ence (kon' fid ens) n.
    Self-reliance.
14. confidential   con FID ential (kon fi den' chal) adj.
    In the nature of a secret; as, confidential information.
15. fealty   FEAL ty (fee' al tee) n.
    Loyalty; fidelity to duty.

16. **fidelity**   FID elity (fi del' it ee) n.
                     Faithfulness; fealty.
17. **infidel**   in FID el (in' fid el) n.
                     One who has no faith.
18. **infidelity** in FID elity (in fi del' it ee) n.
                     Faithlessness; disloyalty.
19. **perfidy**   per FID y (per' fid ee) n.
                     Disloyalty; treachery; deceit.
20. **perfidious** per FID ious (per fid' ee us) adj.
                     Treacherous; deceitful; as, a perfidious *friend.*

word analysis

CONFEDERACY—No. 7
    CON—Prefix =with; together
    FEDER (fidere)—Latin Root =trust; have faith
    ACY—Suffix =state of

practical exercises

1. Supply the missing words:
   His self-........................... was based on solid preparation
   for the job. Due to the .... of one of the
   members all their .... plans were revealed.

2. Analyze No. 10.

3. Choose the number of the word which best expresses the
   italicized word:
   a. *confederate* (1) enemy   (2) accomplice
      (3) judge   (4) statement   (5) juror   ....
   b. *creditor* (1) debtor   (2) manager   (3) porter
      (4) one who trusts   (5) customer   ....
   c. *accident* (1) misfortune   (2) wedding
      (3) surprise   (4) resentment   (5) jest   ....
   d. *guinea* (1) brush   (2) suitcase   (3) car
      (4) gold coin   (5) silver case   ....
   e. *honor* (1) insult   (2) defend   (3) enjoy
      (4) call upon   (5) esteem highly   ....
   f. *demand* (1) forbid   (2) permit   (3) request
      (4) insist   (5) owe   ....

KEY NO. 69

O—➤

OPUS · OPER

work

is the Root *OPUS, OPER* meaning WORK. It comes from the Latin word *OPUS, OPERA* (plural). While the original meaning is closest to the Latin word No. 19 and the plural is in use mostly as a singular word meaning No. 1 (plural is operas), this root has become a word for any work which is planned, acted on, and carried through. So we OPERate and have OPERations, and everything seems to be moving in an OPERational manner, with OPERators and coOPERators.

1. opera
OPER a (op' e ra) n.
A drama which has been set to music and is sung instead of spoken.

2. operatic
OPER atic (op e rat' ik) adj.
Resembling an opera; having qualities of opera.

3. operable
OPER able (op' e ra b'l) adj.
Can be treated by an operation.

4. operameter
OPER ameter (op er am' e ter) n.
An instrument for counting the rotations of a wheel in a machine.

5. operalogue
OPER alogue (op' er a log) n.
A lecture on opera which presents a summary of the story.

6. operate
OPER ate (op' e rate) v.
To labor; function; to perform surgery.

7. operatee
OPER atee (op er a tee') n.
The patient on whom an operation is performed.

8. operation
OPER ation (op e ray' shun) n.
An action done as part of practical work.

9. operational
OPER ational (op e ray' shun al) adj.
Relating to work performed.

10. operative
OPER ative (op' e rat iv) adj.
Having the power to act; causing operation.

11. operatize
OPER atize (op' er a tize) v.
To form into an opera.

12. operator
OPER ator (op' e rate or) n.
One who works and produces.

13. operatory
OPER atory (op' er a toe ri) n.
A place where work is done; laboratory.

14. operetta   OPER etta (op e ret' a) n.
                    A light, musical drama.

15. operettist   OPER ettist (op e ret' ist) n.
                    One who composes an operetta.

16. operose   OPER ose (op' e rose) adj.
                    Requiring labor; laborious; diligent.

17. cooperate   co OPER ate (koe op' e rate) v.
                    To work together for a common purpose.

18. cooperation   co OPER ation (koe op e ray' shun) n.
                    The act of working together for mutual benefit.

19. opus   OPUS (o' pus) n.
                    A musical composition; as, OPUS 25.

20. opuscule   OPUS cule (o pus' kyul) n.
                    A small, petty work.

word analysis

OPERATIONAL—No. 9
    OPERA (opus)—Latin Root =work
    TION—Suffix =act of
    AL—Suffix =relation to

practical exercises

1. Supply the missing words:
    .... is a fundamental principle in a demo-
cratic society. I called the .... to notify her that
the phone was out of order.

2. Analyze No. 6.

3. Use one word to express the phrase:
   a. believing too easily   ....
   b. relating to secret matters   ....
   c. a personal incident   ....
   d. a writer of operettas   ....
   e. to demand payment of a loan   ....
   f. a gold coin worth about 2 shillings   ....
   g. an unfortunate happening   ....
   h. to make things on a large scale   ....
   i. money owing to another   ....
   j. faith in a good result   ....

KEY NO. 70

○━━⚡

IVE

causing
making

is the Suffix *IVE*, meaning CAUSING; MAKING. We call IVE a causatIVE —the word carries in itself the key which means CAUSING, *IVE*. I am certain that you have noticed that the words listed are getting longer and longer. In word building we add to the root such pieces that change the meaning of the word grammatically, and give us an opportunity to express ourselves with exactitude. Scientific names are long for the same reason. Every element is a KEY in the name.

1. declarative   declarat IVE (de klar′ at iv) adj.
       Tending to make a statement.

2. derogative   derogat IVE (de rog′ at iv) adj.
       Tending to lessen value or respect.

3. affirmative   affirmat IVE (a fir′ mat iv) adj.
       Tending to agree; as, an affirmative *reply.*

4. additive   addit IVE (ad′ it iv) adj.
       Tending to add or be added.

5. subtractive   subtract IVE (sub trak′ tiv) adj.
       Tending to take away.

6. aggressive   aggress IVE (a gres′ iv) adj.
       Tending to push oneself forward.

7. appreciative   appreciat IVE (a pre′ shat iv) adj.
       Tending to understand; to value.

8. assertive   assert IVE (a sert′ iv) adj.
       Tending to claim one's rights and opinions.

9. authoritative   authoritat IVE (au thor′ i tate iv) adj.
       Causing obedience; as, an authoritative *command.*

10. cohesive   cohes IVE (koe hee′ siv) adj.
       Making things stick together; as, a cohesive *force.*

11. commemorative   commemorat IVE (ko mem′ o rat iv) adj.
       Causing to be remembered.

12. conjunctive   conjunct IVE (kon junk′ tiv) adj.
       Causing union.

13. abusive   abus IVE (a byu′ siv) adj.
       Causing insult; tending to mistreat.

14. accumulative   accumulat IVE (a kyu′ myu late iv) adj.
       Causing to pile up.

15. digestive   digest IVE (die jes′ tiv) adj.
           Causing digestion.

16. cooperative   cooperat IVE (koe op′ e rat iv) adj.
           Tending to work together.

17. deliberative   deliberat IVE (de lib′ e rate iv) adj.
           Tending to be careful; as, a deliberative manner.

18. evocative   evocat IVE (e vok′ at iv) adj.
           Tending to call forth an image.

19. exhaustive   exhaust IVE (eg zo′ stiv) adj.
           Making every kind of test; as, an exhaustive study.

20. expletive   explet IVE (ek′ splet iv) adj.
           Adding words and phrases, often to fill in extra space.

word analysis

COOPERATIVELY—No. 16+LY
     CO (com)—Prefix =with; together
     OPER (opus)—Root =work
     ATE—Suffix =make; cause
     IVE—Suffix =cause
     LY—Suffix =manner

practical exercises

1. Supply the missing words:
     "In my Father's House there are many Mansions." The word *there* is an .... It is unnecessary in the sentence. As, for instance in, "Many Mansions are in my Father's House."

2. Analyze Adoptive.

3. Key review. Match keys with their meanings:

a. cred	1. trust	....
b. fed, fid	2. causing	....
c. an (prefix)	3. one	....
d. uni	4. teeth	....
e. manu	5. condition	....
f. inter	6. hand	....
g. dent	7. conquer	....
h. vinc	8. between	....
i. tude	9. native of	....
j. ive	10. believe	....
k. an, ian	11. not	

0—➤

**CULE · ICLE
LING**

very small

is really three keys, all meaning the same thing, VERY SMALL. They are the Suffixes *CULE, ICLE, LING*. With these Suffixes added the thing spoken of is diminished, made small not only in size but also in significance. Nos. 4 and 10 use *ICLE;* the rest of the first ten words, *CULE;* and the last ten, *LING. LING* often has a gentle, endearing quality, as in Nos. 11, 13, 16, 17 and 18. Youth is tenderly called a sapLING.

1. crepuscule   crepus CULE (kre pus' kyul) n.
   Dim light; half light; twilight.

2. articulate   arti CUL ate (ar tik' yu late) v.
   To pronounce each little sound carefully.

3. minuscule   minus CULE (min' us kyul) adj.
   Very small; petty; insignificant.

4. article   art ICLE (art' i k'l) n.
   A small thing; a detail; a piece of writing on a particular topic.

5. animalcule   animal CULE (an i mal' kyul) n.
   A minute animal, usually microscopic.

6. reticule   reti CULE (ret' i kyul) n.
   A small net handbag.

7. ridicule   ridi CULE (rid' i kyul) n.
   Small, mocking laughter.

8. molecule   mole CULE (mol' e kyul) n.
   A tiny particle of matter.

9. molecular   mole CUL ar (mo lek' ye lar) adj.
   In the nature of a molecule.

10. funicle   fun ICLE (fue' ni k'l) n.
    A small cord; a bundle of threadlike fibers.

11. darling   dar LING (dar' ling) n.
    A dear one, favorite.

12. duckling   duck LING (duk' ling) n.
    A little baby duck.

13. fledgling   fledg LING (flej' ling) n.
    A baby bird; an inexperienced person.

14. gosling   gos LING (goz' ling) n.
    A baby goose.

15. hireling   hire LING (hire' ling) n.
    One hired to do a job for petty motives.

142

16. **nestling**   nest LING (nest' ling) n.
                      A bird still in the nest, unable to fly.
17. **princeling**   prince LING (prin' sling) n.
                      A prince of a small country.
18. **sapling**   sap LING (sap' ling) n.
                      A very young tree; youth.
19. **underling**   under LING (un' der ling) n.
                      An underdog; of the lowest status.
20. **worldling**   world LING (worl' dling) n.
                      One devoted to the world and its pleasures.

word analysis

MINUSCULE—No. 3
    MINUS—Root =less; least
    CULE—Suffix =very small

practical exercises

1. Supply the missing words:
    Richard III had the two ....(s) murdered in
the Tower. "It is not in our stars, but in ourselves that we
are ....(s)" (Shakespeare).

2. Analyze No. 5.

3. Indicate the pronunciation by placing the accent mark ('):
        induct   discourse (verb)   discourse (noun)
        antiknock   recede   dissolve
        replace   antiquated   reminisce
        animalcule   fledgling   molecule

KEY NO. 72

URE

**state of
act
process
rank**

is the Suffix *URE*. It means STATE OF, ACT, PROCESS, RANK. It makes a noun out of an adjective. See *overt, literat, temperat* and *signat*. It is good to remember this for conveniently changing a part of speech. Besides it gives a very fine form to a word, both in writing and in speech.

1. censure   cens URE (sen' chur) v.
        To find fault with; to blame.

2. aperture   apert URE (ap' er chur) n.
        An opening; a hole; as, an aperture in a wall.

3. culture   cult URE (kul' chur) n.
        Result of development in education, art, and mode of life.

4. exposure   expos URE (ek spoe' zhur) n.
        State of being laid open; bare of protection or concealment.

5. immature   immat URE (im a tyur') adj.
        Unripe; adolescent.

6. future   fut URE (fyu' chur) n.
        That time which is yet to come.

7. judicature judicat URE (jude' i ka chur) n.
        Court of justice; judges collectively.

8. legislature legislat URE (lej' i slay chur) n.
        The collective body of persons who make the law.

9. overture   overt URE (o' ver chur) n.
        The opening piece of music in an opera; an introductory piece.

10. literature literat URE (lit' e ra chur) n.
        The collective body of writings of the highest rank.

11. picture   pict URE (pik' chur) n.
        A representation through painting, drawing, or photography.

12. prefecture prefect URE (pre' fek chur) n.
        The official residence of the prefect.

13. primogeniture primogenit URE (prie mo jen' i tur) n.
        The state of being the first born.

14. posture   post URE (pos' chur) n.
        State of one's bearing; carriage.

15. pressure   press URE (presh' ur) n.
                       Force; painful force which causes distress.
16. procedure   proced URE (pro see' jur) n.
                       Manner or method of a course of action.
17. tenure   ten URE (ten' yur) n.
                       The act or right of holding.
18. temperature   temperat URE (tem' pe ra chur) n.
                       The degree of heat or cold.
19. signature   signat URE (sig' na chur) n.
                       The seal of approval or of right.
20. rupture   rupt URE (rup' chur) n.
                       A break; as, a rupture of a vein.

word analysis

TENURE—No. 17
    TEN (tenere)—Latin Root =to hold
    URE—Suffix =state of

practical exercises

1. Supply the missing words:
    His .... to constant .... made
his .... of office doubtful. He refused to add
his .... to the bill.

2. Analyze No. 16.

3. Read the following excerpt underlining all those words that
contain keys that you have already learned.

    A tradesman who had long dunned him for a note of
three hundred guineas **fou**nd him, one day, counting gold,
and demanded payment.

    "No," said Fox, "I owe this money to Sheridan. It is a
debt of honor; if an accident should happen to me, he
would have nothing to show."

    Said the Creditor, "Then I will change my debt for a
debt of honor," and he tore the note into pieces.

    Fox thanked the man for his confidence, and paid him,
saying, "Your debt is of older standing. And now Sheridan
must wait."

    (An anecdote about the great English statesman, John Fox,
as related by Ralph Waldo Emerson.)

KEY NO. 73

o—⚷

FIX

fix

is the Root FIX. It comes from the Latin *figere, fixus,* and it means just that, *FIX*. It is a word commonly used and nearly always by itself, without Prefixes or Suffixes. The list contains words which seem strange at first, but we can grow accustomed to them.

1. fix   FIX (fiks) n.
         A difficult position; a dilemma.

2. fixate   FIX ate (fik′ sate) v.
         To become fixed.

3. fixation   FIX ation (fik say′ shun) n.
         The state of being attached; fixed.

4. fixative   FIX ative (fik′ sat iv) adj.
         Causing to be fixed; attached.

5. fixator   FIX ator (fiks ay′ tor) n.
         A thing that holds something in place.

6. fixature   FIX ature (fik′ sa ture) n.
         A preparation used to fix or stiffen something.

7. fixedly   FIX edly (fik′ sed lee) adv.
         In the manner of being fastened to; as, looking at a person fixedly.

8. fixity   FIX ity (fik′ sit ee) n.
         Quality of being fastened firmly in place.

9. fixer   FIX er (fik′ ser) n.
         One who adjusts claims.

10. fixture   FIX ture (fiks′ chur) n.
         Furnishings fastened firmly in place, as shelves, a counter.

11. affix   af FIX (a fiks′) v.
         To fix or fasten in any way; to seal.

12. affix   af FIX (af′ iks) n.
         That which is attached to a word to produce another; as, a prefix or a suffix.

13. affixal   af FIX al (af′ ik sal) adj.
         In the nature of an affix.

14. affixation   af FIX ation (af ik say′ shun) n.
         The process of affixing a seal or a signature.

15. affixion   af FIX ion (a fik′ shun) n.
         Affixation; Nos. 14 and 15 are synonyms.

16. affixer   af FIX er (a fiks′ er) n.
         The official whose duty it is to affix a seal or a signature.

17. affixture   af FIX ture (a fiks' ture) n.
                  Act of affixing; attachment.
18. transfix   trans FIX (trans fiks') v.
                  To hold motionless; as, to transfix *with horror.*

word analysis

AFFIXER—No. 16
    AF (ad)—Prefix =to; toward
    FIX (figere)—Latin Root =fix
    ER—Suffix =one who

practical exercises

1. Supply the missing words:
    Prefixes and Suffixes are ....(ed) to words to
    change their meanings. The .... of the man's
    stare was annoying. At the sound of the air raid warning
    she was ....(ed) with terror.

2. Analyze No. 8.

3. Change the nouns in column 1 to adjectives and adverbs:
    Example: ration   ....rational........   ......rationally......
    a. recreation   ....
    b. sensation   ....
    c. education   ....
    d. emotion   ....
    e. promotion   ....
    f. function   ....
    g. option   ....

KEY NO. 74

ISH

origin
nature
resembling

is the Suffix *ISH*. It means ORIGIN, as in No. 11, Ir*ISH*; NATURE, as in No. 10, amateur*ISH*; RESEMBLING, as in No. 9, clown*ISH*. In the last two there is an uncomplimentary element. Usually *ISH* makes adjectives of nouns. Sometimes verbs have this Suffix for no apparent reason, as per*ISH*, nour*ISH*, etc.

1. boorish   boor ISH (boor' ish) adj.
   A lout; a churl; as, a boorish man.
2. ghoulish   ghoul ISH (gu' lish) adj.
   Like a ghoul.
3. brutish   brut ISH (brut' ish) adj.
   Like a brute; rough.
4. foolish   fool ISH (foo' lish) adj.
   Like a fool; somewhat ridiculous.
5. waspish   wasp ISH (was' pish) adj.
   Sharp; stinging; as, a waspish tongue.
6. womanish   woman ISH (wom' a nish) adj.
   Like a woman; feminine.
7. Scottish   Scott ISH (skot' ish) adj.
   Native of Scotland.
8. childish   child ISH (chile' dish) adj.
   Like a child; somewhat immature.
9. clownish   clown ISH (klow' nish) adj.
   Like a clown; somewhat silly or foolish.
10. amateurish   amateur ISH (am a tur' ish) adj.
    Like an amateur; a nonprofessional.
11. Irish   Ir ISH (ire' ish) adj.
    Native of Ireland.
12. bookish   book ISH (book' ish) adj.
    Inclined to reading; as, a bookish fellow.
13. Swedish   Swed ISH (swede' ish) adj.
    Native of Sweden.

word analysis

AMATEURISH—No. 10
    AMAT (amo)—Root =love
    EUR (er)—Suffix =one who
    ISH—Suffix =nature of

practical exercises

1. Supply the missing words:

   As an .... performance it was good enough.
   Her .... tongue stung many a friend. A
   .... of trumpets announced the arrival of the
   King's Court.

2. Analyze No. 4.

3. Use one word for the phrase:
   a. opposite parts of the globe   ....
   b. a struggle against a person   ....
   c. a tiny particle of matter   ....
   d. causing someone to stand out   ....
   e. work together for a common purpose   ....
   f. a woman in whom one can confide   ....
   g. all the group having one opinion   ....

KEY NO. 75

O—↦

GNOSI · COGNOSC

know

is the Root *GNOSI, COGNOSC* which comes from the Latin, *noscere* and *cognoscere*. They both mean KNOW. And I am *COGNI*zant of the fact that, if you re*COGNI*ze all the keys, you too will be a *COGNOSC*ente.

1. agnosy   a GNOS y (ag' no si) n.
    State of not knowing; ignorance.

2. agnosia   a GNOSI a (ag no' si a) n.
    Inability to recognize familiar objects.

3. agnostic   a GNOS tic (ag nos' tik) n.
    One who professes ignorance about the certainty that God exists.

4. agnosticism   a GNOS ticism (ag nos' ti siz um) n.
    The doctrine that God is unknowable.

5. cognition   COGNI tion (kog nish' un) n.
    The act of knowing.

6. cognizable   COGNI zable (kog' ni za b'l) adj.
    Can be known.

7. cognize   COGNI ze (kog nize') v.
    To know; to perceive.

8. cognizance   COGNI zance (kog' ni zans) n.
    Notice; understanding.

9. cognizant   COGNI zant (kog' ni zant) adj.
    Knowing; being aware.

10. cognosce   COGNOSC e (cog nos') v.
    Inquire into; to determine.

11. cognoscente   COGNOSC ente (kon yoe shent' ee) n.
    One who is "in the know"; a connoisseur.

12. recognize   re COGNI ze (rek' og nize) v.
    To know again; as, recognize a face.

13. incognito   in COGNI to (in cog' ni to) adj.
    Not known; as, the King went about the city incognito.

14. prognosis   pro GNOSIS (prog no' sis) n.
    A forecast; foretelling the course of a disease.

15. prognose   pro GNOS e (prog nose') v.
    To give a prognosis of a disease.

16. prognostic   pro GNOS tic (prog nos' tik) adj.
    Foretelling; knowing beforehand.

17. prognosticable   pro GNOS ticable (prog nos' ti ka b'l) adj.
    Can be foretold.

18. prognosticate   pro GNOS ticate (prog nos' ti kate) v.
      To foreshow from symptoms.
19. prognostication   pro GNOS tication (prog nos ti kay' shun) n.
      A prediction; forecast.
20. prognosticator   pro GNOS ticator (prog nos' ti kate or) n.
      One who can predict; prognose.

word analysis

RECOGNIZABLE—No. 7+RE+ABLE
    RE—Prefix =again
    COGN (cognoscere)—Latin Root =know
    IZE—Suffix =make
    ABLE—Suffix =can do

practical exercises

1. Supply the missing words:
    The young Prince liked to walk about the city ....
    In that guise he was not ....

2. Analyze No. 7.

3. By adding a key make a word which matches a phrase or a sentence:
    Example: Like a woman   woman..........   ....ish....
    a. knowing again   ....cognize   ....
    b. appearing as one unknown   ....cognito   ....
    c. acting like a clown   clown..........   ....
    d. if he puts the official seal on documents he's the
        .... fix..........   ....
    e. in this parish he is the rect..........   ....
    f. an error which is rectifi..........   ....

KEY NO. 76

RECT · RECTI

is the Root *RECT, RECTI*, which means STRAIGHT; RIGHT. It is simple and most diRECT and goes exactly where it indicates, RIGHT to the point, no two ways about it.

straight
right

1. rectangle   RECT angle (rek' tan g'l) n.
A right-angled parallelogram.

2. rectangled   RECT angled (rek tan' guld) adj.
Separated into rectangles.

3. rectangular   RECT angular (rek tan' gyu lar) adj.
Having edges that meet at right angles.

4. rectangulate   RECT angulate (rek tang' yu late) v.
To move at right angles to each other.

5. rectangulometer RECT angulometer (rek tang yu lom' e ter) n.
Instrument for measuring right angles.

6. rectify   RECTI fy (rek' ti fie) v.
To make right; to correct an error.

7. reckon   REC kon (rek' on) v.
To count; to calculate.

8. reckoning   REC koning (rek' o ning) n.
An account; the sum total.

9. recto   RECT o (rek' toe) n.
A right-hand page.

10. rector   RECT or (rek' tor) n.
A clergyman; one who directs.

11. rectifiable   RECTI fiable (rek' ti fie a b'l) adj.
Can be made right; as, a rectifiable error.

12. rectificator RECTI ficator (rek' ti fi kay tor) n.
One who can make things right; a rectifier.

13. rectory   RECT ory (rek' to ree) n.
The house where the clergyman lives; the parsonage.

14. rectilinear   RECTI linear (rek ti lin' ee ar) adj.
Formed by straight lines.

15. rectitude   RECTI tude (rek' ti tyud) n.
Uprightness; righteousness.

16. direct   di RECT (di rekt') v.
To show the right way; to guide.

17. director   di RECT or (di rek' tor) n.
One who shows the right way.

152

18. direction   di RECT ion (di rek' shun) n.
                   The act of directing.
19. directive   di RECT ive (di rek' tiv) n.
                   An order; instruction as to procedure.
20. indirect   indi RECT (in di rekt') adj.
                   Not in a straight line or course.

word analysis

RECTIFICATOR—No. 12
     RECTI—Root =right
     FIC (facere)—Latin Root =to make
     OR—Suffix =one who

practical exercises

1. Supply the missing words:
   In the morality play *Everyman,* man is summoned to bring
   with him a "sure ...." The ....
   gave a .... for the .... of the cam-
   paign.

2. Analyze No. 6.

3. Choose the number of the word which best expresses the
   italicized word:
   a. *recognition*   (1) thoughtfulness   (2) timeliness
         (3) pomp   (4) knowing again   (5) report   ....
   b. *rectitude*   (1) righteousness   (2) announcement
         (3) history   (4) experiment   (5) latitude   ....
   c. *fixator*   (1) paper   (2) ruler   (3) pen
         (4) glue   (5) eraser   ....
   d. *animalcule*   (1) hippopotamus   (2) giraffe
         (3) horse   (4) dinosaur   (5) mouse   ....
   e. *anesthesia*   (1) orange   (2) anemia
         (3) champion   (4) ether   (5) doctor   ....
   f. *literature*   (1) temperature   (2) picture
         (3) Iliad   (4) prisoner   (5) jealousy   ....

KEY NO. 77

o━┳

BIO

life

is the Root *BIO* which means LIFE. An important key as it treats the most important of all subjects, LIFE. The word list is a fine preparation for the enjoyment of a lecture or an article of a BIOlogical nature.

1. biogenesis   BIO genesis (bie o jen' e sis) n.
   The development of living organisms from life that exists.

2. biogenesist   BIO genesist (bie o jen' e sist) n.
   An expert in biogenesis.

3. biogenetic   BIO genetic (bie o je net' ik) adj.
   Pertaining to the development of life from life that exists.

4. biology   BIO logy (bie ol' o jee) n.
   The study of living organisms.

5. biogeny   BIO geny (bie oj' e ni) n.
   The development of life.

6. biogeography   BIO geography (bie o jee og' ra fee) n.
   The area of biology that deals with the distribution of plants and animals.

7. biognosis   BIO gnosis (bie og no' sis) n.
   The investigation of life.

8. biography   BIO graphy (bie og' ra fee) n.
   The written story of the life of a particular person.

9. biographer   BIO grapher (bie og' ra fer) n.
   One who writes about the life of another.

10. biographee   BIO graphee (bie og ra fee') n.
    The person whose life is written about.

11. autobiography   auto BIO graphy (aut o bie og' ra fee) n.
    One's own life story written by oneself.

12. biologist   BIO logist (bie ol' o jist) n.
    An expert in biology.

13. bios   BIO s (bie' os) n.
    Organic nature among plants and animals.

14. biosis   BIO sis (bie o' sis) n.
    The way of life among living organisms; vitality.

15. biostatics   BIO statics (bie o stat' iks) n.
    The study of living organisms and their functions.

16. biota   BIO ta (bie ote′ a) n.
           Animal and plant life of a region; the fauna
           and flora of an area.
17. biostatistics   BIO statistics (bie o sta tis′ tiks) n.
           Vital measurements.
18. biopsy   BIO psy (bie′ op see) n.
           Examination of diseased tissue removed
           from a body.
19. biostratigraphy   BIO stratigraphy (bie o stra tig′ ra fi) n.
           Condition and order of sedimentary rocks.
20. biopsychology   BIO psychology (bie o sie kol′ o ji) n.
           Psychology as related to biology.

word analysis

BIOGRAPHER—No. 9
    BIO (bios)—Greek Root =life
    GRAPH (graphein)—Greek Root =write
    ER—Suffix =one who

practical exercises

1. Supply the missing words:
    The .... gave to his .... all the
information on .... and all the ....
which he had collected in years of work. This was a valu-
able contribution to ....

2. Analyze No. 4.

3. Read the following excerpt underlining all those words that
contain keys you have already learned.

CITY HOST TODAY TO BIOCHEMISTS

    The Sixth International Congress of Biochemists will con-
vene here today. Six thousand biochemists, including 15
Nobel laureates, are expected to attend.

    They will discuss the chemistry of life—molecular dy-
namics of aging, heredity, natural resistance to disease, the
transmission of nerve impulses, regulation of body proc-
esses by enzymes, action of antibiotics against bacteria and
tumors, and the storage and use of energy in the body. . . .

          (From *The New York Times,* July 26, 1964.)

KEY NO. 78

0—⚡

PEL · PULS

drive
push
throw

is *PEL, PULS,* a Root which comes from the Latin *pellere, pulsus,* and it means DRIVE; PUSH; THROW. It is a key that takes seven Prefixes to give full range of its violence. There isn't a peaceful word on the list nor is there a quiet moment in its usage. Inner and outer turmoil accompanies this key. Of course, if that is the impression wanted, there's nothing better, but be certain that that is the word you want before you use *PEL* or *PULS.*

1. impulsion   im PULS ion (im pul' shun) n.
     An uncontrollable impulse to act; as, an im-pulsion to shoot.

2. pulse   PULS e (puls) n.
     Beat; heartbeat.

3. pulsation   PULS ation (pul say' shun) n.
     The regular heartbeat; throbbing; as, the pul-sations of the wind.

4. compel   com PEL (kom pel') v.
     To urge; force.

5. compulsion   com PULS ion (kom pul' shun) n.
     The state of being forced; driven.

6. compulsive   com PULS ive (kom pul' siv) adj.
     Being forced; as, compulsive eating.

7. compulsory   com PULS ory (kom puls' o ree) adj.
     Acting under compulsion; as, compulsory edu-cation.

8. expel   ex PEL (ek spel') v.
     Drive out; throw out; as, expel from school.

9. repel   re PEL (re pel') v.
     Drive back; as, repel the enemy.

10. propel   pro PEL (pro pel') v.
     Push forward; as, the use of steam to propel ships.

11. impel   im PEL (im pel') v.
     To force; to urge; as, facts impel the jury to judge him guilty.

12. dispel   dis PEL (dis pel') v.
     To scatter; to drive away; as, dispel doubt.

13. impulsive   im PULS ive (im pul' siv) adj.
     Driven to act quickly; as, an impulsive nature.

14. **repulsive**   re PULS ive (re pul′ siv) adj.
    Disgusting; as, repulsive *language.*
15. **repulse**   re PULS e (re puls′) n.
    The action of driving back; rejection; as, his
    proposal was repulsed.
16. **propulsive**   pro PULS ive (pro pul′ siv) adj.
    Tending to push forward.
17. **propulsion**   pro PULS ion (pro pul′ shun) n.
    State of being pushed forward.
18. **repellent**   re PEL lent (re pel′ ent) adj.
    Driving back; as, water-repellent *fabrics.*
19. **expulsion**   ex PULS ion (ek spul′ shun) n.
    State of being expelled, thrown out.

word analysis

PROPULSION—No. 17
    PRO (pro, before)—Greek Prefix =forward
    PULS (pello)—Latin Root =push
    SION—Suffix =state; act

practical exercises

1. Supply the missing words:
    For repeated misdemeanors he was .... from
    the school. A surging wave ....(led) the boat
    against the rocks.

2. Analyze No. 4.

3. Use one word for the phrase:
    a. sudden action motivated by some inner force   ....
    b. one who sets things right   ....
    c. a condition foretold   ....
    d. the subject of a biography   ....
    e. the rank of the first-born   ....

SPOND · SPONS

pledge
answer

is the Root *SPOND*, *SPONS*, meaning PLEDGE; ANSWER. It comes from the Latin *spondeo*, *spondere*, *sponsus*, meaning to pledge. In that verb you get the explanation of the two spellings of the key. Knowing that the key Root means "Pledge" and "covenant" gives one the full, rich meaning of the word reSPONSibility. It means not only to pledge, but to REpledge. Please notice in No. 16, the key *IR* before the KEY *RE*. *IR* is an assimilated *IN* before *r*.

1. sponsor   SPONS or (spon' sor) n.
                 One who assumes responsibility for a project; as, a sponsor *of a charity.*

2. sponsor   SPONS or (spon' sor) v.
                 To assume responsibility; to promise support.

3. sponsorship   SPONS orship (spon' sor ship) n.
                 The state of being a sponsor.

4. sponsorial   SPONS orial (spon sore' ee al) adj.
                 Relating to a sponsor.

5. respond   re SPOND (re spond') v.
                 To answer in kind; as, respond *to an appeal.*

6. response   re SPONS e (re spons') n.
                 An answer; as, an immediate response.

7. responsive   re SPONS ive (re spon' siv) adj.
                 Causing to answer; as, a responsive *nature.*

8. respondent   re SPOND ent (re spon' dent) n.
                 One who responds.

9. responder   re SPOND er (re spon' der) n.
                 One who answers a communication.

10. responsible re SPONS ible (re spon' si b'l) adj.
                 Answerable; trustworthy to carry out obligations.

11. responsibility re SPONS ibility (re spon si bil' it ee) n.
                 Reliability; as, seeing one's responsibility.

12. correspond   corre SPOND (kor e spond') v.
                 To communicate by letter; sending and receiving letters.

13. correspondence corre SPOND ence (kor e spon' dens) n.
                 State of corresponding; letters.

14. correspondent   corre SPOND ent (kor e spon' dent) n.
One who communicates with another.

15. unresponsive   unre SPONS ive (un re spon' siv) adj.
Not answering; opposite of No. 7.

16. irresponsible   irre SPONS ible (ir e spon' si b'l) adj.
Not reliable; does not respond to the call of duty.

word analysis

SPONSORSHIP—No. 3
    SPONS (spondere)—Latin Root = to pledge
    OR—Suffix = one who
    SHIP—Suffix = state of

practical exercises

1. Supply the missing words:
    The .... to his appeal was excellent and he was asked to be the .... and assume complete ....

2. Analyze No. 5.

3. Choose the number of the word which best expresses the italicized word:
    a. *irresponsible* (1) capable (2) unworthy
       (3) juvenile (4) answerable
       (5) not keeping a pledge   ....
    b. *compulsion* (1) liberty (2) innocence
       (3) withered (4) mixture (5) force   ....
    c. *bachelor* (1) knight (2) guinea (3) conflict
       (4) unmarried man (5) spinster   ....
    d. *indifferent* (1) sincere (2) careful
       (3) unconcerned (4) cautious (5) amazing   ....
    e. *expelled* (1) invited (2) promoted
       (3) rewarded (4) put out (5) punished   ....
    f. *direction* (1) guidance (2) deceit (3) shock
       (4) property (5) ambition   ....

KEY NO. 80

0—⚷

CEDE · CEED
CESS

go
yield
surrender

is the Root *CEDE, CEED, CESS*, which comes from the Latin *cedere* which means GO; YIELD; SURRENDER. The differences in the spelling are due to the usual problem of the various spellings of the Latin Root. In addition, there is the extra odd spelling in No. 19 where we have *CEASE* instead of any of the others.

1. cede   CEDE (sede) v.
   Yield; admit; as, cede *a point in an argument.*
2. accede   ac CEDE (ak sede') v.
   To go along with; agree to.
3. concede   con CEDE (kon sede') v.
   Yield to; agree to.
4. secede   se CEDE (se sede') v.
   Go apart; separate; as, secede *from the Union.*
5. intercede   inter CEDE (int er sede') v.
   Go between two litigants.
6. precede   pre CEDE (pre sede') v.
   Go before; as, the leader will precede *the rest.*
7. recede   re CEDE (re sede') v.
   Go back; as, the tide begins to recede.
8. precedent   pre CEDE nt (pres' ed ent) n.
   That which went before; as, a precedent *for an opinion.*
9. procedure   pro CED ure (pro see' jure) n.
   The manner of going forward.
10. abscess   abs CESS (ab' ses) n.
    A localized collection of pus due to infection.
11. ancestor   an CES tor (an' ses tor) n.
    One who came before, as father or grandfather.
12. intercession   inter CESS ion (int er sesh' un) n.
    Act of going between.
13. recession   re CESS ion (re sesh' un) n.
    Act of going back.
14. procession   pro CESS ion (pro sesh' un) n.
    Act of going forward.
15. success   suc CESS (suk ses') n.
    The reaching of a goal; achievement.

16. exceed   ex CEED (ek seed') v.
                    To go beyond the ordinary; beyond the average.

17. succeed   suc CEED (suk sede') v.
                    To achieve; to reach the goal.

18. process   pro CESS (pros' es) n.
                    The going forward; the movement forward.

19. decease   de CEASE (de sese') v.
                    To go away; to depart from life; to die.

20. accession   ac CESS ion (ak sesh' un) n.
                    The going to; as, the accession *to the throne.*

word analysis

SECESSION
    SE—Prefix =apart; separate
    CESS (cedere)—Latin Root =to go
    ION—Suffix =state; act of

practical exercises

1. Supply the missing words:
    It is difficult to .... between two people who both insist that they are right. President Franklin D. Roosevelt set a .... for more than two terms in office.

2. Analyze No. 6.

3. Syllabicate and indicate which syllable receives the greatest stress by placing the accent mark ('):

        indifferently   precedent (noun)
        disfiguration   conflict (noun)
        sincere   mixture
        bachelor   preparatory
        regret   spontaneity

KEY NO. 81

O—⚡

POLY

many

is the Root *POLY* and it means MANY. A great many words are built with this Root and you will have no trouble remembering it. You yourself will, if you wish, be able to make up words with it, if not serious ones which Webster will wish to include in his International Dictionary, then humorous ones. Word No. 15 is sometimes used for "jargon." But the Polyglot Bible, written in nine languages by Brian Walton, is a tremendous achievement in language and religious literature.

1. polyanthus   POLY anthus (pol ee an' thus) n.
     A type of plant, especially primrose, which has many flowers.

2. polydactyl   POLY dactyl (pol i dak' til) adj.
     Having more than the normal number of fingers or toes.

3. polychord   POLY chord (pol' i kord) n.
     A viol-shaped instrument with ten strings.

4. polychotomous   POLY chotomous (pol y kot' o mus) adj.
     Having many branches; many parts.

5. polychotomy   POLY chotomy (pol i kot' o mee) n.
     Division into many parts or branches.

6. polychresty   POLY chresty (pol i kres' ti) n.
     Usefulness for many purposes; as, a word of many meanings.

7. polymorphic   POLY morphic (pol i mor' fik) adj.
     Having many forms.

8. polychromatic   POLY chromatic (pol i kro mat' ik) adj.
     Having many colors.

9. polynomial   POLY nomial (pol i no' mee al) n.
     A sum of two or more.

10. polyclinic   POLY clinic (pol i klin' ik) n.
     A hospital where a variety of diseases are treated.

11. polydemic   POLY demic (pol i dem' ik) adj.
     Native to many countries.

12. polyesthesia   POLY esthesia (pol i es thee' zhi a) n.
     A condition in which a single object touching the body seems to be felt in many places.

13. polyethnic	POLY ethnic (pol i eth' nik) adj.
	Inhabited by many races.
14. polygamy	POLY gamy (po lig' a me) n.
	The custom of plural wives or husbands.
15. polyglot	POLY glot (pol' i glot) n.
	One who knows many languages; a linguist.
16. polygon	POLY gon (pol' i gon) n.
	A (closed plane) figure with many angles.
17. polygraphy	POLY graphy (pol' i gra fi) n.
	Literary productiveness; writing on a variety of subjects.
18. polyhedron	POLY hedron (pol i hee' dron) n.
	A solid figure having many plane faces.
19. polyneuritis	POLY neuritis (pol i nu rie' tis) n.
	Inflammation of many nerves at once.
20. polyarchy	POLY archy (pol' i ar ki) n.
	A government ruled by many persons.

word analysis

POLYGON—No. 16
    POLY—Prefix =many
    GON (gonos)—Greek Root =angle
POLYGLOT—No. 15
    POLY—Prefix =many
    GLOT (glotta)—Greek Root =tongue

practical exercises

1. Supply the missing words:
    A .... speaks many languages; he is a linguist.
    But *polyglot* is also an adjective, as the ....
    Bible.

2. Analyze No. 20.

3. By supplying missing KEYS, make a word which expresses
    a phrase or sentence:
    a. abnormally large number of teeth— ....dontia
    b. made of many races— ...... ethnic
    c. the manner of going ahead— pro..........ure
    d. a state of being thrown out— ....sion
    e. being sorry for— re..........
    f. letters received and answered— corre..........ence

163

KEY NO. 82

O━━x

APO

away from

is the Prefix *APO* which means AWAY FROM. This is a useful key leading to acquaintance with interesting words and worlds. Oddly enough, *APO* is found in the most modern words and also in the most ancient. No. 9 is used in modern science. No. 2 and No. 7 refer to ancient religious writings.

1. apobiotic   APO biotic (ap o bie ot′ ik) adj.
   Pertaining to any change that diminishes the vital energy of tissue.

2. apocalypse   APO calypse (a pok′ a lyps) n.
   Religious literature; a revelation.

3. apocalyptic   APO calyptic (a pok a lyp′ tik) n.
   Relating to the apocalypse.

4. apocenter   APO center (ap′ o sen ter) n.
   The point of an orbit the most distant from the center of attraction.

5. apocope   APO cope (a pok′ o pee) n.
   A cutting off; as, the end letters of a word.

6. apocrustic   APO crustic (ap o krus′ tik) adj.
   Able to drive away; repellent.

7. apocrypha   APO crypha (a pok′ ri fa) n.
   Writings of doubtful authority.

8. apocryphal   APO cryphal (a pok′ ri fal) adj.
   Relating to the Apocrypha.

9. apogee   APO gee (ap′ o je) n.
   The point in the orbit of a heavenly body farthest from the earth.

10. apology   APO logy (a pol′ o jee) n.
    An attempt to make amends; an excuse.

11. apologetic   APO logetic (a pol o jet′ ik) adj.
    In the nature of an apology.

12. apoplexy   APO plexy (ap′ o plek see) n.
    Sudden loss of consciousness; a stroke.

13. apoplectic   APO plectic (ap o plek′ tik) adj.
    In the nature of a stroke; highly excited.

14. apostasy   APO stasy (a pos′ ta see) n.
    A defection from one's faith.

15. apostate   APO state (a pos′ tate) n.
    One who abandons his faith.

16. apostle APO stle (a pos' el) n.
One who is sent away on a mission; as, the disciples of Jesus.

17. apostrophe APO strophe (a pos' tro fee) n.
A mark used to indicate the omitting of a letter; as, in the contraction "can't."

18. apotype APO type (ap' o tipe) n.
Type specimen used as the basis of information.

19. apotheosis APO theosis (a poth ee o' sis) n.
Release from earthly life; deification.

20. apothegm APO thegm (ap' o them) n.
A short saying that teaches; as, "Man proposes and God disposes" or "Time and tide wait for no man."

word analysis

APOCRUSTIC—No. 6
  APO—Prefix =away from
  CRUST (kroust)—Greek Root =repel
  IC—Suffix =nature of

practical exercises

Read the following excerpt underlining all those words that contain keys you have already learned.

The wide-open blue eyes looked up at Geoffrey's without any uneasiness or sign of recognition; the child could make no visible audible claim on its father; and the father felt a strange mixture of feelings, a conflict of regret and joy, that the pulse of that little heart had no response for the half-jealous yearning in his own, when the blue eyes turned away from him slowly, and fixed themselves on the weaver's queer face, which was bent low down to look at them, while the small hand began to pull at Marner's withered cheek with loving disfiguration.

"You'll take the child to the parish tomorrow?" asked Geoffrey, speaking as indifferently as he could.

"Who says so?" said Marner, sharply. "Will they make me take her?"

"Why, you wouldn't like to keep her, should you—an old bachelor like you?"

(From *Silas Marner* by George Eliot.)

KEY NO. *83*

o–➤

PER

through

is the Prefix *PER* which means THROUGH. It is a very useful key. Small as it is, it speaks a mouthful, and every time. Whether it is a matter of paying toll PER capita, or taking down words PER minute, working for a PERcentage, or making coffee in your PERcolator, this little key is working for you. It is a great favorite in Latin phrases.

1. per annum   PER annum (per an' um) adv.
In each year; for each year.

2. per capita   PER capita (per kap' it a) adv.
For each head; by each unit of population.

3. perforated   PER forated (per' fo rate ed) adj.
Bored through; as, perforated *paper.*

4. perennial   PER ennial (pe ren' ee al) adj.
Through the years; year after year.

5. peradventure   PER adventure (per ad ven' chur) n.
A matter of chance; uncertainty.

6. peregrinate   PER egrinate (per' e gri nate) v.
To walk through; to travel; especially, on foot.

7. perambulate   PER ambulate (pe ram' byu late) v.
Walk through; traverse; promenade.

8. perceive   PER ceive (per seve') v.
To understand; to take cognizance of.

9. perception   PER ception (per sep' shun) n.
Act of knowing truths; insight; awareness.

10. perceptive   PER ceptive (per sep' tiv) adj.
Having keen perception.

11. percolate   PER colate (per' ko late) v.
To drip through; to filter.

12. percent   PER cent (per sent') n.
The parts in the hundred.

13. percentage   PER centage (per sent' ij) n.
Rate of interest; so many per hundred.

14. percurrent   PER current (per kur' ent) adj.
Running through; as the midrib of a leaf.

15. percussion   PER cussion (per kush' un) n.
The striking of sound; as, the drum and the piano are percussion *instruments.*

16. percussive   PER cussive (per kus' iv) adj.
Operated by percussion; as, the drumbeat has percussive *force.*

17. peremptory   PER emptory (pe remp' to ree) adj.
                   Final; with authority; as, a peremptory *command.*
18. perfection   PER fection (per fek' shun) n.
                   Thoroughly made; state of complete development.

word analysis

PERCOLATE—No. 11
    PER—Prefix =through
    COLA (colare)—Latin Root =to filter
    ATE—Suffix =make

practical exercises

1. Supply the missing words:
    Plants like cosmos and marigolds are called ....
because they bloom year after year without reseeding. It is
possible to buy sheets of paper which have already been
............................(d).

2. Analyze No. 8.

3. Key review. Match keys with their meanings:

a. spond	1. through	....
b. bio	2. away	....
c. per	3. many	....
d. cogno	4. pledge	....
e. apo	5. push	....
f. rect	6. life	....
g. poly	7. know	....
h. pels, puls	8. right	....

KEY NO. 84

O—⚡

**CAUSE · CUSE
CUS**

cause
motive

is the Root *CAUSE, CUSE, CUS,* which comes from the Latin *causa,* CAUSE; MOTIVE. It is very simple and retains its original form and meaning. Notice in the pronunciation guide that the *s* has the sound of *z* as well as *s.* Remember which is which.

1. cause	CAUSE (kauz) v.	

        To make happen.

2. because   be CAUSE (be kauz') conj.
        For that reason.

3. accusable   ac CUS able (a kyuz' a b'l) adj.
        Can be accused of wrong-doing.

4. accusative   ac CUS ative (a kyu' zat iv) adj.
        Producing accusations; accusatory.

5. accuser   ac CUSE r (a kyu' zer) n.
        One who charges another with wrong-doing.

6. accusatory   ac CUS atory (a kyu' za tore ee) adj.
        In the nature of an accusation; as, accusatory *evidence.*

7. excuse   ex CUSE (ek skyuze') v.
        To attempt to remove the blame; exonerate.

8. excuse   ex CUSE (ek skyus') n.
        The reason for an action.

9. excusator   ex CUS ator (eks kue zay' tor) n.
        An apologist.

10. excusive   ex CUS ive (eks kue' siv) adj.
        Inclined to excuse; to exonerate.

11. cause   CAUSE (kauz) n.
        Reason; motive; as, cause *for murder.*

12. causation   CAUS ation (kau zay' shun) n.
        The act of causing; motivation.

13. causeless   CAUSE less (kauz' les) adj.
        Without reason; as, causeless *hatred.*

14. causable   CAUS able (kauz' a b'l) adj.
        Can be caused.

15. causal   CAUS al (kau' zal) adj.
        Relating to motive.

16. causality   CAUS ality (kau zal' it ee) n.
        Agency; connection between cause and effect.

17. accuse	ac CUSE (a kyuz') v.
	To charge with wrong-doing; to blame.
18. accusation	ac CUS ation (ak yu zay' shun) n.
	A charge of wrong-doing; as, an accusation of theft.
19. excusable	ex CUS able (ek skyu' za b'l) adj.
	Can be excused.
20. inexcusable	inex CUS able (in ek skyu' za b'l) adj.
	Cannot be excused.

word analysis

INEXCUSABLY—No. 20+LY
   IN—Prefix =not
   EX—Prefix =out
   CUS (cause)—Root =cause
   ABL (able)—Suffix =can do
   LY—Suffix =manner of

practical exercises

1. Supply the missing words:
      The .... was .... and ....
      In vain he looked for an .... but the court
      would not ....him.

2. Analyze No. 5.

3. Make a word for the phrase by adding missing keys:
      a. having reason for an accusation— accusat..........
      b. cannot be excused— ....cus..........
      c. a matter of chance— ....adventure
      d. command through authority— ....emptory
      e. away from the truth, perhaps— ....cryphal
      f. having many angles— ....gon
      g. with faith in his success— con..........ently
      h. a quality of ancient days— ....quity

KEY NO. 85

O—➤

HUM · HUMAN

earth
ground
man

is the Root *HUM, HUMAN*, which comes from the Latin *humus*, EARTH, GROUND, and the Latin *humanus*, which means MAN. It is interesting to follow the changes of idea in this key. It begins with HUM-us, earth; then becomes HUMble, lowly; finally to HUMAN, Man. But we must never forget the origin of man: "Dust thou art and to dust thou must return."

1. humus	HUM us (hyu' mus) n.	*Earth; ground.*
2. humanities	HUMAN ities (hyu man' i teze) n.	*Studies and interests of a cultural type which enrich the spirit of mankind.*
3. humate	HUM ate (hyu' mate) n.	*A salt of a humic acid.*
4. exhume	ex HUM e (egz yume') v.	*Take out of the ground; unearth; disinter.*
5. exhumate	ex HUM ate (eks hyu' mate) v.	*To exhume; disinter.*
6. exhumation	ex HUM ation (eks hu may' shun) n.	*The act of taking out of the ground; disinterment.*
7. humble	HUM ble (hum' b'l) adj.	*Lowly; unpretentious; as, an* humble *person.*
8. humbly	HUM bly (hum' blee) adv.	*Meekly; unpretentiously.*
9. humic	HUM ic (hyu' mik) adj.	*Derived from the soil; as,* humic *acid.*
10. humicubation	HUM icubation (hyu mik yue bay' shun) n.	*Act of lying on the ground in penitence; self-abasement.*
11. humility	HUM ility (hyu mil' it ee) n.	*The quality of lowliness; meekness.*
12. humiliate	HUM iliate (hyu mil' ee ate) v.	*To humble; to shame; to abase.*
13. humiliation	HUM iliation (hyu mil ee ay' shun) n.	*Feeling of shame; degradation.*
14. human	HUMAN (hyu' man) adj.	*Belonging or relating to man.*
15. humanify	HUMAN ify (hyu man' i fie) v.	*Make into a man.*

170

16. humane   HUMAN e (hyu mane') adj.
                   Marked by sympathy, compassion for other human beings and animals.

17. humanize   HUMAN ize (hyu' ma nize) v.
                   Make human; render humane.

18. inhuman   in HUMAN (in hyu' man) adj.
                   Lacking the qualities of a humane being.

19. humanity   HUMAN ity (hyu man' it ee) n.
                   The quality of being human.

word analysis

HUMICUBATION—No. 10
    HUM (humus)—Latin Root =earth
    CUB (cubare)—Latin Root =lie down
    TION—Suffix =act of; state of

practical exercises

1. Supply the missing words:
    The Social Studies, Languages, Arts, and Philosophy are called the .... There is nothing sadder on earth than man's in............................ to man.

2. Analyze No. 19.

3. Choose the number of the word which most nearly expresses the italicized word:
    a. *humanity* (1) quality of a wolf (2) silkiness
       (3) sulkiness (4) quality of a human being
       (5) bearish   ....
    b. *humble* (1) arrogant (2) bold (3) inquisitive
       (4) disgraceful (5) lowly   ....
    c. *performance* (1) action (2) honor
       (3) prestige (4) outrage (5) distress ....
    d. *exhume* (1) bury (2) hide (3) dig out
       (4) supply (5) explain   ....
    e. *humiliate* (1) abate (2) enhance (3) subdue
       (4) make ashamed (5) decorate   ....

KEY NO. 86

0—⚷

MOB · MOT MOV

move

is the Root *MOB, MOT, MOV*, all meaning MOVE. They come from the Latin words *mobilis, movere, motus,* all meaning move, and in them you get the reason for the changes in spelling. In a sense this book of keys is a powerful motor for vocabulary enrichment. Each key serves as a small stimulus and adds its strength to the others until they become a source which will never let you down. Remember these keys and you will never lose.

1. mobile	MOB ile (mo′ bele) adj.	
	Capable of moving.	
2. mobilize	MOB ilize (mo′ bi lize) v.	
	To assemble for movement; as, mobilize forces.	
3. mobilization	MOB ilization (mo bi li zay′ shun) n.	
	The act of assembling for action.	
4. mobility	MOB ility (mo bil′ it ee) n.	
	The quality of being able to move.	
5. motion	MOT ion (mo′ shun) n.	
	Movement; action; as, make a motion.	
6. motionless	MOT ionless (mo′ shun les) adj.	
	Without motion.	
7. motive	MOT ive (mote′ iv) n.	
	Cause; inducement to move; stimulus to act.	
8. motivation	MOT ivation (mote i vay′ shun) n.	
	The reason for an action; cause; inducement.	
9. mover	MOV er (mu′ ver) n.	
	One who moves.	
10. motor	MOT or (mote′ or) n.	
	That which imparts motion; source of mechanical power.	
11. motorcade	MOT orcade (mote′ or kade) n.	
	A group of vehicles going together.	
12. automobile	auto MOB ile (au′ to mo bele) n.	
	A motor vehicle; self-moving.	
13. automotive	auto MOT ive (au to mote′ iv) adj.	
	Self-moving; self-propelling.	
14. demote	de MOT e (de mote′) v.	
	Move away; move down in rank; degrade.	

172

15. emotional   e MOT ional (e mo' shun al) adj.
                   Moved strongly by feelings; as, an emotional
                   act.

16. motivate   MOT ivate (mote' i vate) v.
                   Move to action; as, anger will motivate
                   crime.

17. immobile   im MOB ile (im o' bil) adj.
                   Not moving; motionless.

18. demobilization de MOB ilization (de mo bi li zay' shun) n.
                   The act of disbanding the armed forces.

19. motordrome   MOT ordrome (mote' or drome) v.
                   A course for racing automobiles.

20. promotion   pro MOT ion (pro mo' shun) n.
                   A move to a higher position; an advance-
                   ment.

word analysis

AUTOMOTIVE—No. 13
    AUTO—Prefix =self
    MOT (motus)—Latin Root =move
    IVE—Suffix =causing

practical exercises

1. Supply the missing words:
      There is "in the mind of man .... and spirit
    that impels." (Wordsworth) A .... preceded
    the car of the President.

2. Analyze No. 14.

3. Key review. Match keys with their meanings:
    a. mot   1. out   ....
    b. ex   2. not   ....
    c. e   3. move   ....
    d. mov   4. out   ....
    e. cus, cause   5. motive   ....
    f. ec   6. move   ....
    g. mob   7. earth   ....
    h. hum   8. not   ....
    i. il   9. move   ....
    j. ir   10. out   ....

KEY NO. 87

O—x

PRE

before

is the Prefix *PRE* which means BE-FORE. The use of this key is very simple. I *PRE*dict a fine vocabulary, but it's really up to *YOU*.

1. preamble — PRE amble (pree' am b'l) n.
   An introduction; as, the Preamble *to the Constitution.*

2. precaution — PRE caution (pre kau' shun) n.
   Care taken beforehand.

3. precede — PRE cede (pre sede') v.
   To go before.

4. precedent — PRE cedent (pres' ed ent) n.
   Something similar which happened before.

5. predecessor — PRE decessor (pred' e ses or) n.
   One who preceded another in office.

6. predict — PRE dict (pre dikt') v.
   Foretell; as, predict *the weather.*

7. precipitate — PRE cipitate (pre sip' i tate) v.
   To act hurriedly; to throw headlong.

8. preeminent — PRE eminent (pree em' i nent) adj.
   Supreme; above all others; as, a preeminent *speaker.*

9. prelude — PRE lude (prel' yude) n.
   A musical or dramatic introduction.

10. premonition — PRE monition (pre mo nish' un) n.
    A forewarning; an omen.

11. preoccupied — PRE occupied (pree ok' yu pide) adj.
    Already occupied; very busy.

12. preparatory — PRE paratory (pre par' a tore ee) adj.
    Introductory; as, a preparatory *school.*

13. prejudice — PRE judice (prej' ud is) n.
    Judgment before proof is given.

14. presage — PRE sage (pres' ij) v.
    To predict; prophesy.

15. preside — PRE side (pre zide') v.
    To occupy the leading place; as, preside *at a meeting.*

16. preserve — PRE serve (pre zerv') v.
    To keep secure from injury; to protect.

174

17. presume   PRE sume (pre zume') v.
                 To take to oneself a right before it has been
                 granted.

18. pretender   PRE tender (pre ten' der) n.
                 One who makes a claim; as, a pretender to a
                 throne.

19. prevention   PRE vention (pre ven' chun) n.
                 The act of intervening before trouble; as, pre-
                 vention of crime.

20. precocious   PRE cocious (pre koe' shus) adj.
                 Having ripened very early; as, a precocious
                 child.

word analysis

PREVENTION—No. 19
    PRE—Prefix =before
    VEN (venire)—Latin Root =come
    TION—Suffix =act of

practical exercises

1. Supply the missing words:
    Education against .... will help ....
religious persecution. An ounce of .... goes a
long way toward cure.

2. Analyze No. 3.

3. Read the following excerpt underlining all those words that
contain keys you have already learned.

    a) Scientists are still discovering awesome aspects of the
March 27 Alaskan earthquake. Last week, for example, the
United States Geological Survey reported finding an unin-
habited island that was thrust upward more than 30 feet
by the shock. A strip of sea floor some 1,350 feet wide was
exposed when Montague Island, in Prince William Sound,
"shot up" geologists said. What may brighten the pros-
pect. . . .

    b) Although scientists are sure that at least some human
cancers are caused by viruses, no virus has yet been re-
covered from a human tumor and been shown to have
caused it. . . .

                         (From *The New York Times*, July, 1964.)

is the Root *MIS, MISO,* which means WRONG, BAD, HATE. We all make *MIS*takes and *MIS* is the key that says it's wrong. Consider word No. 10. *Mis*chief is trouble. The *mis*chievous fellow is a troublemaker, usually a poor student. Smart ones have no time for *mis*chief. Perhaps the *mis*chievous fellow would like to be the leader, the *chief.* But he cannot be the *chief* since he does not *achieve* good work. He wants attention, so he goes in for *mis*chievous acts, *achievement* of the wrong kind.

1. misadventure
MIS adventure (mis ad ven' chur) n.
An accident; misfortune.

2. misalliance
MIS alliance (mis a lie' ans) n.
An improper union; esp., an improper marriage.

3. misanthrope
MIS anthrope (mis' an thrope) n.
A hater of mankind.

4. misappropriate
MIS appropriate (mis a pro' pree ate) v.
To use wrongly; esp., for one's own benefit.

5. misbegotten
MIS begotten (mis be got' en) adj.
Born out of wedlock; ill-born.

6. misbehavior
MIS behavior (mis be hay' vyor) n.
Improper conduct.

7. miscalculate
MIS calculate (mis kal' kyu late) v.
To make an error in counting.

8. miscarriage
MIS carriage (mis kar' ij) n.
Wrong handling; as, a miscarriage of justice.

9. miscast
MIS cast (mis kast') v.
To give an actor a role not suited to him.

10. mischief
MIS chief (mis' chif) n.
An act which results in damage or injury.

11. misconception
MIS conception (mis kon sep' shun) n.
An erroneous idea; wrong interpretation.

12. miscreant
MIS creant (mis' kree ant) n.
An evil-doer; one who is vicious in behavior.

13. misgivings
MIS givings (mis giv' ings) n.
Doubt about the result of some action.

14. misnomer	MIS nomer (mis no' mer) n.
	The wrong name.
15. misguide	MIS guide (mis gide') v.
	To lead in the wrong direction.
16. misogynist	MIS ogynist (mi soj' i nist) n.
	A hater of women.
17. misopedia	MIS opedia (mis o pee' di a) n.
	A morbid dislike of one's own children.
18. misrepresent	MIS represent (mis rep re zent') v.
	To give a false impression of.
19. mistrial	MIS trial (mis trie' al) n.
	A trial of no effect because of some error in the proceedings.
20. misinterpretation	MIS interpretation (mis in ter pre tay' shun) n.
	Misunderstanding.

word analysis

MISOGYNIST—No. 16
    MISO (misein)—Root = to hate
    GYN (gyne)—Root = a woman
    IST—Suffix = one who

practical exercises

1. Supply the missing words:
       When court proceedings do not result in a just verdict we call it a .... of justice. The actor was hopelessly .... as Shylock.

2. Analyze No. 9.

3. With the help of a key make one word express the phrase:
    a. one who hates mankind— ....anthrope
    b. one who hates women— ....ogynist
    c. an abnormal dislike for children, even one's own— ....opedia
    d. a feeling of being brought low— ....iliation
    e. a moving vehicle, using an engine— ....ile
    f. a showing beforehand— ....view
    g. care against accident— ....caution

KEY NO. 89

o—⇥

LIC · LICIT

permit

is the Root *LIC, LICIT* from the Latin *licēre* which means to PERMIT. This is a tricky key. LICense can so easily slip away from the law and authority to disorder. Keep the meaning clear.

1. license   LIC ense (lise' ens) n.
                 Freedom to act; a permit; as, a driver's license.

2. licensed   LIC ensed (lies' ensd) adj.
                 Permitted; authorized.

3. licensee   LIC ensee (lise en see') n.
                 The one to whom a license is granted.

4. licenser   LIC enser (lise' en ser) n.
                 The one who grants the license.

5. licensor   LIC ensor (lie' sen ser) n.
                 Legal way of saying No. 4.

6. licensure   LIC ensure (lise' en shur) n.
                 The granting of licenses; especially, to those who practice various professions.

7. licentiate   LIC entiate (lie sen' chee at) n.
                 One who is licensed to practice a profession.

8. licentiation   LIC entiation (lie sen shi ay' shun) n.
                 The act of granting a license; especially, to practice medicine.

9. licentious   LIC entious (lie sen' chus) adj.
                 Taking liberties; disregarding rules; especially, in morals.

10. licentiously   LIC entiously (lie sen' chus lee) adv.
                 Immorally.

11. licentiousness   LIC entiousness (lie sen' chus ness) n.
                 The state of immorality.

12. licit   LIC it (lis' it) adj.
                 Permitted; lawful; conceded.

13. illicit   il LIC it (il is' it) adj.
                 Unlawful; illegal.

14. illicitly   il LIC itly (il is' it lee) adv.
                 Unlawfully; illegally.

15. illicitness   il LIC itness (i lis' it nes) n.
                 The state of being unauthorized by law.

16. license plate   LIC ense plate (lie' sens plate) n.
                 A plate or tag showing that a permit has been granted.

17. **unlicensed** un LIC ensed (un lise′ ensd) adj.
       Not permitted; unlawful.

word analysis

ILLICITLY—No. 14
    IL (in)—Prefix =not
    LICIT (licēre)—Latin Root =to permit
    LY—Suffix =manner of

practical exercises

1. Supply the missing words:
       "............ .... they mean when they cry liberty."
    (John Milton) A bribe passed from the .... to
    the ...., and a .... passed from
    .... to ....

2. Analyze No. 13.

3. Indicate the pronunciation of the following words by placing
   the accent mark (′):

    license   predecessor
    licentious   precede
    misanthrope   humiliating
    misogynist   humble
    preeminence   mobilization

KEY NO. 90

0—⚡

CAPIT · CAPT

head
chief
leader

is the Root *CAPIT, CAPT* which means HEAD; CHIEF; LEADER. It comes from the Latin word *caput*, head. No. 15 needs to explain its presence in this list. The rancher's wealth, or CAPital, depends on the head of cattle he has. Now, if you can imagine him talking about his capital investment in cattle, while, perhaps, he is chewing at a plug of tobacco, the word CAPital can come out C**T*L. Try it.

1. capital   CAPIT al (kap′ it al) n.
                  Amount of accumulated goods; also property; money.
2. capitalize   CAPIT alize (kap′ it al ize) v.
                  Convert into capital; make a profit.
3. capitate   CAPIT ate (kap′ i tate) adj.
                  Forming a head; suddenly enlarged.
4. decapitate   de CAPIT ate (de kap′ i tate) v.
                  Cut the head off.
5. capitation   CAPIT ation (kap i tay′ shun) n.
                  A tax imposed by the numbering of heads; poll tax.
6. Capitol   CAPIT ol (kap′ it ol) n.
                  The chief building in Washington in which Congress holds sessions.
7. Capitoline   CAPIT oline (kap′ it ol ine) n.
                  The smallest of the seven hills upon which Rome stands.
8. capitular   CAPIT ular (ka pich′ u lar) adj.
                  Relating to a heading, a chapter, or a section of a book.
9. capitulate   CAPIT ulate (ka pich′ u late) v.
                  To surrender; to give up, as it were, the head.
10. capitulation CAPIT ulation (ka pich u lay′ shun) n.
                  The surrender.
11. captain   CAPT ain (kap′ tin) n.
                  The head; the chief; as, the rank of captain.
12. captaincy   CAPT aincy (kap′ tin see) n.
                  Rank or commission of captain.
13. caption   CAPT ion (kap′ shun) n.
                  The heading of a chapter or a section.

180

14. cap à pie — CAP à pie (kap a pee') adv.
    (French) From head to foot.
15. cattle — CA(P)T tle (kat' 'l) n.
    Animals; the rancher's chief property is cattle.
16. recapitulate — re CAPIT ulate (ree ka pich' u late) v.
    To repeat or restate briefly.
17. recapitulation re CAPIT ulation (ree ka pich u lay' shun) n.
    The act of repeating or restating briefly.
18. recapitalize — re CAPIT alize (ree kap' it al ize) v.
    To change the capital of.
19. decapitation — de CAPIT ation (de kap i tay' shun) n.
    The act of decapitating.
20. per capita — per CAPIT a (per kap' it a) adv.
    (Latin) By each head; equally to each and every individual.

word analysis

DECAPITATE—No. 4
    DE—Prefix = from; away
    CAPIT (caput)—Latin Root = head
    ATE—Suffix = make

practical exercises

1. Supply the missing words:
       When Samuel Johnson struggled against death he cried, "I will not .... (give in)!" During the French Revolution many of the aristocrats were ....(d) by the guillotine.

2. Analyze No. 2.

3. Choose the number of the word which best expresses the italicized word:
    a. *irregularity* (1) balance (2) symbol (3) perfection (4) secret (5) imperfection ....
    b. *emotion* (1) lesson (2) strong feeling (3) curiosity (4) language (5) voyage ....
    c. *humiliating* (1) praising (2) advancing (3) teaching (4) debasing (5) exciting ....
    d. *license* (1) permit (2) price (3) award (4) action (5) trespass ....
    e. *continue* (1) reason (2) explain (4) foresee (4) keep on (5) pretend ....

KEY NO. 91

O—➤

STA · STIT
SIST · STET

stand

is the Root *STA, STIT, SIST, STET,* meaning STAND. The reason for these various spellings is simply that the related Latin and Greek roots have varied spellings—*stare, sistere, stiti, steti, status.* All these mean STAND. I notice there is no word with *STET* on the list. But ob*STET*-rics might have been added and there are others. *STET,* let it remain, is sometimes spelled STEAD. Often the final *t* in *STIT* is omitted (as in No. 10), for the sake of euphony. Remember?

1. assist   as SIST (a sist′) v.
       To stand by with help.

2. circumstance   circum STA nce (sir′ kum stans) n.
       A situation; a happening.

3. stamina   STA mina (stam′ i na) n.
       Power to withstand, to endure.

4. constant   con STA nt (kon′ stant) adj.
       Fixed; steady; as, constant as a star.

5. desist   de SIST (de zist′) v.
       Cease; discontinue; quit.

6. distant   di STA nt (dis′ tant) adj.
       Standing far off; as, a distant hill.

7. ecstasy   ec STA sy (ek′ sta see) n.
       A state of being out of oneself for joy; rapture.

8. interstices   inter STI ces (in ter′ sti seze) n.
       Spaces between; cracks; as, the interstices of a wall.

9. obstacle   ob STA cle (ob′ sta k'l) n.
       That which stands in the way; a hindrance.

10. obstinate   ob STI nate (ob′ sti nat) adj.
       Standing against; stubborn.

11. persist   per SIST (per sist′) v.
       Stand firmly; unyielding; continue.

12. resist   re SIST (re zist′) v.
       Withstand; as, resist all obstacles.

13. consist   con SIST (kon sist′) v.
       To have the quality of; to be made of; as, coke consists mainly of carbon.

14. stanchion   STA nchion (stan′ chun) n.
       A standing brace or support.

15. standard	STA ndard (stan' dard) n.
	A degree of quality which must be main-tained.
16. stage	STA ge (staje) n.
	A platform for actors to stand on.
17. subsist	sub SIST (sub sist') v.
	To endure; as, to subsist on charity.
18. substance	sub STA nce (sub' stans) n.
	The real nature of a thing which keeps it what it is.
19. substitute	sub STI tute (sub' sti tute) v.
	To stand in for another; take the place of.

word analysis

SUBSISTENCE—No. 17 +ence
    SUB—Prefix =under
    SIST (sistere)—Latin Root =stand
    ENCE—Suffix =quality of

practical exercises

1. Supply the missing words:
    In the last few yards of a race it is .... that
    counts. In every .... there must be a ....
    of character to .... many ....(s).

2. Analyze No. 11.

3. Key review. Match KEYS with their meanings:

a. capit	1. stand	....
b. lic	2. earth	....
c. mis	3. cause	....
d. mov	4. answer	....
e. hum	5. head	....
f. cus	6. permit	....
g. per	7. move	....
h. apo	8. through	....
i. spond	9. away from	....
j. sta	10. hate	....

KEY NO. 92

0—⚡

**DUC · DUCE
DUCT**

is the Root *DUC, DUCE, DUCT*, which comes from the Latin *ducere*, meaning LEAD. It will indeed LEAD you to many places, people, subjects.

lead

1. abduct   ab DUCT (ab dukt') v.
   To take away by force; kidnap.

2. deduct   de DUCT (de dukt') v.
   To take away from; as, deduct *ten percent of the price.*

3. deductible   de DUCT ible (de duk' ti b'l) adj.
   Can be taken off; as, tax deductible.

4. educate   e DUC ate (ej' u kate) v.
   To develop; teach; lead out from ignorance.

5. induce   in DUC e (in dyuse') v.
   To lead into; persuade.

6. induction   in DUC tion (in duk' shun) n.
   The act of leading into an official position; as, induction *into the army.*

7. inductometer   in DUCT ometer (in duk tom' e ter) n.
   Equipment used to measure electrical induction.

8. introduction   intro DUC tion (in tro duk' shun) n.
   The act of bringing together.

9. inductile   in DUCT ile (in duk' til) adj.
   Inflexible; unyielding; not easily led.

10. produce   pro DUCE (pro dyuse') v.
    To bring forth; lead forward.

11. product   pro DUCT (prod' ukt) n.
    Anything produced by growth, labor, thought.

12. productive   pro DUCT ive (pro duk' tiv) n.
    Causing to bring forth; creative.

13. production   pro DUC tion (pro duk' shun) n.
    The act of bringing forth; creation.

14. reduce   re DUCE (re dyuse') v.
    To lead to a lower position or price; as, reduce *to poverty.*

15. reduction   re DUC tion (re duk' shun) n.
    A lowering; as, a reduction *in price.*

16. seduce   se DUCE (se dyuse') v.
    To lead apart; lead astray; corrupt.

17. conducive   con DUC ive (kon dyue' siv) adj.
                   Tending to promote; as conducive *to good health.*

18. ducat   DUC at (duk' at) n.
                   A gold coin used in some European countries.

19. aqueduct   aque DUCT (ak' we dukt) n.
                   An artificial channel for bringing a large quantity of water from one place to another.

20. traduce   tra DUCE (tra dyuse') v.
                   To disgrace unjustly; to slander.

word analysis

INTRODUCTION—No. 8
    INTRO—Prefix =inward
    DUC (ducere)—Latin Root =to lead
    TION—Suffix =act of; state of

practical exercises

1. Supply the missing words:
    "The treaty we have signed does not .... the nuclear stockpiles; it does not halt .... of nuclear weapons." (Secretary Rusk)

2. Analyze No. 16.

3. Read the following excerpt underlining all those words that contain keys you have already learned.

    "Now Thomasin," she [Mrs. Yeobright] said sternly, "what's the meaning of this disgraceful performance?"

    Thomasin looked as if quite overcome by her aunt's change of manner. "It means just what it seems to mean: I am—not married," she replied faintly. "Excuse me for humiliating you, aunt, by this mishap. I am sorry for it. But I cannot help it."

    "Me? Think of yourself first."

    "It was nobody's fault. When we got there the parson wouldn't marry us because of some trifling irregularity in the license."

    "What irregularity?"

    "I don't know. Mr. Wildeve can explain. I did not think when I went away this morning that I should come back like this." It being dark, Thomasin allowed her emotion to escape her by the silent way of tears, which could roll down her cheek unseen.

         (From *The Return of the Native* by Thomas Hardy.)

KEY NO. 93

O—🗝

OMNI

all

is the Root *OMNI* which comes from the Latin *omnis* meaning ALL. It is really an OMNIbus of a word, for everything can be tacked on to it. The humor of saying English words with a Latin ending, like No. 9, is called macaronic, burlesque, as it were. But it is not humor to the doctors who use that kind of Latin in their prescriptions. It makes the ailing Latin professors laugh and that does them more good than the prescriptions. The joke is on the doctor, but he doesn't know it.

1. omniana   OMNI ana (om ni ay' na) n.
       Bits of information from everywhere.

2. omnibus   OMNI bus (om' ni bus) n.
       A conveyance for all; providing transportation for many.

3. omnicompetent   OMNI competent (om ni kom' pe tent) adj.
       Legally competent in all matters.

4. omnicorporeal   OMNI corporeal (om ni kor poe' ree al) adj.
       Including all bodies.

5. omnifarious   OMNI farious (om ni far' ee us) adj.
       Of all sorts; of many varieties.

6. omnify   OMNI fy (om' ni fie) v.
       Enlarge; make universal.

7. omnigenous   OMNI genous (om nij' e nus) adj.
       Of all types of kinds.

8. omnigraph   OMNI graph (om' ni graf) n.
       A device for teaching radio telegraph operators.

9. omnium-gatherum   OMNI um-gatherum (om' ni um gath' er um) n.
       A collection of all things, people.

10. omnimeter   OMNI meter (om nim' e ter) n.
       Instrument for measuring all angles.

11. omnimodous   OMNI modous (om nim' o dus) adj.
       Of every kind.

12. omniparent   OMNI parent (om nip' a rent) adj.
       Being the origin of all.

13. omnipotent   OMNI potent (om nip' ot ent) adj.
       All powerful; having unlimited authority.

14. omniscient	OMNI scient (om nish' ent) adj.
	All knowing; having complete understanding.
15. omnist	OMNI st (om' nist) n.
	A believer in all religions.
16. omnipresent	OMNI present (om ni prez' ent) adj.
	Present everywhere; ubiquitous.
17. omnivorous	OMNI vorous (om niv' or us) adj.
	Eating everything; taking in everything.
18. omnium	OMNI um (om' ni um) n.
	Total; as, my omnium.

word analysis

OMNISCIENT—No. 14
OMNI (omnis)—Latin Root =all
SCI (scire)—Latin Root =to know
ENT—Suffix =one who

practical exercises

1. Supply the missing words:
   During the Middle Ages the Pope's position was all
   but .... The hippopotamus is another animal
   which is ....

2. Analyze No. 2.

3. Add the KEY and complete the word:
   a. carrying all— ....bus
   b. knowing all— ....scient
   c. all powerful— ....potent
   d. measuring all— ....meter
   e. eating all— ....vorous
   f. all kinds— ....genous
   g. water channel— aque..........
   h. disgrace unjustly— tra..........
   i. staying power— ....mina

KEY NO. 94

0━┱

FORC · FORT

strong

FORTUNA

**fortune
chance**

presents two Roots: *FORC, FORT* meaning STRONG and *FORTUNA* meaning FORTUNE, CHANCE. Be careful not to confuse the two! Words 1 to 13 all have an element of strength in their meanings; words 14 to 18 involve an element of chance. Read *Les Misérables*, by Victor Hugo, and you will get a powerful idea of word No. 9. Remember the keys!

1. fort
   FORT (fort) n.
   A stronghold for protection.

2. fortalice
   FORT alice (fort' al is) n.
   A small fort.

3. forte
   FORT e (fort) n.
   One's strong point; as, writing is his forte.

4. fortification
   FORT ification (fort i fi kay' shun) n.
   A stronghold.

5. fortissimo
   FORT issimo (for tis' i moe) adj.
   Using the utmost loudness.

6. fortitude
   FORT itude (fort' i tude) n.
   Strength of mind and character to endure.

7. fortress
   FORT ress (for' tres) n.
   A fortified place.

8. force
   FORC e (fors) n.
   Power; strength; pressure.

9. forçat
   FORÇ at (for sa') n.
   In France, a convict condemned to hard labor.

10. effort
    ef FORT (ef' ort) n.
    The putting forth of strength; as, an effort of will.

11. comfortable
    com FORT able (kom' fort a b'l) adj.
    Giving strength and ease.

12. enforce
    en FORC e (en fors') v.
    Put force in; use pressure; as, enforce law.

13. effortless
    ef FORT less (ef' ort les) adj.
    Without force; without pressure.

14. fortuitous
    FORTU itous (for tyue' it us) adj.
    Happening by chance; unexpected.

15. Fortuna
    FORTUN a (for tue' na) n.
    The goddess of fortune, of chance.

188

16. fortunate   FORTUN ate (forch' u nat) adj.
             Having good luck.
17. unfortunate   un FORTUN ate (un forch' u nat) adj.
             Unlucky; as, an unfortunate *accident.*
18. misfortune   mis FORTUN e (mis for' chun) n.
             Bad luck; disaster.

word analysis

UNFORTUNATE—No. 17
    UN—Prefix =not
    FORTUN (fortuna)—Latin Root =chance
    ATE—Suffix =quality

practical exercises

1. Supply the missing words:
    Everyone is endowed with a secret weapon which enables him to endure life with .... In *Les Misérables* the hero is condemned to .... for stealing a loaf of bread.

2. Analyze No. 12.

3. COMPOUND SUFFIX: The Suffix *ITY* can be combined with the Suffix *AN* and *OUS*. In the following a noun becomes an adjective and then becomes a noun again. Observe the changes in spelling. The adjective gives a clue.

	noun	adjective	noun
Example:	man	hum*an*	human*ity*
Example:	fierceness	feroci*ous*	feroc*ity*
Example:	precox	precoci*ous*	precoc*ity*
Example:	pomp	pomp*ous*	pompos*ity*
a.	urb (city)	urb*an*	....
b.	virtue	virtu*ous*	....
c.	velox (speed)	veloci*ous*	....
d.	word	verbose	....
e.	....	prolix	....

is the Root *CHRON* which means TIME. It comes from the Greek word *chronos*. The awareness of events CHRONologically gives us a perspective of history impossible without it. Whether an event came before or after assumed real significance with the appearance of CHRONicles. This is a very valuable key.

1. chronic   CHRON ic (kron' ik) adj.
   Continuing for a long time; as, a chronic invalid.

2. chronicle   CHRON icle (kron' i k'l) n.
   A record of events in order of time.

3. chronicler   CHRON icler (kron' i kler) n.
   A historian; as, a chronicler of events.

4. chronology   CHRON ology (kro nol' o jee) n.
   The science of recording events by period and by date.

5. chronologist   CHRON ologist (kro nol' o jist) n.
   An expert in the science of chronology.

6. chronologize   CHRON ologize (kro nol' o jize) v.
   To give to time its period and to an event its date.

7. chronologer   CHRON ologer (kro nol' o jer) n.
   Another name for a chronologist.

8. chronobarometer   CHRON obarometer (kron o ba rom' e ter) n.
   Barometer connected with clock work.

9. chronocyclegraph   CHRON ocyclegraph (kron o sie' k'l graf) n.
   A photograph showing the course of motion by timed flashes.

10. chronograph   CHRON ograph (kron' o graf) n.
    An instrument to measure and record time.

11. chronography   CHRON ography (kro nog' ra fee) n.
    A record of past time; history.

12. chronomancy   CHRON omancy (kron' o man si) n.
    Divination to determine the right time for action.

13. chronologic   CHRON ologic (kron ol oj' ik) adj.
    Relating to chronology.

14. chronologically   CHRON ologically (kron ol oj' i ka lee) adv.
    According to periods of time; as, chronologically speaking.

15. chronometer	CHRON ometer (kro nom' et er) n. *Instrument to keep time.*
16. chronopher	CHRON opher (kron' o fer) n. *An instrument which signals the correct time.*
17. chronoscope	CHRON oscope (kron' o skope) n. *Instrument which measures minute intervals of time.*
18. chronoscopy	CHRON oscopy (kron os' ko pi) n. *The study of brief intervals of time by means of a chronoscope.*
19. synchronous	syn CHRON ous (sin' kro nus) adj. *Happening at the same time.*
20. chronothermal	CHRONO thermal (kron o ther' mal) adj. *Relating to time and temperature.*

word analysis

CHRONOTHERMAL—No. 20
    CHRONO (chronos)—Root =time
    THERM (thermos)—Root =heat
    AL—Suffix =relating to

practical exercises

1. Supply the missing words:
    Without the science of .... history would be a confused jumble of events, and we need the .... to create order in the world of events.

2. Analyze No. 6.

3. Use one word for each phrase:
    a. a record of events in order of time   ....
    b. strength of character to endure   ....
    c. eats everything like a pig   ....
    d. give to each event its exact date   ....
    e. endurance to follow through to the end   ....
    f. begin again from the beginning   ....
    g. the state of immorality   ....
    h. take one meaning when another is intended   ....

KEY NO. 96

0—🔨

FLECT · FLEX

bend

is a Root, *FLECT, FLEX*, from the Latin, *flectere*, to BEND. Roots which combine easily with other keys are the most interesting. This key with its various spellings is one of these. The word list uses eighteen keys to combine with *FLEX, FLECT, FLICK* and every combination makes a good word which you can easily make your own.

1. flex   FLEX (fleks) v.
         To bend; as, to flex *the arm.*

2. flexible   FLEX ible (flek′ si b′l) adj.
         Able to bend.

3. flexibility   FLEX ibility (flek si bil′ it ee) n.
         Quality of being able to bend.

4. flexile   FLEX ile (flek′ sil) adj.
         Flexible; tractable; as, a flexile *nature.*

5. flection   FLECT ion (flek′ shun) n.
         The act of bending.

6. flexor   FLEX or (flek′ sor) n.
         A muscle which serves to bend a limb.

7. flexuose   FLEX uose (flek′ shu os) adj.
         Relaxed; adaptable; not rigid.

8. flexuous   FLEX uous (fleksh′ u us) adj.
         Having many bends, turns.

9. genuflection   genu FLECT ion (jen yu flek′ shun) n.
         The bending of the knee.

10. deflect   de FLECT (de flekt′) v.
         Bend away; as, deflect *the missile from its target.*

11. inflection   in FLECT ion (in flek′ shun) n.
         The rise and fall of the voice, as, the inflection *of his voice.*

12. reflect   re FLECT (re flekt′) v.
         Turn back and forth in the mind; as, to reflect *on an idea.*

13. reflection   re FLECT ion (re flek′ shun) n.
         An image thrown back; as, a reflection *in a mirror.*

14. reflexive   re FLEX ive (re flek′ siv) adj.
         Bent back on itself; as, a reflexive *pronoun.*

15. reflective   re FLECT ive (re flek′ tiv) adj.
         Thoughtful; as, a reflective *mind.*

16. reflector   re FLECT or (re flek' tor) n.
    That which reflects light.
17. circumflexion circum FLEX ion (sir kum flek' shun) n.
    A bending around and around.
18. reflectoscope re FLECT oscope (re flek' toe skope) n.
    *A magic lantern, a device that places an image
    on a screen.*

word analysis

GENUFLECTION—No. 9
    GENU—Root =knee
    FLECT (flectere)—Root =to bend
    ION—Suffix =act of; state of

practical exercises

1. Supply the missing words:
    "The eye sees not itself but by ...." (Shake-
    speare) Harry strained his .... muscle. Her
    voice had a pleasing ....

2. Analyze No. 10.

3. Use one word for each phrase:
    a. the act of bending the knee   ....
    b. in the manner of a chronology   ....
    c. not a regular thing   ....
    d. a hater of mankind   ....
    e. do away with by law   ....
    f. a lowering in price   ....
    g. of practically no significance   ....

KEY NO. 97

o—x

METER

measure

is the Root *METER*, which means to MEASURE. This is a universal key and everything in life is *METER*ed out to us. Again our list is full of interesting scientific words and we find much to make us feel at home. In words No. 7, 8, 9, 10, 11, 19, 20 we find old and newly made friends. There is today a weight reducer called METRECAL. It meters out calories.

1. mete
METE (met) v.
To measure; to assign by measure.

2. meter
METER (mete' er) n.
A measure; the official measure of certain commodities; as, a gas meter.

3. barometer
baro METER (ba rom' et er) n.
Instrument to record atmospheric pressure.

4. meterage
METER age (me' ter ij) n.
Act of measuring.

5. metrical
METR ical (me' tri kal) adj.
Relating to measuring; to metering.

6. chronometer
chrono METER (kro nom' et er) n.
An instrument which measures time.

7. gravimeter
gravi METER (gra vim' et er) n.
Instrument for measuring weight and density.

8. gyrometer
gyro METER (jie rom' e ter) n.
A rotary speed indicator.

9. megameter
mega METER (meg am' e ter) n.
An instrument which measures longitude by observation of the stars.

10. macrometer
macro METER (ma krom' e ter) n.
An instrument for measuring size and distance of objects.

11. isoperimeters
isoperi METER s (i so pe rim' e ters) n.
Figures with equal perimeters.

12. plegometer
plego METER (ple gom' e ter) n.
An instrument for measuring and recording the force of blows.

13. speedometer
speedo METER (spe dom' et er) n.
Instrument for measuring speed.

14. pedometer
pedo METER (pe dom' et er) n.
Instrument for measuring distance walked.

15. perimeter	peri METER (pe rim' et er) n.
	The distance around a closed plane figure.
16. thermometer	thermo METER (ther mom' et er) n.
	An instrument for measuring heat.
17. seismometer	seismo METER (size mom' et er) n.
	Instrument to determine movement of the ground during an earthquake.
18. voltameter	volta METER (vol tam' et er) n.
	Instrument to measure volts in an electric circuit.
19. hypermetric	hyper MET ric (hie per me' trik) adj.
	Exceeding the common measure.
20. heliothermometer	heliothermo METER
	(he li o ther mom' e ter) n.
	Instrument to measure solar radiation.

word analysis

ISOPERIMETER—No. 11
    ISO—Prefix =equal
    PERI—Prefix =around
    METE (meter)—Root =measure
    ER—Suffix =that which

practical exercises

1. Supply the missing words:
        Life . . . . (s) out to each one of us good fortune and bad. When the tidal wave hit Alaska, the .... registered earth tremors under the sea.

2. Analyze No. 6.

3. From the following list of keys select the key needed for the missing word. Give meaning of key used:
   FLECT—CHRON—FORT—OMNI—DUC—STA—CAPIT—SIST—LIC—CUS—METER
   a. He looked at his re..........tion in the mirror.   ....
   b. He showed great ....itude in his accident.   ....
   c. A scientific name for a watch is ....
   d. His bad manners are inex..........able.   ....
   e. The fighting was so fierce that re..........ance was   ....
       impossible.   ....
   f. He thinks he is ....scient.   ....
   g. The re..........tions at the sale were amazing.   ....
   h. In former times de..........ation was a common pun-   ....
       ishment.   ....

195

is the Prefix *PERI* meaning AROUND. As usual, every key opens not only one door, but many doors. The key *PERI* is no exception. On your list are words useful in medicine, anatomy, geology, mathematics, dentistry, publications, and, of course, space science. In the last, especially, I have been helped by the keys *PERI*, AROUND, and *APO*, AWAY. I used to be confused by *PERI*gee and *APO*gee. I couldn't remember which was far from the sun, which near. Now I know.

1. **pericarp**   PERI carp (per' i karp) n.
   Around the fruit; the covering skin or shell.
2. **pericentric** PERI centric (per i sen' trik) adj.
   Deposited around the center.
3. **periclitate** PERI clitate (pe rik' li tate) v.
   To expose to danger.
4. **pericranium** PERI cranium (per i kray' nee um) n.
   Around the skull.
5. **pericardium** PERI cardium (per i kard' ee um) n.
   Around the heart.
6. **periosteal**   PERI osteal (per ee os' tee al) adj.
   Situated around the bone.
7. **perigee**   PERI gee (per' i jee) n.
   That point in the orbit of a satellite nearest to the earth.
8. **perihelion**   PERI helion (per i hele' yon) n.
   That point in the orbit of a comet or a planet nearest to the sun.
9. **perigon**   PERI gon (per' i gon) n.
   An angle that is round.
10. **perimeter**   PERI meter (pe rim' et er) n.
    The distance around a closed plane figure.
11. **perinephritis** PERI nephritis (per i ne frie' tis) n.
    Inflammation of the tissues around the kidneys.
12. **period**   PERI od (per' ee od) n.
    A period of time (a going around).
13. **periodic**   PERI odic (per ee od' ik) adj.
    Occurring at regular, stated times.
14. **periodical** PERI odical (per ee od' i k'l) n.
    A publication which appears at fixed times.

15. periodicity   PERI odicity (per ee o dis' it ee) n.
         The quality of recurring regularly.
16. periodontal   PERI odontal (per ee o dont' al) adj.
         Around the tooth.
17. periotic   PERI otic (per ee ote' ik) adj.
         Around the ear.
18. peripatetic   PERI patetic (per i pa tet' ik) adj.
         Walking around; itinerant.
19. periphery   PERI phery (pe rif' e ree) n.
         A line around a surface; as, the circumference
         of a circle.
20. peripheral   PERI pheral (pe rif' e ral) adj.
         Relating to the periphery.

word analysis

PERIOSTEAL—No. 6
    PERI—Prefix =around
    OSTE (osteo)—Latin Root=bone
    AL—Suffix =relating to

practical exercises

1. Supply the missing words:
     Aristotle liked to walk about when he was giving his lec-
    tures, and thus he was often called the ....
    philosopher. The opposite of the apogee is the ....

2. Analyze No. 8.

3. Choose the number of the word which best expresses the
    meaning of the italicized word:
    a. *period*   (1) epoch   (2) necessity   (3) degree
       (4) comparison   (5) despair   ....
    b. *perimeter*   (1) distance around   (2) area
       (3) anecdote   (4) triangle   (5) thermometer   ....
    c. *omnibus*   (1) omniscient   (2) perigee
       (3) gyrometer   (4) carry all   (5) fortitude   ....
    d. *authority*   (1) diameter   (2) expert   (3) design
       (4) era   (5) student   ....
    e. *incredulity*   (1) cheerfulness   (2) believer
       (3) unbeliever   (4) patience   (5) direction   ....

KEY NO. 99

O—x

SUPER · SUPR

over
above
beyond
greater in quality

is the Prefix *SUPER, SUPR* meaning OVER, ABOVE, BEYOND, GREATER IN QUALITY. *SUPR* indicates the *SUPER*lative. There you are, on your way to having a SUPER vocabulary!

1. superable   SUPER able (sue' pe ra b'l) adj.
   Can be overcome; conquerable.

2. superabundant SUPER abundant (sue pe ra bun' dant) adj.
   Above the needed amount; excessive.

3. supercilious   SUPER cilious (sue per sil' ee us) adj.
   Over-bearing; proud; haughty.

4. superfine   SUPER fine (sue per fine') adj.
   Of an exceptional quality.

5. superfluent   SUPER fluent (sue per' flue ent) adj.
   Flowing freely, richly.

6. superintendent SUPER intendent (sue pe rin ten' dent) n.
   One in charge; overseer.

7. superlunary   SUPER lunary (sue per lue' na ree) adj.
   In a position above the moon.

8. superhuman   SUPER human (sue per hyu' man) adj.
   Having powers beyond mankind.

9. superman   SUPER man (sue' per man) n.
   A man with extraordinary powers.

10. superiority   SUPER iority (su per ee or' it ee) n.
    Excellence; preeminence.

11. supernatural   SUPER natural (sue per nach' u ral) adj.
    Above and beyond all nature.

12. superimpose   SUPER impose (sue pe rim poze') v.
    To place one thing over another.

13. supervise   SUPER vise (sue' per vize) v.
    To oversee; to superintend.

14. superlative   SUPER lative (su per' lat iv) adj.
    In the highest degree; the best.

15. supralateral   SUPRA lateral (sue pra lat' er al) adj.
    Placed high up on the side.

16. supraliminal   SUPRA liminal (sue pra lim' in al) adj.
    Lying above the threshold of consciousness.

17. supreme   SUPR eme (su preme') adj.
    Superior; of the highest quality.

18. supremely   SUPR emely (su preme' lee) adv.
           In the highest degree; as, supremely *happy.*
19. supremacy   SUPR emacy (su prem' a see) n.
           State of being supreme.

word analysis

SUPERIMPOSE—No. 12
    SUPER—Prefix =over
    IM (in)— Prefix =into
    POSE (ponere)—Latin Root =to place
SUPERFLUENT—No. 5
    SUPER—Prefix =over
    FLU (fluere)—Latin Root =flow
    ENT—Suffix

practical exercises

1. Supply the missing words:
      The .... folly of mankind today is the vain
    race for .... in space flying. It ....(s)
    .... burdens on man and makes for ....
    attitudes in nations which have some success.

2. Analyze No. 1.

3. Key review. Match keys with their meanings:
     a. meter   1. around   ....
     b. super   2. shut   ....
     c. clus   3. earth   ....
     d. peri   4. answer   ....
     e. licit   5. move   ....
     f. hum   6. above; beyond   ....
     g. spons   7. permit   ....
     h. mob   8. measure   ....

KEY NO. *100*

O⚊⚊x

PARA

**beside
alongside
position**

is the Prefix *PARA* which means BESIDE, ALONGSIDE, POSITION. There are other words with this key which it would be well for you to know, words such as *PARA*noia, delusions of greatness; *PARA*phernalia, goods; *PARA*mount, etc. There is also a name which you would do well to remember, *PARA*celsus, a Swiss physician who did a great deal for modern medicine. Paracelsus preceded Dr. Lister in the hard fight against blood-poisoning after surgical operations.

1. parallel

PARA llel (par′ a lel) adj.
Lying evenly side by side; as, parallel lines.

2. parabasis

PARA basis (pa rab′ a sis) n.
An important ode by the chorus in old Greek comedy.

3. parabiosis

PARA biosis (par a bie o′ sis) n.
Union of two organisms.

4. parabola

PARA bola (pa rab′ o la) n.
A plane curve; shaped like a bowl.

5. parablepsy

PARA blepsy (par′ a blep si) n.
Vision that is abnormal.

6. paracentral

PARA central (par a sen′ tral) adj.
Lying near the center.

7. parachronism

PARA chronism (par ak′ roe niz um) n.
An error in chronology; a date set too late.

8. Paraclete

PARA clete (par′ a klete) n.
A helper; comforter; a term applied to the Holy Spirit.

9. paradigm

PARA digm (par′ a dime) n.
An example; a model.

10. parable

PARA ble (par′ a b′l) n.
A story told to emphasize a point; a fable.

11. paradox

PARA dox (par′ a doks) n.
An opinion which seems contradictory and sometimes is.

12. paradromic

PARA dromic (par a drom′ ik) adj.
Running parallel.

13. parody

PAR ody (par′ od ee) n.
An imitation mocking an author's style.

14. paracusia   PARA cusia (par a que' si a) n.
                   Any hearing disorder.

15. paralysis   PARA lysis (pa ral' a sis) n.
                   Loss of the function of motion.

16. paragraph   PARA graph (par' a graf) n.
                   *A section of a composition which completes
                   one topic.*

17. paragon   PARA gon (par' a gon) n.
                   A model of perfection.

18. paraphrase   PARA phrase (par' a fraze) n.
                   *A restatement of a text, giving the meaning
                   in another form.*

19. paradental   PARA dental (par a den' tal) adj.
                   Near a tooth.

20. parachromatism PARA chromatism (par a kro' ma tiz um) n.
                   Color blindness.

word analysis

PARABIOSIS—No. 3
    PARA—Root =one beside the other
    BIO—Root =life
    OSIS—Suffix =disease

practical exercises

1. Supply the missing words:
        What the cartoon does to ridicule the mannerisms of peo-
    ple, the .... does in the literary world. ....
    leaves the limbs in one position, without change or function.
    Siamese twins are an example of ....

2. Analyze No. 1.

3. Add keys to incomplete words and match them with the
   phrases they express:
   a. ....lysis   1. work of a .... degree   ....
   b. ....llel   2. the market slumped ....
   c. ....odically   3. no .... between them   ....
   d. ....emacy   4. .... to record temperature   ....
   e. thermo..........   5. .... of the right arm   ....
   f. ....lative   6. fought for the ....

201

KEY NO. *101*

o—⚷

GRAD · GRED
GRESS

step
degree
walk

is the Root, *GRAD, GRED, GRESS*, meaning STEP, DEGREE, WALK. This key is a most interesting one to us in this stage of our vocabulary building. No sooner do we put two keys together to make a word (see No. 10) than we can think of another key and still another one to add to it (see Word Analysis). And all by adding one key at a time. The Latin adverb *Gradatim!* beautifully expresses the method of this book. One KEY A DAY! STEP BY STEP! brings you to SUCCESS!

1. gradal   GRAD al (grade′ al) adj.
   Relating to grade or degree.
2. gradate   GRAD ate (gray′ date) v.
   To blend into another color.
3. gradation   GRAD ation (gray day′ shun) n.
   Act or process of grading; gradual advance.
4. gradient   GRAD ient (grade′ ee ent) n.
   A gentle slope.
5. gradiometer   GRAD iometer (gray di om′ e ter) n.
   An instrument used in civil engineering.
6. gradual   GRAD ual (graj′ u al) adj.
   Proceeding by small steps and degrees.
7. grado   GRAD o (gra′ do) n.
   (Music) A degree of the scale.
8. gradometer   GRAD ometer (grade om′ e ter) n.
   An instrument for measuring slopes.
9. aggressive   ag GRESS ive (a gres′ iv) adj.
   Tending to attack; to encroach.
10. congress   con GRESS (kon′ gres) n.
    A getting together; a body of lawmakers.
11. digress   di GRESS (die gres′) v.
    Step aside; wander off the subject.
12. egress   e GRESS (ee′ gres) n.
    The way out; exit.
13. ingredient   in GRED ient (in grede′ ee ent) n.
    One of the elements which enter into a mixture; as, the ingredients of a cake.
14. gressorial   GRESS orial (gre sore′ ee al) adj.
    Adapted for walking.

202

15.	progress	pro GRESS (pro gres') v.
		To go forward; advance.
16.	degrade	de GRAD e (de grade') v.
		Put a step lower; debase.
17.	graduation	GRAD uation (graj u ay' shun) n.
		Promotion to a degree.
18.	gradienter	GRAD ienter (gray' di en ter) n.
		An instrument for leveling.
19.	degree	de GREE (de gree') n.
		A step in advancement; a gradation.
20.	graduated	GRAD uated (graj' u ate ed) adj.
		Marked for contents at various levels; as, a graduated glass.

word analysis

CONGRESSIONAL—No. 10+IONAL
   CON—Prefix =with
   GRESS (gressus)—Latin Root =walk
   SION—Suffix =act of; state of
   AL—Suffix =relating to

practical exercises

1. Supply the missing words:
    To proceed ....ly is better than a spectacular spurt of effort. All students look forward to ....

2. Analyze No. 12.

3. Syllabicate and indicate which syllable is most greatly stressed by placing the accent mark (').

aggressive	progress (noun)	gradiometer
paralysis	incredulity	period
authorities	insisted	superlative
comparison	crystal	preserves
omnibus	omniscient	omnipotent

KEY NO. 102

o—⚷

DOM

quality
realm
office
state

is the Suffix *DOM* which has a Romany, Gypsy origin. It means QUALITY; REALM; OFFICE; STATE. It often indicates an area that is a way, a world all its own.

1. Anglo-Saxondom — Anglo-Saxon DOM (an glo sak' son dom) n.
   The land occupied by Anglo-Saxons.

2. newspaperdom — newspaper DOM (nuz' pae per dom) n.
   The world of the press.

3. boredom — bore DOM (bord' om) n.
   State of being bored.

4. Christendom — Christen DOM (kris' en dom) n.
   The Christian world.

5. dukedom — duke DOM (dyuke' dom) n.
   The rank of a duke.

6. earldom — earl DOM (earl' dom) n.
   The rank of an earl.

7. freedom — free DOM (free' dom) n.
   State of being free.

8. halidom — hali DOM (hal' id om) n.
   State of holiness; sanctity.

9. kingdom — king DOM (king' dom) n.
   Kingship; the realm of a king.

10. martyrdom — martyr DOM (mart' ird om) n.
    Condition of being sacrificed to a cause.

11. officialdom — official DOM (o fish' al dom) n.
    Dignity of officials.

12. professordom — professor DOM (pro fes' or dom) n.
    Rank of professor; status in education.

13. random — ran DOM (ran' dom) adj.
    State of aimlessness; as, a random choice.

14. serfdom — serf DOM (serf' dom) n.
    The state of the near-slave.

15. stardom — star DOM (stard' om) n.
    The status of an important person in the theatre.

16. whoredom — whore DOM (hore' dom) n.
    The state of idolatry; harlotry.

17. wisdom   wis DOM (wiz' dom) n.
                      The state of knowledge.

18. Yankeedom   Yankee DOM (yan' kede om) n.
                      The world of the Northerner.

word analysis

HALIDOM—No. 8
    HALI (Halig)—Root =sacred
    DOM—Suffix =state

practical exercise

Read the following excerpt underlining all those words that contain keys you have already learned.

It was the best of times, it was the worst of times, it was the age of wisdom, it was the age of foolishness, it was the epoch of belief, it was the epoch of incredulity, it was the season of light, it was the season of darkness, it was the spring of hope, it was the winter of despair, we had everything before us, we had nothing before us, we were all going direct to Heaven, we were all going direct the other way—in short the period was so far like the present period, that some of its noisiest authorities insisted on its being received, for good or for evil, in the superlative degree of comparison only.

There was a king with a large jaw and a queen with a plain face, on the throne of England; there was a king with a large jaw and a queen with a pretty face on the throne of France. In both countries it was clearer than crystal to the lords of the State preserves of loaves and fishes that things in general were settled forever.

      (from *The Tale of Two Cities* by Charles Dickens.)

KEY NO. 103

o—►

CIAN

**having a
certain skill or art**

is the Suffix *CIAN* which is really an extension of the Suffix *AN*, NATIVE TO. *CIAN* means HAVING A CERTAIN SKILL OR ART. The beautiCIAN is one who knows how to create beauty. The PolitiCIAN knows how to manipulate politics; the musiCIAN knows how to create music; and so on with the rest of the list. Bear that in mind when you see *CIAN*, *TIAN*, ONE WHO.

1. logician   logi CIAN (lo jish' an) n.
   An expert in the science of logic.

2. musician   musi CIAN (myu zish' an) n.
   One skilled in music.

3. beautician   beauti CIAN (byue tish' an) n.
   An expert in beauty care.

4. dietician, or   dieti CIAN (die e tish' an) n.
   dietitian   *An expert in foods and nutrition.*

5. statistician   statisti CIAN (stat i stish' an) n.
   An expert in compiling statistics.

6. technician   techni CIAN (tek nish' an) n.
   An expert in the industrial arts.

7. pyrotechnician   pyrotechni CIAN (pie ro tek nish' an) n.
   An expert at displaying fireworks.

8. magician   magi CIAN (ma jish' an) n.
   One skilled in magic.

9. mathematician   mathemati CIAN (math e ma tish' an) n.
   One skilled in mathematics.

10. mortician   morti CIAN (mor tish' an) n.
    An undertaker.

11. electrician   electri CIAN (e lek trish' an) n.
    One versed in the practice of electricity.

12. obstetrician   obstetri CIAN (ob ste trish' an) n.
    A physician whose specialty is delivering babies.

13. patrician   patri CIAN (pa trish' an) n.
    One nobly born in ancient Roman society; aristocrat.

14. pediatrician   pediatri CIAN (pede ee a trish' an) n.
    A physician whose specialty is the care of children.

15. physician   physi CIAN (fi zish' an) n.
    Another name for a doctor of medicine.

16. optician   opti CIAN (op tish' an) n.
One whose specialty is making eyeglasses and other optical instruments.

17. politician   politi CIAN (pol i tish' an) n.
An expert in politics.

word analysis

PYROTECHNICIAN—No. 7
    PYRO (pyros)—Greek Root =fire
    TECHNI (technikos)—Greek Root =art; skill
    CIAN—Suffix =one who

practical exercises

1. Supply the missing words:
    In Greece and in Rome the nobly born belonged to the .... class of society. A great responsibility for the health of the community rests on the ....

2. Analyze No. 1.

3. In the following list add the suffix which means ONE WHO has skill in the field of work mentioned:
    a. beauty   ....
    b. electricity   ....
    c. statistics   ....
    d. logic   ....
    e. optics   ....
    f. technics   ....
    g. music   ....
    h. diet   ....

is the root *NUMBER, NUMER* which means exactly what it looks like, NUMBER. How lucky we are that we live in a world where we express numbers by numbers and not by letters as the Latins did. I've copied out an example using Roman numbers and the corresponding Arabic numbers:

| MCCLXXXIX | 1289 |
| +MXXXVIII | +1038 |

NUMERation has certainly been made easy for us with the Arabic NUMERals and the Hebrew base of ten.

1. numberless	NUMBER less (num' ber les) adj. *Without number; as,* numberless *stars.*
2. numeral	NUMER al (nume' e ral) adj. *Relating to a number; as,* numeral *adjective.*
3. numeral	NUMER al (nume' e ral) n. *A figure expressing a number; as, a Roman* numeral.
4. numberable	NUMBER able (num' be ra b'l) adj. *Can be numbered.*
5. numeration	NUMER ation (nue me ray' shun) n. *Act of counting.*
6. numerant	NUMER ant (nue' mer ant) n. *Used in counting.*
7. numerate	NUMER ate (nue' me rate) v. *To count over; to enumerate.*
8. numerology	NUMER ology (nue me rol' o jee) n. *A study of the mystic significance of numbers.*
9. numerous	NUMER ous (nume' e rus) adj. *Of great number; plentiful.*
10. numerosity	NUMER osity (nue mer os' i ty) n. *State of being numerous.*
11. numerical	NUMER ical (nue mer' i k'l) adj. *Expressed by numbers.*
12. numerative	NUMER ative (nue' mer ay tive) adj. *Relating to numeration; as, a* numerative *system.*
13. numerist	NUMER ist (nue' mer ist) n. *A numerologist.*

14. numerator   NUMER ator (nue′ me rate or) n.
                     The upper number in a fraction.

15. enumerate   e NUMER ate (e nue′ me rate) v.
                     Count, one by one.

16. innumerable   in NUMER able (in ume′ e ra b'l) adj.
                     Not able to be counted.

17. renumber   re NUMBER (re num′ ber) v.
                     Give to each another, a different number.

18. unnumbered   un NUMBER ed (un num′ berd) adj.
                     Have not been counted; as, unnumbered votes.

19. supernumerary   super NUMER ary (sue per nue′ me rar ee) adj.
                     Exceeding the needed number; as, a super- *numerary officer.*

20. denumerable   de NUMER able (de nume′ e ra b'l) adj.
                     Countable.

word analysis

INNUMERABILITY—No. 16+ility
     IN—Prefix =not
     NUMER—Root =number
     ABIL (able)—Suffix =can do
     ITY—Suffix =quality of

practical exercises

1. Supply the missing words:
     When one views the heavens through a telescope, he becomes certain of the .... of the stars. The play needed only twelve actors, and one .... He was told .... times not to smoke.

2. Analyze No. 19.

3. Make adverbs of the following adjectives:
     a. numerable   ....
     b. numerological   ....
     c. numerous   ....
     d. numerical   ....
     e. numerative   ....
     f. innumerable   ....
     g. supernumerary   ....
     h. numberless   ....

o—►

TRACT · TRAH

draw
pull

is the Root *TRACT*, *TRAH* meaning DRAW, PULL. It comes from the Latin *trahere*, to draw, pull. *TRAH* is rarely used. *TRACT* lends itself readily to combination with other keys, as you see from the list. *ABLE*, *ILE*, *ITY*, *TION*, *AT*, *IVE*, *OR*, *ABS*, *CON*, *DE*, *DIS*, *EX*, *RE*, *SUB*, *PRO*—all old friends, more or less, a fine reunion. Just think of the performance when all these get into the act. What a company! And what a performance you'll be able to give when you recognize them one and all!

1. tractable   TRACT able (trak' ta b'l) adj.
     Can be handled.

2. tractile   TRACT ile (trak' til) adj.
     Can be drawn out; tensile.

3. tractability   TRACT ability (trak ta bil' it ee) n.
     The quality which makes handling possible.

4. intractable   in TRACT able (in trak' ta b'l) adj.
     Cannot be handled; inflexible.

5. traction   TRACT ion (trak' shun) n.
     The act of pulling, hauling.

6. attract   at TRACT (a trakt') v.
     To draw toward; to allure.

7. attractive   at TRACT ive (a trak' tiv) adj.
     Alluring; as, an attractive beauty.

8. tractor   TRACT or (trak' tor) n.
     An automotive machine for farm work that pulls equipment.

9. abstract   abs TRACT (ab strakt') v.
     To draw away; as, to abstract the wallet from the purse.

10. contract   con TRACT (kon' trakt) n.
     An agreement that draws together; as, both signed the contract.

11. contractual   con TRACT ual (kon trak' chu al) adj.
     Relating to an agreement signed.

12. contraction   con TRACT ion (kon trak' shun) n.
     A drawing together; shrinkage.

13. detract   de TRACT (de trakt') v.
     To draw away from; as, detract from a person's good name.

14. distract   dis TRACT (dis trakt') v.
         To draw away; as, distract *the mind.*

15. extract   ex TRACT (eks trakt') v.
         To draw out; as, extract *a tooth.*

16. retract   re TRACT (re trakt') v.
         To draw back; as, retract *the accusation.*

17. subtract   sub TRACT (sub trakt') v.
         To take away; as, subtract *5 from 9.*

18. subtrahend   sub TRAH end (sub' tra hend) n.
         The number to be drawn away from another;
         as, in a subtraction example.

19. protract   pro TRACT (pro trakt') v.
         Draw further; drag out; as, protract *a case.*

20. protractive   pro TRACT ive (pro trak' tiv) adj.
         Causing delay; as, protractive *tactics in court.*

word analysis

SUBTRAHEND—No. 18
     SUB—Prefix =under
     TRAH (trahere)—Latin Root =to draw
     END—Suffix =that which

practical exercises

1. Supply the missing words:
     .... of teeth is a painful experience. The claim could not be established because all .... evidence had been ....(ed) from the files.

2. Analyze No. 9.

3. Add necessary keys to complete words:
     a. He loved her to dis..........tion.
     b. She would not re ..... the ac..........ation.
     c. The ex..........tion of the tooth was soon done.
     d. Whenever she could she would ....tract from his good name.
     e. After number.......... ....tractions, nothing was left in the account.

KEY NO. *106*

PEND · PEN

hang

is the Root *PEND, PEN* which comes from the Latin *pendere*, meaning to HANG. This is a very simple key, easily recognizable, and takes simple Suffixes and Prefixes to play around with. At the same time it does its duty for widening of the vocabulary horizon, enrichment of comprehension and subject areas.

1. pendent   PEND ent (pen' dent) adj.
     Hanging; as, "pendent drops of ice."

2. pendant   PEND ant (pen' dant) n.
     A piece of jewelry that hangs; as, a pearl pendant in each ear.

3. pending   PEND ing (pen' ding) adj.
     Hanging over; as, a pending suit for libel.

4. pendule   PEND ule (pen' dule) n.
     A small hanging ornament; as, a locket.

5. pendulous   PEND ulous (pen' ju lus) adj.
     Hanging down; drooping.

6. pendulum   PEND ulum (pen' ju lum) n.
     A freely swinging piece of machinery; as, the pendulum of a clock.

7. pendulate   PEND ulate (pen' due late) v.
     To swing; undulate.

8. pendulosity   PEND ulosity (pen due los' i ti) n.
     The quality of hanging down; pendulousness.

9. pendency   PEND ency (pen' den see) n.
     State of being undecided; as the pendency of a trial.

10. dependent   de PEND ent (de pen' dent) adj.
     Hanging on to something for support.

11. dependability   de PEND ability (de pen da bil' it ee) n.
     A quality one can hang on to; reliability.

12. independent   inde PEND ent (in de pen' dent) adj.
     Not hanging on anyone.

13. impending   im PEND ing (im pend' ing) adj.
     Hanging over one, as a doom.

14. interdependent   interde PEND ent (int er de pen' dent) adj.
     Hanging on to each other and helping each other.

15. independence   inde PEND ence (in de pen' dens) n.
> *State of being free; not holding on to any-thing.*

16. suspended   sus PEND ed (su spend' ed) adj.
> *Hanging from; as, the pendulum is suspended from a fixed point.*

17. suspension   sus PEN sion (su spen' shun) n.
> *State of hanging; debarred for a time; as, suspension from school.*

18. perpendicular   per PEND icular (per pen dik' yu lar) adj.
> *Hanging straight down at right angles.*

19. appendage   ap PEND age (ap end' dij) n.
> *A thing which hangs on; as, a useless appendage.*

20. appendix   ap PEND ix (a pen' diks) n.
> *Extra material attached to a book.*

word analysis

SUSPENDED—No. 16
> SUS—Prefix =under
> PEND (pendere)—Latin Root =hang
> ED—Suffix =forms the past participle.

practical exercises

1. Supply the missing words:
> In the winter some animals live in a state of .... animation. The Colonies declared their .... from England on July 4, 1776. The appendix is an unnecessary ....

2. Analyze No. 2.

3. Choose the number of the word which most nearly expresses the italicized word:
> a. *calculate*   (1) resist   (2) numerate   (3) place   (4) attract   (5) retain   ....
> b. *attraction*   (1) system   (2) motion   (3) pull toward   (4) mathematics   (5) mistake   ....
> c. *tides*   (1) earth   (2) orbit   (3) waters   (4) resistance   (5) gravitation   ....
> d. *suspended*   (1) moving   (2) calculated   (3) hanging from   (4) entering   (5) spacious   ....
> e. *position*   (1) mass   (2) orbit   (3) motion   (4) system   (5) place   ....

ASTER, ASTRO, a Root which comes from the Greek *astron,* means STAR. This is an important key in our times, as no one is more in the public eye than the ASTROnaut.

star

1. asterisk   ASTER isk (as' te risk) n.
   A tiny star; used in printing to note something special.

2. asteroid   ASTER oid (as' te roid) adj.
   Like a star; resembling a star.

3. asterozoa   ASTER ozoa (as ter o zo' a) n.
   The starfish family.

4. astrology   ASTRO logy (a strol' o jee) n.
   A study of the stars as having influence on human destiny.

5. astrologer   ASTRO loger (a strol' o jer) n.
   One who practices astrology.

6. astrological   ASTRO logical (as tro loj' i k'l) adj.
   Relating to astrology.

7. astronomy   ASTRO nomy (a stron' o mee) n.
   Science of the heavenly bodies.

8. astronomer   ASTRO nomer (a stron' o mer) n.
   One versed in astronomy.

9. astronomical   ASTRO nomical (as tro nom' i k'l) adj.
   Relating to astronomy; enormous.

10. astrophil   ASTRO phil (as' tro fil) n.
    One interested in star lore; an amateur astronomer.

11. astrophysics   ASTRO physics (as tro fiz' iks) n.
    Astronomy and physics combined to understand the heavens.

12. astronaut   ASTRO naut (as' tro naut) n.
    A space traveler.

13. astronautics   ASTRO nautics (as tro naut' iks) n.
    The science of creating spaceworthy vehicles.

14. astrosphere   ASTRO sphere (as' tro sfer) n.
    The sphere of the stars.

15. astrograph   ASTRO graph (as' tro graf) n.
    A photographic telescope.

16. astrography   ASTRO graphy (as trog' ra fi) n.
    Description and mapping out of the heavens.

17. astrometry ASTRO metry (as trom' e tri) n.
  The measuring of the heavenly bodies.

18. astrometer ASTRO meter (as trom' e ter) n.
  Instrument for measuring heavenly bodies.

19. astrolabe ASTRO labe (as' tro labe) n.
  An instrument to observe the positions of the heavenly bodies.

20. astrotheology ASTRO theology (as tro the ol' o ji) n.
  A theology based upon the observation of the heavens.

word analysis

ASTROLOGICAL—No. 6
  ASTRO (astron)—Greek Root =star
  LOG (logos)—Greek Root =word; study
  IC—Suffix =like; nature of
  AL—Suffix =relating to

practical exercises

1. Supply the missing words:
  .... is a science but .... is a pseudo-science. Astronautics is to the .... what .... is to the astrophysicist.

2. Analyze No. 17.

3. Read the following excerpt underlining all those words that contain keys you have already learned.

  Ranger 7's performance was a triumph of science. It was a great leap forward in lunar astronomy, providing in a few minutes knowledge about the moon that was far beyond man's reach in all the centuries before. It also was a crucial and successful test for the United States space program, since it was one of the essential preliminaries in the actual journey to the moon that is set for this decade.

  So the nation was heartened. . . . We had made a historical achievement and everything else for a while seemed small by comparison. Even if depressing problems remained, we had at least demonstrated what concerted national effort could accomplish in one area, raising the hope that it might succeed also in others.

  (From *The New York Times*, Aug. 2, 1964.)

KEY NO. 108

O—➤

IST

**one who
that which**

is the Suffix *IST* which means ONE WHO; THAT WHICH. It is easily added to nouns as, art—art*IST*. To that can be added the Suffix *IC* and we have an adjective, art*IS-TIC*. To that can be added the compound suffix *ALLY* and we have the adverb, art*ISTICALLY*. So to the little word art is added a double compound suffix. It is truly amazing how flexible and accommodating these keys are. They are ready at all times and in all places to extend themselves and to give their influence where it helps.

1. accompanist   accompan IST (a komp' a nist) n.
   One who plays an accompaniment to a soloist.
2. alarmist   alarm IST (a lar' mist) n.
   One who excites alarms needlessly.
3. artist   art IST (art' ist) n.
   One who creates a work of art; a painter, musician.
4. biologist   biolog IST (bie ol' o jist) n.
   One versed in biology, the science of living things.
5. bigamist   bigam IST (big' a mist) n.
   One married to two wives at the same time.
6. chemist   chem IST (kem' ist) n.
   One well versed in chemistry, the science of the composition of substances.
7. dentist   dent IST (dent' ist) n.
   One who practises dentistry, the care of teeth.
8. evangelist   evangel IST (ee van' je list) n.
   One who rouses religious fervor.
9. violinist   violin IST (vie o lin' ist) n.
   One who is an artist with the violin.
10. humanist   human IST (hyue' ma nist) n.
   One who is interested in human values.
11. legalist   legal IST (lee' ga list) n.
   One who is expert in law and legal procedures.
12. monarchist   monarch IST (mon' ar kist) n.
   One who believes in monarchy as a government.

216

13. naturalist   natural IST (nach' u ra list) n.
                  One who is expert in nature studies.
14. optometrist   optometr IST (op tom' e trist) n.
                  One who prescribes corrective lenses and exercises to improve defective vision.
15. pianist   pian IST (pee an' ist) n.
                  One who is an artist at the piano.
16. racist   rac IST (ray' sist) n.
                  One who has racial prejudices.
17. sociologist   sociologist (so see ol' o jist) n.
                  One who is versed in sociology, the study of the affairs and institutions of society.
18. terrorist   terror IST (ter' or ist) n.
                  One who uses fear as a weapon of power.
19. geologist   geolog IST (jee ol' o jist) n.
                  One who works in the field of geology, the study of the history of the earth as recorded in rocks.
20. cellist   cell IST (chel' ist) n.
                  One who is an artist with the cello.

word analysis

ARTISTICALLY—No. 3+IC+AL+LY
    ART (ars)—Latin Root =art
    IST—Suffix =one who
    IC—Suffix =like
    AL—Suffix =relating to
    LY—Suffix—adverbial ending

practical exercises

1. Supply the missing words:
   In Spain the ....(s) are waiting for Franco to give up his hold on the country. The .... to the .... was also a fine ....

2. Analyze No. 7.

3. USE the suffix *IST* with the suffix *IC*, and the compound suffix *ICALLY* where necessary to complete words:
   a. like an artist— art..........
   b. played the violin— art.......... ....
   c. He is a human.......... with a human.......... point of view; he views the situation ....
   d. being a lawyer, he treats the matter ....
   e. disapprove of the terror.......... tactics

o━┳

AUTO · AUT

self

is the Root *AUTO, AUT*—which means SELF. It comes from the Greek *autos* meaning self, same. This key is the most important to ourselves because it is our very SELF. Our bodies are automated and they give us a great deal of self-service: breathing, digesting, thinking—all with practically no aid from ourselves. Word No. 8 is particularly interesting. It meant a great deal to Louis Pasteur, although in his day "spontaneous generation" was the phrase used. When you reach KEY NO. 230 you will read a thumbnail sketch of Louis Pasteur.

1. autograph   AUTO graph (aut' o graf) n.
           A person's signature.

2. autobiography   AUTO biography (aut o bie og' ra fee) n.
           The story of one's life written by oneself.

3. autocrat   AUTO crat (aut' o krat) n.
           An absolute monarch; a despot.

4. autocratic   AUTO cratic (aut o krat' ik) adj.
           In the nature of an autocrat; despotic.

5. autocracy   AUTO cracy (au tok' ra see) n.
           State governed by absolute rule; supremacy.

6. autarch   AUT arch (au' tark) n.
           An absolute ruler; a despot.

7. autarchy   AUT archy (au' tar kee) n.
           Absolute rule; despotism.

8. autogenesis   AUTO genesis (aut o jen' e sis) n.
           Born from oneself; spontaneously generated.

9. autognosis   AUTO gnosis (au tog no' sis) n.
           Self-knowledge; self-understanding.

10. autoignition   AUTO ignition (au to ig nish' un) n.
           Self-kindling; spontaneous ignition.

11. autoinfection   AUTO infection (aut o in fek' shun) n.
           Infection caused from within one's own body.

12. autointoxication   AUTO intoxication (aut o in tok si kay' shun) n.
           Self-infection.

13. automat   AUTO mat (aut' o mat) n.
           A self-service cafeteria.

14. automatic   AUTO matic (aut o mat' ik) adj.
                       Having self-acting and self-regulating mechanism.

15. automation   AUTO mation (aut o may' shun) n.
                       An industrial system using machinery that runs itself.

16. automaton   AUTO maton (au tom' at on) n.
                       A self-operating figure; a mechanical man.

17. automobile   AUTO mobile (aut o mo bele') n.
                       A vehicle containing its own means of propulsion.

18. automotive   AUTO motive (aut o mote' iv) adj.
                       Self-moving; as, an automotive *machine.*

19. autonomy   AUTO nomy (au ton' o mee) n.
                       Self-government; independence of action.

20. autonomous   AUTO nomous (au ton' o mus) adj.
                       Self-governing; independent in action.

word analysis

AUTOGENESIS—No. 8
     AUTO (autos)—Greek Root =self
     GEN (genes)—Greek Root =produced; generated
     ESIS—Suffix =process

practical exercises

1. Supply the missing words:
     In industry today much .... equipment is
needed. Oliver Wendell Holmes wrote a book called "The
.... of the Breakfast Table," containing some
very delightful pieces. A popular star is constantly besieged for his ....

2. Analyze No. 6.

3. Use one word for each phrase:
    a. the process of using machines instead of
       manpower   ....
    b. poisoning due to disease germs in the body   ....
    c. a mechanical figure, like a robot   ....
    d. devouring everything   ....
    e. independent, self-government is the goal   ....

KEY NO. *110*

○━➤

ILE

**relating to
suited for
capable of**

is the Suffix *ILE* which means RE-LATING TO; SUITED FOR; CAPA-BLE OF. It is a tidy little key and says much in its three letters. Where it is seen it carries much weight, either in praise or blame. It can be a good recommendation or a bad one. It is a very revealing key, and tells all very simply, without hedging. Senior citizens do not want to be called senILE, and a boy does not want to be called puerILE. AgILE is a compliment, but facILE isn't. Don't be too easy. Watch *ILE*.

1. domicile   domic ILE (dom' i sile) n.
   A place for home and family.
2. docile   doc ILE (dos' il) adj.
   Easy to teach; amenable; as, a docile *child.*
3. agile   ag ILE (aj' il) adj.
   Suited to quick motion; graceful in movement.
4. ductile   duct ILE (duk' til) adj.
   Can be led; tractable.
5. fertile   fert ILE (fert' il) adj.
   Capable of being fruitful.
6. fragile   frag ILE (fraj' il) adj.
   Can be broken easily; frail.
7. imbecile   imbec ILE (im' be sil) adj.
   Tending to be mentally weak; as, imbecile *conduct.*
8. mercantile   mercant ILE (mer' kan tele) adj.
   Relating to business; commercial.
9. juvenile   juven ILE (ju' ven ile) adj.
   Relating to youth; as, juvenile *delinquency.*
10. infantile   infant ILE (in' fan tile) adj.
    Relating to infancy; as, infantile *behavior.*
11. mobile   mob ILE (moe' bil) adj.
    Capable of being moved.
12. prehensile   prehens ILE (pree hen' sil) adj.
    Capable of grasping; as, the prehensile *tail of a monkey.*
13. projectile   project ILE (pro jek' til) adj.
    Capable of being thrown.
14. senile   sen ILE (sene' ile) adj.
    Relating to old age; as, senile *weakness.*

15. reptile   rept ILE (rep' til) n.
             An animal that crawls; as, a snake.
16. puerile   puer ILE (pyu' er il) adj.
             Suited to a child; childish.
17. sterile   ster ILE (ster' il) adj.
             Tending to be barren; free from germs.
18. tactile   tact ILE (tak' til) adj.
             Capable of being touched; as, tactile *qualities.*
19. volatile   volat ILE (vol' at il) adj.
             Capable of flying; light; buoyant.
20. versatile   versat ILE (ver' sat il) adj.
             Capable of varying; having various talents; as,
             a versatile *genius.*

word analysis

PREHENSILE—No. 12
     PREHENS (prehendere)—Latin Root =wrapping around;
                                    grasp
     ILE—Suffix =suited for

practical exercises

1. Supply the missing words:
     The monkey is an animal with a .... tail.
We are much concerned with .... delinquency.
For her age she was remarkably .... The box
of china was marked ....

2. Analyze No. 5.

3. Use the correct word to express each phrase:
   a. always flying about   ....
   b. suited for a baby   ....
   c. suitable for youth   ....
   d. free from germs   ....
   e. is easily broken   ....
   f. fit for an idiot   ....
   g. suited for a child   ....

KEY NO. 111

0—➤

**POS · PON
POUND**

place
set

is the Root *POS, PON, POUND* which means PLACE; SET. It comes from the Latin *ponere, positus* which means PLACE; SET. Please look at No. 6 post*PON*e. The syllable POST does not mean the same as No. 5. The *post* in *postPON*e is simply a Prefix that means after, or later, and it has nothing to do with this key.

1. posit
POS it (poz' it) v.
Set firmly in place; assert; declare.

2. position
POS ition (po zish' un) n.
The manner in which a thing is placed; office.

3. positive
POS itive (poz' it iv) adj.
Definitely laid down; as, a positive law.

4. positor
POS itor (poz' i tor) n.
One who asserts or affirms.

5. post
POS t (poste) n.
A place; station; position; as, a soldier's post.

6. postpone
post PON e (poste pone') v.
Place later; delay; as, postpone the wedding.

7. posture
pos ture (pos' chur) n.
Placement of the limbs of the body; carriage.

8. posture
POS ture (pos' chur) v.
To assume a position; to pose.

9. composition
com POS ition (kom po zish' un) n.
Combination of parts to form a whole.

10. deponent
de PON ent (de pon' nent) n.
One who gives evidence in writing.

11. expose
ex POS e (ek spoze') v.
Set forth; show for all to see; as, expose a fraud.

12. exposure
ex POS ure (ek spoe' zhur) n.
The act of laying bare; as, exposure of all facts.

13. expound
ex POUN d (ek spound') v.
Set forth; explain; as, expound a theory.

14. impound
im POUN d (im pound') v.
To seize and hold in custody; as, to impound stray cattle.

15. propound
pro POUN d (pro pound') v.
To propose; to offer; as, propound a question.

222

16. depose   de POS e (de poze) v.
              To remove from office; as, depose *the chairman.*
17. impose   im POS e (im poze') v.
              To place on; as, impose *a penalty.*
18. propose   pro POS e (pro poze') v.
              To offer; to suggest; as, propose *marriage.*
19. proposal   pro POS al (pro poe' zal) n.
              An offer; as, a proposal *of marriage.*
20. proposition   pro POS ition (prop o zish' un) n.
              A statement offered for consideration.

word analysis

POSTPONEMENT—No. 6+MENT
     POST—Prefix =after; later
     PONE (ponere)—Latin Root =place; set
     MENT—Suffix =state of

practical exercises

1. Supply the missing words:
     Good .... is necessary for attractive personal
appearance. The ....('s) evidence asserted, under
oath, threatened more ....(s)
of the facts in the case.

2. Analyze No. 11.

3. Choose the number of the word which most nearly expresses
the italicized word:
     a. *postpone*   (1) discriminate   (2) delay
        (3) distinguish   (4) accuse   (5) remove   ....
     b. *proposition*   (1) ridicule   (2) university
        (3) idea   (4) presented   (5) decision   ....
     c. *positive*   (1) doubtful   (2) evident   (3) negative
        (4) definite   (5) informal   ....
     d. *century*   (1) year   (2) month   (3) era
        (4) week   (5) 100 years   ....
     e. *depose*   (1) abhor   (2) exhaust   (3) retain
        (4) distress   (5) dismiss   ....

KEY NO. *112*

O—➤

MITT · MISS

send

is the Root *MITT, MISS* which comes from the Latin *mittere, missus* meaning to SEND. The Latin Root accounts for the two spellings and the double letters in the English words. In the list you will find words made with earlier keys. How simple they seem now! How easy it is to understand the words made of those keys! One of these days you will find it very easy to know the longest word in the English language. *Just keep going* with the keys!

1. mission   MISS ion (mish' un) n.
   A duty one is sent to perform; as, sent on a mission.
2. missile   MISS ile (mis' il) n.
   Something which can be sent through the air.
3. missive   MISS ive (mis' iv) n.
   A note which can be sent by messenger.
4. admission   ad MISS ion (ad mish' un) n.
   Entrance; the permission to enter.
5. commit   com MIT (ko mit') v.
   To send; to entrust; as, commit yourself to a noble cause.
6. dismissed   dis MISS ed (dis misd') adj.
   Sent away; discharged.
7. emissary   e MISS ary (em' i sar ee) n.
   A messenger sent on a mission.
8. intermission   inter MISS ion (int er mish' un) n.
   A break between two parts of a performance; as, during intermission.
9. intermittent   inter MIT tent (int er mit' ent) adj.
   Coming and going; irregular.
10. remiss   re MISS (re mis') adj.
    Careless; as, service here is remiss.
11. remit   re MIT (re mit') v.
    Pay back; pardon.
12. remittance   re MITT ance (re mit' ans) n.
    Payment; as, enclose a remittance.
13. submit   sub MIT (sub mit') v.
    Give up; surrender.
14. submission   sub MISS ion (sub mish' un) n.
    Act of surrender.

15. transmit   trans MIT (trans mit') v.
                    Send across; as, transmit *news by cable.*
16. transmissible trans MISS ible (trans mis' i b'l) adj.
                    Can be sent across.
17. transmission trans MISS ion (trans mi' shun) n.
                    The act of sending across.
18. transmitter trans MITT er (trans mit' er) n.
                    One who or that which transmits.
19. emit   e MIT (ee mit') v.
                    To send out; as, emit *cries of horror.*
20. permit   per MIT (per mit') v.
                    To allow; as, liberty will not permit *license.*

word analysis

INTERMISSION—No. 8
    INTER—Prefix =between
    MISS (mittere)—Latin Root =to send
    SION—Suffix =state of

practical exercises

1. Supply the missing words:
    Having completed his .... he returned to his
    base of operations. No one knows how characteristics are
    .... from parent to child. At the concert they
    met friends during the ....

2. Analyze No. 11.

3. Supply the KEYS needed to complete words, or supply a com-
    plete word:
    a. She was bright but re.......... in attendance.
    b. He resented his ....al from his job.
    c. He acted as ....ary between the hostile brothers.
    d. This is not trans..........ible by wireless.
    e. She was careful to carry out her ....ment.

KEY NO. 113

0—x

POP

people

is the Root *POP* which comes from *populi*, Latin for PEOPLE. The word People did not mean to the ancient Romans what it means for us today. Today we hold the word in the greatest respect and every single party and every single government in the world seeks the approval of the people. In those days the word was held in contempt. Even when Julius Caesar made merely a show of wanting POPular approval, to him *POPuli* meant the illiterate, the vulgar, the common people.

1. populace   POP ulace (pop' yu las) n.
   The people.

2. Vox populi, (vox pop' yu lie vox day)
   vox Dei
   The voice of the people, the voice of God.

3. popular   POP ular (pop' yu lar) adj.
   Relating to the people; as, the popular vote.

4. popularity   POP ularity (pop yu lar' it ee) n.
   The quality of being liked by many people.

5. popularism   POP ularism (pop' yu lar iz um) n.
   A democratic movement.

6. popularist   POP ularist (pop' yu lar ist) n.
   One who believes in popularism.

7. popularize   POP ularize (pop' yu la rize) v.
   To cater to popular taste.

8. populate   POP ulate (pop' yu late) v.
   Furnish with people; as, populate a desert area.

9. population   POP ulation (pop yu lay' shun) n.
   The number of people in an area.

10. populationist POP ulationist (pop yu lay' shun ist) n.
    One who advocates population control.

11. populous   POP ulous (pop' yu lus) adj.
    Full of inhabitants; as, New York is a populous city.

12. populator   POP ulator (pop' yu lay tor) n.
    That which causes increase in population.

13. populism   POP ulism (pop' yu liz um) n.
    Doctrines advocated by the Populist party.

14. Populist   POP ulist (pop' yu list) n.
    A member of the Populist party.

226

15. populicide   POP ulicide (pop' yu li side) n.
                            The slaughter of populations; genocide.
16. unpopular   un POP ular (un pop' yu lar) adj.
                            Unpleasing to many people.
17. depopulate   de POP ulate (de pop' yu late) v.
                            To cut down the population.
18. repopulate   re POP ulate (re pop' yu late) v.
                            Fill up again with people.
19. depopulator   de POP ulator (de pop' yu lay tor) n.
                            That which causes a decrease in population.

word analysis

POPULICIDE—No. 15
    POPULI—Latin Root =people
    CIDE (cadeo)—Latin Root =kill

practical exercises

1. Supply the missing words:
     His .... was due to the fact that he was a
     liberal .... In ancient warfare the victors
     abandoned the conquered .... to slaughter or
     slavery.

2. Analyze No. 11.

3. Key review. Match keys with their meanings:
     a. mit   1. make   ....
     b. pop   2. one who   ....
     c. ile   3. place   ....
     d. ante   4. people; public   ....
     e. ate   5. before   ....
     f. pos, pon   6. send   ....
     g. ist   7. suited for   ....

is the Root *LEG* meaning LAW, from the Latin *lex, legis.* An odd thing is that *lex* is used only in Latin phrases, like *lex mercatorum*—Commercial Law. In the list all the words are with *LEG* and *LEGIS.* Please note No. 8, a verb, with the accent on the 2nd syllable. No. 7 is a noun and accent is on the first syllable. Notice No. 20, where *il* is an assimilated *in* before *legal.* For the sake of euphony, remember?

1. legal   LEG al (lee' gal) adj.
       Lawful; according to law; as, a legal *holiday.*

2. legalism   LEG alism (lee' gal iz um) n.
       Strict adherence to the law.

3. legalistic   LEG alistic (lee ga lis' tik) adj.
       Strictly according to law.

4. legality   LEG ality (le gal' it ee) n.
       The quality of being strictly legal.

5. legalize   LEG alize (lee' ga lize) v.
       Make lawful; as, legalize *citizenship.*

6. legacy   LEG acy (leg' a see) n.
       A gift of property left by will; an inheritance.

7. legate   LEG ate (leg' at) n.
       A delegate; an official messenger; an ambassador.

8. legate   LEG ate (le gate') v.
       To bequeath a legacy.

9. legatee   LEG atee (leg a tee') n.
       The one to whom a legacy is bequeathed.

10. legator   LEG ator (le gate' or) n.
       One who bequeaths the legacy.

11. legist   LEG ist (le' jist) n.
       One skilled in law; jurist.

12. legislate   LEG islate (lej' i slate) v.
       To enact a law; to cause to become a law.

13. legislative   LEG islative (lej' i slate iv) adj.
       Having the power to make a law; as, legislative *assembly.*

14. legislature   LEG islature (lej' i slay chur) n.
       A body of persons who can make laws.

15. legislator   LEG islator (lej' i slate or) n.
       A member of the legislature.

16. legislatress   **LEG** islatress (lej i slay' tres) n.
A female member of the legislature.

17. legislation   **LEG** islation (lej i slay' shun) n.
The enactment of law by the legislature.

18. legitimate   **LEG** itimate (le jit' i mat) adj.
Legal; according to the law; as, legitimate *business.*

19. legitimize   **LEG** itimize (le jit' i mize) v.
Make legal.

20. illegal   il **LEG** al (il ee' gal) adj.
Unlawful; illegitimate.

word analysis

LEGALIZE—No. 5.
     LEG (lex)—Root =law
     AL—Suffix =relating to
     IZE—Suffix =make

practical exercises

1. Supply the missing words:
     The millionaire left a huge .... but the
     .... failed to appear. When all the ....
     measures had been passed, the will was made ....

2. Analyze No. 20.

3. Use one word for each phrase:
     a. not according to law   ....
     b. the opposite of illegal   ....
     c. property bequeathed by a will   ....
     d. a group of people chosen to enact laws   ....
     e. make a matter lawful   ....
     f. cut down the number of inhabitants   ....

KEY NO. 115

o—x

HELIO

sun

is the Root *HELIO* which comes from the Greek *helios*, SUN. From this key we enrich our vocabulary with words from photography, sun worship, the science of the sun, sunbathing, sun-therapy and sunflowers. In Greek Mythology Helios, the Sungod, drove his sun-chariot across the sky every morning. In our day suntherapy cures rickets, tuberculosis, and is a preventative of many ills. The fragrant heliotrope is a garden favorite, and sunflower seeds are healthful.

1. heliocentric   HELIO centric (he lee o sen' trik) adj.
Having relation to the center of the sun.

2. heliochrome   HELIO chrome (he' lee o krome) n.
A naturally colored photograph.

3. heliochromoscope   HELIO chromoscope
(he li o kro' mo skope) n.
Instrument to produce photos in natural colors.

4. heliochromy   HELIO chromy (he' li o kro mi) n.
Color photography.

5. heliodon   HELIO don (he' li o don) n.
A device to illustrate what seems to be the Sun's motion.

6. heliodor   HELIO dor (he' li o dor) n.
Yellow beryl found in South Africa.

7. heliofugal   HELIO fugal (he li of' yu gal) adj.
Tending away from the sun.

8. heliograph   HELIO graph (he' lee o graf) n.
An instrument for using the sun's rays; as, a mirror for telegraphing.

9. heliogram   HELIO gram (he' lee o gram) n.
The message transmitted by heliograph.

10. helioid   HELIO id (he' li oid) adj.
Like the sun.

11. heliolatry   HELIO latry (he lee ol' a tree) n.
Sun worship.

12. heliology   HELIO logy (he li ol' o ji) n.
Science of the sun.

13. heliophilous   HELIO philous (he li of' i lus) adj.
Sun-loving.

14. heliophobic	HELIO phobic (he li o foe' bik) adj.
	Fearing the sun; shade-loving.
15. heliophyte	HELIO phyte (he' li o fite) n.
	Plant growing in sunlight.
16. helioscope	HELIO scope (he' li o skope) n.
	A dark lens telescope to view the sun while protecting the eyes.
17. heliosis	HELIO sis (he li o' sis) n.
	Sunburn; sunstroke.
18. heliotherapy	HELIO therapy (he li o ther' a pi) n.
	Use of sunbaths to cure disease.
19. heliothermometer	HELIO thermometer (he li o ther mom' e ter) n.
	Instrument to measure the intensity of solar radiation.
20. heliotrope	HELIO trope (hele' ee o trope) n.
	A plant which turns to the sun.

word analysis

HELIOFUGAL—No. 7
    HELIO (helios)—Greek Root = sun
    FUG (fugare)—Latin Root = run away
    AL—Suffix = relating to

practical exercises

1. Supply the missing words:
    Sunflowers and marigolds are called ....(s) because they turn to the sun. They are also called .... for the same reason. On the other hand some flowers are called .... because they shun the sun and require shade.

2. Analyze No. 14.

3. Syllabicate and indicate which syllable is most greatly stressed by placing the accent mark ('):

astronaut	random	supernumerary
astronautics	pyrotechnician	subtrahend
asteroid	innumerable	perpendicular
	prehensile	

KEY NO. *116*

O—x

AMB · AMBI

**around
about
both**

is the Prefix *AMB, AMBI* which means AROUND, ABOUT, BOTH. It comes from the Latin *ambo, ambio, ambitio.* This last, which is the basis for No. 4 and No. 5, means "a going about," especially by candidates who solicit votes. It seems that our election campaigns have a long and honorable lineage.

1. amble   AMB le (am' b'l) v.
   Walk leisurely about.

2. ambidexter   AMBI dexter (am bi dek' ster) n.
   One who uses both hands with skill.

3. ambidextrous AMBI dextrous (am bi dek' strus) adj.
   Using both hands with skill.

4. ambition   AMBI tion (am bish' un) n.
   Eagerness for achievement and honor.

5. ambitious   AMBI tious (am bish' us) adj.
   Eager for achievement and honor.

6. ambiguity   AMBI guity (am bi gyue' it ee) n.
   The quality of uncertainty in meaning.

7. ambiguous   AMBI guous (am big' yu us) adj.
   Having a double meaning; as, an ambiguous word.

8. ambiparous   AMBI parous (am bip' a rus) adj.
   Having both leaves and flowers.

9. ambit   AMBI t (am' bit) n.
   Bounds set up extending to the limit of a place.

10. ambient   AMBI ent (am' bee ent) adj.
    Moving around; surrounding on all sides; as, the ambient air.

11. ambilateral AMBI lateral (am bi lat' er al) adj.
    Relating to both sides; bilateral.

12. ambivalence AMBI valence (am biv' a lens) n.
    Repulsion and attraction to an object at the same time.

13. ambivalent   AMBI valent (am biv' a lent) adj.
    Repelled and attracted at the same time.

14. ambivert   AMBI vert (am' bi vert) n.
    A person whose nature combines those of the introvert and extrovert.

15. ambisinister AMBI sinister (am bi sin' is ter) adj.
    Left-handed; clumsy with both hands.

16. ambitendency AMBI tendency (am bi ten' den si) n.
                   *A case of having both tendency and counter-
                   tendency.*
17. amburbial   AMB urbial (am bur' bi al) adj.
                   Relating to a circuit of a city.
18. perambulator per AMB ulator (pe ram' byu late or) n.
                   One who travels around; baby carriage.
19. ambulance   AMB ulance (am' byu lans) n.
                   A vehicle to transport the injured.

word analysis

AMBURBIAL—No. 17
    AMB (ambulare)—Latin Root = Walk around
    URB (urbs)—Latin Root = city
    AL—Suffix = relating to

practical exercises

1. Supply the missing words:
       "Sir, your wit .... well—it goes about easily."
       (Shakespeare) "He has .... to attempt and skill
       to win." (Wordsworth) The ancient Oracles spoke..........(ly).

2. Analyze No. 10.

3. Prefixes may also be compound and can be recognized together.
   Example: UN+IN = Not lived in: ....*unin*habited....
   a. no inspiration in it   ....
   b. not asked to come in   ....
   c. did not mean to do it   ....
   d. not much brain in him   ....
   e. does not know the facts   ....
   f. doesn't carry much weight   ....
   g. not of a curious mind   ....

KEY NO. *117*

0—⚡

RIDI · RISI · RI

laughter

is the Root *RIDI, RISI, RI*, meaning LAUGHTER. It comes from *ridere, risus*. The Romans were not, I'm afraid, a gay and happy people. Their *ridi* and *risi* were, for the most part, the laughter which mocks and hurts, not the laughter which heals and helps. The only words which are pleasant in laughter with this Root are RIant, RIantly, and RIancy. You may have heard the heartbreaking laughter of "Ridi, Pagliaccio . . ." "Laugh, Clown, laugh . . ." in the opera.

1. ridibund   RIDI bund (ri' di bund) adj.
      Tending to laughter.
2. ridicule   RIDI cule (rid' i kyule) n.
      Laughter at the expense of another; mockery.
3. ridicule   RIDI cule (rid' i kyule) v.
      To mock; as, to ridicule *another.*
4. ridiculer   RIDI culer (rid' i kyule er) n.
      One who mocks another.
5. ridiculosity   RIDI culosity (ri dik yu los' i ti) n.
      The state of being ridiculous.
6. ridiculous   RIDI culous (ri dik' yu lus) adj.
      Laughable; as, a ridiculous *dress.*
7. ridiculousness RIDI culousness (ri dik' yu lus nes) n.
      Absurdity; inviting of mockery.
8. ridiculously   RIDI culously (ri dik' yu lus lee) adv.
      In a manner which invites ridicule.
9. riant   RI ant (rie' ant) adj.
      Smiling; gay; laughing.
10. risible   RISI ble (riz' i b'l) adj.
      Disposed to laugh.
11. risibility   RISI bility (riz i bil' it ee) n.
      The quality of being able to laugh; a sense of humor.
12. riantly   RI antly (rie' ant ly) adv.
      Laughingly; gaily.
13. derision   de RIS ion (de rizh' un) n.
      Mocking laughter.
14. risibles   RISI bles (ri' zi b'lz) n.
      Likely to laugh.

15. risibleness   RISI bleness (ri' zi b'l nes) n.
                   A disposition toward laughter.

16. deride   de RID e (de ride') v.
                   Make mock of; jeer at.

17. derisive   de RISI ve (de rie' siv) adj.
                   Causing mocking laughter.

18. derisively   de RISI vely (de rie' siv lee) adv.
                   Mockingly, as, he laughed derisively.

word analysis

RIANTLY—No. 12
     RI (ridi)—Latin Root =laughter
     ANT—Suffix =that which
     LY—Suffix =in the manner of

practical exercises

1. Supply the missing words:
     The clown sprawled .... over the tiny car. He
   was .... by the other members of the troupe.

2. Analyze No. 3.

3. Key review. Match keys with their meanings:
     a. ridi   1. sun   ....
     b. tract   2. star   ....
     c. ambi   3. around   ....
     d. peri   4. hang   ....
     e. helio   5. laugh   ....
     f. pend   6. draw   ....
     g. astra   7. move about; both   ....

KEY NO. 118

O—x

VOC · VOK

voice
call

is the Root *VOC, VOK* which comes from the Latin *vox, vocis* meaning VOICE, and *vocare* meaning to CALL. From VOICE we get words relating to human sounds. From CALL we get Nos. 14, 15, 16, 17, 18, 19, and 20. All are from the same key.

1. vocable   VOC able (voe' ka b'l) n.
     A human sound; a word.

2. vocal   VOC al (voe' kal) adj.
     Relating to the voice; oral.

3. vocalic   VOC alic (voe kal' ik) adj.
     Rich in vowel sounds; as, Gaelic is very vocalic.

4. vocalion   VOC alion (voe kay' li on) n.
     A musical instrument with organ-like tones.

5. vocabulary   VOC abulary (voe kab' yu lar ee) n.
     A collection of words and phrases.

6. vocabulist   VOC abulist (voe kab' u list) n.
     A maker of vocabularies; a lexicographer.

7. vocalize   VOC alize (voe' ka lize) v.
     To sing; to give utterance.

8. vocation   VOC ation (voe kay' shun) n.
     A call to serve in a particular profession.

9. vocational   VOC ational (voe kay' shun al) adj.
     Relating to a vocation: as, vocational *guidance.*

10. sotto voce   sotto VOC e (sot o voe' chee) adv.
     In an undertone; an aside.

11. vociferant   VOC iferant (voe' sif' e rant) adj.
     Noisy; loud.

12. vociferous   VOC iferous (voe sif' e rus) adj.
     Clamorous; making an outcry.

13. vociferously   VOC iferously (voe sif' e rus lee) adv.
     Noisily; as, he argued vociferously.

14. avocation   a VOC ation (av o kay' shun) n.
     A second calling; a hobby.

15. convocation   con VOC ation (kon vo kay' shun) n.
     A calling together; an assembly.

16. invocation   in VOC ation (in vo kay' shun) n.
     Solemn prayer; divine blessing.

17. invoke   in VOK e (in voke') v.
     To plead; to supplicate.

18. evoke   e VOK e (e voke') v.
               Call out from the past; as, evoke *a memory.*
19. evocative   e VOC ative (e vok' at iv) adj.
               Causing to recall the past.
20. provoke   pro VOK e (pro voke') v.
               To call forth anger; as, provoke *his wrath.*

word analysis

VOCIFEROUSLY—No. 13
     VOC (vocis)—Latin Root =voice
     FER (ferre)—Latin Root =to bear; carry
     OUS—Suffix =having; full of
     LY—adv. Suffix =in the manner of

practical exercises

1. Supply the missing words:
     The play ....(d) a time long gone. Electra had
     ample .... for anger and she ....(d)
     the curses of the gods.

2. Analyze No. 17.

3. Choose the number of the word which most nearly expresses
the italicized word:
     a. *provoke*   (1) examine   (2) ridicule   (3) dismiss
         (4) invent   (5) exasperate   ....
     b. *ignorance*   (1) knowledge   (2) study
         (3) license   (4) lack of knowledge
         (5) ambiguity   ....
     c. *ambition*   (1) wish to please   (2) ambience
         (3) satisfaction   (4) invocation   (5) aspiration   ....
     d. *ambiguous*   (1) doubletalk   (2) vocal
         (3) plain talk   (4) creditable   (5) dismissed   ....
     e. *heliosis*   (1) nightmare   (2) heresy
         (3) imprisonment   (4) sunburn   (5) graft   ....

KEY NO. 119

O—➤

CAP · CEP · CEPT

**take
receive**

is the Root *CAP, CEP, CEPT* which means TAKE, RECEIVE. It comes from the Latin *capere, cepi, ceptus.* Do not confuse this *CAP* with the Root which means *head.* You must be careful now when you see the key *CAP* that you know exactly which is which. You will have no problem with *CEP* or *CEPT.*

1. capable   CAP able (kay' pa b'l) adj.
                 Able to receive knowledge; clever.

2. capias   CAP ias (kay' pee as) n.
                 A writ for arrest.

3. capstan   CAP stan (kap' stan) n.
                 An apparatus used on shipboard for moving heavy weights.

4. capsule   CAP sule (kap' sul) n.
                 A tiny case for holding medication; a pill.

5. caption   CAP tion (kap' shun) n.
                 A heading; a subtitle.

6. captation   CAP tation (kap tay' shun) n.
                 Effort to get something by flattery.

7. captious   CAP tious (kap' shus) adj.
                 Calculated to entrap; as, by captious questions.

8. captive   CAP tive (kap' tiv) n.
                 One who has been seized and enslaved.

9. captor   CAP tor (kap' tor) n.
                 One who seizes and enslaves.

10. capture   CAP ture (kap' chur) v.
                 To get possession of; as, to capture a criminal.

11. captivate   CAP tivate (kap' ti vate) v.
                 To seize; as, captivate someone with charm.

12. accept   ac CEPT (ak sept') v.
                 To receive; to agree to.

13. deception   de CEP tion (de sep' shun) n.
                 A taking by fraud; deceit.

14. exception   ex CEP tion (ek sep' shun) n.
                 Something left out of general use; as, an exception to the rule.

15. intercept   inter CEPT (int er sept') v.
                 To take aside before arrival; to hinder.

16. conception   con CEP tion (kon sep' shun) n.
                 The process of forming ideas.

238

17. receptacle   re CEPT acle (re sep' ta k'l) n.
                      That which receives and holds; a small container.

18. susceptible   sus CEPT ible (sus sep' ti b'l) adj.
                      Impressionable; as, susceptible *to beauty.*

19. perceptive   per CEPT ive (per sep' tiv) adj.
                      Having the faculty of perception; discerning.

20. precept   pre CEPT (pree' sept) n.
                      A maxim; a principle by which one lives.

word analysis

SUSCEPTIBLE—No. 18
    SUS (sub)—Latin Prefix =under
    CEPT (capere)—Latin Root =take
    IBLE—Suffix =can do

practical exercise

Read the following excerpt underlining all those words that contain keys you have already learned.

The ancient Greeks believed that Helios, the first Sungod, drove his sun-chariot across the sky every morning and returned in a golden boat every evening. In the 16th century people laughed at this myth. They believed that the sun moved around the earth without the help of Helios.

When Galileo told them that the earth moved around the sun he provoked a storm of ridicule. He was dismissed from his professorship at the University of Pisa. He went to Padua, and then to Florence. There he was accused by the dread Inquisition for daring to have an opinion which differed from that of the Church, and he was condemned to death.

In order to save his life, Galileo, humiliated and heartbroken, publicly admitted his sin. "I confess that my error was one of ambition and ignorance. I declare and swear that the earth does not move around the sun."

Under his breath he muttered, "And yet it moves."

Galileo could not keep his great mind hidden from the world. His advanced ideas brought him imprisonment. There he wrote his book, *The Laws of Motion.* Friends smuggled it out and had it printed. Too blind to read, he held it in his arms on his deathbed. It was his legacy to modern science.

KEY NO. _120_

GRAPH

write

is the Root _GRAPH,_ meaning to WRITE. It comes from the Greek _graphein._ The list of words here used is truly a monument to man's skill and ingenuity—even genius! Aloys Senefelder invented lithoGRAPHy about 1796. Samuel Johnson, the first English lexicographer, presented his great work, the _Dictionary,_ in 1775. Since then there have been many inventions and new words have been invented to name them. The key is all.

1. graph   GRAPH (graf) n.
                Something written; a diagram; a chart.

2. graphite   GRAPH ite (graf' ite) n.
                A soft, black carbon used for pencils.

3. graphology   GRAPH ology (gra fol' o jee) n.
                A study of handwriting to determine character.

4. graphomania   GRAPH omania (graf o may' ni a) n.
                A morbid mania for writing.

5. graphomotor   GRAPH omotor (graf o moe' ter) adj.
                Relating to movements used in writing.

6. graphometer   GRAPH ometer (graf om' e ter) n.
                An instrument used for measuring angles.

7. calligraphy   calli GRAPH y (ka lig' ra fee) n.
                Elegant handwriting.

8. holograph   holo GRAPH (hol' o graf) n.
                A document written wholly by the person who signs it.

9. homograph   homo GRAPH (hom' o graf) n.
                Two words spelled the same but with different meanings; as, fair: a market and fair: beautiful.

10. hydrography   hydro GRAPH y (hie drog' ra fee) n.
                A study of the world's water surfaces.

11. lexicographer   lexico GRAPH er (lek si kog' ra fer) n.
                One who writes a dictionary.

12. lithography   litho GRAPH y (lith og' ra fee) n.
                Process of reproducing writing; as, from designs on stone.

13. mimeograph   mimeo GRAPH (mim' ee o graf) n.
                An apparatus for making copies of written material.

14. orthography   ortho GRAPH y (or thog' ra fee) n.
                Writing with correct penmanship and spelling.

15. phonograph phono GRAPH (foe' no graf) n.
An instrument for reproducing recorded sound.
16. photograph photo GRAPH (fote' o graf) n.
A picture taken by the process of photography.
17. radiograph radio GRAPH (rade' ee o graf) n.
An image produced by action of X-rays.
18. monograph mono GRAPH (mon' o graf) n.
An article written on a single subject.
19. geography geo GRAPH y (jee og' ra fee) n.
A study of the earth and its people.
20. telegraphy tele GRAPH y (te leg' ra fee) n.
Communication by signals from afar.

word analysis

LEXICOGRAPHER—No. 11
  LEXICO (lexicon)—Latin Greek Root =word book
  GRAPH (graphein)—Greek Root =to write
  ER—Suffix =one who

practical exercises

1. Supply the missing words:
   The universal use of the typewriter has robbed ....
   of its importance and, in general, ... has suffered. Rarely is a .... seen, and the signature
   of the writer is the only personal touch.

2. Analyze No. 9.

3. Syllabicate and indicate which syllable is most greatly stressed
   by placing the accent mark ('):

   calligraphy   graphomania   lexicographer
   monograph   telegraphy   homograph
   inquisition   ridicule   populace
                      orthography

241

KEY NO. *121*

0—🗝

CISE

cut

CIDE

kill

is a double key. Here you will meet the Root *CISE* which means CUT and comes from the Latin *caedere, caesus*. The first eight words on the list are derived from this root. The next group of words are constructed with the Suffix *CIDE* which means to KILL. It developed from the Latin word meaning CUT, and thus both forms are treated together.

1. incise   in CISE (in size') v.
   Cut into; as, incise *an abscess or infection.*
2. concise   con CISE (kon sise') adj.
   Cut short; all non-essentials cut off.
3. circumcise   circum CISE (sir' kum size) v.
   To cut around.
4. caesura   CAES ura (se zhur' a) n.
   A cut or break in line of verse.
5. decide   de CIDE (de side') v.
   To cut off uncertainty; reach a decision.
6. decisive   de CIS ive (de sie' siv) adj.
   Causing one to reach a decision.
7. excision   ex CIS ion (ek sizh' un) n.
   The cutting out; removing of.
8. precise   pre CISE (pre sise') adj.
   Cut exactly right; cut with precision.
9. microbicide   microbi CIDE (mi kroe' bi side) n.
   An agent which kills microbes.
10. autocide   auto CIDE (au' to side) n.
    The killing of self and others in an automotive vehicle.
11. fratricide   fratri CIDE (fra' tri side) n.
    The killing of one's brother.
12. homicide   homi CIDE (hom' i side) n.
    The killing of a human being.
13. genocide   geno CIDE (jen' o side) n.
    The killing of a race of people.
14. infanticide   infanti CIDE (in fant' i side) n.
    The killing of one's infant.
15. patricide   patri CIDE (pa' tri side) n.
    The killing of one's father.
16. suicide   sui CIDE (sue' i side) n.
    The killing of oneself.

17. matricide   matri CIDE (ma' tri side) n.
  The killing of one's mother.

word analysis

EXCISION—No. 7
  EX—Prefix =out; from
  CIS (caesus)—Latin Root =cut
  SION—Suffix =act of

practical exercises

1. Supply the missing words:
  The most .... work is done with ....
  instruments. As soon as the .... of the abscess
  was completed, the patient felt .... better.

2. Analyze No. 5.

3. Key review. Match keys with their meanings:

a. sta	1. take	....
b. pre	2. cut	....
c. mot	3. write	....
d. graph	4. all	....
e. omni	5. people	....
f. vox	6. movement	....
g. cide	7. before	....
h. populi	8. voice	....
i. cept	9. stand	....

KEY NO. 122

O—⚷

TEST

to bear witness

is the Root *TEST* (Latin, *testari*) meaning, to BEAR WITNESS. Do not confuse this root *TEST* with the word which means examination. It is true that when you take an examination you are a witness for your own knowledge and, unless you cheat, you are showing what you do or don't know. However, here the word means a solemn telling of the truth of what you know, bearing witness for truth's sake. Also notice the word con*TEST* (No. 17): the accent is on the *TEST*. Con*TEST* is merely a competition.

1. testate   TEST ate (tes' tate) adj.
                Leaving a valid will which has been witnessed.
2. testament   TEST ament (tes' ta ment) n.
                A will; an agreement of faith.
3. testamur   TEST amur (tes tay' mur) n.
                A certificate attesting to proficiency; as, a diploma.
4. testate   TEST ate (tes' tate) v.
                To make a will.
5. intestate   in TEST ate (in tes' tate) adj.
                Not leaving a will; as, dying intestate.
6. testation   TEST ation (tes tay' shun) n.
                The act of making a will.
7. testator   TEST ator (tes' tate or) n.
                One who bequeaths his property by a will.
8. testatrix   TEST atrix (te' stay triks) n.
                A female testator.
9. testatory   TEST atory (tes' ta to ri) adj.
                Of the nature of testimony.
10. testimony   TEST imony (tes' ti moe nee) n.
                A solemn declaration.
11. testification TEST ification (tes ti fi kay' shun) n.
                The act of bearing witness.
12. testify   TEST ify (tes' ti fie) v.
                To bear witness; as, testify *in a case.*
13. testimonial TEST imonial (tes ti moe' nee al) n.
                Evidence; testimony.
14. detest   de TEST (de test') v.
                To loathe; to abhor; as, we detest *evil.*

244

15. attest   at TEST (a test') v.
           Certify; affirm; bear witness to.
16. attestant   at TEST ant (at tes' tant) n.
           One who bears witness to; affirms.
17. contest   con TEST (kon test') v.
           Argue against; as, they are going to contest *the will.*
18. contestable   con TEST able (kon test' a b'l) adj.
           Can be argued against; challengeable.
19. protest   pro TEST (pro test') v.
           Bear witness against; as, protest *the verdict.*
20. testamentary TEST amentary (tes ta ment' a ree) adj.
           Relating to a will; as, testamentary *letters.*

word analysis

ATTESTANT—No. 16
    AT (ad)—Prefix =to
    TEST (testari)—Latin Root =to bear witness
    ANT—Suffix =one who

practical exercises

1. Supply the missing words:
     The will was bitterly ....(ed). In sworn .... the records of the forgery were disclosed and the witness ....(ed) to the validity of the dead man's last will and ....

2. Analyze No. 12.

3. To the following key Roots add the compound Prefix IN+AD, IN+AC, IN+AP, IN+AT and the compound Suffix IBLE+LY, IVE+LY, ENT+LY or AL+LY, whichever is best.
    Example: *IN AD* miss *IBLE LY*   ....inadmissibly....
    a. ....vis.......... ....
    b. ....cess.......... ....
    c. ....proach.......... ....
    d. ....vert.......... ....
    e. ....tent.......... ....

KEY NO. *123*

○──➤

TEND · TENS TENT

stretch strain

is the Root *TEND, TENS, TENT* which comes from the Latin meaning STRETCH; STRAIN. The Latin Root has three spellings—*tendo, tensus, tentus.* Therefore the English words based on this Root have the three spellings. A very pleasant word for us today is No. 20 on the list. Every relaxation of strained relations in the world gives us a hope for final peace.

1. intend
: in TEND' (in tend') v.
To plan; aim to do; as, I intend *to succeed.*

2. intendance
: in TEND ance (in ten' dans) n.
Control; management; superintendence.

3. intendancy
: in TEND ancy (in ten' dan si) n.
The office of a manager.

4. intention
: in TENT ion (in ten' chun) n.
Purpose; as, the intention *is honorable.*

5. intently
: in TENT ly (in tent' ly) adv.
With concentration; as, listening intently.

6. intendment
: in TEND ment (in tend' ment) n.
The true meaning; insight; as, the intendment *of the law.*

7. tense
: TENS e (tens) adj.
Strained; nervous.

8. tension
: TENS ion (ten' chun) n.
Strain; nervousness.

9. intensity
: in TENS ity (in ten' sit ee) n.
Quality of strain.

10. intensify
: in TENS ify (in ten' si fie) v.
Make more intense; strengthen.

11. intensifier
: in TENS ifier (in ten' si fie er) n.
One who intensifies.

12. intensification
: in TENS ification (in ten si fi kay' shun) n.
The state of increased tension.

13. intent
: in TENT (in tent') adj.
Absorbed; earnest; as, intent *on the problem.*

14. intensive
: in TENS ive (in ten' siv) adj.
Emphasizing; as, the intensive *pronoun himself.*

246

15. attention   at TENT ion (a ten' chun) n.
                              Concentration upon; as, pay attention to the speaker.

16. inattention   inat TENT ion (in a ten' chun) n.
                              Lack of attention.

17. unintentionally unin TENT ionally (un in tench' un al ee) adv.
                              Without meaning to; as, unintentionally rude.

18. distend   dis TEND (dis tend') v.
                              Stretch out.

19. detention   de TENT ion (de ten' chun) n.
                              The holding back; as, detention in jail.

20. detente   de TENT e (day tant') n.
                              Relaxation of strained relations.

word analysis

DETENTION—No. 19
    DE—Prefix =from; away
    TENT (tentus)—Latin Root =strain
    TION—Suffix =act of; state of

practical exercises

1. Supply the missing words:
    Her name was .... omitted from the guest list. She was furious and paid no heed to our .... efforts at conciliation.

2. Analyze No. 18.

3. Choose the number of the word which best expresses the italicized word:
    a. *detente* (1) relaxation of tension among nations
             (2) tension (3) cooperation (4) understanding
             (5) pity   ....
    b. *vigilant* (1) asleep (2) dreamy
             (3) unconcerned (4) watchful
             (5) not pressed   ....
    c. *resounding* (1) extremely loud (2) noisy
             (3) echoing (4) singing (5) thundering ....
    d. *extenuate* (1) clash (2) delay (3) pardon
             (4) decide (5) forget   ....
    e. *purchase* (1) sell (2) borrow (3) extenuate
             (4) buy (5) give away   ....

KEY NO. *124*

○━┱

SUB

**under
beneath**

is the Prefix *SUB* which means UN-DER, BENEATH. This is a very use-ful key, with history both ancient and modern right down to our own SUB-way. Please note the difference in accent of No. 7 and No. 8. They are the same word, but one is a noun the other a verb. Notice also the change in spelling of Nos. 9 and 10. The Latin verb *mergere*, to plunge, be-comes *mersus* in the past participle. *SUB*urban comes from *urbs*, city. In ancient Rome the city was built on the hill for a position of safety. Out-lying districts were below.

1. subaltern   SUB altern (su bal' tern) n.
     Under another; inferior in rank.
2. subcutaneous SUB cutaneous (sub kyu tay' nee us) adj.
     Under the skin.
3. subdivide   SUB divide (sub di vide') v.
     To cut up into small lots.
4. subdue   SUB due (sub dyue') v.
     To overcome; vanquish.
5. subconscious SUB conscious (sub kon' chus) adj.
     Under the conscious level of the mind.
6. subfluvial   SUB fluvial (sub flue' vi al) adj.
     Placed under a river; as, a tunnel.
7. subject   SUB ject (sub ject') v.
     To place under control of another.
8. subject   SUB ject (sub' ject) n.
     A topic to write about; the underling of a king.
9. submerge   SUB merge (sub merj') v.
     To plunge under; as, submerge under a wave.
10. submersion   SUB mersion (sub mer' zhun) n.
     The act of placing completely under water.
11. submission   SUB mission (sub mish' un) n.
     The act of putting oneself under the control of another.
12. subpoena   SUB poena (su pee' na) n.
     A writ placing one under threat of punishment unless one appears in court.
13. subscribe   SUB scribe (sub skribe') v.
     To underwrite; sign one's name under a contract; as, to subscribe to a magazine.

14. subsidize   SUB sidize (sub' si dize) v.
                    To aid with public funds; as, subsidize *a national theater.*

15. substantiate   SUB stantiate (sub stan' chee ate) v.
                    To make firm with support; as, substantiate *the man's claims.*

16. subterfuge   SUB ter fuge (sub' ter fyuje) n.
                    Deception; as, he escaped by a subterfuge.

17. substitute   SUB stitute (sub sti tute') n.
                    Someone who takes the place of another; as, a substitute *teacher.*

18. subterraneous   SUB terraneous (sub te ray' nee us) adj.
                    Under ground; as, a subterraneous *passage.*

19. subversive   SUB versive (sub ver' siv) adj.
                    Tending to undermine the government.

word analysis

SUBMERSION—No. 10
    SUB—Prefix =under
    MERS (mergere, mersus)—Latin Root =dip; plunge
    SION—Suffix =result of

practical exercises

1. Supply the missing words:
    "In all .... and humility York does present himself to your Highness." (Shakespeare) The political party was accused of being .... and the leader was given a .... to appear in court.

2. Analyze No. 11.

3. Add keys to complete the words:
    a. under the skin— ....cutane..........
    b. plunge under— ....merge
    c. put oneself under— ....ject
    d. under punishment by court order— ....poena
    e. take the place of another— sub..........ute
    f. tending to undermine the government— ....versive

KEY NO. 125

SCRIB · SCRIP

write

is the Root *SCRIB, SCRIP* which comes from the Latin *scribere, scriptus,* which means to WRITE. Here again there are two spellings, because the Latin verb has two spellings. In ancient days before printing had been invented the error in a manuscript was *SCRIB*al, now we call it a misprint and blame the printer. Word No. 17 needs a bit of explanation. Formerly, workers were not always paid in cash but in certificates or bonds. That was called paying with scrip.

1. scribable   SCRIB able (skribe' a b'l) adj.
   Can be written upon; can receive the markings of a stylus or pen.
2. scribacious   SCRIB acious (skrie bay' shus) adj.
   Addicted to writing; fond of writing.
3. scribble   SCRIB ble (skri' b'l) n.
   Meaningless marks on paper.
4. subscription   sub SCRIP tion (sub skrip' shun) n.
   A purchase order; sign one's name for acceptance.
5. scribblemania   SCRIB blemania (skrib' el may' ni a) n.
   A mania for making meaningless marks on paper.
6. ascribe   a SCRIB e (a skribe') v.
   To refer to; attribute; as, ascribe *success to hard work.*
7. circumscribe   circum SCRIB e (cir kum skribe') v.
   To draw a line around; set limits to.
8. conscript   con SCRIP t (kon skript') v.
   To enroll into military service; to draft.
9. conscript   con SCRIP t (kon' skript) n.
   One drafted into military service.
10. description   de SCRIP tion (de skrip' shun) n.
    A representation in words of something seen.
11. inscription   in SCRIP tion (in skrip' shun) n.
    Words engraved on a stone or monument.
12. scrivener   SCRIV ener (skriv' e ner) n.
    A public writer; a scribe.
13. superscription   super SCRIP tion (su per skrip' shun) n.
    Writing above an inscription.

14. prescription   pre SCRIP tion (pre skrip' shun) n.
Written directions from a doctor for prepara-
tion of a medicine by a druggist.

15. script   SCRIP t (skript) n.
Written characters; also short for manuscript,
used in the theater.

16. scribe   SCRIBE (skribe) n.
A public writer acting as a clerk.

17. scrip   SCRIP (skrip) n.
A list; paper money; a means.

18. Scripture   SCRIP ture (skrip' chur) n.
Any sacred writings; especially, the Bible.

19. transcript   tran SCRIP t (trans' kript) n.
A copy of something in writing, typing, or
printing.

word analysis

SUBSCRIPTION—No. 4
    SUB—Prefix =under
    SCRIP (scriptus)—Latin Root =to write
    TION—Suffix =act of

practical exercise

Read the following excerpt underlining all those words that contain keys you have already learned.

    Three millions of people, armed in the holy cause of liberty, and in such a country as that which we possess, are invincible by any force which our enemy can send against us. Besides, sir, we shall not fight our battles alone. There is a just God who presides over the destinies of nations; and who will raise up friends to fight our battles for us. The battle, sir, is not to the strong alone; it is to the vigilant, the active, the brave. Besides, sir, we have no election. If we, the brave, were base enough to desire it, it is now too late to retire from the contest. There is no retreat but in submission and slavery! Our chains are forged, their clanking may be heard on the plains of Boston. The war is inevitable—and let it come! I repeat it, sir, let it come!

        (From Patrick Henry's speech, March 23, 1775.)

KEY NO. 126

O—x

POST

**after
behind
following**

is the Prefix *POST* which means AFTER, BEHIND. There is another word *post* which has to do with mailing, postage, and Post Office. But that word is not this key. The key *POST* means AFTER, BEHIND, or FOLLOWING. When you meet a word with *POST* just take a second to see whether the sentence has anything to do with mailing. If it has you need go no further—it is not our key. One thing that always means our key, *POST*, AFTER, is P.M., *POST* meridian, *afternoon.*

1. postern   POST ern (pose' tern) adj.
   Situated at the back, rear; as, the postern gate.
2. posterity   POST erity (po ster' it ee) n.
   Those who come after; descendants.
3. postfix   POST fix (post fiks') v.
   To add to end of syllable or word; affix.
4. postgeniture   POST geniture (post jen' i tur) n.
   The state of being born after another.
5. postgraduate   POST graduate (post graj' u at) adj.
   Relating to studies after graduation.
6. posthumous   POST humous (pos' chu mus) adj.
   After death; often said of writings published after the author's death.
7. posterior   POST erior (po ster' ee or) adj.
   Later in time; coming after.
8. postlude   POST lude (post' lude) n.
   The closing piece on the program.
9. postmarital   POST marital (post mar' i tal) adj.
   Relating to after the marriage.
10. Post meridian   POST meridian (post me rid' ee an) adj.
    After the sun has passed the meridian; P.M.
11. postmortal   POST mortal (post mor' tal) adj.
    Relating to after death.
12. postmortem   POST mortem (post mort' em) adj.
    After death; as, a postmortem examination.
13. postmutative   POST mutative (post mue' ta tiv) adj.
    Causing changes by the use of suffixes.
14. postnatal   POST natal (post nate' al) adj.
    Referring to the period immediately after birth.

252

15. post-obit   POST- obit (poe stoe′ bit) adj.
Happening after death; as, a post-obit gift.

16. postorbital   POST orbital (poe stor′ bit al) adj.
Situated behind the socket of the eye.

17. postpone   POST pone (post pone′) v.
Delay; set the date back.

18. postponement POST ponement (post pone′ ment) n.
A delay; holding back until a later date.

19. postprandial   POST prandial (post pran′ dee al) adj.
After the feast; after the meal.

20. postscript   POST script (post′ skript) n.
A note added to a letter after it has been signed.

word analysis

POSTPONEMENT—No. 18
    POST—Prefix =after
    PONE (ponere)—Latin Root =place; set
    MENT—Suffix =state of

practical exercises

1. Supply the missing words:
    Most of the author's works were published ....
and he achieved .... fame. The prelude and
interlude were lovely but the .... was the best.

2. Analyze No. 14.

3. Add a key to complete the word which expresses the idea:
    a. fame after death— ....humous fame
    b. addition to the end of a letter— ....script
    c. one who continues to study after graduation— ....graduate
    d. death to insects— insecti.........
    e. the underwriting of the cost of a magazine— ....scrip.........

KEY NO. 127

O—⚡

MON · MONO

one

is a Prefix *MON, MONO* which means ONE. It comes from the Greek *monos* which means ALONE. *MON, MONO* opens the door on marital customs of ancient days, when polygamy was the custom, permitting both many wives and many husbands. Civilization has complicated many things, but it has certainly simplified life by doing away with polygamy and polyandry. One spouse is about all the average civilized person can manage. Wisely we leave multiples to children.

1. monad
MON ad (moe' nad) n.
A unit; one.

2. monandry
MON andry (mon' an dree) n.
The custom of having only one husband at a time.

3. monogyny
MON ogyny (mo noj' y nee) n.
A society which establishes the law of one wife only.

4. monarch
MON arch (mon' ark) n.
The ruler of an empire.

5. monarchy
MON archy (mon' ar kee) n.
A government which has only one ruler.

6. monastery
MON astery (mon' a ster ee) n.
A religious institution in which monks live.

7. monochord
MONO chord (mon' o kord) n.
An instrument of ancient days that had only one string.

8. monocle
MONO cle (mon' o k'l) n.
An eyeglass for one eye.

9. monody
MON ody (mon' od ee) n.
A funeral lament sung by one voice; a dirge.

10. monogamy
MONO gamy (mo nog' a mee) n.
One marriage, as opposed to bigamy or polygamy.

11. monodrama
MONO drama (mon' o dram a) n.
A play with one actor.

12. monologue
MONO logue (mon' ol og) n.
A discourse by one person; soliloquy.

13. monocycle
MONO cycle (mon' o sie k'l) n.
A velocipede with one wheel; unicycle.

14. monochrome   MONO chrome (mon' o krome) n.
                   A painting of a single color.

15. monocracy   MONO cracy (mo nok' ra see) n.
                   Government by one ruler; an autocracy.

16. monochromatic   MONO chromatic (mon o kroe' mat ik) adj.
                   Of one color only.

17. monotone   MONO tone (mon' o tone) n.
                   One tone of unvaried pitch.

18. monotony   MONO tony (mo not' on ee) n.
                   Sameness; as, a monotonous voice.

19. monodynamic   MONO dynamic (mon o di nam' ik) adj.
                   Having one power or talent.

20. monoblepsia   MONO blepsia (mon o blep' si a) n.
                   A condition in which vision is normal only when one eye is used.

word analysis

MONOCHROMATIC—No. 16
     MONO (monos)—Prefix =one
     CHROMAT (chromos)—Greek Root =color
     IC—Suffix =like

practical exercises

1. Supply the missing words:
     Krapp's Last Tape was a splendid ...., being a one-character play. The opposite of .... is bigamy and .... is the opposite of polyandry.

2. Analyze No. 7.

3. Use one word for the phrase:
     a. a drama with one actor   ....
     b. a recitation by one person   ....
     c. a funeral dirge sung by one voice   ....
     d. a velocipede with one wheel   ....
     e. a government with one ruler   ....
     f. an ancient instrument with one string   ....

KEY NO. 128

O—⚷

MAL

bad
evil

is a Prefix *MAL* meaning BAD; EVIL. I'm sure that the opposite comes to your mind immediately—*BENE*. If you refer to the list for that KEY you will find that many of the words are just the same except that *MAL* is used instead of *BENE*. How long will it take you to learn the key, *MAL*? One instant? Good. One key learned makes 20 words earned. Remember Mrs. MALaprop? *MAL* is the key to her MALfortune. Remember your keys and you'll never be a Mr. or Mrs. MALaprop. The key is all.

1. maladroit   MAL adroit (mal a droit') adj.
   Clumsy; awkward; inept.
2. malady   MAL ady (mal' ad ee) n.
   Sickness; disease.
3. malapert   MAL apert (mal a pert') adj.
   Ill-bred; impudent.
4. malapropos   MAL apropos (mal ap ro poe') adj.
   Inappropriate; not fitting.
5. malapropism MAL apropism (mal' a prop iz um) n.
   Humorous misuse of words.
6. malaria   MAL aria (ma lar' ee a) n.
   A disease carried by a mosquito.
7. malcontent   MAL content (mal' kon tent) adj.
   Rebellious; discontented; bad tempered.
8. malediction   MAL ediction (mal e dik' shun) n.
   Slander; curse.
9. malefaction   MAL efaction (mal e fak' shun) n.
   An evil deed.
10. malefactor   MAL efactor (mal' e fak tor) n.
    One who commits an evil deed; evildoer.
11. malevolent   MAL evolent (ma lev' o lent) adj.
    Wishing evil to others.
12. malevolence   MAL evolence (ma lev' o lens) n.
    The state of wishing evil to others; ill will; viciousness.
13. malfeasance   MAL feasance (mal feze' ans) n.
    Evil conduct; especially by a public official.
14. maltreated   MAL treated (mal trete' ed) adj.
    Badly treated; abused.

256

15. malice   MAL ice (mal' is) n.
             Ill-will; as, "with malice toward none."
16. malicious   MAL icious (ma lish' us) adj.
             Full of ill-will.
17. malpractice MAL practice (mal prak' tis) n.
             Professional misconduct.
18. malignant   MAL ignant (ma lig' nant) adj.
             Injurious; extremely evil; tending to produce death.
19. malign   MAL ign (mal ine') v.
             To utter slander of; to defame, unjustly.
20. maliferous   MAL iferous (ma lif' er us) adj.
             Disease bringing; productive of evil.

word analysis

MALEVOLENCE—No. 12
    MAL—Prefix =evil
    VOL (volere)—Latin Root =to wish
    ENCE—Suffix =act of

practical exercises

1. Supply the missing words:
    The doctor was sued for .... She was afraid
    that her .... was .... On board
    ship they suffered constantly from ....

2. Analyze No. 1.

3. Choose the number of the word which best expresses the italicized word:
   a. *malignant*   (1) beautiful   (2) growing
        (3) inventive   (4) monotonous   (5) cancerous   ....
   b. *humidity*   (1) vivacity   (2) malice   (3) gravity
        (4) dampness   (5) solidity   ....
   c. *submerge*   (1) postpone   (2) plunge under water
        (3) subscribe   (4) induce   (5) prevail   ....
   d. *transcript*   (1) copy of a record   (2) suburb
        (3) mission   (4) superman   (5) rigidity   ....
   e. *distended*   (1) broken   (2) torn   (3) stretched
        (4) snapped   (5) scribbled.   ....

KEY NO. *129* is the Root *GRAV, GRAVI, GRAV-ITO*, meaning HEAVY, WEIGHTY. It comes from the Latin *gravis* which means HEAVY. It is also necessary to avoid confusion with words that are based on the Root *GRAVEL* meaning PEBBLY GROUND. You will have a weighty decision to make when you encounter words with *GRAV* in them; your dictionary will help you!

O━➤

GRAV · GRAVI
GRAVITO

heavy
weighty

1. grave   GRAV e (grave) adj.
               Serious; weighty.

2. aggravate   ag GRAV ate (ag' ra vate) v.
               To make heavier; increase.

3. gravidate   GRAV idate (grav' i date) v.
               To make heavy; impregnate.

4. gravimeter GRAV imeter (gra vim' et er) n.
               An instrument to measure the weight of liquids.

5. gravely   GRAV ely (grave' ly) adv.
               Seriously; heavily.

6. graveolent GRAV eolent (gra vee' o lent) adj.
               Smelly; unpleasant.

7. gravid   GRAV id (grav' id) adj.
               Heavy with child; pregnant.

8. gravific   GRAV ific (gra vif' ik) adj.
               Weight-producing.

9. gravitationally GRAVI tationally (grav it a' shun al ee) adv.
               In the manner of gravitating.

10. gravimetry GRAV imetry (gra vim' e tree) n.
               The measurement of weight and density.

11. gravimetric GRAV imetric (grav i me' trik) adj.
               Relating to measurements by weight.

12. gravitate   GRAV itate (grav' i tate) v.
               To obey the law of gravitational attraction.

13. gravitation GRAV itation (grav i tay' shun) n.
               Tendency to be drawn to something on a lower level.

14. gravity   GRAV ity (grav' it ee) n.
               Weight; seriousness.

15. gravitative GRAV itative (grav' i tate iv) adj.
               Tending to gravitate.

258

16. gravitational   **GRAV** itational (grav i tay′ shun al) adj.
           Relating to the tendency of bodies to fall to
           the earth.

17. gravic   **GRAV** ic (grav′ ik) adj.
           Relating to gravitation.

18. gravitater   **GRAV** itater (grav′ i tate er) **n.**
           That which gravitates.

word analysis

GRAVITATION—No. 13
    GRAVITA (gravitas)—Latin Root =weight; heaviness
    TION—Suffix =state of

practical exercise

Read the following excerpt underlining all those words that contain keys you have already learned.

    Some people's idea of free speech is that they are free to say what they like but if anyone says anything back that is an outrage. . . . This house is not only a machine for legislation . . . it is a great forum for debate. . . . The House of Commons stands for freedom and law and this is the message which the Mother of Parliaments has proved herself capable of proclaiming to the world at large. . . . It is difficult to explain to those who do not understand our ways. They cannot easily be made to understand why we consider that the intensity, passion, intimacy, informality, and spontaneity of our debates constitute the personality of the House of Commons and endow it at once with its focus and its strength. . . . The object of Parliament is to substitute argument for fisticuffs. . . . The truth is incontrovertible. Panic may resent it; ignorance may deride it; malice may distort it, but there it is . . . I do not consider that prefixing the words, "I am informed . . ." relieves me of all responsibility.

    (Churchill speaks. From *The New York Times,* Aug. 2, 1964.)

KEY NO. 130

O—⚷

OID

like
resembling

is the Suffix *OID* which means LIKE; RESEMBLING. It comes from the Latin *oides*, and Greek *eides*, with the same meanings. It is a very easy key to use. Use *OID* to show resemblance. Anyone can do it. Does anything resemble a key? Then it's KEY-*OID*. If you like that you can even use a compound Suffix and say KEY-*OID-AL*. You can do that to every word on the list. Store up the compound suffixes. They help to strengthen your vocabulary.

1. gynecoid   gynec OID (jin' e koid) adj.
     Resembling a female in function.

2. asteroid   aster OID (as' te roid) adj.
     Like a star.

3. dentoid   dent OID (den' toid) adj.
     Like a tooth.

4. helioid   heli OID (he' li oid) adj.
     Like the sun.

5. hypnotoid   hypnot OID (hip' no toid) adj.
     Resembling hypnotism.

6. geoid   ge OID (jee' oid) n.
     The figure of the earth.

7. geoidal   ge OID al (jee oi' dal) adj.
     Having the quality of the figure of the earth.

8. anthropoid   anthrop OID (an' thro poid) adj.
     Resembling man.

9. lipoid   lip OID (lip' oid) adj.
     Like fat.

10. neuroid   neur OID (nue' roid) adj.
     Resembling a nerve.

11. Negroid   Negr OID (nee' groid) adj.
     Resembling the Negro race in traits.

12. osteoid   oste OID (os' te oid) adj.
     Resembling bone.

13. ostreoid   ostre OID (os' tree oid) adj.
     Oysterlike.

14. spheroid   spher OID (sfer' oid) adj.
     Like a sphere.

15. thyroid   thyr OID (thire' oid) n.
     A large gland below the pharynx in the neck, shaped like a shield.

16. typhoid	typh OID (tie' foid) n.
	A disease resembling typhus.
17. cycloid	cycl OID (sie' kloid) adj.
	Arranged in circles.
18. fibroid	fibr OID (fie' broid) adj.
	Composed of fibrous tissue.
19. tabloid	tabl OID (tab' loid) n.
	A newspaper with a small format.

word analysis

CONICOIDAL
    CON (cone)—Greek Root =cone
    IC—Suffix =like
    OID (oides)—Latin Suffix =resembling
    AL—Suffix =relating to

practical exercises

1. Supply the missing words:

    The small-sized newspapers which have adopted a picture-frame format are called ....(s). When the doctors saw a disease resembling typhus they called it ....

2. Analyze No. 4.

3. Key review. Match keys with their meanings:

a. tend	1. witness	....
b. test	2. one	....
c. sub	3. after	....
d. scrib	4. heavy	....
e. post	5. under	....
f. pos, pon	6. evil	....
g. mono	7. stretch	....
h. mal	8. resembling	....
i. gravi	9. place	....
j. oid	10. write	....

o—⚷

CREA

create

is the Root *CREA* which comes from the Latin *creare* which means to CREATE. This is one of the most important words in our language or in any language. Our world and we in it, together with all the qualities of heart and mind, depend on the *CREA*tion of scientist as well as artist. One artist, Joseph Haydn (see below), had a wife who did not care for music. She liked to cut up his musical compositions into strips and use them for hair curlers.

1. creant   CREA nt (kree′ ant) adj.
         Creating; having the urge to create.

2. create   CREA te (kree ate′) v.
         Bring into existence; produce; as, create *a song.*

3. creation   CREA tion (kree ay′ shun) n.
         The act of creating.

4. creational   CREA tional (kree ay′ shun al) adj.
         Relating to creation.

5. creationary   CREA tionary (kree ay′ shun ar i) adj.
         Having the nature of creation.

6. creative   CREA tive (kree ate′ iv) adj.
         Having the power to produce; as, creative *ability.*

7. creator   CREA tor (kree ate′ or) n.
         One who creates; maker.

8. creature   CREA ture (kree′ chur) n.
         Anything created; a creation.

9. re-create   re CREA te (re kree ate′) v.
         Bring to existence again; refresh; revive.

10. recreation   re CREA tion (rek ree ay′ shun) n.
         The act of refreshing; renewal by food, exercise, or rest.

11. recreational   re CREA tional (rek ree ay′ shun al) adj.
         Having the nature of refreshing.

12. recreationist   re CREA tionist (rek ree ay′ shun ist) n.
         One seeking recreation.

13. procreate   pro CREA te (pro′ kree ate) v.
         To beget offspring; to generate.

14. procreation   pro CREA tion (pro kree ay′ shun) n.
         The act of begetting; generation.

15. procreant   pro CREA nt (pro' kree ant) adj.
                    Fruitful; productive.
16. procreative   pro CREA tive (pro' kree ate iv) adj.
                    Having the power to procreate.
17. procreatory   pro CREA tory (pro' kree a to ri) adj.
                    Procreative.
18. uncreative   un CREA tive (un kree ay' tiv) adj.
                    Lacking creative power; unimaginative.

word analysis

RECREATIONIST—No. 12
    RE—Prefix =again; back
    CREA (creare)—Latin Root =to create
    TION—Suffix =act of
    IST—Suffix =one who

practical exercises

1. Supply the missing words:
    Joseph Haydn wrote a magnificent Oratorio called "The
    ...." Every normal child is born with a lively,
    .... imagination which, if not thwarted can
    help him to work ....(ly).

2. Analyze No. 18.

3. Use one strong word instead of the phrase:
    a. having an urge to create
    b. those who have been created
    c. make to exist again
    d. one who creates
    e. the begetting of children
    f. unethical procedures in a profession
    g. situated behind the orbit

KEY NO. *132*

0—x

**PHIL · PHILA
PHILO · PHILE**

love

is the Root *PHIL, PHILA, PHILO, PHILE* which means LOVE. It comes from the Greek *philos* which means loving. There are a great many words with this root since there are many things to love. This list gives you a good sampling: man, the arts both creative and practical, self, others, learning, wisdom, even the humble plant which wants nothing more than a tree to climb on. Truly *PHIL* makes the world go round!

1. philadelphy   PHIL adelphy (fil a del′ fi) n.
   Love for all men as brothers.

2. philanderer   PHIL anderer (fi lan′ der er) n.
   A male flirt.

3. philanthropist   PHIL anthropist (fi lan′ thro pist) n.
   A lover of mankind; a generous giver to human welfare.

4. philatelist   PHIL atelist (fi lat′ el ist) n.
   A stamp collector.

5. Philathea   PHILA thea (fi lay′ thee a) n.
   An international organization of Bible classes for women.

6. philematology   PHILE matology (fi lee ma tol′ o ji) n.
   The science of kissing.

7. philharmonic   PHIL harmonic (fil har mon′ ik) adj.
   Relating to an organization concerned with music.

8. philhippic   PHIL hippic (fil hip′ ik) adj.
   Loving horses.

9. philodemic   PHIL odemic (fil o dem′ ic) adj.
   Loving the people.

10. philodendron   PHIL odendron (fil o den′ dron) n.
    A climbing green-leaved plant that is cultivated because of its beautiful leaves.

11. philosophy   PHIL osophy (fi los′ o fee) n.
    Love of wisdom; pursuit of wisdom.

12. philodox   PHILO dox (fil′ o doks) n.
    One who loves the opinions he himself holds.

13. philogeant   PHIL ogeant (fil o jee′ ant) n.
    A lover of all good things.

14. philogynist   PHIL ogynist (fi loj′ i nist) n.
    One who is fond of women.

15. philologist PHIL ologist (fi lol' o jist) n.
           A student, scholar, and lover of languages.
16. philomath PHILO math (fil' o math) n.
           A lover of learning.
17. philomuse PHILO muse (fil' o muze) n.
           A lover of poetry and the arts.
18. philotechnist PHILO technist (fil o tek' nist) n.
           A lover of the practical arts.
19. philotheism PHILO theism (fil' o thee iz um) n.
           Love of God.
20. philter PHIL ter (fil' ter) n.
           A love potion.

word analysis

PHILANTHROPIST—No. 3
    PHIL (philos)—Greek Root =love
    ANTHROPOS—Greek Root =mankind
    IST—Suffix =one who

practical exercises

1. Supply the missing words:
    A .... is the opposite of a ....,
and a misogynist is the opposite of a .... William Penn was imbued with .... when he named his city Philadelphia.

2. Analyze No. 17.

3. Key review. Match keys with their meanings:
    a. mitt, miss   1. law   ....
    b. pop   2. head   ....
    c. lex, leg   3. laugh   ....
    d. helio   4. send   ....
    e. ambi   5. stretch   ....
    f. ridi, risi, ri   6. call   ....
    g. voc, vok, vox   7. people   ....
    h. cap, cep   8. take   ....
    i. caput   9. both   ....
    j. tendo, tent   10. sun   ....

KEY NO. 133

O—⚷

SOPH

wisdom

is the Root *SOPH* which means WIS-DOM. It comes from the Greek *sophos*. The list points up the fact that the SOPH laughs at true wisdom at the very moment when he himself tries to appear wise. The poor SOPH-omore is hard put to it pretending to be wise when he has only just come out of the freshman class. His SO-PHistication sits uneasily on his im-maturity. SOPHocles was the writer of the great Greek tragedies *Antigone, Electra, Oedipus Rex*. SOPHocles lived up to his name.

1. sophic   SOPH ic (sof′ ik) adj.
     Full of wisdom; intellectual.

2. sophical   SOPH ical (sof′ i kal) adj.
     Relating to wisdom.

3. sophiology   SOPH iology (sof i ol′ o ji) n.
     The science of human ideas.

4. sophism   SOPH ism (sof′ iz um) n.
     An argument deceptively reasonable, but hiding a fallacy.

5. sophist   SOPH ist (sof′ ist) n.
     One who reasons falsely.

6. sophistry   SOPH istry (sof′ i stree) n.
     Deceptive reasoning.

7. sophistical   SOPH istical (so fis′ ti k'l) adj.
     In the nature of sophistry; deceptive.

8. sophisticate   SOPH isticate (sof is′ ti kate) v.
     Falsify; to make worldly-wise.

9. sophisticated   SOPH isticated (so fis′ ti kat ed) adj.
     Worldly-wise; artificial.

10. sophistication   SOPH istication (so fis ti kay′ shun) n.
     A state of worldliness; artificiality.

11. unsophisticated   un SOPH isticated
     (un so fis′ ti kate ed) adj.
     Not artificial; not worldly-wise.

12. sophisticator   SOPH isticator (so fis′ ti kay tor) n.
     One who falsifies, sophisticates.

13. unsophisticatedness   un SOPH isticatedness
     (un so fis ti kate′ ed nes) n.
     Naturalness.

14. sophomore   SOPH omore (sof' om or) n.
                                Student in the second year of high school or college.

15. sophomoric   SOPH omoric (sof o more' ik) adj.
                                Like a sophomore; immature.

16. Sophoclean   SOPH oclean (sof' o klee an) adj.
                                Relating to the great Greek playwright called "The wise one."

17. philosopher   philo SOPH er (fi los' o fer) n.
                                One who loves wisdom.

18. philosophism   philo SOPH ism (fi los' o fiz um) n.
                                Sophistry; falsification. ·

19. unsophisticate   un SOPH isticate (un so fis' ti kate) n.
                                A person who is not sophisticated.

word analysis

SOPHISTICATION—No. 10
    SOPH (sophos)—Greek Root =wisdom
    IST—Suffix =one who
    IC—Suffix =like
    TION—Suffix =state of

practical exercises

1. Supply the missing words:
    The specious reasoning of the .... makes wrong seem right and right, wrong. The .... of the .... is nothing but ....

2. Analyze No. 17.

3. Syllabicate and indicate which syllable is most greatly stressed by placing the accent mark ('):

sophomore	sophist	sophiologist
sophistication	philatelist	philodendron
creational	procreatory	anthropoid

KEY NO. 134

O━━┱

HYPO

sub
under
less

is the Prefix *HYPO* which means SUB; UNDER; LESS. It is an amazingly rich key and has access to many doors in many places. You will find that it opens the way to understanding terms of anatomy, zoology, music, medicine, botany, psychiatry, right in this short list. There are many other words which you will wish to find for yourself. You will find keys you know repeated in new words and you will find keys that mean the opposite of keys already learned. Watch pronunciation in HYPOcrite.

1. hypo   HYPO (hie' po) n.
   Short for hypodermic.
2. hypobenthos   HYPO benthos (hie po ben' thos) n.
   Deep sea fauna.
3. hypobulia   HYPO bulia (hie po bue' li a) n.
   Increasing disability to make decisions or to act.
4. hypochondria   HYPO chondria (hie po kon' dree a) n.
   Morbid anxiety about one's health.
5. hypochromia   HYPO chromia (hie po kroe' mi a) n.
   Deficiency in pigmentation.
6. hypochrosis   HYPO chrosis (hie po kroe' sis) n.
   Anemia caused by lack of hemoglobin.
7. hypocotyl   HYPO cotyl (hie' po kot yl) n.
   That part of the plant below the cotyledons; the stem.
8. hypocrisy   HYPO crisy (hip ok' ri see) n.
   Outward show; deceit.
9. hypocrite   HYPO crite (hip' o krit) n.
   One who plays a part to win favor; a dissembler.
10. hypocytosis   HYPO cytosis (hie po sie toe' sis) n.
    Lack of red corpuscles in the blood.
11. hypoderma   HYPO derma (hie po der' ma) n.
    The tissue under the epidermis that strengthens it.
12. hypodermic   HYPO dermic (hie po der' mik) n.
    An injection under the skin.
13. hypodiapason   HYPO diapason (hip o die a pay' zon) n.
    An octave measuring downward.

14. hypoglottis   HYPO glottis (hie po glot' is) n.
                       The under side of the tongue.

15. hypomania   HYPO mania (hie po may' nee a) n.
                       A mild manic excitement.

16. hypoplasia   HYPO plasia (hie po play' zha) n.
                       A condition of arrested development of limb or organ.

17. hypopraxia   HYPO praxia (hie po prak' si a) n.
                       Lack of sufficient activity.

18. hypotaxia   HYPO taxia (hie po tak' si a) n.
                       Loss of control of the will.

19. hypothesis   HYPO thesis (hie poth' e sis) n.
                       Something assumed for the sake of argument.

20. hypothetical   HYPO thetical (hie po thet' i k'l) adj.
                       Assumed for the sake of argument; as, a hypothetical *question.*

word analysis

HYPOTHETICAL—No. 20
     HYPO—Prefix =sub; under; less
     THET (thesis)—Greek Root =subject
     IC—Suffix =like
     AL—Suffix =relating to

practical exercises

1. Supply the missing words:
     "...................... is the homage which vice pays to virtue."
(French—La Rochefoucauld) The ....(c) suffers from imaginary ailments. Hypothetical is the adjective form of ....

2. Analyze No. 15.

3. Choose the number of the word which best expresses the italicized word:
     a. *maladroit*   (1) clever   (2) clumsy   (3) patient
        (4) false   (5) nearby   ....
     b. *sophisticated*   (1) sincere   (2) plodding
        (3) obstinate   (4) artificial   (5) lazy   ....
     c. *hypocrisy*   (1) naivete   (2) falseness
        (3) sincerity   (4) boastfulness   (5) charity   ....
     d. *rigid*   (1) flexible   (2) liquid   (3) stiff
        (4) easily   (5) intolerable   ....

KEY NO. 135

0—➤

SYS · SYL
SYM · SYN

with
together
along with

is the Prefix *SYS, SYL, SYM, SYN*,
all meaning WITH, TOGETHER,
ALONG WITH. *SYL* is used before
the letter *l*; *SYM* is used before the
letter *m*; *SYN* is used before the
letter *n*. It's the old story of assimilation and labials causing the
changes for the sake of euphony. Remember?

1. syllable   SYL lable (sil' a b'l) n.
   One or more letters which together form one sound.

2. monosyllable   mono SYL lable (mon' o syl a b'l) n.
   A word of one syllable, as "no."

3. syllogism   SYL logism (sil' o jiz um) n.
   A formal argument with a major and minor premise and a conclusion.

4. syllogist   SYL logist (sil' o jist) n.
   One skilled in syllogistic reasoning.

5. system   SYS tem (sys' tem) n.
   A planned arrangement of procedures; method.

6. systematic   SYS tematic (sys tem at' ik) adj.
   Arranged methodically according to a system.

7. symbol   SYM bol (sim' bol) n.
   Something that stands as a visible sign of something else; as, a lion is a symbol of courage.

8. symbolize   SYM bolize (sim' bo lize) v.
   To represent by a symbol.

9. symmetry   SYM metry (sim' e tree) n.
   A balanced arrangement in size and form.

10. symmetrical   SYM metrical (si me' tri k'l) adj.
    Arranged in interchangeable parts.

11. sympathy   SYM pathy (sim' pa thee) n.
    Going along with others in feeling; as, sympathy for the homeless.

12. sympathetic   SYM pathetic (sym pa thet' ik) adj.
    Having mutual feelings; as, sympathy for others.

13. symphony   SYM phony (sim' fo nee) n.
    A harmony of sound; musicians playing in harmony.

270

14. synchronize   SYN chronize (sin' kro nize) v.
               To make happen at the same time.
15. syncopation   SYN copation (sin ko pay' shun) n.
               A temporary displacement of the regular accent.
16. syndactyl   SYN dactyl (sin dak' tal) adj.
               Having webbed feet; as, ducks.
17. syndicate   SYN dicate (sin' di kat) n.
               An association of persons for business.
18. syndrome   SYN drome (sin' drome) n.
               Signs and symptoms coming together at the same time.
19. synonym   SYN onym (sin' o nim) n.
               Two words which have practically the same meaning; as, system and method.
20. synthesis   SYN thesis (sin' the sis) n.
               A combination of parts to form a whole.

word analysis

SYMPATHETIC—No. 12
    SYM—Prefix =with
    PATH (pathos)—Greek Root =suffer; feel
    ETIC—Suffix =like

practical exercises

1. Supply the missing words:
    The English language is partly a .... of prefixes, suffixes and roots from the Latin and Greek. It is a great pleasure to listen to the work of a fine .... orchestra.

2. Analyze No. 9.

3. Use one word for each phrase:
    a. to make happen at the same time   ....
    b. a methodical arrangement of doing things   ....
    c. a balanced arrangement in size and form   ....
    d. an unproven idea which is under discussion   ....
    e. a combination of parts to make a whole   ....
    f. the tendency of an object to be drawn to a
       lower level   ....

THE · THEO

god

is the Root *THE; THEO* which comes from *theos* meaning GOD. There has not been room on the list for names like Theodore and Theodora which have the gracious meaning of "gift from God." The only word with a Prefix is No. 19. The *a* is really *ab* which means away; away from.

1. thearchy   THE archy (thee' ar ki) n.
   Government under God.
2. theocracy   THEO cracy (the ok' ra see) n.
   Government directed by priests or clergy representing God.
3. theocentric   THEO centric (thee o sen' trik) adj.
   Assuming God to be the center.
4. theocrat   THEO crat (the' o krat) n.
   One who favors a theocracy.
5. theocratic   THEO cratic (the o krat' ik) adj.
   Relating to a theocracy.
6. theocratically   THEO cratically (the o krat' i ka lee) adv.
   In the manner of a theocracy.
7. theodicy   THE odicy (the od' i see) n.
   A defense of God's justice.
8. theody   THE ody (thee' od i) n.
   A hymn in praise of God.
9. theogamy   THEO gamy (the og' a mi) n.
   The marriage of gods.
10. theolatry   THEO latry (the ol' a tri) n.
    Worship of God.
11. theologaster   THEO logaster (the ol o gas' ter) n.
    A theological quack.
12. theology   THEO logy (the ol' o jee) n.
    The study of the elements of religion.
13. theologist   THEO logist (the ol' o jist) n.
    One versed in the study of religion.
14. theologize   THEO logize (the ol' o jize) v.
    Be occupied with religion.
15. theologian   THEO logian (the o lo' jan) n.
    A theological scholar. Same as No. 13.
16. theomania   THEO mania (the o may' ni a) n.
    A condition in which the patient imagines himself to be God.

272

7. theomancy   THEO mancy (the' o man si) n.
                   Divination by responses of divinely inspired
                   oracles.

8. theomastix   THEO mastix (the o mas' tiks) n.
                   A scourge to mortals designated by the di-
                   vinity.

9. atheist   a THE ist (ay' the ist) n.
                   One who does not believe in the existence of
                   God.

word analysis

THEIST—No. 19
    A—Prefix =away; away from
    THE (theos)—Greek Root =God
    IST—Suffix =one who

practical exercises

Supply the missing words:

    The .... and the .... have no
common ground for .... discussion. The service
concluded with a beautiful .... sung by the
choir.

Analyze No. 1.

Choose the number of the word which best expresses the
italicized word:

a. *calculate* (1) ponder (2) compute (3) refuse
    (4) deny (5) accept   ....

b. *resistance* (1) pleasure (2) expectation
    (3) strong feeling against (4) trial
    (5) patience   ....

c. *suspended* (1) lofty (2) glorious (3) hanging
    (4) certified (5) assured   ....

d. *gravitation* (1) science (2) interest (3) finance
    (4) solidity (5) attraction   ....

e. *speculate* (1) ponder (2) fight (3) admit
    (4) submit (5) remit   ....

f. *entranced* (1) frightened (2) dismissed
    (3) delighted (4) swayed (5) beaten   ....

g. *accumulation* (1) gathering together (2) money
    (3) taxes (4) freedom (5) poetry   ....

273

KEY NO. *137*

O—x

ANA

up
back
again
excessive
too much

is the Prefix *ANA*. It has several important meanings: 1) UP as in No. 4, ANAcatharsis; 2) BACK as in No. 7, ANAchronism; 3) AGAIN as in No. 11, ANAlepsis, be well again; 4) EXCESSIVE, TOO MUCH as in No. 8, ANAcusia, quite deaf.

1. anabasis ANA basis (a nab' a sis) n.
   A journey upward; a military advance.
2. anabiosis ANA biosis (an a bie o' sis) n.
   The state of suspended animation.
3. anabiotic ANA biotic (an a bie ot' ik) adj.
   Relating to anabiosis.
4. anacatharsis ANA catharsis (an a ka thar' sis) n.
   Severe vomiting.
5. anacephalize ANA cephalize (an a sef' a lize) v.
   To review; recapitulate.
6. anachorism ANA chorism (a nak' o riz um) n.
   A thing out of place in terms of geography.
7. anachronism ANA chronism (a nak' ro niz um) n.
   An error in order of time.
8. anacusia ANA cusia (an a kue' zhi a) n.
   Complete deafness.
9. anadipsia ANA dipsia (an a dip' si a) n.
   Excessive desire to drink.
10. anagenesis ANA genesis (an a jen' e sis) n.
    Restoration of tissue.
11. analeptic ANA leptic (an al ep' tik) adj.
    Restorative; giving strength.
12. analogy ANA logy (a nal' o jee) n.
    A resemblance between two situations.
13. analogue ANA logue (an' al og) n.
    A situation which corresponds to another.
14. analogous ANA logous (a nal' o gus) adj.
    Corresponding to; as, an analogous case.
15. anagram ANA gram (an' a gram) n.
    *A word formed from the scrambled letters o
    another word.*
16. analyze ANA lyze (an' al ize) v.
    Examine all elements; as, analyze a word.

274

17. analysis   ANA lysis (a nal' i sis) n.
                   Separation into elements.
18. analytic   ANA lytic (an al it' ik) adj.
                   Treating of analysis.
19. analytically   ANA lytically (an al it' i k'l lee) adv.
                   In the manner of analysis.
20. ananym   ANA nym (an' a nim) n.
                   The spelling of a name backward for use as
                   a pseudonym; as, Mr. Draw for Mr. Ward.

word analysis

ANACHRONISM—No. 7
   ANA—Prefix =back; backward
   CHRON (chronos)—Greek Root =time
   ISM—Suffix =doctrine; theory

practical exercise

Read the following excerpt underlining all those words that contain keys you have already learned.

"Just give me the mass, the position and the motion of a system of heavenly bodies at any given moment and I will calculate their future positions and motions by a set of rigid and unerring mathematical calculations. I will calculate the tides and the motions of the waters and the earth. For the earth attracts the moon and the moon attracts the earth . . . the force of each in turn tends to keep both in a state of perpetual resistance. Attraction and reaction—reaction and attraction. The great masses of the planets and the stars remain suspended in space and retain their orbits only through this mysterious law of universal gravitation."

He was entranced with the world.

"The fact that the universe is so beautifully designed in accordance with such harmonious laws must presuppose the existence of a Divine Wisdom, the hand of a Divine Creator. . . . I can frame no hypothesis about Him. I am a scientist and I do not speculate on theological matters. I deal not with God, but with His observable laws."

Newton was a philosopher, and he was the humblest of men.

"Knowledge is an accumulation of vision. If I have seen farther it is by standing on the shoulders of giants."

(Sir Isaac Newton, in his own words, tells what he can do.)

KEY NO. 138

O—⚔

ISM

doctrine
system
manner
condition
act
characteristic

is the Suffix *ISM*. It means DOC-
TRINE; SYSTEM; MANNER. CON-
DITION, ACT, or, CHARACTER-
ISTIC. It has the quality of enlargement, and it carries you from the
particular to the general, from the
individual to the mass. Take the word
Nazi and you have an individual who
is associated with Nazism. But take
Nazism and you have a system of
government which murdered millions
and millions of people of all national-
ities. Take Charis and you have one
of the Graces, Charity. Take Charism
and you have a divine or spiritual
gift.

1. accidentalism   accidental ISM (ak si den′ tal iz um) n.
     The theory that accidents happen without
     cause.

2. alcoholism   alcohol ISM (al′ ko ho liz um) n.
     A condition of addiction to alcoholic drinks.

3. Americanism   American ISM (A mer′ i ka niz um) n.
     A characteristic of the American image.

4. baptism   bapt ISM (bap′ tiz um) n.
     Doctrine of ablution as a sign of purification

5. barbarism   barbar ISM (bar′ bar iz um) n.
     The manner of a barbarian.

6. colloquialism   colloquial ISM (ko lo′ kwee a liz um) n.
     An informal style of speech.

7. despotism   despot ISM (des′ po tiz um) n.
     A system of government that allows the ruler
     to govern absolutely.

8. exorcism   exorc ISM (ek′ sor siz um) n.
     The act of driving out an evil spirit.

9. heroism   hero ISM (her′ o iz um) n.
     A courageous manner of acting.

10. jingoism   jingo ISM (jin′ go iz um) n.
     A chauvinistic manner; aggressive policy dis
     playing readiness to fight.

11. Nazism   Naz ISM (Nat′ siz um) n.
     Doctrine of the fascists of Germany.

12. nihilism   nihil ISM (nie′ hil iz um) n.
     The doctrine of denial of the moral and
     spiritual objectives of man.

13. charisma   char ISM a (ka riz' ma) n.
                   A divine gift.
14. plagiarism   plagiar ISM (play' ji riz um) n.
                   *The act of using as one's own the words and
                   ideas which belong to others.*
15. Quakerism   Quaker ISM (Kway' ke riz um) n.
                   The doctrine of the Quakers.
16. realism   real ISM (ree' a liz um) n.
                   *The doctrine that allows only concern with
                   fact and reality.*
17. romanticism   romantic ISM (ro mant' i siz um) n.
                   *The tendency toward the romantic imagina-
                   tion and sentiment.*
18. Stoicism   Stoic ISM (Stoe' i siz um) n.
                   The doctrine of the Greek Stoics.
19. terrorism   terror ISM (ter' or iz um) n.
                   *The system of government that uses terror to
                   intimidate.*
20. totalitarianism totalitarian ISM (to tal i tar' ee a niz um) n.
                   *The system of government that is based on
                   authoritarian control.*

word analysis

ACCIDENTALISM—No. 1
    AC (ad)—Prefix =to; toward
    CID (cadere)—Latin Root =to fall
    ENT—Suffix =that which
    AL—Suffix =relating to
    ISM—Suffix =doctrine; system

practical exercises

1. Supply the missing words:
       The power of Nazism lay in the .... inherent
   in its .... Slang expressions often, by their
   frequent use, become ....(s).
2. Analyze No. 17.
3. Use one word for each phrase:
   a. method of managing all details   ....
   b. philosophy of the strong man among the
      Greeks   ....
   c. government by dictatorship   ....
   d. informal style of speech   ....

277

KEY NO. *139*

o—⚡

VERS · VERT

turn

is the Root *VERS*, *VERT* which means TURN. *VERS* comes from *versare* and *VERT* comes from *vertere*. Both are Latin and mean TURN. The key does not tell you *where* to turn, that is told you by another key, a Prefix placed before the Root. From No. 8 through No. 18 you are given a signal, which way to turn. Exactly like a sign on the highway, to make a left turn or a right one, the Prefixes tell you—away, to, against, with, from, in, through, under and back. You can't go wrong with keys.

1. versatile   VERS atile (ver' sat il) adj.
   Having aptitude for many skills; able to turn from one thing to another.

2. versatility VERS atility (ver sa til' it ee) n.
   The quality of skill along many lines.

3. versation   VERS ation (ver say' shun) n.
   A turning; twisting.

4. versative   VERS ative (ver' sa tiv) adj.
   Adaptable; versatile.

5. version   VERS ion (ver' zhun) n.
   A changed form; an adaptation; a translation.

6. versus   VERS us (ver' sus) prep.
   Against; as, in a legal action of Jones versus Smith.

7. vortex   VOR tex (vor' teks) n.
   A double motion of whirling and pulling down; a whirlpool.

8. controversial contro VERS ial (kon tro ver' shal) adj.
   Open to dispute; as, a controversial issue.

9. averse   a VERS e (a vers') adj.
   Turned against; as, averse to seeing him.

10. advertise   ad VERT ise (ad' ver tize) v.
    Turn attention toward; as, advertise a sale.

11. divert   di VERT (di vert') v.
    Turn attention away from; as, divert the mind.

12. invert   in VERT (in vert') v.
    Turn upside down; as, to divide by a fraction, invert and multiply.

278

13. conversant   con VERS ant (kon vers′ ant) adj.
                        Acquainted with; as, conversant *with the subject.*

14. obverse   ob VERS e (ob′ vers) adj.
                        Facing the opponent.

15. reverse   re VERS e (re vers′) v.
                        Turn back.

16. pervert   per VERT (per vert′) v.
                        To turn to improper use; corrupt.

17. subversive   sub VERS ive (sub ver′ siv) adj.
                        Causing to undermine; as, a subversive *group.*

18. reversible   re VERS ible (re ver′ si b′l) adj.
                        Can be reversed.

19. vertigo   VERT igo (vert′ i go) n.
                        A dizzy spell when everything seems to be turning.

20. vertiginous   VERT iginous (ver tij′ i nus) adj.
                        Dizzy; affected with vertigo.

word analysis

CONTROVERSIAL—No. 8
    CONTRO (contra)—Latin Prefix =against
    VERS (versus)—Latin Root =turn
    AL—Suffix =relating to

practical exercises

1. Supply the missing words:
    It is necessary to eliminate all .... activities in order to have security. Peace is a .... hope. In the division of fractions we .... and multiply.

2. Analyze No. 14.

3. Key review. Match keys with their meanings:

a. circum	1. about	....
b. clud, clus	2. know	....
c. clam, claim	3. very small	....
d. co	4. divide	....
e. cede, cess	5. around	....
f. cogno	6. together	....
g. cule, icle, ling	7. shut	....
h. cred	8. surrender; go	....
i. dent	9. believe	....
j. di	10. tooth	....

KEY NO. *140*

0—➤

PED · POD

foot

is the Root *PED, POD*. Both mean FOOT. *PED* comes from the Latin *ped*. *POD* comes from the Greek *podos*. Here's a complication. On the list, words No. 1, 2, 3, 4, 5, 6, 7, 8 are concerned with children. You are right to ask where children come in with *PED*, which means FOOT. Here's the answer: in Greek *paidos* means *boy*. Someone walked (*agogos*) the boy to school, on foot. *Paidos* became *PED;* his companion became a teacher (*PED*agogue); the doctor who cared for the boy became a *PED*iatrician. See?

1. pedagogue   PED agogue (ped' a gog) n.
   One who leads a child; a teacher.
2. pedantry   PED antry (ped' an tree) n.
   Display of learning.
3. pediatrician   PED iatrician (ped ee a trish' an) n.
   A doctor who specializes in the care of children.
4. pediatrics   PED iatrics (pede ee a' triks) n.
   That branch of medicine devoted to the care of children.
5. pedodontia   PED odontia (pee do don' shi a) n.
   Treatment of the teeth of children.
6. pedophilia   PED ophilia (pee do fil' i a) n.
   Inordinate love for children.
7. pedotrophy   PED otrophy (pe dot' ro fi) n.
   The art of properly rearing children.
8. pedology   PED ology (pee dol' o jee) n.
   Child study.
9. pedigerous   PED igerous (pe dij' er us) adj.
   Having feet.
10. pedestal   PED estal (ped' est al) n.
    The base of a statue or monument.
11. pedestrian   PED estrian (pe des' tree an) n.
    One who travels on foot.
12. pedometer   PED ometer (pe dom' et er) n.
    An instrument to measure distance walked.
13. pedomotive   PED omotive (ped o moe' tiv) adj.
    Moved by the power of the foot.

14. pedal PED al (ped' al) adj.
   Relating to the foot.

15. podiatry POD iatry (po die' a tree) n.
   That branch of medicine which treats of diseases of the foot.

16. podiatrist POD iatrist (po die' a trist) n.
   One who practices podiatry.

17. pedograph PED ograph (ped' o graf) n.
   An instrument that records topography when held by a pedestrian as he walks.

18. pedomotor PED omotor (pe dom' ot or) n.
   Machine driven by the power of the feet; as, a bicycle, skates.

19. podium POD ium (pode' ee um) n.
   A platform; dais.

20. pedialgia PED ialgia (ped i al' ji a) n.
   Neuralgia in the foot.

word analysis

PEDODONTIA—No. 5
   PED (paidos)—Greek Root =child
   DONT—Root =teeth
   IA—Suffix =end of scientific names

practical exercises

1. Supply the missing words:
   As the .... strolled through the park, he saw a child ....(ing) along on a bicycle. A bicycle is a ....

2. Analyze No. 14.

3. Choose the number of the word which best expresses the meaning of the italicized word:
   a. *vertigo* (1) dizziness (2) nausea (3) headache (4) short breath (5) sore throat ....
   b. *pedestrian* (1) mountain climber (2) cyclist (3) horseman (4) air pilot (5) walker ....
   c. *podium* (1) ingrowing toenail (2) dish closet (3) foot bath (4) platform (5) foot ....
   d. *convertible* (1) devisable (2) painstaking (3) can be turned (4) rigid (5) excusable ....
   e. *diversion* (1) test (2) ambition (3) system (4) entertainment (5) anxiety ....

281

KEY NO. 141

O—➤

TACT · TANG
TIG
TAG · TING

touch

is the Root *TACT, TANG, TIG, TAG, TING* meaning TOUCH. All these variations come from the conjugation of the Latin *tango, tetigi, tactus, tangere*. If you study the keys carefully you will have a sure *touch* for the right word in every *contingency*.

1. tact
    TACT (takt) n.
      A feeling of what is appropriate; as, the hostess showed tact.

2. tactful
    TACT ful (takt' ful) adj.
      Having tact.

3. tactics
    TACT ics (tak' tiks) n.
      Clever maneuvering; strategy in management.

4. tactician
    TACT ician (tak ti' shun) n.
      An expert at tactics.

5. tactical
    TACT ical (tak' tik al) adj.
      Relating to tactics; as, a tactical error.

6. tactile
    TACT ile (tak' til) adj.
      Pertaining to the sense of touch.

7. tactus
    TACT us (tak' tus) n.
      The sense of touch.

8. tactility
    TACT ility (tak til' it ee) n.
      Perceptibility by touch.

9. tangent
    TANG ent (tan' jent) n.
      A straight line which touches a circle at a single point.

10. tangential
    TANG ential (tan jen' shul) adj.
      Touching at one point.

11. tangible
    TANG ible (tan' ji b'l) adj.
      Capable of being touched; perceptible.

12. tangled
    TANG led (tan' guld) adj.
      Intertwined; snarled; as, tangled in lies.

13. contiguous
    con TIG uous (kon tig' yu us) adj.
      Touching; as, contiguous property.

14. contingent
    con TING ent (kon tin' jent) adj.
      Possible but not certain; dependent on something else.

15. contingency
    con TING ency (kon tin' jen see) n.
      Uncertainty; possibility.

16. contact   con TACT (kon′ takt) n.
         A touching; an association; as, an important
         contact.
17. contagion   con TAG ion (kon tay′ jun) n.
         Transmission of disease.
18. contagious   con TAG ious (kon tay′ jus) adj.
         Catching; as, a contagious *disease.*
19. intangible   in TANG ible (in tan′ ji b′l) adj.
         Cannot be touched; as, spiritual matters are
         intangible.
20. intangibility   in TANG ibility (in tan ji bil′ it ee) n.
         The quality of not being touchable.

word analysis

INTANGIBILITY—No. 20
     IN—Prefix =not
     TANG (tangere)—Latin Root =to touch
     IBIL (ible)—Suffix =able
     ITY—Suffix =quality of

practical exercises

1. Supply the missing words:
     "What a .... web we weave when first we
     practice to deceive." "Do not build certain rules on the
     .... of human actions." (Aristotle)

2. Analyze No. 9.

3. Read the following excerpt underlining all those words that
     contain keys you have already learned.
         Warnings are made regularly about keeping potentially
     poisonous chemicals out of the reach of children. And
     regularly there are reports of children becoming accidentally
     poisoned.
         Because this happens even when parents are cautious the
     Children's Hospital Medical Center in Boston put out an
     announcement last week urging parents to equip the family
     first-aid kit with a kind of universal antidote—a syrup called
     Ipecac, which tastes good (cherry flavor) but will induce
     vomiting and clearance from the system. It can be obtained
     by prescription and should be administered only under di-
     rection by a doctor.
                 (From *The New York Times*, Aug. 2, 1964.)

KEY NO. 142

0—⟶

JUS · JUR

law

is a Root, *JUS, JUR,* meaning LAW. JURIS means "of Law," from Roman Law. Please notice change of accent in con*jure* and con*jurer*. Also notice the use of *ad* and *ab;* ad*jure* and ab*jure.* The prefix here is most important to the meaning of the word. Also notice spelling. In No. 9 the suffix meaning one who, is spelled ER. There is a word, not in this list, where the suffix meaning one who is OR, as in con*jur or*, a conspirator. Even though it is not on the list, bear in mind the difference between a con*jurer*, magician, and con*jur or*, conspirator.

1. juror	JUR or (jur' or) n.	
	One who serves by law on a jury.	
2. jury	JUR y (jur' ee) n.	
	A group of twelve who are sworn to give a just verdict.	
3. justice	JUS tice (jus' tis) n.	
	A just judgement; as, justice *must be served.*	
4. justification	JUS tification (jus ti fi kay' shun) n.	
	Just cause for action.	
5. adjustment	ad JUS tment (a just' ment) n.	
	Settlement; as, an amicable adjustment.	
6. conjure	con JUR e (kon' jur) v.	
	To swear together; to imagine; to entreat; as, conjure *the king to be merciful.*	
7. adjure	ad JUR e (a jur') v.	
	To bind as if by solemn oath.	
8. abjure	ab JUR e (ab jur') v.	
	To swear away under oath; reject.	
9. conjurer	con JUR er (kon' jur er) n.	
	A magician; a trickster.	
10. abjuration	ab JUR ation (ab ju ray' shun) n.	
	A renunciation by solemn oath.	
11. adjuration	ad JUR ation (aj u ray' shun) n.	
	A solemn appeal.	
12. adjustive	ad JUS tive (a jus' tiv) adj.	
	Tending to put into proper order.	
13. adjuratory	ad JUR atory (a jur' a tor ee) adj.	
	Tending to solemn appeal; begging.	

14. abjuratory   ab JUR atory (ab jur' a to ri) adj.
                 Containing a disavowal.
15. jurisdiction   JUR isdiction (jur is dik' shun) n.
                 The legal right and power to hear and determine a cause.
16. juryman   JUR yman (jur' ee man) n.
                 A juror.
17. jurist   JUR ist (jur' ist) n.
                 One who is versed in law.
18. jurisprudence   JUR isprudence (jur i sprude' ens) n.
                 Law; that which is recognized in law.
19. juristic   JUR istic (ju ris' tik) adj.
                 Relating to jurisprudence.

word analysis

JURISDICTION—No. 15
     JURIS—Root =law
     DIC (dicere)—Latin Root =to speak
     TION—Suffix =act of

practical exercises

1. Supply the missing words:
     The more versed a lawyer is in .... the better lawyer he is. Without a warrant the law has no .... in a man's home. There is no .... for cruelty.

2. Analyze No. 7.

3. Add key to complete word expressing phrase:
     a. to place on a throne— ....throne
     b. most mighty— mighti..........
     c. not held back— ....strained
     d. being well suited for ....com..........
     e. government by one ruler ....arch..........
     f. legal authority ....dic..........
     g. one who swears by oath to serve on a jury— ....or

KEY NO. 143

O—x

TEMPO · TEMPOR

time

is the Root *TEMPO, TEMPOR* which means TIME. It comes from the Latin *tempus, temporis*. Do not confuse this Root with one which is spelled "temper." That is something entirely different. Words like *temperature* or *temperate* have nothing to do with TIME—*TEMPOR*. Another word which looks similar is *tempt*. This, too, has nothing to do with TIME—*TEMPOR*. So, when a word has TEMP in it, just take a hard look at the next letter. Not *e*, not *t*, but *o*.

1. tempo

TEMPO (tem' po) n.
Rate of speed. The plural is "tempi."

2. pro tem

pro TEM (pro tem') adv.
For the time being.

3. temporal

TEMPOR al (tem' po ral) adj.
Limited by time; earthly life.

4. temporality

TEMPOR ality (tem po ral' it ee) n.
The quality of being limited by time.

5. temporary

TEMPOR ary (tem' po rar ee) n.
For the time being; as, a temporary job.

6. temporize

TEMPOR ize (tem' po rize) v.
To comply with the time or circumstance.

7. temporariness

TEMPOR ariness (tem po rar' ee ness) n.
Impermanence; as, the temporariness of life.

8. temporizer

TEMPOR izer (tem' po rize er) n.
One who temporizes.

9. temporization

TEMPOR ization (tem po ri zay' shun) n.
The act of temporizing.

10. temporarily

TEMPOR arily (tem po rar' i lee) adv.
For the present; as, she lives here temporarily.

11. contemporary

con TEMPOR ary (kon tem' po rar ee) n.
Those who live at the same time; as, Hitler and Mussolini.

12. contemporaneous

con TEMPOR aneous
(kon tem po ray' nee us) adj.
Happening at the same time.

286

3. contemporaneously con TEMPOR aneously
                    (kon tem po ray' nee us lee) adv.
                    At the same time.

4. extempore   ex TEMPOR e (ek stem' po ree) adv.
                    On the spur of the moment; impromptu;
                    unprepared.

5. extemporaneous   ex TEMPOR aneous
                    (ek stem po ray' nee us) adj.
                    Unprepared; improvised.

6. extemporaneously ex TEMPOR aneously
                    (ek stem po ray' nee us lee) adv.
                    Impromptu.

word analysis

EMPORIZATION—No. 9
    TEMPOR (tempus)—Latin Root =time
    IZE—Suffix =cause (to pass)
    TION—Suffix =act of

practical exercises

Supply the missing words:
    When the President has a .... disability the
vice-president becomes President .... He had
a remarkable facility for .... speaking.

Analyze No. 3.

Choose the word which best expresses the italicized word:
a. *enthrone* (1) decorate (2) congratulate
   (3) arrest (4) deny (5) place on a throne   ....
b. *temporal* (1) lively (2) heavenly (3) final
   (4) impermanent (5) early   ....
c. *scepter* (1) cane (2) umbrella (3) seal
   (4) crown (5) staff of power   ....
d. *mercy* (1) misery (2) hunger (3) cruelty
   (4) indifference (5) compassion   ....
e. *strained* (1) limited (2) lost (3) unwanted
   (4) denied (5) poor   ....

KEY NO. 144

0—⚷

TRIB

pay
bestow

is the Root *TRIB* which comes from the Latin *tribuere*, to PAY; BESTOW. These two meanings seem to be contradictory, but both imply giving. To PAY tribute to a hero means to BESTOW honor on him. To PAY tribute to the conqueror means to BESTOW money on him. The two meanings come from the same root; to know which is being used you must read the text.

1. tribute — TRIB ute (trib′ yute) n.
   A fine paid to a conquering power.

2. tributary — TRIB utary (trib′ yu tar ee) n.
   A stream of water which flows into a larger river.

3. attribute — at TRIB ute (a trib′ yute) v.
   To regard as the cause of; blame for; ascribe to.

4. attribute — at TRIB ute (a′ tri byute) n.
   A high quality; as, the attribute for which he is noted is honesty.

5. attributive — at TRIB utive (a trib′ yute iv) adj.
   Ascribing a characteristic.

6. contribute — con TRIB ute (kon trib′ yute) v.
   To give money to a cause, or give service.

7. contributory — con TRIB utory (kon trib′ yu tore ee) adj.
   Giving to an endeavor; as, contributory labor.

8. contribution — con TRIB ution (kon tri byu′ shun) n.
   An offering; a tax; a thing given to a cause.

9. contributional — con TRIB utional (kon tri byu′ shun al) adj.
   Relating to a contribution.

10. contributorial — con TRIB utorial (kon trib ue toe′ ri al) adj.
    Of or relating to a contributor.

11. distribute — dis TRIB ute (dis trib′ yute) v.
    To divide among many; to allot; to deal out.

12. distribution — dis TRIB ution (dis tri byu′ shun) n.
    The sharing; the allotment.

13. distributive — dis TRIB utive (dis trib′ yute iv) adj.
    Tending to deal a share to each one.

14. distributively — dis TRIB utively (dis trib′ yute iv lee) adj.
    Separately; giving to each his portion.

15. distributor — dis TRIB utor (dis trib′ yute r) n.
    One who distributes.

288

16. redistribute   redis TRIB ute (rede i strib' yute) v.
                        To distribute over again.

17. redistribution   redis TRIB ution (re dis tri byu' shun) n.
                     / A sharing over again.

18. redistributor   redis TRIB utor (re dis trib' ue tor) n.
                     One who apportions, distributes, again.

19. retribution   re TRIB ution (re tri byu' shun) n.
                     Act of paying back.

word analysis

RETRIBUTION—No. 19
     RE—Prefix = back
     TRIB (tribuere)—Latin Root = to pay
     TION—Suffix = act of

practical exercises

1. Supply the missing words:
     Doctors .... lung cancer to smoking. The
driver was charged with .... negligence. The
Mississippi River has many ....(ies). The death
of the heir caused a .... of the estate.

2. Analyze No. 15.

3. Read the following excerpt underlining all those words that
contain keys you have already learned.
     The quality of mercy is not strain'd.
     It droppeth as the gentle rain from heaven
     Upon the place beneath. It is twice blest:
     It blesseth him that gives and him that takes
     'Tis mightiest in the mightiest; it becomes
     The throned monarch better than his crown.
     His sceptre shows the force of temporal power,
     The attribute to awe and majesty,
     Wherein doth sit the dread and fear of kings;
     But mercy is above this sceptred sway;
     It is enthroned in the hearts of kings;
     It is an attribute to God himself;
     And earthly power doth then show likest God's
     When mercy seasons justice. . . .
         (Portia's speech from *The Merchant of Venice* by Shake-
speare.)

KEY NO. *145*

ARCH

ruler

Is the Root *ARCH* which means RULER. It comes from the GREEK *archos*. From this basic meaning it is associated with chief or head or king or origin in one way or another. You can make many words with ARCH, from ARCHbishop to ARCHfoe, from ARCHfriend to ARCHliar. Sometimes it is pronounced ARCH and sometimes ARK.

1. myriarch   myri ARCH (mir' i ark) n.
   A leader of 10,000 troops.

2. panarchy   pan ARCH y (pan' ar ki) n.
   Government by all; universal rule.

3. anarchy   an ARCH y (an' ar kee) n.
   A state without government.

4. architect   ARCH itect (ar' ki tekt) n.
   The creator of a design or plan for a building.

5. biarchy   bi ARCH y (bie' ar ki) n.
   Government by two people.

6. chiliarch   chili ARCH (kil' i ark) n.
   Chief over a thousand troops.

7. exilarch   exil ARCH (ek' si lark) n.
   Ruler over the Jews in Babylon.

8. ecclesiarch   ecclesi ARCH (e klee' zi ark) n.
   The leader of a church.

9. demarch   dem ARCH (dee' mark) n.
   The mayor in modern Greece.

10. endarchy   end ARCH y (en' dark ee) n.
    Government from an inner center of control.

11. genarch   gen ARCH (jen' ark) n.
    The head of a family.

12. hierarch   hier ARCH (hie' a rark) n.
    A leader in the church.

13. monarch   mon ARCH (mon' ark) n.
    A single ruler, as a king.

14. matriarch   matri ARCH (may' tree ark) n.
    The female head of a tribe or family.

15. patriarch   patri ARCH (pay' tree ark) n.
    The male head of family or tribe.

16. oligarchy   olig ARCH y (ol' i gar kee) n.
    Government in the hands of a few.

17. pentarchy   pent ARCH y (pent' ar kee) n.
    Government by five rulers or five powers.

290

18. polemarch   polem ARCH (pol' e mark) n.
                    A military leader in Athens.

word analysis

PANARCHY—No. 2
    PAN (pantos)—Root =all
    ARCH (archos)—Root =ruler
    Y—Suffix =inclined to

practical exercises

1. Supply the missing words:
    Throughout the ages most governments have tried to
    avoid .... A city planner relies heavily on a(n)
    ....

2. Analyze No. 3.

3. Syllabicate and indicate which syllable is most greatly stressed
   by placing the accent ('):

attribute (n.)	attribute (v.)	retribution
distributor	tactician	temporal
enthroned	seasons	temporaneous
contemporary	abjuratory	justification
adjutant	conjuror	suffice

KEY NO. *146*

**DROME
DROMOS**

running

is the Root *DROME, DROMOS* which comes from the Greek and means RUNNING. Sometimes this key is spelled *DROMOUS* and is found at the end of a word. Then it is called a Suffix, but that is very rare. I'm certain you know that there is the two-humped camel as well as the dromedary. The dromedary is the swift one and can run a hundred miles in one day's travel. It is my guess that because of this speed, he was given a name with *DROME*, running, in it.

1. dromos
DROMOS (drom' os) n.
A long narrow course for foot racing. A large specially prepared area.

2. dromedary
DROME dary (drom' e dar y) n.
A swiftly running camel.

3. prodromal
pro DROM al (pro drom' al) adj.
Precursory; as, prodromal *stages of disease.*

4. dromedarian
DROME darian (drom e dar' i an) n.
One who rides a dromedary.

5. dromograph
DROMO graph (drom' o graf) n.
A chart for recording speed changes.

6. dromometer
DROMO meter (dro mom' e ter) n.
An apparatus for measuring speed.

7. dromotropic
DROMO tropic (drom o trop' ik) adj.
Affecting the cardiac muscle.

8. airdrome
air DROME (air' drome) n.
Airport.

9. prodromous
pro DROMO us (prod' ro mus) n.
A preliminary publication; introductory work.

10. hydrodromica
hydro DROM ica (hie dro drom' i ka) n.
The swimming bugs.

11. hippodromist
hippo DROM ist (hi pod' ro mist) n.
A circus rider or trainer.

12. hydrodrome
hydro DROME (hie' dro drome) n.
A boatlike vessel used to skim the surface of the water.

13. motordrome
motor DROME (mote' r drome) n.
A track for races of automotive vehicles.

14. dromomania
DROMO mania (dro mo ma' ni a) n.
Exaggerated longing for travel.

15. syndrome   syn DROME (sin' drome) n.
      Concurrence of signs and symptoms.
16. syndromic   syn DROM ic (sin drome' ik) adj.
      Like a syndrome.
17. hippodrome   hippo DROME (hip' o drome) n.
      A track for horse and chariot racing.
18. prodrome   pro DROME (pro' drome) n.
      An early warning of disease.

word analysis

PRODROMAL—No. 3
    PRO—Prefix =forward
    DROM (dromos)—Greek Root =running
    AL—Suffix =relating to

practical exercises

1. Supply the missing words:
    For its strength and speed the .... has been
called "the ship of the desert." For huge spectacles in action
the best showplace is the .... A .... is
a vessel that skims through water.

2. Analyze Hippodrome.

3. Give a word for the phrase:
   a. a swiftly running camel   ....
   b. a racetrack for automotive vehicles   ....
   c. a concurrence of symptoms of disease ....
   d. a small stream flowing into a larger one ....
   e. state the cause of (place accent mark) ....
   f. act of paying back for a good or an evil ....

KEY NO. *147*

0—➤

ALI · ALLO
ALTER

other

is the Root *ALI, ALLO, ALTER,* all meaning OTHER. In spite of the various spellings they are still one key and a very useful one. It opens doors to criminology, law, medicine, metallurgy, botany and the delicate matter of forgery (No. 10). Never a dull moment!

1. **alias**   ALI as (a' lee as) n.
   An assumed name, usually to escape the law.

2. **alibi**   ALI bi (al' i bie) n.
   Proof of being elsewhere at the time of a crime.

3. **alien**   ALI en (a' lee en) n.
   A foreigner; not a citizen.

4. **alienable**   ALI enable (ale' ye na b'l) adj.
   Can be transferred to another.

5. **inalienable**   in ALI enable (in ale' ye na b'l) adj.
   Cannot be taken away; as, inalienable *rights.*

6. **alienist**   ALI enist (a' lee en ist) n.
   One who treats diseases of the mind; a psychiatrist.

7. **allogamy**   ALLO gamy (a log' a me) n.
   Reproduction by cross-fertilization.

8. **alienate**   ALI enate (a' lee e nate) v.
   To transfer to another; to estrange.

9. **alienation**   ALI enation (a lee e nay' shun) n.
   The act of transferring to another; as, alienation *of affections.*

10. **allograph**   ALLO graph (al' o graf) n.
    The signing of another's name; forgery.

11. **allotypical**   ALLO typical (al o tip' i kal) adj.
    Relating to other types.

12. **allolalia**   ALLO lalia (al o lay' li a) n.
    A form of aphasia in which other words are spoken than those intended.

13. **allonym**   ALLO nym (al' o nim) n.
    The name of another person used by an author.

14. **allonymous**   ALLO nymous (a lon' i mus) adj.
    Using another's name for one's own work.

15. **alter**   ALTER (al' ter) v.
    To change somewhat.

16. alteration   ALTER ation (al ter ay' shun) n.
          A change; as, an alteration *in plan was necessary.*
17. alter ego   ALTER ego (al' ter e ·go) n.
          A second self; a bosom friend.
18. altercate   ALTER cate (al' ter kate) v.
          To dispute; to wrangle.
19. alternate   ALTER nate (al' ter nat) adj.
          By turns, now one, now another; as, an alternate *rhyme scheme.*
20. alternative   ALTER native (al ter' nat iv) n.
          Another choice; as, I had no alternative.

word analysis

INALIENABLE—No. 5
    IN—Prefix =not
    ALI (alius)—Root =other
    EN—Suffix =made of
    ABLE—Suffix =can do

practical exercises

1. Supply the missing words:
    A famous .... was called in to decide whether the prisoner was sane or insane. Shakespeare says that "love is not love that alters when it .... finds."

2. Analyze No. 16.

3. Supply the keys needed to complete the words:
    a. using the name of another person— ....nym
    b. proof of being somewhere else at time stated— ....bi
    c. act of making a change in a dress— ....ation
    d. to use first one and then another— ....nate
    e. rights which cannot be taken away— ....alien.......... rights
    f. have a dispute on a difference of opinion— ....cate

KEY NO 148

O—🔑

EPI

upon
beside
among

is the Prefix *EPI* which means UPON, BESIDE, AMONG. No. 15 is a good word to know, as many people have this condition and just call it running eyes. If the tearduct were not obstructed, the tears would run through it instead of running over on the cheeks.

1. epicarp   EPI carp (ep' i karp) n.
              The outer layer of the fruit.
2. epidemic   EPI demic (ep i dem' ik) n.
              A spreading among the people; as, a disease that is contagious.
3. epidermis EPI dermis (ep i der' mis) n.
              Outer layer of skin.
4. epiglottis EPI glottis (ep i glot' is) n.
              A thin cartilage behind the tongue.
5. epigram   EPI gram (ep' i gram) n.
              A clever, pithy saying.
6. epigraph   EPI graph (ep' i graf) n.
              A quotation placed at the beginning of a work to suggest theme.
7. epigraphy EPI graphy (ep i' gra fee) n.
              Science of interpreting ancient writings.
8. episode   EPI sode (ep' i sode) n.
              A separate incident in a long narrative.
9. epistle   EPI stle (e pis' l) n.
              Piece of writing in the form of a letter.
10. epistolography EPI stolography (e pis to log' ra fi) n.
              The art of letter writing.
11. epileptic EPI leptic (ep i lep' tik) n.
              One ill with a disturbance of the nervous system.
12. epilepsy   EPI lepsy (ep' i lep see) n.
              A disease of the nervous system that is revealed by convulsions and loss of consciousness.
13. epithet   EPI thet (ep' i thet) n.
              An expression which gives a good description; as, Sophocles, the wise one.
14. epitaph   EPI taph (ep' i taf) n.
              An inscription on a gravestone.

15. epiphora	EPI phora (e pif′ o ra) n.
	Watering from the eyes caused by obstruction of the tearduct.
16. epitome	EPI tome (e pit′ o mee) n.
	An abridged summary of a topic or work.
17. epitomize	EPI tomize (e pit′ o mize) v.
	To make an epitome of; abridge.
18. epizeuxis	EPI zeuxis (ep i zuke′ sis) n.
	Emphatic repetition; as, "Peace! Peace! But there is no peace!"
19. epilogue	EPI logue (ep′ i log) n.
	The concluding section of a work.
20. epithalamium	EPI thalamium (ep i tha lay′ mee um) n.
	A poem in honor of bride and groom.

word analysis

EPIDEMIC—No. 2
    EPI—Prefix = upon; among
    DEM (demos)—Greek Root = people
    IC—Suffix = like; nature of

practical exercises

1. Supply the missing words:
     Oscar Wilde was famous for his brilliant ....
     Patrick Henry's famous, "The gentlemen cry 'Peace! Peace!' but there is no Peace!" is an example of ...., emphatic repetition.

2. Analyze Archangel.

3. Choose the number of the word which best expresses the italicized word:
     a. *episode* (1) incident (2) story (3) sepulcher
          (4) mariner (5) epistle ....
     b. *epithet* (1) a short description (2) Iliad
          (3) letter (4) a contagious disease (5) fruit ....
     c. *epidermis* (1) foundation (2) the outer skin
          (3) grave (4) quotation (5) epistle ....
     d. *epileptic* (1) art of writing a letter (2) ocean
          (3) foundation (4) conception (5) a sick man ....

MAR · MARI
MER

sea
pool

is the Root *MAR, MARI, MER* meaning SEA, POOL. It comes from the Latin *mare* which means SEA. The SEA was of the greatest importance to the Romans. Mare Liberum, the open sea; Mare Clausum, the closed Sea; and Mare Nostrum, our sea, which is now called the Mediterranean Sea. All the words on this list have a musical sound, from MERmaid to MARina. "The Ancient Mariner" sounds much more musical than "The Old Sailor" which means the same thing.

1. mere   MERE (meer) n.
         Lake; pool.

2. mermaid   MER maid (mer′ made) n.
         Fabled marine creature, half fish, half woman.

3. merman   MER man (mer′ man) n.
         The male of the marine creatures.

4. marine   MAR ine (ma rene′) adj.
         Relating to the sea.

5. marine   MAR ine (ma rene′) n.
         A sailor, serving on shipboard.

6. maritime   MAR itime (mar′ i time) adj.
         Relating to commerce and navigation.

7. mariner   MAR iner (mar′ i ner) n.
         A sailor; as, in a poem by Coleridge, "The Rime of the Ancient Mariner."

8. mare liberum   MAR e liberum (mar′ e lib′ er um)
         The open sea; open to all nations.

9. marinist   MAR inist (ma rene′ ist) n.
         One interested in relation between land and sea.

10. marinorama   MAR inorama (mar i no ra′ ma) n.
         A panoramic presentation of a view of the sea.

11. marsh   MAR sh (marsh) n.
         Wet land; swamp; morass.

12. marshy   MAR shy (mar′ shee) adj.
         Swampy.

13. mare nostrum	MAR e nostrum (mar' e nos' trum) n.
	Latin; "Our Sea." The name which the Romans gave to the Mediterranean Sea.
14. marfire	MAR fire (mar' fire) n.
	The phosphorescence on the sea.
15. marina	MAR ina (ma ree' na) n.
	A dock for mooring and refitting boats of various types.
16. Margaret	MAR garet (mar' ga ret) n.
	A female name meaning a pearl.
17. Marginella	MAR ginella (mar ji nel' a) n.
	Sea-snails.
18. marigenous	MAR igenous (ma rij' ee nus) adj.
	Produced in or by the sea.

word analysis

MARINORAMA—No. 10
>   MAR (mare)—Latin Root =sea
>   INE—Suffix =relating to
>   ORAMA (horama)—Greek Root =view

practical exercises

1. Supply the missing words:

>   Samuel Taylor Coleridge wrote *The Rime of the Ancient* .... The Romans called the Mediterranean Sea .... nostrum, our sea.

2. Analyze No. 7

3. Read the following excerpt underlining all those words that contain keys you have already learned.

>   Report of record sales and earnings by G.M. epitomizes wave of prosperity. . . . Disclosures of the big automotive profits might, however, stiffen the union's position in the current bargaining. That is the major worry in business and economic circles. While the auto companies might easily absorb a fairly sizable wage settlement without severe financial consequences for themselves, any such generous pact might become a target or pattern for a host of other industries less able to afford it. This could lead to renewed inflationary pressures spawned by a wage-price spiral. . . . The labor settlement might be around 25 cents an hour, including work-rule changes and other fringe benefits.

>   (From *The New York Times*, July 26, 1964.)

is the Root *SIMIL*, *SIMUL*, which comes from the Latin meaning LIKE, RESEMBLING. The second meaning, *SIMUL*, has a fine meaning in the words so far. But beginning with No. 11 *SIMUL* suggests deception. It is no longer honest and sincere. The meaning assumes a tricky, artificial look.

1. similar
   SIMIL ar (sim' i lar) adj.
   Resembling in many respects.

2. similarity
   SIMIL arity (sim i lar' it ee) n.
   Resemblance; as, similarity in views.

3. similative
   SIMIL ative (sim' i lay tiv) adj.
   Indicating a likeness.

4. simile
   SIMIL e (sim' i le) n.
   A figure of speech that compares two things that are unlike; as, "I wandered lonely as a cloud." (Wordsworth)

5. similitude
   SIMIL itude (si mil' i tude) n.
   Resemblance.

6. similitudenize
   SIMIL itudenize (si mil i tue' de nize) v.
   To make resemblances.

7. similize
   SIMIL ize (sim' i lize) v.
   To compare; to copy.

8. similor
   SIMIL or (sim' i lor) n.
   An alloy resembling gold in color.

9. simultaneous
   SIMUL taneous (sie mul tay' nee us) adj.
   Happening at the same time.

10. simultaneously
   SIMUL taneously
   (sie mul tay' ne us lee) adv.
   Happening concurrently.

11. simulate
   SIMUL ate (sim' yu late) v.
   Pretend; put on an act to make a certain impression.

12. simulacrum
   SIMUL acrum (sim yu lak' rum) n.
   An image; a likeness of an image.

13. simulacral
   SIMUL acral (sim yu lay' kral) adj.
   Resembling a simulacrum.

14. simulator
   SIMUL ator (sim' yu late or) n.
   One who simulates.

15. simulation
   SIMUL ation (sim yu lay' shun) n.
   Pretence; counterfeit display.

16. simulatory   SIMUL atory (sim' yu la to ri) adj.
         Pretending; putting up a show.
17. simulative   SIMUL ative (sim' yu lay tiv) adj.
         Showing a tendency to simulation.
18. simulant   SIMUL ant (sim' yu lant) n.
         One who puts on an act.
19. dissimilar   dis SIMIL ar (dis im' i lar) adj.
         Not showing any resemblance.
20. assimilate   as SIMIL ate (a sim' i late) v.
         To make similar to; as, assimilate *the* d *in*
         ad *with the* l *of* lege *to form* allege.

word analysis

SIMILARITY—No. 2
    SIMIL—Root = resembling
    AR—Suffix = that which
    ITY—Suffix = quality of

practical exercises

1. Supply the missing words:
      The .... between the sisters was remarkable.
One was frank and simple, and the other ....
friendliness with those she did not like. It was impossible
to .... one with the other.

2. Analyze No. 5.

3. Key review. Match keys with their meanings:

a. port	1. many	....
b. pro	2. hang	....
c. pello	3. through	....
d. poly	4. love	....
e. per	5. push	....
f. pre	6. foot	....
g. pend	7. forward	....
h. pos	8. before	....
i. philo	9. carry	....
j. ped	10. place	....

KEY NO. 151

O—⚹

SE

apart
aside
without

is the Prefix *SE* which means APART; ASIDE; WITHOUT. This key has an interesting personality, aside from its function as a prefix meaning ASIDE, APART. In Latin *SE* is the ablative case of *SUI* and means *by itself, apart, aside.* Now please look at our list. Nearly every word means exactly that, to be ASIDE, APART. Emily Dickinson, the classic example of a poet who wanted to be *by herself,* SEquestered herself from society.

1. seclude   SE clude (si klude') v.
       Set apart; aside.

2. seclusion   SE clusion (si klue' zhun) n.
       State of being shut apart; alone.

3. secure   SE cure (si kyur') v.
       Set aside carefully; to protect.

4. security   SE curity (si kyur' it ee) n.
       Condition of being protected; apart from danger.

5. secret   SE cret (se' kret) n.
       A thing apart; hidden.

6. secrete   SE crete (si krete') v.
       To hide away; store away; as, to secrete stolen goods.

7. secretion   SE cretion (si kree' shun) n.
       Matter stored away for functional use.

8. secretive   SE cretive (see' kret iv) adj.
       Disposed to keep secrets; as, secretive by nature.

9. sequestration   SE questration (seek wes tra' shun) n.
       Separation; retirement from society.

10. secretary   SE cretary (sek' re tar ee) n.
       One entrusted with secrets; a confidential employee.

11. secern   SE cern (si sern') v.
       To set apart; to discriminate.

12. secede   SE cede (si sede') v.
       Withdraw; to separate oneself from government.

13. secession   SE cession (si sesh' un) n.
       State of withdrawal from government.

302

14. sedition	SE dition (si dish' un) n.
	Conduct tending to treason.
15. seditionist	SE ditionist (si dish' un ist) n.
	One who practices acts of sedition.
16. seduce	SE duce (si duse') v.
	To lead astray by fraud.
17. seductive	SE ductive (si duk' tiv) adj.
	Attractive; causing to be led astray.
18. select	SE lect (se lekt') v.
	To choose one from many and set it apart.
19. segregate	SE gregate (seg' re gate) v.
	To cut off from the general mass; seclude.
20. separate	SE parate (sep' a rate) v.
	To disunite; to disconnect; to sever from others.

word analysis

SEGREGATE—No. 19
  SE—Prefix =apart; aside
  GREG (gregis)—Root =flock; herd
  ATE—Suffix =make

practical exercises

1. Supply the missing words:

Emily Dickinson, the poet, lived in .... for many years. No one seems to know the reason for her .... from society. That .... died with her.

2. Analyze No. 17.

3. Supply the word that each phrase explains:
   a. one occupied with navigation ....
   b. singled out for honors ....
   c. completely unknown and without honor ....
   d. at the same moment ....
   e. the mind completely filled up ....
   f. speech of some kind ....

KEY NO. *152*

o→⚷

CATA

down

is the Prefix *CATA* which means DOWN, just the opposite of *ANA*, up. You will find quite a few scientific words in the list and you will feel very much advanced to have them in your vocabulary. And, indeed, you are advanced to know the keys *CATA* and *ANA*.

1. catabasis   CATA basis (ka tab' a sis) n.
     A going down; decline in health.

2. catachresis   CATA chresis (kat a kree' sis) n.
     A misuse of words; mixed metaphor.

3. cataclysm   CATA clysm (kat' a kliz m) n.
     A downward sweep of water; flood; disaster.

4. cataclysmic   CATA clysmic (kat a kliz' mik) adj.
     In the nature of a cataclysm.

5. catacomb   CATA comb (kat' a kome) n.
     Underground burial place.

6. catafalque   CATA falque (kat' a falk) n.
     A raised platform for the coffin of one deceased.

7. catagenesis   CATA genesis (kat a jen' e sis) n.
     Evolution going back, and not forward.

8. catalyst   CATA lyst (kat' a list) n.
     A combination which starts a reaction.

9. cataract   CATA ract (kat' a rakt) n.
     A large waterfall; a clouding of the lens of the eye.

10. catakinesis   CATA kinesis (kat a ki nee' sis) n.
     A state when energy is down.

11. catalepsy   CATA lepsy (kat' al ep sy) n.
     A nervous disorder which keeps limbs rigid.

12. catalogue   CATA logue (kat' a log) n.
     Lists of names set down; registered.

13. catapult   CATA pult (kat' a pult) n.
     An ancient apparatus for hurling stones.

14. catasta   CATA sta (ka tas' ta) n.
     Platform on which slaves were shown for sale.

15. catastasis   CATA stasis (ka tas' ta sis) n.
     Climax in a drama.

16. catastrophe   CATA strophe (ka tas' tro fee) n.
     A moment of tragedy.

17. catatonia   CATA tonia (kat a to' nee a) n.
     A severe type of mental disorder.

18. catarrh   CATA rrh (ka tar') n.
                  Inflammation of the mucous membrane.
19. catastrophic CATA strophic (kat a strof' ik) adj.
                  In the nature of a great disaster.

word analysis

CATASTROPHIC—No. 19
    CATA—Prefix =down; low
    STROPHE (strephein)—Greek Root =twist
    IC—Suffix =like

practical exercises

1. Supply the missing words:
      Shakespeare is guilty of using a mixed metaphor or
      .... when he lets Hamlet say, ". . . take up
arms against a sea of troubles . . ." *Arms* and *sea* do not
belong together. Julius Caesar suffered from ....,
commonly called "falling sickness."

2. Analyze No. 12.

3. Choose the number of the word which best expresses the
italicized word:
    a. *monument*   (1) money   (2) memorial
       (3) pressure   (4) delay   (5) patience   ....
    b. *conception*   (1) drama   (2) dream   (3) idea
       (4) valley   (5) suitcase   ....
    c. *tremor*   (1) journey   (2) incident   (3) features
       (4) shaking   (5) energy   ....
    d. *conscious*   (1) fainting   (2) bedridden
       (3) amused   (4) aware   (5) asleep   ....
    e. *ambitious*   (1) lazy   (2) lacks initiative
       (3) greedy   (4) timid   (5) zealous   ....
    f. *intimate*   (1) forget   (2) purchase   (3) destroy
       (4) ridicule   (5) personal   ....

is the Root *STRU, STRUCT,* meaning BUILD. It comes from the Latin *struere, structus,* meaning build. As the Root implies, every word with it is a word of action.

build

1. structure	STRUCT ure (struk' chur) n.	*A building; an arrangement.*
2. structural	STRUCT ural (struk' chur al) adj.	*Relating to structure; as, a structural error.*
3. construction	con STRUCT ion (kon struk' shun) n.	*The act of bringing together all the elements of a building.*
4. destructive	de STRUCT ive (de struk' tiv) adj.	*Tending to hinder; to destroy.*
5. industry	indu STRY (in' dus tree) n.	*Diligence at one's job; productive business.*
6. construe	con STRU e (kon strue') v.	*To explain; to arrange words and phrases so as to make sense.*
7. industrious	indu STRI ous (in dus' tree us) adj.	*Energy and zeal to work.*
8. instructor	in STRUCT or (in struk' ter) n.	*One who teaches; a teacher.*
9. instruction	in STRUCT ion (in struk' shun) n.	*Teaching; information; education.*
10. instructive	in STRUCT ive (in struk' tiv) adj.	*Tending to teach; enlightening.*
11. instrument	in STRU ment (in' stru ment) n.	*A tool to build with.*
12. instrumental	in STRU mental (in stru ment' al) adj.	*Relating to an instrument helpful in building.*
13. instrumentalist	in STRU mentalist (in strue men' tal ist) n.	*One who plays on a musical instrument.*
14. obstruct	ob STRUCT (ob strukt') v.	*Build against; prevents building.*
15. obstruction	ob STRUCT ion (ob struk' shun) n.	*That which blocks; clogs; hinders.*
16. obstructive	ob STRUCT ive (ob struk' tiv) adj.	*Hindering; opposing; blocking.*
17. reconstruct	recon STRUCT (re kon strukt') v.	*Build over again; make over.*

18. reconstruction   recon STRUCT ion (re kon struk' shun) n.
Rebuilding; remaking.

19. reconstructionist   recon STRUCT ionist
                     (re kon struk' shun ist) n.
                     One who wants rebuilding.

word analysis

RECONSTRUCTIONIST—No. 19
     RE—Prefix =again
     CON—Prefix =with
     STRUC (structus)—Latin Root =build
     TION—Suffix =act of
     IST—Suffix =one who

practical exercise

Read the following excerpt underlining all those words that contain keys you have already learned.

"Old and young we dream of graves and monuments," murmured the stranger Youth. "I wonder how the mariners feel when the ship is sinking, and they, unknown and undistinguished, are to be buried together in the ocean—that wide and nameless sepulcher!"

For a moment, the old woman's ghastly conception so engrossed the minds of her hearers, that a sound, abroad in the night, rising like the roar of a blast, had grown broad, deep and terrible before the fated group were conscious of it. The house, and all within it, trembled; the foundations of the earth seemed to be shaken, as if this awful sound were the peal of the last trump. Young and old exchanged one wild glance, and remained an instant, pale, affrighted, without utterance, or power to move. Then the same shriek burst out simultaneously from all their lips.

"The Slide! The Slide!"

The simplest words must intimate, but not portray, the unutterable horror of the catastrophe. The victims rushed from their cottage and sought refuge in what they deemed a safer spot. . . . Alas! they had quitted their security, and had fled right into the pathway of destruction.

(From *The Ambitious Guest* by Nathaniel Hawthorne.)

KEY NO. 154

○━�

ACER · ACID
ACRI

bitter
sour
sharp

is the Root *ACER, ACID, ACRI* which means BITTER, SOUR, SHARP. There is a difference, however, in the bitterness of each one. *ACER* has a sharpness to it like a needle. *ACID* has a sourness. *ACRI* has a sting, like smoke that chokes. So, if you want the word to pierce like a needle, use No. 13. If you want to express vinegar, use No. 4. If you want to choke or sting, use No. 18. Each has its own personality.

1. acerate   ACER ate (as' e rate) adj.
                Shaped like a needle; as, acerate *leaves.*
2. acerb   ACER b (a serb') adj.
                Bitter to the taste; tart.
3. acidifiant   ACID ifiant (a sid' i fie ant) n.
                That which acidifies; acid making.
4. acidity   ACID ity (a sid' it ee) n.
                The quality of sourness.
5. acerbic   ACER bic (a ser' bik) adj.
                Bitter; harsh; irritating.
6. acid   ACID (as' id) n.
                A sour substance.
7. acidemia   ACID emia (as i dee' mi a) n.
                Condition of too much acid in the blood.
8. acrimonious ACRI monious (ak ri moe' nee us) adj.
                Nagging, quarrelsome bitterness.
9. acidic   ACID ic (a sid' ik) adj.
                Acid-forming; as, acidic *foods.*
10. acidiferous ACID iferous (as i dif' er us) adj.
                Containing or producing acid.
11. acidify   ACID ify (a sid' i fie) v.
                Make acid; make bitter; make sour.
12. acidification ACID ification (a sid i fi kay' shun) n.
                Act of making sour; acid.
13. acerbity   ACER bity (a ser' bit ee) n.
                Bitterness; sharpness of tongue.
14. acerbate   ACER bate (as' er bate) v.
                Embitter; irritate.
15. acidimeter ACID imeter (as i dim' et er) n.
                Instrument to measure amount of acid.

16. acidosis   ACID osis (as i doe' sis) n.
                     Condition of the blood having an abnormal
                     amount of acid.
17. acrid   ACRI d (ak' rid) adj.
                     Stingingly bitter; as, the acrid *sting of smoke.*
18. acridity   ACRI dity (a krid' it ee) n.
                     Bitterness; as, the bitter acridity *of smoke.*
19. acrimony   ACRI mony (ak' ri moe nee) n.
                     Bitterness, not of taste, but of feeling.

word analysis

ACIDIFEROUS—No. 10
    ACID—Root =sour
    FER (ferre)—Latin Root =to bear; yield
    OUS—Suffix =having; full of

practical exercises

1. Supply the missing words:
     Voltaire was known for his ...., his biting
     wit. The patient showed symptoms of .... and
     the doctor prohibited all .... foods.

2. Analyze No. 4.

3. Add a key and complete the word expressing the phrase:
     a. nagging and quarrelsome— ....monious
     b. foods which are acid forming— acidi..........
     c. the act of bending the knee— genu..........
     d. in the manner of recording time— ....log..........
     e. an unusual, irregular thing— an..........y
     f. a hater of women— mis..........ist
     g. to slander unjustly— tra..........

is the Root *MICRO* meaning SMALL, MINUTE. It comes from the Greek *mikros* meaning tiny. When you see *MICRO* you will immediately think of its opposite number *MACRO*, which you will have soon.

1. microaudiphone   MICRO audiphone (mie kro au' di fone) n.
    An instrument to make slight sounds audible.

2. microlith   MICRO lith (mie' kro lith) n.
    A tiny stone implement.

3. microbe   MICRO be (mie' krobe) n.
    A minute organism; a germ.

4. microbicide   MICRO bicide (mie kroe' bi side) n.
    Any agent which destroys microbes.

5. microcephalous   MICRO cephalous (mie kro sef' a lus) adj.
    Having an abnormally small head.

6. microcosm   MICRO cosm (mie' kro koz um) n.
    A small world.

7. microcosmography   MICRO cosmography
    (mie kro koz mog' ra fi) n.
    A description of man as a microcosm.

8. microdont   MICRO dont (mie' kro dont) adj.
    Having small teeth.

9. microgram   MICRO gram (mie' kro gram) n.
    One millionth of a gram.

10. micrograph   MICRO graph (mie' kro graf) n.
    An instrument for writing and engraving minutely.

11. micrographer   MICRO grapher (mie krog' ra fer) n.
    A specialist in micrography.

12. microbarograph   MICRO barograph (mie kro bar' o graf) n.
    An instrument for recording small and rapid changes.

13. micrology   MICRO logy (mie krol' o ji) n.
    The art of handling microscopic objects.

14. micromania   MICRO mania (mie kro may' ni a) n.
    A delusion that one's body has become very small.

15. micromelia   MICRO melia (mie kro mee' li a) n.
A condition where the extremities are abnormally undeveloped.

16. micrometer   MICRO meter (mie krom' et er) n.
Instrument for measuring minute distances.

17. micromotion   MICRO motion (mi kro mo' shun) adj.
Relating to the study of microscopic motions.

18. microphone   MICRO phone (mie' kro fone) n.
Instrument to intensify slight sounds.

19. microscope   MICRO scope (mie' kro skope) n.
Instrument to examine objects too small to be seen by the naked eye.

word analysis

MICROAUDIPHONE—No. 1
     MICRO (mikros)—Root =small
     AUDI (audire)—Root =to hear
     PHONE—Root =*sound*

practical exercises

. Supply the missing words:
     A .... reveals a world too small to be seen by the naked eye The invention of the .... is a boon to those who are hard of hearing. In a land of giants a man may suffer from ....

. Analyze No. 8.

. Syllabicate and indicate which syllable is most greatly stressed by placing the accent mark ('):

substantiate	simultaneous	micrology
micrometer	simultaneously	subcutaneous
maritime	marine	simulacrum
	sequestration	

KEY NO. 156

○—⚡

**HYDRO · HYDRA
HYDR**

water

is the Root *HYDRO, HYDRA,
HYDR* meaning WATER. Many
words using this key have 3, 4, or 5
syllables, but you already know what
some of them mean. You're like a
clever surgeon, knowing where to cut
apart and where to sew together. You
know that a HYDRAngea needs water; you know a prune is dry because
it has been deHYDRAted.

1. hydragogue   HYDRA gogue (hie′ dra gog) adj.
         *Causing the expelling of serum as in
         dropsy.*

2. hydragogy   HYDRA gogy (hie′ dra goe ji) n.
         *Conveyance of water through channels
         artificially.*

3. hydrangea   HYDRA ngea (hie drane′ je) n.
         A beautiful plant that needs much water.

4. hydrant   HYDR ant (hie′ drant) n.
         *A pipe with spout from which water may
         be drawn.*

5. hydrate   HYDR ate (hie′ drate) n.
         A compound of water plus one element.

6. hydraulic   HYDR aulic (hie dra′ lik) adj.
         Acting by water power.

7. hydraulics   HYDR aulics (hie dra′ liks) n.
         Use of water in driving machinery.

8. hydrophobia   HYDRO phobia (hie dro fo′ bi a) n.
         Morbid fear of water.

9. hydrophone   HYDRO phone (hie′ dro fone) n.
         *Instrument that detects sound of water
         flowing in pipes.*

10. hydropic   HYDRO pic (hie drop′ ik) adj.
         Said of one suffering from dropsy.

11. hydroplane   HYDRO plane (hie′ dro plane) n.
         *A seaplane; a boat that can rise or light
         on water.*

12. hydropropulsion   HYDRO propulsion
         (hie dro pro pul′ shun) n.
         Propulsion by means of jet propeller.

13. hydroscope   HYDRO scope (hie′ dro skope) n.
         *A device for enabling one to see through
         great depths to the sea bed.*

14. hydrosphere	HYDRO sphere (hie' dro sfere) n. *The water vapor in the atmosphere.*
15. hydrostat	HYDRO stat (hie' dro stat) n. *A device to regulate the amount of water in a reservoir or boiler.*
16. hydrostatics	HYDRO statics (hie dro stat' iks) n. *The principles of statics applied to water and other liquids.*
17. hydrostatician	HYDRO statician (hie dro sta tish' an) n. *An expert in hydrostatics.*
18. hydrotherapist	HYDRO therapist (hie dro ther' a pist) n. *One who practices hydrotherapy.*
19. hydrotherapy	HYDRO therapy (hie droe ther' a pee) n. *Treatment of disease by the scientific use of water.*
20. dehydrate	de HYDR ate (dee hie' drate) v. *To remove water; as,* dehydrate *foods.*

word analysis

HYDROPROPULSION—No. 12
HYDRO (hydros)—Root = water
PRO—Prefix = forward
PUL (pello)—Latin Root = push
SION—Suffix = act of

practical exercises

1. Supply the missing words:
.... blooms need plenty of water. A ....
press acts by water power. The dried fruits are ....(d)
and therefore not so healthful as the fresh ones.

2. Analyze No. 20.

3. Add the correct key to the incomplete words:
   a. a branch of engineering using water power— ....aulics
   b. treatment of disease by water cures— ....therapy
   c. morbid fear of water, as in rabies— ....phobia
   d. the area in a neighborhood— ....viron..........
   e. the study of the mind— psycho..........
   f. an instrument for intensifying slight sounds— ....phone
   g. a tiny stone instrument— ....lith

313

KEY NO. 157

O—x

GERM

vital part

is the Root *GERM* and it has no other meaning than itself, the thing it is, the mass of living substance that it is: the GERM. Whether of vegetation or of idea, the GERM is the vital part, and the incipient stage is as important as the final stage, if, indeed, not more important. Whether we call it GERM, bacteria or microbe, the important question is *"Are you for human life or bad? Are you for disease or for health"?*

1. germ — GERM (jerm) n.
   Seed; living substance; as, the germ of an idea.
2. germal — GERM al (jer' mal) adj.
   Relating to a germ.
3. germane — GERM ane (jer mane') adj.
   Akin; closely allied.
4. germanity — GERM anity (jer man' i ti) n.
   Quality of kinship; relationship.
5. germicide — GERM icide (jer' mi side) n.
   An agent that destroys germs.
6. germifuge — GERM ifuge (jer' mi fuje) adj.
   Driving out germs.
7. germinable — GERM inable (jer' mi na b'l) adj.
   Having the capacity to germinate.
8. germinal — GERM inal (jerm' in al) adj.
   Relating to a germ cell; early stage.
9. germinant — GERM inant (jerm' i nant) adj.
   Beginning to grow; sprouting.
10. germinate — GERM inate (jer' mi nate) v.
    To grow; to sprout.
11. germination — GERM ination (jer mi nay' shun) n.
    The process of germinating.
12. germinative — GERM inative (jer' mi nate iv) adj.
    Causing to grow; tendency to grow.
13. germule — GERM ule (jer' mule) n.
    A tiny germ.
14. germin — GERM in (jer' min) v.
    To bud; to bud into.
15. germless — GERM less (jerm' les) adj.
    Free from germs.
16. germproof — GERM proof (jerm' prufe) adj.
    Germ repellent.

17. germy	GERM y (jer' mi) adj.
	Inclined to have germs.
18. germiparity	GERM iparity (jer mi par' i ti) n.
	Reproduction by germs.
19. germinator	GERM inator (jer' mi nay tor) n.
	A device for testing the capacity of seeds to germinate.
20. germling	GERM ling (jerm' ling) n.
	A young sporophyte; a new plant which produces spores.

word analysis

GERMINATIVE—No. 12
   GERMIN (germinare)—Latin Root =to grow; to sprout
   AT (ate)—Suffix =make
   IVE—Suffix =cause; tend to

practical exercises

1. Supply the missing words:
      The quality of a ...., even of a .... is more important than its capacity for .... For if that quality is harmful to health, it will give small comfort to test its .... strength.

2. Analyze No. 13.

3. Key review. Match keys with their meanings:

a. struct	1. upon	....
b. cata	2. resembling	....
c. se	3. sea	....
d. simul	4. run	....
e. mare	5. apart	....
f. epi	6. pay out	....
g. alter	7. down	....
h. drome	8. build	....
i. acro	9. other	....
j. trib	10. top	....

KEY NO. 158

GEN

race
kind of

is the Root *GEN (genus)* meaning RACE; KIND OF. The science of genetics has opened up a world of thought and knowledge of man. Naturally, in order to learn and follow, the vocabulary must keep pace with the developments and knowledge attained. All growth and development are accompanied by language, and keeping pace with the language is the purpose of this book. Every new thought has a key to unlock its treasures. The key itself becomes a treasure to be cherished. He who has no key stays out!

1. genarch   GEN arch (jen' ark) n.
                Head of family, tribe, or race.
2. gendarme   GEN darme (zhan darm') n.
                Cavalry man in command of a squad.
3. gender   GEN der (jen' der) n.
                Kind; sort; sex—masculine, feminine, neuter.
4. genitals   GEN itals (jen' i tals) n.
                The reproductive organs.
5. genealogy   GEN ealogy (jee nee al' o jee) n.
                The study of family lines; pedigree.
6. genealogist GEN ealogist (jee nee al' o jist) n.
                One who traces genealogies.
7. gene   GEN e (jene) n.
                One of the elements in hereditary development.
8. genius   GEN ius (jee' nyus) n.
                Great natural endowment; as, Milton was a genius.
9. generable   GEN erable (jen' e ra b'l) adj.
                Can be generated.
10. general   GEN er al (jen' e ral) adj.
                Relating to all kinds; as, a general thing.
11. generic   GEN eric (je ner' ik) adj.
                Belonging to race or kind; as, a generic name.
12. generation GEN eration (jen e ray' shun) n.
                Process of producing offspring.
13. genesis   GEN esis (jen' e sis) n.
                Development into being.

14. genetics   GEN etics (je net' iks) n.
                     The study of heredity.

15. genre   GEN re (zhan' re) n.
                     A species; a kind; a type.

16. genuine   GEN uine (jen' yu win) adj.
                     Pure; unalloyed; as, a genuine ruby.

17. genus   GEN us (jene' us) n.
                     Stock; category; classification.

18. genial   GEN ial (jee' nyal) adj.
                     Favorable to growth; kindly; as, a genial person.

19. progeny   pro GEN y (proj' e nee) n.
                     Offspring; descendants; children.

20. indigenous   indi GEN ous (in dij' e nus) adj.
                     Inborn; innate.

word analysis

CONGENIAL—No. 18+CON
    CON—Prefix =together
    GEN (genus)—Latin Root =growth
    AL—Suffix =relating to

practical exercises

1. Supply the missing words:
    He hired a .... to construct a family tree.
    Increasing interest in science should result in a healthy
    young .... Some people believe that marriage
    should be more related to ....

2. Analyze No. 10.

3. Choose the number of the word which most nearly expresses
the meaning of the italicized word:
    a. *hydrophobia*   (1) fear of high places   (2) courage
        (3) want   (4) fear of water   (5) accident   ....
    b. *putrefaction*   (1) growth   (2) allergy
        (3) geniality   (4) rottenness   (5) crops   ....
    c. *brilliant*   (1) dim   (2) wealthy   (3) enormous
        (4) small   (5) flashing   ....
    d. *microbe*   (1) animal   (2) vegetable
        (3) bacteria   (4) kingdom   (5) mineral   ....
    e. *spontaneous*   (1) result of labor
        (2) result of planning   (3) from sudden impulse
        (4) fruitless   (5) dry   ....

KEY NO. 159

0━━x

**SPEC · SPECT
SPECTRO**

watch
see
observe

is the Root *SPEC, SPECT, SPEC-TRO,* which means WATCH, SEE, OBSERVE. It comes from the Latin *spectare* and *specto.* From a simple SPECTacle we slip into science and space science which employs "out of the world" vocabulary.

1. spectacle
SPECT acle (spek' ta k'l) n.
A show; as, a gorgeous spectacle.

2. spectacular
SPECT acular (spek tak' yu lar) adj.
Appealing to the sight; thrilling.

3. spectator
SPECT ator (spec' tate er) n.
One who looks on; an observer.

4. specter
SPECT er (spek' ter) n.
A disembodied spirit; a ghost.

5. spectral
SPECT ral (spek' tral) adj.
Relating to a specter; ghostlike.

6. spectrogram
SPECTRO gram (spek' tro gram) n.
A photograph.

7. spectrum
SPECT rum (spek' trum) n.
*Wavelengths of color, from red to violet;
an afterimage.*

8. spectroscope
SPECTRO scope (spek' tro skope) n.
An instrument used to analyze spectra.

9. spectrophone
SPECTRO phone (spek' tro fone) n.
The science of analyzing spectra.

10. spectrology
SPECTRO logy (spek trol' o ji) n.
The science of spectrums.

11. spectrohelioscope
SPECTRO helioscope
(spek tro he' li o skope) n.
*An instrument for the observation of the
sun.*

12. spectroheliograph
SPECTRO heliograph
(spek tro hee' li o graf) n.
*An instrument which combines use of
spectroscope, camera and telescope.*

13. spectrometry
SPECTRO metry (spek trom' e tree) n.
The measuring of wavelengths of rays.

14. spectrophobia
SPECTRO phobia (spek tro foe' bi a) n.
Fear of ghosts.

15. species	SPEC ies (spee' sheze) n.
	Kinds; varieties; types.
16. special	SPEC ial (spesh' ul) adj.
	Relating to some particular quality.
17. specialist	SPEC ialist (spesh' u list) n.
	One who is expert in a special activity.
18. specimen	SPEC imen (spes' i men) n.
	A sample of a certain kind or thing.
19. specious	SPEC ious (spee' shus) adj.
	Pleasing to the eye but deceptive.

word analysis

SPECTROHELIOGRAPH—No. 12
   SPECTRO (spectare)—Latin Root =observe
   HELIO—Greek Root =sun
   GRAPH (graphein)—Root =to write

practical exercises

1. Supply the missing words:
      The boy was what is called in slang, a tough ....
      Evil takes on .... forms.

2. Analyze No. 13.

3. Read the following excerpt underlining all those words that contain keys you have already learned.

   Ability test called subject to misuse. Minority group children could lose out on training opportunities through misuse of standard mental tests, psychologists said today. . . . Most conventional tests are designed to measure learning abilities of children from middle-class environments who have certain advantages that stem from those environments, the group report said. When these same tests are turned to forecasting the learning abilities of children from less advantageous circumstances, the report continued, the results are often not valid.

                   (From *The New York Times,* July 19, 1964.)

KEY NO. *160*

O—➤

STEREO

solid

is the Root *STEREO*, which means SOLID. It comes from the Greek *stereos* which means a solid body. Years ago the Root *STEREO* was mainly associated with a *STEREO*pticon, which is an optical instrument for throwing pictures on a screen. Today, with the advent of motion pictures and the *STEREO*scope, and its use with a phonograph, illustrated lectures are given in the classroom with great profit to the student.

1. stereo   STEREO (ster′ ee oe) n.
   An abbreviated way of referring to a stereotype or stereophonic system.

2. stereotype   STEREO type (ster′ ee o tipe) v.
   To fix in lasting form.

3. stereogram   STEREO gram (ster′ ee o gram) n.
   A picture of objects in relief.

4. stereotomy   STEREO tomy (ster ee ot′ o me) n.
   The art of cutting solids.

5. stereometry   STEREO metry (ster ee om′ e tri) n.
   Art of finding the volume of a solid figure.

6. stereotype   STEREO type (ster′ ee o tipe) n.
   Anything reproduced without variation.

7. stereopticon   STEREO pticon (ster ee op′ ti kon) n.
   An instrument to put the images produced by transparent slides on a screen.

8. stereoscope   STEREO scope (ster′ ee o skope) n.
   Instrument which gives to pictures the impression of solidity.

9. stereoscopic   STEREO scopic (ster ee o skop′ ik) adj.
   Like a stereoscope.

10. stereoscopy   STEREO scopy (ster ee os′ ko pee) n.
    Science which deals with stereoscopic effects and methods.

11. stereopsis   STEREO psis (ster ee op′ sis) n.
    Stereoscopic vision.

12. stereoscopism   STEREO scopism (ster ee os′ ko piz um) n.
    Stereoscopic effects.

13. stereoscopist   STEREO scopist (ster ee os′ ko pist) n.
    A person skilled in stereoscopy.

14. stereotyper   STEREO typer (ste′ re o typ er) n.
    One who stereotypes.

15. stereoplasm   STEREO plasm (ster′ ee o plaz um) **n.**
                     The solid part of cell protoplasm.

16. stereochemistry STEREO chemistry (ster ee o kem′ i stree) **n.**
                     A science dealing with the arrangement of
                     atoms and molecules in space.

17. stereomatrix   STEREO matrix (ster ee o may′ triks**)** **n.**
                     Mold used in stereotyping.

18. stereome   STEREO me (ster′ ee ome) **n.**
                     Strengthening tissue in plants.

19. stereograph   STEREO graph (ster′ ee o graf) **n.**
                     Stereographic art.

20. stereography   STEREO graphy (ster ee og′ ra fee) **n.**
                     Picture prepared for the stereoscope.

word analysis

STEREOMETRY—No. 5
     STEREO (stereos)—Greek Root =solid
     METR (meter)—Root =measure
     Y—Suffix =inclined to; tend to

practical exercises

1. Supply the missing words:
     Pictures taken by a .... seem to have three
dimensions instead of being flat like pictures taken by an
ordinary camera. ....(ic) movies are very ex-
citing.

2. Analyze No. 2.

3. Key review. Match KEYS with their meanings:
     a. re   1. rank   ....
     b. rect   2. together   ....
     c. ridi, risi   3. back, again   ....
     d. ship   4. answer   ....
     e. spond   5. wisdom   ....
     f. scrib   6. under   ....
     g. sym, syn, sys   7. right   ....
     h. soph   8. write   ....
     i. sub   9. resemble   ....
     j. simil, simul   10. laugh   ....

O⟶x

**HEMI · DEMI
SEMI**

half

is the Prefix *HEMI, DEMI, SEMI*
meaning HALF. However, there is a
difference in the interpretation which
each one has of the word. When we
say HEMIsphere we don't really
mean half of the sphere, we mean one
side, right side or left side. When we
say DEMI we mean less or not quite,
as DEMImillionaire. When we say
SEMI we mean partly, as SEMI-
civilized; SEMIbarbarous. There is an
amusing combination of the three
in music—hemisemidemiquavers, short
notes sung in trills.

1. hemialgia   HEMI algia (hem i al' ji a) n.
        Pain on one side of the head.

2. hemihedron   HEMI hedron (hem i hed' ron) n.
        A crystal having half of the usual number
        of faces.

3. hemiepilepsy   HEMI epilepsy (hem i ep' i lep si) n.
        Convulsions on one side only.

4. hemiplegia   HEMI plegia (hem i plee' jee a) n.
        Paralysis on one side only.

5. hemisphere   HEMI sphere (hem' i sfir) n.
        Half of the globe.

6. hemidystrophy   HEMI dystrophy (hem i dis' tro fi) n.
        One half of body less developed than the
        other.

7. demimillionaire   DEMI millionaire (dem i mil' yun are) n.
        One having less than a million.

8. demivoice   DEMI voice (dem' i vois) n.
        Less than full voice.

9. demimonde   DEMI monde (dem' ee mond) n.
        A woman of doubtful reputation.

10. demitone   DEMI tone (dem' i tone) n.
        Halftone; semitone.

11. demisemitone   DEMI semitone (dem' i sem i tone) n.
        Quartertone.

12. demisuit   DEMI suit (dem' i sute) n.
        Half armor; not all parts protected.

13. demitasse   DEMI tasse (dem' ee tas) n.
        A very small cup, usually for after dinner
        coffee.

14. semiautomatic   SEMI automatic (sem i ot o mat' ic) adj.
                    Not completely automatic.

15. semicircle   SEMI circle (sem' i sir k'l) n.
                    A half circle.

16. semicivilized   SEMI civilized (sem i siv' i lized) adj.
                    Only partly civilized.

17. semidiapason   SEMI diapason (sem i die a pay' zon) n.
                    A diminished octave.

18. semimonthly   SEMI monthly (sem i month' lee) adj.
                    Twice in a month.

word analysis

DEMISEMITONE—No. 11
    DEMI—Prefix =half
    SEMI—Prefix =half
    TONE—Root word =sound

practical exercises

1. Supply the missing words:
    In some of the new nations .... tribes re-
tard advancement. Some singers rehearse in a ....
in order to save their voices for the performance.

2. Analyze No. 15.

3. Use one word for the phrase:
  a. to sing in halftones   ....
  b. to stand firm against attack   ....
  c. to hold on to one's place in line ....
  d. published two a month   ....
  e. to force the enemy out of a good position ....
  f. running after those who are running away ....

KEY NO. *162*

0—⚷

DIC · DICT

say
declare

is the Root *DIC, DICT* which means SAY, DECLARE. It is a good key to own and opens the door to many needed words. You will recognize it without difficulty. Notice the change in pronunciation of words 13–17. The *c* sound is entirely omitted. *DICT =DIT.*

1. dictate — DIC tate (dik′ tate) v.
   Command; proclaim; as, dictate *a law.*

2. dictator — DICT ator (dik′ tate r) n.
   One who commands; an absolute ruler.

3. dictation — DICT ation (dik tay′ shun) n.
   Authoritative command; as, yield to dictation.

4. diction — DIC tion (dik′ shun) n.
   Language; choice of words; as, fine diction.

5. dictionary — DIC tionary (dik′ shu nare ee) n.
   A reference book of words.

6. dictum — DICT um (dik′ tum) n.
   The statement of a dictator.

7. dictatorship — DICT atorship (dik tate′ or ship) n.
   The rule of a dictator.

8. dictatorial — DICT atorial (dik ta tore′ ee al) adj.
   In the nature of a dictator.

9. contradict — contra DICT (kon tra dikt′) v.
   To speak against; declare wrong.

10. indicate — in DIC ate (in′ di kate) v.
    To point out; as, indicate *an error.*

11. indication — in DIC ation (in di kay′ shun) n.
    A sign of; as, an indication *of favor.*

12. indicator — in DIC ator (in′ di kate r) n.
    That which points to something.

13. indict — in DICT (in dite′) v.
    To charge with some offense.

14. indictment — in DICT ment (in dite′ ment) n.
    A charge; as, an indictment *of murder.*

15. indictable — in DICT able (in dite′ a b'l) adj.
    Can be charged, as with crime.

16. indicter — in DICT er (in dite′ er) n.
    One who makes the charge of offense.

17. indictee — in DICT ee (in die tee′) n.
    The one who is charged with offense.

18. indicative — in DIC ative (in dik′ at iv) adj.
    Pointing out; bringing to notice.

19. prediction   pre DICT ion (pre dik' shun) n.
                  A prophecy.
20. malediction   male DICT ion (mal e dik' shun) n.
                  Words of ill-will; a curse.

word analysis

CONTRADICTION—No. 9+ION
    CONTRA—Prefix =against
    DIC (dicere)—Latin Root =to speak
    TION—Suffix =act of

practical exercises

1. Supply the missing words:
    The evidence flatly .... the defense of the
    ...., The general used the .... of
    a ...., and he aroused the resentment of the
    audience by his .... approach to the subject.

2. Analyze No. 5.

3. By adding the correct keys the words will express the phrases:
    a. the opposite of what was said— contra..........tion
    b. one who makes a charge against another— in..........er
    c. a charge against another— in...........................
    d. pain on one side of the head— ....algia
    e. paralyzed on one side of the body only— ....plegia
    f. sample to show quality or characteristics— ....imen

KEY NO. *163*

0—⚷

AGI · AGO · AG

**move
go
do**

is the Root *AGI, AGO, AG* which means to MOVE, GO, DO. This is a lively key, always on the go. Every now and then the feminine form of a word is used as in No. 11. "ESS" is also feminine. No. 7 is well known, from the washing machine to the whole world where life goes on. The washing machine needs a quarter; man needs keys to the language.

1. agent   AG ent (ay′ jent) n.
   One who does business for another; representative.

2. agency   AG ency (ay′ jen see) n.
   The office or function of an agent; as, an employment agency.

3. agenda   AG enda (a jen′ da) n.
   The program of work to be done.

4. agential   AG ential (ay jen′ chul) adj.
   Relating to the affairs of an agency.

5. agile   AG ile (aj′ il) adj.
   Quick; active; as, an agile wit.

6. agility   AG ility (a jil′ it ee) n.
   Quickness; activity.

7. agitate   AG itate (aj′ i tate) n.
   Keep moving; excite; as, to agitate for rights.

8. agitation   AG itation (aj i ta′ shun) n.
   Excitement; disturbance; as, civil rights agitation.

9. agitative   AG itative (aj′ i tay tiv) adj.
   Causing agitation.

10. agitator   AG itator (aj′ i tate r) n.
    One who stirs up the public.

11. agitatrix   AG itatrix (aj i tay′ trix) n.
    A female agitator.

12. antagonist   ant AGO nist (an tag′ o nist) n.
    One who opposes another; an opponent.

13. antagonize   ant AGO nize (an tag′ o nize) v.
    To act in opposition to; annoy.

14. agitant   AG itant (aj′ i tant) n.
    One who is active in a course of action.

15. agogics   AG ogics (a goj′ iks) n.
    Theory of relation between emphasis and length of tone.

16. agog   AG og (a gog') adj.
                Eager; astir; as, all agog at the news of war.
17. pedagogue   ped AGO gue (ped' a gog) n.
                A teacher.
18. pedagogy   ped AGO gy (ped' a goj ee) n.
                The study of teaching methods.
19. synagogue   syn AGO gue (sin' a gog) n.
                A Jewish place of assembly for worship.
20. demagogue   dem AGO gue (dem' a gog) n.
                *One who stirs people up for personal politics
                or profit.*

word analysis

AGITATIVE—No. 9
    AGI (agere)—Latin Root =to move
    ATE—Suffix =make; cause
    IVE—Suffix =causing

practical exercises

1. Supply the missing words:
    "The mind of man is ....(d) by various prob-
    lems." (Samuel Johnson) At ninety William Cullen Bryant
    still had the .... of youth. A political ....
    is not popular in this country.

2. Analyze No. 1.

3. Choose the number of the word which most nearly expresses
   the meaning of the italicized word:
    a. *pedagogy* (1) dentistry (2) art (3) music
        (4) methods of teaching (5) sports   ....
    b. *indictment* (1) invitation (2) nuisance
        (3) roadster (4) anger (5) a legal charge   ....
    c. *semicircle* (1) half circle (2) right angle
        (3) cube (4) physics (5) agitation   ....
    d. *specie* (1) bankcheck (2) vegetation
        (3) mineralogy (4) hard money
        (5) paper money   ....
    e. *acerbity* (1) geniality (2) wit (3) anecdote
        (4) antidote (5) bitterness   ....

327

KEY NO. *164*

o—🔑

JUNCT · JOIN

join

is the Root *JUNCT, JOIN* and it means just that: JOIN. This word list is a very fine illustration of the value of knowing the keys to our language. Only the key *JOIN* of the whole list can stand alone. All the twenty words are built up by the keys which are joined together. Fifteen keys are represented in this list. Twelve of them you have learned formally, each on its own page. Only three have not been listed but even these you have met in the WORD ANALYSIS. Good going!

1. junction   JUNCT ion (junk' shun) n.
     Act of joining; place of meeting.

2. juncture   JUNCT ure (junk' chur) n.
     A joining; a concurrence of circumstances.

3. junctive   JUNCT ive (junk' tiv) adj.
     Tending to join.

4. adjoining   ad JOIN ing (ad join' ing) adj.
     Attached; as, adjoining *houses.*

5. adjunct   ad JUNCT (aj' unkt) n.
     Something added; someone who assists another.

6. adjunctive   ad JUNCT ive (a junk' tiv) adj.
     Tending to join together.

7. abjunctive   ab JUNCT ive (ab junk' tiv) adj.
     Tending to dissever.

8. conjoin   con JOIN (kon join') v.
     Unite; as, conjoin *in wedlock.*

9. conjoiner   con JOIN er (kon join' er) n.
     One who or that which is brought together.

10. conjunctive   con JUNCT ive (kon junk' tiv) adj.
     Tending to join together.

11. conjunction   con JUNCT ion (kon junk' shun) n.
     A part of speech which joins words or sentences as, in one and two, and is a conjunction.

12. conjuncture   con JUNCT ure (kon junk' chur) n.
     A coming together; as, a conjuncture *of events.*

13. conjunctiva   con JUNCT iva (kon junk tie' va) n.
     The mucous membrane which lines the inner surface of the eyelids.

328

14. conjunctivitis con JUNCT ivitis (kon junk ti vite′ is) n.
        Inflammation of the conjunctiva.
15. disjoint   dis JOIN t (dis joint′) v.
        Separate.
16. disjunctive   dis JUNCT ive (dis junk′ tiv) adj.
        Tending to separate; to disjoin.
17. enjoin   en JOIN (en join′) v.
        To lay an order upon; to command; to forbid;
        as, to enjoin by oath.
18. enjoinder   en JOIN der (en join′ der) n.
        That which is enjoined, or forbidden.
19. injunction   in JUNCT ion (in junk′ shun) n.
        Act of enjoining; a restraining order.
20. interjunction inter JUNCT ion (in ter junk′ shun) n.
        A mutual joining.

word analysis

CONJUNCTION—No. 11
    CON—Prefix =with; together
    JUNCT—Root =join
    TION—Suffix =state of; act of

practical exercises

1. Supply the missing words:
    "Adam and Eve disobeyed that high .... not
to eat that fruit." (John Milton) "Learning is an ....
to oneself." (Shakespeare) The .... connects
parts of a sentence.

2. Analyze No. 3.

3. The six following keys give a clear picture of what the change
of prefix can do to the change of meaning of the same root.
    Example: the Root is JUNCT+ION, a joining. *AB*junction,
    a parting. To each JUNCTION, prefix the correct key to
    give the meaning:

a. ad	+	junction	=	joining..........
b. con	+	junction	=	joining..........
c. dis	+	junction	=	joining..........
d. in	+	junction	=	joining..........
e. inter	+	junction	=	joining..........
f. sub	+	junction	=	joining..........

KEY NO. *165*

O—⚷

PICT · PICTO

paint

is the Root *PICT, PICTO,* meaning to PAINT, to make a picture. All the words made with this Root figure largely in pictures and picture-making of all kinds. You may have a perfectly valid question to ask about the spelling of this root, PICTO and PICT. Why does PAINT have an *n* and the pictures have *c*? The Latin verb has both—*pingere* and *pictus.*

1. picture   PICT ure (pik′ chur) n.
   A representation through the art of painting, drawing, or photography.

2. pictograph   PICTO graph (pic′ to graf) n.
   Writing with pictures or symbols.

3. pictography   PICTO graphy (pik tog′ ra fee) n.
   Picture writing.

4. pictoradiogram   PICTO radiogram (pik to ray′ di o gram) n.
   A picture transmitted by radiophotography.

5. pictorial   PICTO rial (pik tore′ ee al) adj.
   Relating to pictures; as, pictorial *style.*

6. pictorialism   PICTO rialism (pik to′ ri al iz um) n.
   The use of pictorial style.

7. pictorialize   PICTO rialize (pik to′ ri al ize) v.
   To represent by pictures.

8. picture   PICT ure (pik′ chur) v.
   Make a mental image; as, I will picture *the meeting in my mind.*

9. pictural   PICT ural (pik′ tur al) adj.
   Pictorial.

10. picturedom   PICT uredom (pik′ tur dom) n.
    The world of motion pictures.

11. picturedrome   PICT uredrome (pik′ tur drome) n.
    A moving-picture theater.

12. picturesque   PICT uresque (pik chu resk′) adj.
    Just like a picture, as, a picturesque *scene.*

13. picturesquely   PICT uresquely (pik chu resk′ lee) adv.
    In a picturesque manner.

14. picturer   PICT urer (pik′ tur er) n.
    A painter.

15. picturesqueness   PICT uresqueness (pik chu resk′ nes) n.
    The quality of being like a picture.

16. pictury   PICT ury (pik′ tur i) adj.
    Tending to look like a picture.

17. depict   de PICT (de pikt') v.
                        To form a likeness; to portray; describe.
18. depicture   de PICT ure (de pik' chur) v.
                        To depict; to imagine.
19. depiction   de PICT ion (de pik' shun) n.
                        The act of depicting; representing.

word analysis

PICTURESQUENESS—No. 15
     PICT (pingere)—Latin Root =to paint
     URE—Suffix =process; act
     ESQUE—Suffix =like
     NESS—Suffix =quality of

practical exercises

1. Supply the missing words:
     A motion .... magazine keeps one informed
   of all the news in .... He paddled the canoe
   into a most .... spot and there we had a
   ....picnic.
2. Analyze No. 5.
3. By adding keys to a simple root word, a new and stronger
   word is created.
     Example: EN+rich+ment=state of becoming rich. To the
        following root words add these two KEYS:
     a. ....joy..........   ....
     b. ....dear..........   ....
     c. ....dow..........   ....
     d. ....force..........   ....
     e. ....act..........   ....
     f. ....ploy..........   ....
     g. ....barrass..........   ....

KEY NO. 166

0—🗝

LIBER · LIVER

free

is the Root *LIBER, LIVER,* which means FREE. It comes from the Latin word LIBERtas, meaning liberty. The Spanish word for liberty is similar, LIBERtad. The spellings *b* and *v* come from the Latin verb li*b*ero, li*b*eravi, li*b*eratus, which means to set free. Do not confuse this key with the LIBER which means book, or LIBRA, which means balance, weigh.

1. liberal	LIBER al (lib′ e ral) adj.	
	Relating to liberty; free.	
2. liberalize	LIBER alize (lib′ e ra lize) v.	
	To make more free; as, to liberalize the mind from prejudice.	
3. liberalization	LIBER alization (lib e ra li zay′ shun) n.	
	Act of liberalizing.	
4. liberalism	LIBER alism (lib′ e ra liz um) n.	
	A doctrine of generous freedoms.	
5. liberalist	LIBER alist (lib′ e ra list) n.	
	One who believes in liberalism.	
6. liberality	LIBER ality (lib e ral′ it ee) n.	
	A generosity; broad-mindedness.	
7. liberate	LIBER ate (lib′ e rate) v.	
	To set free.	
8. liberator	LIBER ator (lib′ e rate r) n.	
	One who sets others free.	
9. libertarian	LIBER tarian (lib er tar′ ee an) n.	
	One who believes in the doctrine of free will; the principles of freedom.	
10. liberticide	LIBER ticide (li ber′ ti side) n.	
	The destruction of liberty.	
11. liberticidal	LIBER ticidal (li ber ti side′ al) adj.	
	Tending to destroy liberty.	
12. libertine	LIBER tine (lib′ er teen) n.	
	A person without morals; a rake.	
13. libertinage	LIBER tinage (lib′ er tee nij) n.	
	Immoral conduct; licentiousness.	
14. deliver	de LIVER (de liv′ er) v.	
	To set free; to set at liberty.	
15. deliverance	de LIVER ance (de liv′ e rans) n.	
	State of being freed; release.	
16. deliverer	de LIVER er (de liv′ er er) n.	
	Liberator.	

17. delivery   de LIVER y (de liv' e ree) n.
                    Freedom; liberation.

word analysis

LIBERTICIDE—No. 10
     LIBER—Latin Root =free
     TY—Suffix =that which
     CIDE (caedere)—Root =to kill

practical exercises

1. Supply the missing words:
     If one is given .... without limitation, re-
sponsibility and discipline can soon descend to ....,
and that soon leads to ...., the death of liberty.

2. Analyze No. 7.

3. Choose the number of the word which best expresses the
meaning of the italicized word:
     a. *resist*   (1) agree   (2) deliver   (3) depict
          (4) oppose   (5) prepare   ....
     b. *column*   (1) thunder   (2) crest   (3) firing
          (4) bullet   (5) a support to a building   ....
     c. *final*   (1) scared   (2) slackened   (3) engaged
          (4) the last   (5) conjoined   ....
     d. *artillery*   (1) cannons   (2) groceries   (3) books
          (4) clothing   (5) pursuit   ....
     e. *minaret*   (1) lodging
          (2) tall, slender tower on a building   (3) awning
          (4) roof   (5) driveway   ....
     f. *eminence*   (1) darkness   (2) bullet
          (3) engagement   (4) death
          (5) quality of being above others   ....

O—➤

HAB · HABIT

have
live

is the Root *HAB, HABIT* meaning HAVE. *HAB* comes from the Latin *habeo*, to HAVE; and HABIT from *habitare*, to LIVE. One of the finest words in our language is No. 19. It has saved the lives and usefulness of countless soldiers by making them *HAVE again* lost faculties. A Latin phrase much used in Law may well be added to our list: *Habeas Corpus.* Literally it means, "You have the body."

1. habit — HABIT (hab' it) n.
A behavior pattern; usage; custom.

2. habeas corpus — HAB eas corpus (hay' bee a skor' pus) n.
You have the body.

3. haberdashery — HAB erdashery (hab' er dash e ree) n.
A store which sells articles of men's wear.

4. habergeon — HAB ergeon (hab' er jun) n.
A short jacket of mail.

5. habile — HAB ile (hab' il) adj.
Able; skillful.

6. habiliments — HAB iliments (ha bil' i ments) n.
Dress furnishings; clothing.

7. habilitate — HAB ilitate (ha bil' i tate) v.
To clothe; to prepare.

8. habilimentation — HAB ilimentation (ha bil i men tay' shun) n.
The clothing industries and arts.

9. habitat — HAB itat (hab' i tat) n.
The natural abode of plant or animal.

10. habitation — HAB itation (hab i tay' shun) n.
Dwelling place; home; residence.

11. habitual — HABIT ual (ha bich' yu al) adj.
Customary; relating to habit; as, habitual industry.

12. habituate — HABIT uate (ha bit' yu ate) v.
To make accustomed to.

13. habitude — HAB itude (hab' i tude) n.
Nature; character; habitual attitude.

14. habitué — HAB itué (ha bich' u way) n.
One who frequents a certain place; as, a habitué of the theater.

15. inhabit — in HAB it (in hab' it) v.
To live in; to establish as resident.

16. inhabitant   in HAB itant (in hab′ it ant) n.
           One who lives permanently in a place.
17. rehabilitate   re HAB ilitate (re ha bil′ i tate) v.
           To make able again; restrengthen.
18. rehabilitation   re HAB ilitation (re ha bil i tay′ shun) n.
           Act of rehabilitating.

word analysis

REHABILITATE—No. 17
     RE—Prefix =back; again
     HABILIT (habilis)—Latin Root =suitable; fit; apt
     ATE—Suffix =make

practical exercise

Read the following excerpt underlining all those words that contain keys you have already learned.

     Towards evening, the attack of the French, repeated and resisted so bravely, slackened in its fury. They had other foes besides the British to engage, or were preparing for a final onset. It came at last; the columns of the Imperial Guard marched up the hill of Saint Jean, at length and at once to sweep the English from the height which they had maintained all day, and in spite of all: unscared by the thunder of the artillery, which hurled death from the English line—the dark rolling column pressed on and up the hill. It seemed almost to crest the eminence, when it began to wave and falter. Then it stopped, still facing the shot. Then at last the English troops rushed from the post from which no enemy had been able to dislodge them, and the guard turned and fled.

     No more firing was heard at Brussels—the pursuit rolled miles away. Darkness came down on the field and the city: and Amelia was praying for George who was lying on his face, dead, with a bullet through his heart.

     (From "The Victory at Waterloo," from *Vanity Fair*, by William Makepeace Thackeray.)

KEY NO. *168*

O—x

FIN · FINIS

end

is a Root, *FIN, FINIS,* meaning END. The Latin word *finis* has become a part of our language and you will often see it after the last sentence of an English book. Word No. 20, *financial,* meaning relating to money, does not seem to belong to this list. What has money to do with FIN meaning end? Actually there is a relation. Finance comes from *finer* which means to end, and also to pay. When you pay your bill the financial matter is ended. Rather farfetched, don't you think? But there it is.

1. final
   FIN al (fine' l) adj.
   Relating to the end; as, the final *addition.*
2. finale
   FIN ale (fin al' ee) n.
   The last section of a musical composition.
3. finalism
   FIN alism (fie' nal iz um) n.
   Theological doctrine.
4. fin de siècle
   FIN de siècle (fan de sya' k'l) n.
   End of the century.
5. finis
   FIN is (fin' is) n.
   End; conclusion.
6. finish
   FIN ish (fin' ish) v.
   To complete; to reach the end.
7. finite
   FIN ite (fie' nite) adj.
   Definitely limited.
8. finitesimal
   FIN itesimal (fin i tes' i mal) adj.
   Defined by a finite ordinal number.
9. finial
   FIN ial (fin' ee al) n.
   The very topmost; a crowning detail.
10. finific
    FIN ific (fi nif' ik) adj.
    A limiting element or quality.
11. finitude
    FIN itude (fin' i tude) n.
    A finite state.
12. finity
    FIN ity (fin' i ti) n.
    The quality of finitude.
13. affinity
    af FIN ity (a fin' it ee) n.
    Attraction; resemblance.
14. confine
    con FIN e (kon fine') v.
    To keep shut in; as, confine *to bed.*

336

15. define   de FIN e (de fine') v.
                To mark the limit; as, to define *the power of the court.*

16. definitive   de FIN itive (de fin' it iv) adj.
                Conclusive; as, a definitive *statement.*

17. infinite   in FIN ite (in' fi nit) adj.
                Without end; limitless.

18. infinity   in FIN ity (in fin' it ee) n.
                Eternity; boundlessness.

19. infinitesimal in FIN itesimal (in fin i tes' i mal) adj.
                So small it cannot be measured.

20. financial   FIN ancial (fin an' chul) adj.
                Relating to money; as, a financial *statement of the account.*

word analysis

INFINITY—No. 18
    IN—Prefix =not
    FIN (finis)—Latin Root =end
    ITY—Suffix =quality of

practical exercises

1. Supply the missing words:
     She took .... pains with her work. Boswell's biography of Samuel Johnson is generally considered .... Man will not accept a .... world.

2. Analyze No. 15.

3. Fill the spaces with words which contain the key *FIN*:
    a. At the end of the story he wrote the word ....
    b. A micro-micro measurement is truly ....
    c. Man's days are ....
    d. In grammar we have articles which are .... as well as indefinite.
    e. He has an .... for the rolling countryside.
    f. Beauty is hard to ....

KEY NO. 169

O—x

**JUD · JUDI
JUDIC**

judge
lawyer

is the Root *JUD*, *JUDI*, *JUDIC* meaning JUDGE; LAWYER. Note how
the Prefixes *AD* and *AB* do their
job. The word is turned upside down
when *AB* is used, the JUDGE can
even throw the case out of court. In
Roman Law the *judex* was just like a
modern arbitrator. Watch the Prefix
carefully before you decide on the
meaning of a word.

1. judge JUD ge (juj) n.
   *A public officer who has the authority to give
   judgment.*

2. judgment JUD gment (juj' ment) n.
   An opinion or decision.

3. judicable JUDIC able (jud' i ka b'l) adj.
   Capable of being judged.

4. judicate JUDIC ate (jue' di kate) v.
   To judge.

5. judicative JUDIC ative (jud' i kate iv) adj.
   Judicial; as, the judicative *faculty.*

6. judicator JUDIC ator (jue' di kay tor) n.
   A judge.

7. judicatory JUDIC atory (jud' i ka tore ee) adj.
   Exercising judicial functions; as, a judicatory
   tribunal.

8. judicature JUDIC ature (jud' i ka chur) n.
   *The act of judging. As, the honor of a judge is
   his* judicature.

9. judicial JUDI cial (ju dish' al) adj.
   Relating to administration of justice; as,
   judicial *power.*

10. judicious JUDI cious (ju dish' us) adj.
    Having sound judgment.

11. judiciously JUDI ciously (ju dish' us lee) adv.
    Wisely; soundly; as, the court ruled judiciously.

12. adjudicate ad JUDI cate (a jud' i kate) v.
    To settle by judicial decree.

13. abjudicate ab JUDI cate (ab jue' di cate) v.
    Reject the case; throw it out of court.

14. adjudicative ad JUDI cative (a jue' di kay tiv) adj.
    Tending to pass judgment.

15. injudicious in JUDI cious (in ju dish' us) adj.
    Not having sound judgment.

16. injudiciously   in JUDI ciously (in ju dish' us lee) adv.
                        Unsoundly; unwisely; unjudiciously.
17. prejudice   pre JUDI ce (prej' ud is) n.
                        Bias; discrimination.
18. prejudicial   pre JUDI cial (prej u dish' al) adj.
                        Biased; damaging without proof.
19. unprejudiced unpre JUDI ced (un prej' ud isd) adj.
                        Not prejudiced.
20. unprejudicial unpre JUDI cial (un pre jue di' shal) adj.
                        Without being biased.

word analysis

INJUDICIOUSLY—No. 16
    IN—Prefix =not
    JUDI (judex)—Root =judge
    CIOUS—Suffix =having; being
    LY—Suffix =in the manner of

practical exercises

1. Supply the missing words:
    A .... must not be .... when he
    passes .... on a case. Justice must be free from
    any taint of ....

2. Analyze No. 2.

3. Write the word that each phrase explains:
    a. to pass judgment   ....
    b. can be judged   ....
    c. having sound judgment   ....
    d. damaging to a case or evidence   ....
    e. having the power to judge   ....

O——x

PRIM · PRIME

first

is the Root *PRIM, PRIME* meaning FIRST. It comes from the Latin word *primus* (masc.), *prima* (fem.). This is a very important key for most people. From the Metropolitan Opera to the ministry of states, to what hangs on the butcher's hook, everyone wants it *PRIME*.

1. primacy   PRIM acy (prime' a see) n.
    State of being first in rank.

2. prima donna   PRIM a donna (prim a don' a) n.
    The first lady of opera.

3. primage   PRIM age (prie' mij) n.
    Extra money paid to the captain by shippers for extra care of their goods.

4. primal   PRIM al (prie' mal) adj.
    First; original.

5. primary   PRIM ary (prie' mar ee) adj.
    First in order of time; as, the primary grades.

6. primarily   PRIM arily (prie mar' i lee) adv.
    In the first place; originally.

7. primate   PRIM ate (prie' mate) n.
    First in rank, quality, authority.

8. primateship   PRIM ateship (prie' mate ship) n.
    Office of a primate; the first in dignity and authority.

9. Primates   PRIM ates (pri' mates) n.
    The order of mammals consisting of man, monkey, etc.

10. primavera   PRIM avera (pree ma vay' ra) n.
    A light wood called white mahogany.

11. prime   PRIME (prime) adj.
    The foremost; the best; as, prime beef.

12. primer   PRIM er (prim' er) n.
    A small, elementary introductory book to teach reading.

13. primeval   PRIM eval (prie me' val) adj.
    Belonging to the first ages; as, "This is the forest primeval. . . ." (Longfellow)

14. primitive   PRIM itive (prim' it iv) adj.
    From the earliest times.

15. primogenitor   PRIM ogenitor (prie moe jen' it ur) n.
    The earliest ancestor.

16. primogeniture PRIMO geniture (prie moe jen' i chur) n.
                 State of being the first-born of parents.
17. primoprime   PRIMO prime (prie' mo prime) adj.
                 The very first; strictly original.
18. primordial   PRIM ordial (prie mord' ee al) adj.
                 Elemental; fundamental; as, primordial *rights.*
19. primatial   PRIM atial (prie ma' shul) adj.
                 Having primacy.

word analysis

PRIMEVAL—No. 13
    PRIM (primus)—Latin Root =first
    EV (aevum)—Root =age
    AL—Suffix =relating to

practical exercises

1. Supply the missing words:
    Longfellow's great poem, *Evangeline,* begins with these
    words: "This is the forest ...." Grandma Moses
    painted in a .... style.

2. Analyze No. 5.

3. To complete the necessary words add the missing keys:
    a. firstborn in the family— primo..........ture
    b. judgment without truth— ....judice
    c. a joining together— con..........tion
    d. finished it at last— ....ally
    e. he was freed from his captivity— de..........ed
    f. no likeness between them— dis..........arity
    g. he was in a state of being half-starved— ....starva..........

is the Prefix *SUR* which means OVER, ABOVE, MORE. This Prefix does not indicate greatness or superiority. In No. 2, it is a belt tied over a saddle; in No. 13, it describes an article of clothing that goes over other clothes

o—⚡

SUR

over
above
more

1. surcharge   SUR charge (sur' charj) n.
       An addition over and above the price.

2. surcingle   SUR cingle (sur' sin g'l) n.
       A belt drawn over the saddle to keep it on the horse.

3. surcoat   SUR coat (sur' kote) n.
       Overcoat.

4. surface   SUR face (sur' fas) n.
       The top layer; as, the surface of the water.

5. surfeit   SUR feit (sur' fit) v.
       To sicken with having too much, with excess.

6. surmise   SUR mise (sur mize') v.
       To guess; to have superficial opinion based on little evidence.

7. surpass   SUR pass (sur pas') v.
       To get ahead of; to transcend.

8. surplice   SUR plice (sur' plis) n.
       A white linen vestment worn over the cassock of a priest.

9. surplus   SUR plus (sur' plus) n.
       Over plus; excess; abundance.

10. surprise   SUR prise (sur prize') v.
       To take unawares.

11. surround   SUR round (su round') v.
       To go around on all sides; encircle.

12. surtax   SUR tax (sur' taks) n.
       An additional tax.

13. surtout   SUR tout (sur tu') n.
       Over all; a man's overcoat.

14. surveillance   SUR veillance (sur vay' lens) n.
       Supervision; the watch over all.

15. survey   SUR vey (sur vay') v.
       Look over with an appraising eye; oversee.

16. surveyor   SUR veyor (sur vay' or) n.
       One who appraises; overseer.

17. survigrous   SUR vigrous (sur vig' rus) adj.
                         Very active; enterprising.

18. survival   SUR vival (sur vie' val) n.
                         Continuing to live; keeping alive.

19. survivor   SUR vivor (sur vie' vor) n.
                         One who remained alive.

20. survive   SUR vive (sur vive') v.
                         Remain alive longer than others.

word analysis

SURVIGROUS—No. 17
    SUR—Prefix =over; more
    VIGR (vigor)—Latin Root =energy
    OUS—Suffix =full of

practical exercises

1. Supply the missing words:
     The .... of the fittest is a theory in evolu-
tion. In his early days George Washington worked as a
.... The judge asked for evidence, not ....

2. Analyze No. 4.

3. Read the following excerpt underlining all those words that
contain keys you have already learned.

     Three years ago last Thursday, residents of Berlin awak-
ened to learn news. During the night Soviet-led Communists
had sealed the border dividing East and West Berlin. Work-
men were erecting the 29-mile-long concrete and barbed-
wire barrier that since has become known in the West as
"the wall of shame." The wall was the boldest Communist
move since the blockade of West Berlin. The apparent Soviet
motives were to stop the exodus of East German refugees—
mostly young people and technicians—which had reached
2,000 a day, and to force the West's acceptance of the
division of Berlin and Germany and thus of the sovereignty
of East Berlin.

     (From "Anniversary of a Wall," *The New York Times,*
Aug., 1964.)

VIV • VIVI • VITA

alive
life

is the Root *VIV, VIVI, VITA* which means ALIVE, LIFE. It comes from the Latin *vita* and *vivus*. The key leads on from the ancient barbaric practice of VIVIsepulture, to the modern barbaric practice of VIVIsection. As we travel we marvel at the VIVIparous guppy; at the salmon which gives us fish eggs for caviar. We rejoice at the discovery of VITAmins and wonder what the ancients did without this knowledge. Of course, they didn't go to the drugstore to buy them, they just ate them in the growing foods.

1. vital	VITA l (vite′ al) adj.	*Relating to life; as,* vital *power.*
2. Vitaglass	VITA glass (vie′ ta glas) n.	*A trademark for glass which allows ultraviolet rays to pass through it.*
3. vitality	VITA lity (vi tal′ i ty) n.	*State and quality of being alive.*
4. vitalize	VITA lize (vite′ al ize) v.	*Endow with life; revive; vivify.*
5. vitals	VITA ls (vite′ alz) n.	*The vital organs; essential parts; as heart, lungs, brain, liver, etc.*
6. vitamin	VITA min (vite′ a min) n.	*One of the essential constituents of foods.*
7. vitaminize	VITA minize (vie′ ta mi nize) v.	*Enrich foods by adding vitamins.*
8. vitaminology	VITA minology (vie ta mi nol′ o ji) n.	*Knowledge treating of the nature of vitamins.*
9. vitascope	VITA scope (vite′ a skope) n.	*A motion picture projector.*
10. vivace	VIV ace (vee vach′ ay) adj.	*In a brisk; lively; spirited manner.*
11. vivacious	VIV acious (vi vay′ shus) adj.	*Full of life; sprightly; as,* vivacious *wit.*
12. vivacity	VIV acity (vi vas′ it ee) n.	*Vital force; animation.*
13. vivarium	VIV arium (vie var′ ee um) n.	*A box, enclosed with glass, in which plants and animals are kept alive indoors.*

344

14. viveur   VIV eur (vee ver') n.
                         One who lives it up.
15. viviparous   VIV iparous (vie vip' a rus) adj.
                         Bearing live young, not eggs.
16. vivisect   VIV isect (viv' i sekt) v.
                         Cut for investigation.
17. vivisection   VIV isection (viv i sek' shun) n.
                         The act of vivisecting for science.
18. vivisepulture VIV isepulture (viv i sep' ul tur) n.
                         The practice of burying people alive.
19. revive   re VIV e (re vive') v.
                         Bring back to life.
20. survive   sur VIV e (sur vive') v.
                         Live through and beyond an ordeal.

word analysis

VIVISECTION—No. 17
     VIVI (vivus)—Latin Root =alive
     SECT (sectus)—Latin Root =cut up
     TION—Suffix =act of

practical exercises

1. Supply the missing words:
     One of the wonders among creatures is the guppy, which is .... Happily, in this century, ... is no longer practiced. However, we do have ....(ion), alas!

2. Analyze No. 14.

3. Choose the number of the word which most nearly expresses the italicized word:
    a. *vivisepulture*   (1) burying alive   (2) generation   (3) growth   (4) survivor   (5) life   ....
    b. *vitascope*   (1) minerals   (2) microbe   (3) phobia   (4) motion picture projector   (5) glass   ....
    c. *viviparous*   (1) vigorous   (2) desperate   (3) anxious   (4) ashamed   (5) bearing live young   ....
    d. *vitality*   (1) height   (2) weight   (3) energy   (4) surplice   (5) gown   ....
    e. *prejudice*   (1) intolerance   (2) friendship   (3) justice   (4) vitamins   (5) pity   ....

KEY NO. *173*

CYCL · CYCLO

**wheel
circle
circular**

is the Root *CYCL, CYCLO*. It comes from the Greek *cyclos,* meaning WHEEL, CIRCLE, CIRCULAR. A bit more about the CYCLOrama, No. 7. This curved background on the stage gives an audience a feeling of being part of the production. CYCLOPS, No. 8, was a hideous monster with a single eye, one of a race of giants. You can read about him in Greek mythology or in Homer's *Odyssey.*

1. cycle   CYCL e (sie′ kul) n.
   A complete course of operations returning to its original state.

2. cyclic   CYCL ic (sie′ klik) adj.
   Moving in circles or cycles.

3. cyclian   CYCL ian (sik′ li an) adj.
   Moving in circles.

4. cyclical   CYCL ical (sie′ kli kal) adj.
   Moving in a circle or cycle.

5. cyclometer   CYCL ometer (sie klom′ et er) n.
   Instrument to measure area of circles.

6. cyclometry   CYCL ometry (sie klom′ e tri) n.
   Science of measuring circles.

7. cyclorama   CYCL orama (sie klo ram′ a) n.
   A spectacle painted on a curved background.

8. Cyclops   CYCL ops (sie′ klops) n.
   A mythical giant with one eye in the middle of his forehead.

9. cyclitis   CYCL itis (si klie′ tis) n.
   Inflammation of the tissue behind the eyeball.

10. cyclograph   CYCLO graph (sie′ klo graf) n.
    An apparatus attached to a bicycle which records the topography of the road.

11. cyclographer   CYCLO grapher (sie klog′ ra fer) n.
    One who writes of a cycle of legends.

12. cycloid   CYCLO id (sie′ kloid) adj.
    Circular or arranged in circles.

13. cyclone   CYCLO ne (sie′ klone) n.
    A wind blowing circularly; a tornado.

14. cyclonology   CYCLO nology (sie klone ol′ o ji) n.
    Study of cyclones.

346

15. cyclonoscope CYCLO noscope (sie kloe' no skope) n.
         Apparatus for finding the center of a cyclone.

16. Cyclopean CYCLO pean (sie klo pee' an) adj.
         Like a Cyclops; having a median eye.

17. cyclopedia CYCLO pedia (sie klo peed' ee a) n.
         The range of human knowledge.

18. cyclopedic CYCLO pedic (sie klo pede' ik) adj.
         Being like an encyclopedia; as, a cyclopedic
         mind.

19. cycloscope CYCLO scope (syk' lo skop) n.
         A machine to measure velocity of rotation.

20. cyclopedist CYCLO pedist (sie klo pee' dist) n.
         One who writes for an encyclopedia.

word analysis

CYCLICAL—No. 4
    CYCL (cyclos)—Root = wheel; circle
    IC—Suffix = like
    AL—Suffix = relating to

practical exercises

1. Supply the missing words:
    Every home needs a good .... for reference.
When H. G. Wells speaks of the .... fate of
the individual life, he means that the end comes full circle,
back to the beginning.

2. Analyze No. 12.

3. Key review. Match keys with their meaning:

a. vis, vid	1. turn	....
b. vinc	2. not	....
c. voc, vok	3. state; process	....
d. vers, vert	4. one	....
e. viv, vita	5. circle	....
f. un	6. see	....
g. ure	7. life	....
h. uni	8. build	....
i. cycl	9. conquer	....
j. struct, strue	10. call	....

KEY NO. 174

O—🔑

INTRO

into
inward

is the Prefix *INTRO* meaning INTO; INWARD. The three keys—INTER, INTRA and INTRO—must be clearly spoken and exactly understood. INTERnational means between *all* the nations of the world. INTRAnational means within one nation. Notice the change in spelling—*intromit* with a *t*, and *intromissable* with an *s!* The reason for that is the change in the spelling of the Latin Root—to send. *Mitto* becomes *missi* and that is carried over to the English words derived from it.

1. introceptive   INTRO ceptive (in tro sep' tiv) adj.
      Capable of receiving into itself.

2. introduce   INTRO duce (in tro dus') v.
      Lead into; present.

3. introduction   INTRO duction (in tro duk' shun) n.
      Act of presenting.

4. introflex   INTRO flex (in tro fleks') v.
      To bend inward.

5. introgression   INTRO gression (in tro gre' shun) n.
      Act of going in; entrance.

6. introject   INTRO ject (in tro jekt') v.
      To throw within; as, introject *new ideas.*

7. introjection   INTRO jection (in tro jek' shun) n.
      Act of throwing oneself into a project.

8. intromit   INTRO mit (in tro mit') v.
      Allow to pass in; insert.

9. introspect   INTRO spect (in tro spekt') v.
      To look within; inward.

10. introspection   INTRO spection (in tro spek' shun) n.
      Act of looking within; self-examination.

11. introspective   INTRO spective (in tro spek' tiv) adj.
      Seeing inwardly.

12. introspectionism   INTRO spectionism
      (in tro spek' shun iz um) n.
      Doctrine that psychology finds its essential data by introspection.

13. introvolution   INTRO volution (in tro vo lue' shun) n.
      Act of involving one thing within another.

14. introvert   INTRO vert (in' tro vert) n.
      One who turns inward; draws in.

348

15. introversion	INTRO version (in tro ver′ zhun) n.
	Act of turning one's thoughts inward.
16. introversive	INTRO versive (in tro ver′ siv) adj.
	Tending to turn inward.
17. introvert	INTRO vert (in′ tro vert) v.
	To turn inward; to draw in.
18. introversible	INTRO versible (in tro ver′ si b'l) adj.
	Capable of being turned inward.
19. intropulsive	INTRO pulsive (in tro pul′ siv) adj.
	Inclined to drive inward.
20. intropression	INTRO pression (in tro presh′ un) n.
	Pressure within.

word analysis

INTROSPECTION—No. 10
  INTRO—Prefix = into; inward
  SPEC (specto)—Root = see; look
  TION—Suffix = act of; state of

practical exercises

1. Supply the missing words:
    Glass in the window ....(s) light without
    cold. She was much given to .... beyond her
    years. The snail's eye stalks are ....

2. Analyze No. 8.

3. Add the missing key so that the word may express the phrase:
    a. throwing oneself into a project   ....
    b. looking within oneself   ....
    c. to bend inward   ....
    d. act of leading into   ....
    e. act of turning inward   ....
    f. arranged in circles   ....

KEY NO. *175*

O—⚷

SIGN · SIGNI

sign
mark
seal

is the Root *SIGN; SIGNI* which comes from the Latin *signum* which means SIGN; MARK; SEAL. It leads to one of the most important, most personal matters which concerns the human being—his *SIGN*ature. It is so important, so *SIGNI*ficant, even more than the person himself without the signature. The bank will not pay you on your face, but it will pay on your *SIGN*ature.

1. sign
   SIGN (sine) v.
   To affix a mark, or a seal, or a name; as, sign a will.

2. signable
   SIGN able (sine' a b'l) adj.
   Can be signed.

3. signal
   SIGN al (sig' nal) n.
   A gesture to call attention.

4. signaler
   SIGN aler (sig' nal er) n.
   One who signals.

5. signalist
   SIGN alist (sig' nal ist) n.
   A signaler.

6. signalize
   SIGN alize (sig' nal ize) v.
   To mark; to make known; to point out.

7. signate
   SIGN ate (sig' nate) adj.
   Pointed out; distinguished; designated.

8. signation
   SIGN ation (sig nay' shun) n.
   Act of signing.

9. signatory
   SIGN atory (sig' na tore ee) n.
   One who signs with another in a joint agreement; as, signatory to a peace pact.

10. signature
    SIGN ature (sig' na chur) n.
    The name of a person written in his own handwriting.

11. signet
    SIGN et (sig' net) n.
    Sign or seal expressing authority; a signet ring.

12. signify
    SIGN ify (sig' ni fie) n.
    To show; to make evident; as, signify agreement.

13. significant
    SIGN ificant (sig nif' i kant) adj.
    Showing full importance; expressive.

14. significance
    SIGN ificance (sig nif' i kans) n.
    Value; importance.

15. insignificant   in SIGN ificant (in sig nif' i kant) adj.
    Having no importance.
16. significantly   SIGN ificantly (sig nif' i kant lee) adv.
    Importantly.
17. design   de SIGN (de zine') n.
    A plan of something to be done; intention.
18. designation   de SIGN ation (dez ig nay' shun) n.
    Selection; appointment for an aim.
19. designated   de SIGN ated (dez' ig na ted) adj.
    Selected; as, for high honors.
20. insignia   in SIGN ia (in sig' nee a) n.
    Distinguishing marks; as, insignia *of authority.*

word analysis

SIGNIFICANT—No. 13
    SIGNI (signum)—Latin Root =sign
    FICI (facio)—Root =make
    ANT—Suffix =one who; that which

practical exercises

1. Supply the missing words:
    At a .... the cab pulled up to the curb.
    An .... detail in the .... of the
    latest will roused suspicions that there had been a change
    of ....

2. Analyze No. 6.

3. Write the word each phrase explains:
    a. to have a very good opinion of   ....
    b. the quality of usefulness   ....
    c. the quality of respect for God   ....
    d. a small crack or break in a wall   ....
    e. a hidden place or corner   ....
    f. the ability to know and understand what
       goes on   ....
    g. the wisdom of common sense   ....

KEY NO. *176*

o—⚡

**INTELLECT
INTELLIG**

**power to know
and think**

is the Root *INTELLECT, INTELLIG* meaning POWER TO KNOW AND THINK. This key is really a combination of INTER, between, and *legere*, to gather, collect. Do not confuse this LEGO with the *lex, leg* which means law. This LEGO comes from *legere, lectus,* to collect.

1. intellect   INTELLECT (int' el ekt) n.
      The human faculty to know and understand.

2. intellectual   INTELLECT ual (int el ek' chu al) adj.
      Relating to the power to know and understand; as, intellectual *faculties.*

3. intellectual   INTELLECT ual (int el ek' chu al) n.
      One who is guided by the power to know; as, he is an intellectual.

4. intellectualize   INTELLECT ualize (int el ek' chu a lize) v.
      To make into rational thoughts.

5. intelligent   INTELLIG ent (in tel' i jent) adj.
      Having the power to think and know; as, an intelligent *man.*

6. intelligently   INTELLIG ently (in tel' i jent ly) adv.
      In the manner of an intelligent person.

7. intelligence   INTELLIG ence (in tel' i jens) n.
      The capacity to understand.

8. intelligible   INTELLIG ible (in tel' i ji b'l) adj.
      Can be understood.

9. intelligibility   INTELLIG ibility (in tel i ji bil' it ee) n.
      Quality of being understandable; clearness.

10. intelligenced   INTELLIG enced (in tel' i jensd) adj.
      Informed.

11. intelligencer   INTELLIG encer (in tel' i jen ser) n.
      An informer; a secret agent.

12. intelligential   INTELLIG ential (in tel i jen' shal) adj.
      Relating to the power to know and think.

13. intellectualist   INTELLECT ualist (in te lek' tu al ist) n.
      One who is devoted to intellectual activity.

14. intelligentsia   INTELLIG entsia (in tel i jen' see a) n.
      The artistic, intellectual class of people.

15. unintelligent   un INTELLIG ent (un in tel' i jent) adj.
      Not using the power to think and understand.

16. unintelligently   un INTELLIG ently (un in tel' i jent ly) adv.
      In an unthinking manner.

17. unintelligible   un INTELLIG ible (un in tel' i ji b'l) adj.
   Not clear; not understood.

word analysis

INTELLECTUAL—No. 2
   INTE (inter)—Prefix =between; among
   LECTU (legere, lectus)—Latin Root =to gather knowledge
   AL—Suffix =relating to

practical exercises

1. See whether you can understand the meaning of the italicized words:

   The *miniature* was no larger than a postcard, but the painting of the tiny picture was *exquisite*. The artist had made a fine portrait in miniature.

2. Read the following excerpt underlining all those words that contain keys you have already learned.

   Philip drew a large miniature-case from his pocket and opened it. Maggie saw her old self leaning at a table, with her black locks hanging down behind her ears, looking into space with strange, dreamy eyes. It was a water-color sketch of real merit as a portrait.

   "O dear!" said Maggie, smiling and flushed with pleasure, "what a queer little girl I was! I remember myself with my hair that way, in that pink frock. I really *was* like a gypsy. I daresay I am now," she added, after a pause. "Am I like what you expected me to be?"

   The words might have been those of a coquette, but the full, bright glance Maggie turned on Philip was not that of a coquette. She really did hope he liked her face as it was now, but it was simply the rising again of her innate delight in admiration and love. Philip met her eyes and looked at her in silence for a long moment before he said, quietly, "No, Maggie."

   The light died out a little from Maggie's face, and there was a slight trembling of the lip. Her eyelids fell lower, but she did not turn away her head, and Philip continued to look at her. Then he said, slowly—"You are very much more beautiful than I thought you would be."

   (From *The Mill on the Floss* by George Eliot.)

KEY NO. 177

o—🗝

LUC · LUM
LUN · LUS

light

is the Root *LUC, LUM, LUN, LUS*. It comes from the Latin *lux, lucis, lumen*. All mean LIGHT. LUMinary, to bring light to the eye; eLUCidate to bring light to the mind, both bring brightness. This is a beautiful key. No. 15, eLUCubrate, pictures a hard worker, perhaps an Abraham Lincoln, who keeps on working after the sun goes down, keeps toiling by candle-light, to get the education which he needs.

1. lucent   LUC ent (lus′ ent) adj.
       Giving light; shining.

2. lucid   LUC id (lue′ sid) adj.
       Clear; bright; filled with light.

3. luculent   LUC ulent (lue′ kyu lent) adj.
       Lucid; clear; evident.

4. Luna   LUN a (lue′ na) n.
       The moon goddess.

5. lunambulism   LUN ambulism (lue nam′ bu liz um) n.
       Sleepwalking induced by the moon.

6. lumen   LUM en (lue′ men) n.
       A unit of light.

7. luminary   LUM inary (lue′ mi nar ee) n.
       A heavenly body; someone who shines in his profession.

8. luminescence   LUM inescence (lue mi nes′ ens) n.
       Brightness; incandescence.

9. luminescent   LUM inescent (lue mi nes′ ent) adj.
       Used in the production of luminescence.

10. luminiferous   LUM iniferous (lue mi nif′ e rus) adj.
       Yielding light; producing light.

11. luminosity   LUM inosity (lue mi nos′ it ee) n.
       The quality of being light.

12. luminous   LUM inous (lue′ mi nus) adj.
       Full of light; brilliant; lustrous.

13. luster   LUS ter (lus′ ter) n.
       Sparkle; gloss; glaze.

14. elucidate   e LUC idate (e lue′ si date) v.
       Bring into the light; make clear; explain.

15. elucubrate   e LUC ubrate (e lue′ kue brate) v.
       Express with great effort; work hard.

16. illuminate   il LUM inate (il ue′ mi nate) v.
                     Bring in light; light up; make bright.
17. translucent   trans LUC ent (tranz luse′ ent) adj.
                     Letting light come through.
18. pellucid   pell LUC id (pe lue′ sid) adj.
                     Easy to fathom or understand; allowing light through.
19. luminaire   LUM inaire (lue′ mi nare) n.
                     A lighting unit with all equipment and accessories.
20. lunatic   LUN atic (lue′ na tik) adj.
                     Moonstruck; insane.

word analysis

LUMINIFEROUS—No. 10
    LUMIN (lumen)—Latin Root =light
    FER (ferre)—Latin Root =to bear
    OUS—Suffix =full of; having

practical exercises

1. Supply the missing words:
    The explanation was not only .... but
.... It was clear from the exquisite ....
effects that this painter was a .... The students
asked the teacher to .... the problem.

2. Analyze No. 1.

3. Use one word for each of the following phrases:
    a. sleepwalking induced by moonlight   ....
    b. make clear to the understanding   ....
    c. make the dim room bright   ....
    d. lets the light go through   ....
    e. the quality of being understood   ....

AMPHI

two
both

is the Prefix *AMPHI* which means TWO; BOTH. In this list you will find some genuine oddities, as No. 16. No. 13 and No. 18 sound rather terrible but they are not, as we ourselves have two nostrils and eat both flesh and vegetable foods. No. 15 and No. 17 are beautiful.

1. amphibia   AMPHI bia (am fib' ee a) n.
    A class of vertebrates having characteristics of both fish and reptiles; as, frogs.
2. amphibious   AMPHI bious (am fib' ee us) adj.
    Capable of living on both land and water.
3. amphibiology AMPHI biology (am fib i ol' o ji) n.
    That branch of zoology which is concerned with animals that live on both land and water.
4. amphibiotic   AMPHI biotic (am fi bie ot' ik) adj.
    Living in water in the early stage, on land in adult life.
5. amphibology AMPHI bology (am fi bol' o jee) n.
    Ambiguity arising from a phrase which can have two constructions.
6. amphibolous   AMPHI bolous (am fib' o lus) adj.
    Capable of having two meanings.
7. amphicarpic   AMPHI carpic (am fi kar' pik) adj.
    Producing two kinds of fruit.
8. amphichroic   AMPHI chroic (am fi kro' ik) adj.
    Producing two colors.
9. amphicrania   AMPHI crania (am fi kray' ni a) n.
    Pain on both sides of the head.
10. amphibolia   AMPHI bolia (am fi boe' li a) n.
    Disease of high fever with fluctuating temperature.
11. amphibolic   AMPHI bolic (am fi bol' ik) adj.
    Uncertain; critical stages in disease.
12. amphilogism AMPHI logism (am fil' o jiz um) n.
    Double talk; ambiguity of speech; equivocation.
13. Amphirhina   AMPHI rhina (am fi rie' na) n.
    Vertebrates with double nasal chambers.
14. amphiscians   AMPHI scians (am fish' i ans) n.
    Inhabitants of the tropics.

356

15. amphitheater AMPHI theater (am fi thee' at er) n.
                    Arena theater in which the audience sits
                    around the stage.
16. amphisbaena AMPHI sbaena (am fis bee' na) n.
                    Fabled serpent with a head on each end.
17. amphora   AMPH ora (am' fo ra) n.
                    An ornamental jar with two handles.
18. amphivorous AMPHI vorous (am fiv' o rus) adj.
                    Eating animal and vegetable foods.
19. amphisarca AMPHI sarca (am fi sar' ka) n.
                    Fruits that are pulpy within, but have a hard
                    rind outside.
20. amphorous AMPH orous (am' fo rus) adj.
                    Having a hollow sound.

word analysis

AMPHILOGISM—No. 12
    AMPHI—Prefix =both; two
    LOG (logos)—Greek Root =word
    ISM—Suffix =system; doctrine

practical exercises

1. Supply the missing words:
    The loving cup which is given to the prize-winning
athlete today is like the beautiful .... which the
Greeks gave in ancient days for heroic deeds. They gave
the performance in the new ....

2. Analyze No. 15.

3. Supply the word to express the following phrases:
    a. fever going up and down   ....
    b. with two nostrils   ....
    c. ornamental jar with two handles   ....
    d. ambiguity of speech   ....
    e. eating both flesh and vegetables   ....
    f. relating to fishes and reptiles   ....

O—⊶

FY

make

is the Suffix *FY* which means MAKE. It is very simple and is added to countless words. *FY* makes a verb, and the past tense is *FIED*. Just change the *y* to *i* and add *ed*. With this rule in mind you can do wonders with many words. Word No. 15 is a humorous word and we must cherish it, as it does much to win the audience over to a speaker or reader. *Transmogrified*, as you see in the word analysis, means taken across from one world to another, completely changed, in an absurd way.

1. vitrify   vitri FY (vi' tri fie) v.
      To make into glass; make vitreous.

2. zincify   zinci FY (zink' i fie) v.
      To coat with zinc; galvanize.

3. calcify   calci FY (kal' si fie) v.
      To harden; to become stony.

4. diversify   diversi FY (di ver' si fie) v.
      To make various in form or color.

5. dulcify   dulci FY (dul' si fie) v.
      To make sweet; to render agreeable; as, dulcify *a medicine.*

6. fortify   forti FY (fort' i fie) v.
      To strengthen; as, to fortify *with troops.*

7. fructify   fructi FY (fruk' ti fie) v.
      To make fruitful.

8. putrefy   putre FY (pyu' tre fie) v.
      To cause to decay; to cause to rot.

9. ratify   rati FY (rat' i fie) v.
      To approve; to confirm; as, to ratify *a treaty.*

10. saponify   saponi FY (sa pon' i fie) v.
      To make into soap.

11. simplify   simpli FY (sim' pli fie) v.
      To make easy to understand.

12. stultify   stulti FY (stul' ti fie) v.
      To make appear stupid.

13. terrify   terri FY (ter' i fie) v.
      To frighten.

14. testify   testi FY (tes' ti fie) v.
      To bear witness.

15. transmogrify   transmogri FY (trans mog' ri fie) v.
>To alter completely; to render grotesque *or* humorous.

16. verify   veri FY (ver' i fie) v.
>To affirm the truth of, with proof.

17. vilify   vili FY (vil' i fie) v.
>To make lower in importance; to insult with abusive language.

18. unify   uni FY (yue' ni fie) v.
>To make as one.

19. amplify   ampli FY (am' pli fie) v.
>To enlarge; expand; as, amplify *sound.*

20. beatify   beati FY (be at' i fie) v.
>To make blissfully happy.

word analysis

TRANSMOGRIFIED—No. 15 (past tense)
>TRANS—Prefix =across
>MOGRI (migrate)—Root =move
>FIED (FY, past tense)—Suffix =make; made

practical exercises

1. Supply the missing words:

>Congress must .... treaties made between the U.S. and other nations. Without refrigeration food will .... It is not wise to depend on facts which have not been ....

2. Analyze No. 14.

3. Key Review. Match keys with their meanings:

a. less	1. hand	......
b. ly	2. law	....
c. ling	3. light	....
d. licit	4. free	....
e. leg	5. small	....
f. liber	6. move	....
g. luc	7. manner	....
h. manu	8. measure	....
i. mob, mov, mot	9. permit	....
j. meter	10. without	....

KEY NO. *180*

O—➤

PHOTO

light

is the Root *PHOTO* which means LIGHT. It comes from the Greek, *phos, photos.* This Root is very much involved in PHOTOgraphy of all kinds; so much, in fact, that we think the word PHOTO means PICTURE. We have completely forgotten the LIGHT without which there can be no picture. We must get into the habit of remembering that *PHOTO* means LIGHT. The word PHOTON (No. 9) will help us. A PHOTON is a unit of light intensity, and pictures are taken with that aid.

1. photobiotic
PHOTO biotic (fote o bie ot' ik) adj.
Requiring light to live.

2. photochromy
PHOTO chromy (foe' to kro mi) n.
Color photography.

3. photodromy
PHOTO dromy (foe tod' ro mi) n.
Movement in the direction of light.

4. photograph
PHOTO graph (fote' o graf) n.
A picture made by the action of light on a sensitized plate.

5. photography
PHOTO graphy (fo tog' ra fee) n.
The process of making photographs.

6. photographer
PHOTO grapher (fo tog' ra fer) n.
One who makes photographs.

7. photographee
PHOTO graphee (foe to graf ee') n.
One whose picture is taken.

8. photogenic
PHOTO genic (fote o jen' ik) adj.
Capable of being photographed well.

9. photon
PHOTO n (foe' ton) n.
A unit of light intensity.

10. photology
PHOTO logy (foe tol' o ji) n.
Science of light; optics.

11. photometer
PHOTO meter (foe tom' et er) n.
An instrument for measuring the intensity of light.

12. photopathy
PHOTO pathy (foe top' a thi) n.
Disease caused by light.

13. photoengraving
PHOTO engraving (fote o en grave' ing) n.
Engraving with the aid of photography.

14. photogram
PHOTO gram (fote' o gram) n.
A photograph of a shadowy nature.

15. photokinesis   PHOTO kinesis (fote o ki nee' sis) n.
                          Movement induced by light.
16. photomicroscope   PHOTO microscope
                          (foe to mie' kro skope) n.
                          A combination of microscope and camera.
17. photocombustion   PHOTO combustion (foe to kom bus' chun) n.
                          Combustion induced by the action of light.
18. photodynamic   PHOTO dynamic (fote o die nam' ik) adj.
                          Intensifying a reaction to light that is toxic.
19. photogastroscope   PHOTO gastroscope
                          (foe to gas' tro skope) n.
                          Instrument for photographing the interior of the stomach.
20. photogrammetry   PHOTO grammetry (fote o gram' e tree) n.
                          Art of making maps from photographs taken from above.

word analysis

PHOTOBIOTIC—No. 1
    PHOTO (photos)—Root =light
    BIO—Root =life
    IC—Suffix =like; nature of

practical exercises

1. Supply the missing words:

    A .... is a clever combination of the three
    elements needed to magnify and .... very tiny
    objects—lens, light and scope.

2. Analyze No. 8.

3. Choose the word or expression which most nearly expresses
the italicized word:

    a. *illumine*   (1) extinguish   (2) introduce
       (3) grow   (4) assist   (5) light up   ....
    b. *revive*   (1) bring back to life   (2) assault
       (3) desert   (4) announce   (5) recall   ....
    c. *surmount*   (1) surrender   (2) overcome
       (3) endow   (4) exchange   (5) decide   ....
    d. *amphibian*   (1) fish   (2) cow   (3) groundhog
       (4) bee   (5) frog   ....

KEY NO. 181

O—⚒

VOLCAN
VULCAN

fire

is the Root *VOLCAN, VULCAN*, which comes from Vulcan, the name of the Roman god of fire. The change in spelling often happens with names. Notice No. 7 and No. 9—both mean the same thing. That is also natural. One medical man calls himself a doctor, another a physician. Still another change! The Roman god of fire comes from the Greek god of metal working—see No. 1 and No. 2.

1. Vulcan   VULCAN (vul' kan) n.
                 Roman god of fire.
2. vulcanist   VULCAN ist (vul' kan ist) n.
                 A metal worker.
3. vulcanization VULCAN ization (vul ka ni zay' shun) n.
                 Act of treating with chemicals to produce the qualities of rubber.
4. volcano   VOLCAN o (vol kay' no) n.
                 A mountain erupting molten lava.
5. volcanic   VOLCAN ic (vol kan' ik) adj.
                 Like a volcano; characteristic of a volcano.
6. volcanism   VOLCAN ism (vol' ka niz um) n.
                 The power of a volcano.
7. volcanist   VOLCAN ist (vol' ka nist) n.
                 One versed in the study of volcanic phenomena.
8. volcanology   VOLCAN ology (vol ka nol' o jee) n.
                 The study of volcanic eruptions.
9. volcanologist VOLCAN ologist (vol ka nol' o jist) n.
                 A specialist in the area of volcanology.
10. volcanite   VOLCAN ite (vol' kan ite) n.
                 A rare rock from a specific volcano.
11. volcanize   VOLCAN ize (vol' ka nize) v.
                 To undergo volcanic heat.
12. volcanologize VOLCAN ologize (vol kan ol' o jize) v.
                 To study volcanic phenomena.
13. vulcanian   VULCAN ian (vul ka' nee an) adj.
                 Relating to work done with iron and other metals.
14. vulcanize   VULCAN ize (vul' ka nize) v.
                 To treat with chemicals in such a way as to produce the qualities of rubber.

362

word analysis

VOLCANOLOGIST—No. 9
    VOLCANO (Vulcan)—Latin Root =fire; volcano
    LOG (logos)—Root =word
    IST—Suffix =one who

practical exercises

1. Supply the missing words:
    The Roman god ...., who was represented
    by the violence of the ...., was, under the
    Greeks, the peaceful god Hephaestus, the ....
    .... dust in the air causes red sunsets.

2. Analyze No. 7.

3. Syllabicate and indicate which syllable is most greatly stressed
    by placing the accent ('):
        elucidate   photopathy
        elucidation   amphitheater
        photogrammetry   amphibian

is the Root *SUME, SUMP*, meaning TAKE, USE, WASTE. It comes from the Latin *sumere, sumptus*. It is interesting to notice how the idea of taking and using began to mean expensive, burdensome, and wasteful. The layman's name for tuberculosis is conSUMPtion, a disease that causes the patient to WASTE away. In ancient Greece and Rome there was a SUMPtuary law which forbade lavish spending.

1. assume — as SUME (a sume') v.
   To take; to use; to suppose; as, I assume it is so.

2. assumption — as SUMP tion (a sump' shun) n.
   The act of taking for granted; as, on the assumption that it is so.

3. assuming — as SUM ing (a sume' ing) adj.
   Taking for granted; arrogant.

4. assumed — as SUM ed (a sumed') adj.
   Taken; as, under an assumed name.

5. assumptive — as SUMP tive (a sump' tiv) adj.
   Assuming, supposing.

6. consume — con SUME (kon sume') v.
   To use up; as, Americans consume millions of cigarettes.

7. consumer — con SUME r (kon sue' mer) n.
   One who consumes goods of some kind.

8. consumption — con SUMP tion (kon sump' shun) n.
   Act of using up; wasting away.

9. consumptive — con SUMP tive (kon sump' tiv) adj.
   Affected by consumption; a wasting away of the body.

10. consumable — con SUM able (kon sue' ma b'l) adj.
    Can be used up.

11. consumedly — con SUME dly (kon sue' med lee) adv.
    Excessively; as, he is consumedly proud of himself.

12. presume — pre SUME (pre zume') v.
    To take upon oneself without leave; as, do not presume too much.

13. presumably — pre SUM ably (pre zue' ma blee) adv.
    Supposedly.

14. presumption   pre SUMP tion (pre zump′ shun) n.
                         Arrogance; audacity.

15. presumptuously pre SUMP tuously (pre zump′ chu us lee)
                         adv.
                         Arrogantly; audaciously.

16. resume   re SUME (re zume′) v.
                         Take up again; as, after intermission the
                         play will resume.

17. sumpter   SUMP ter (sump′ ter) n.
                         A beast of burden.

18. sumption   SUMP tion (sump′ shun) n.
                         A major premise; an assumption.

19. sumptuosity   SUMP tuosity (sump tue os′ i ti) n.
                         Lavish display.

20. sumptuously   SUMP tuously (sump′ chu us lee) adv.
                         Lavishly; expensively.

word analysis

CONSUMPTION—No. 8
    CON—Suffix =with
    SUMP (sumptus)—Latin Root =use; waste away
    TION—Suffix =act of

practical exercises

1. Supply the missing words:
    They planned a series of lectures on the ....
that many people would come. However, there were not
many, as .... they were not interested in the
subject. The .... of the fancy dress ball caused
much comment.

2. Analyze No. 14.

3. Read the following excerpt underlining all those words that
contain keys you have already learned.

    The tsetse fly is a parasite insect that works something
like the malaria-carrying mosquito, picking up an infectious
agent from one beast it bites and passing it on to the next
victim. The infectious agent that the tsetse carries is *Try-
panosoma gambiense* which causes sleeping sickness—for
centuries the scourge of Africa. Swarms of tsetse flies have
turned vast reaches of that continent into a veritable eco-
nomic wasteland.

                  (From *The New York Times*, Aug. 16, 1964.)

KEY NO. 183

O—x

EU

**pleasant
well
good**

is the Prefix *EU* meaning PLEAS-ANT; WELL; GOOD. Look at No. 2 and you will find the charmer for whose sake so many changes have been made in the pronunciation of words—assimilation for the sake of EUPHONY. Euphony is a lovely word to hear and say and read. The last word in the list, EUREKA! is always spoken and written with an exclamation point. It was spoken by Archimedes when he discovered a method of determining the purity of the gold in a king's crown. I hope that when you will have finished this book you will have found a method to an excellent vocabulary and you will exclaim, EUREKA!

1. eulogy
EU logy (yue' lo jee) n.
Words of praise, especially for the dead.

2. euphony
EU phony (yue' fo nee) n.
A pleasant sound.

3. euphonious
EU phonious (yue foe' nee us) adj.
Full of pleasing sound; harmonious.

4. euphemism
EU phemism (yue' fe miz um) n.
The use of a pleasant word instead of one that is harsh or offensive.

5. euphemistic
EU phemistic (yue fe mis' tik) adj.
In the manner of euphemism.
"passing on" instead of "dying."

6. euphemistically
EU phemistically (yue fe mis' ti ka lee) adv.
In the maner of euphemism.

7. eugeny
EU geny (ue' je ni) n.
Nobility of birth.

8. Eudora
EU dora (ue doe' ra) n.
A feminine name meaning "a good gift."

9. Eugene
EU gene (ue jene') n.
A masculine name meaning "well born."

10. eugenics
EU genics (yue jen' iks) n.
Breeding for race improvement.

11. Eulalia
EU lalia (ue lay' li a) n.
A feminine name meaning "pleasant speech."

12. euharmonic
EU harmonic (ue har mon' ik) adj.
Producing perfect harmony.

366

13. euphoria	EU phoria (yue for′ ee a) n.
	A feeling of well-being.
14. eurythmics	EU rythmics (yu rith′ miks) n.
	The art of graceful movements; as those in dancing.
15. eucrasia	EU crasia (ue kray′ zhi a) n.
	A state of physical well-being.
16. eudaemony	EU daemony (ue dee′ mo ni) n.
	A state of happiness; well-being.
17. Eumenides	EU menides (yu men′ i deze) n.
	The gracious ones. The Greek euphemism for the Furies, used in an attempt at appeasing them.
18. eupepsia	EU pepsia (yu pep′ sha) n.
	Good digestion.
19. euthanasia	EU thanasia (yue tha nay′ zhee a) n.
	Painless putting to death; mercy killing.
20. eureka	EU reka (yu ree′ ka) n.
	An expression of triumph, meaning "I have found it!" said by Archimedes.

word analysis

EUTHANASIA—No. 19
    EU—Prefix =pleasing
    THANAS (thanatos)—Greek Root =death
    IA—Suffix =name of medical term

practical exercises

1. Supply the missing words:
    The Greeks used the gentle art of .... when they called the Furies the .... Should the science of .... be applied to human beings as well as to the breeding of horses?

2. Analyze No. 2.

3. Use one word for each of the following phrases.
    a. full of pleasing sound ....
    b. graceful movements in dancing ....
    c. producing perfect harmony ....
    d. I have found it! ....
    e. breeding for race improvement ....
    f. takes a good photograph ....

KEY NO. *184*

HEMA · HEMO

blood

is the Root *HEMA, HEMO* which means BLOOD. It comes from the Greek *haima.* You have realized by this time that though the learning of the key is a very simple matter, it brings you into association with very high verbal society. You will not be able to carry on the conversation but you will become a fine, intelligent listener, and that is half the art of the conversationalist.

1. hemachrome   HEMA chrome (hee' ma krome) n.
   The coloring matter of the blood.
2. hematic   HEMA tic (hi mat' ik) adj.
   Containing blood; affecting blood.
3. hematid   HEMA tid (hee' ma tid) n.
   A red blood corpuscle.
4. hemal   HEMA l (he' mal) adj.
   Pertaining to the blood or blood vessels.
5. hemogastric   HEMO gastric (hee mo gas' trik) adj.
   Accompanied by hemorrhaging into the stomach.
6. hemoglobin   HEMO globin (he' mo gloe bin) n.
   An element in the red corpuscles.
7. hemachrosis   HEMA chrosis (hee ma kroe' sis) n.
   Increased redness in the blood.
8. hemachate   HEMA chate (hem' a kate) n.
   A stone like the bloodstone.
9. hemoid   HEMO id (hee' moid) adj.
   Like blood.
10. hemorrhage   HEMO rrhage (hem' o rij) n.
    Intense bleeding; discharge of blood from blood vessels.
11. hemorrhagic   HEMO rrhagic (hem o raj' ik) adj.
    Bleeding intensely.
12. hemorrhoids   HEMO rrhoids (hem' o roids) n.
    Dilated veins liable to discharge blood.
13. hemophilia   HEMO philia (he mo fil' ee a) n.
    Bleeding which cannot be controlled.
14. hemoptoe   HEMO ptoe (he mop' toe ee) n.
    Hemorrhage of the lungs.
15. hemospasia   HEMO spasia (hee mo spay' zhi a) n.
    Draining off blood.

16. hemostat   HEMO stat (he' mo stat) n.
                An instrument which stops hemorrhage.
17. hemostasis HEMO stasis (he mos' ta sis) n.
                The checking of flowing blood.
18. hemotoxic   HEMO toxic (hee mo tok' sik) adj.
                Causing blood-poisoning.
19. hematose   HEMA tose (hem' a tose) adj.
                Bloody; full of blood.
20. hemotropic HEMO tropic (hee mo trop' ik) adj.
                Affecting the blood.

word analysis

HEMOTOXIC—No. 18
    HEMO (haima)—Greek Root =blood
    TOX (toxon)—Root =poison
    IC—Suffix =like; nature of

practical exercises

1. Supply the missing words:
    An internal .... is dangerous to life. In
    former, less medically advanced times, ... was
    a common remedy for many ills.

2. Analyze No. 9.

3. Add the compound Suffix MENT+TION to Roots, thereby
   making strong words. For the sake of euphony place *a* between
   ment and *tion*—ment+a+tion.
   Example: FER+mentation=fermentation=intensive growth
   a. documentation   ....
   b. ornamentation   ....
   c. argu ....
   d. frag...........................   ....
   e. imple........................... ....
   f. regi...........................
   g. supple...........................
   h. seg...........................

KEY NO. *185*

SCOPE

watch
see

is the Root *SCOPE* which comes from *scopos*, meaning WATCH; SEE. The number of instruments which *SCOPE* one thing or another increases every day it seems. Soon there will be no need to read about anything because we'll be able to see it. We'll just reach out for a handy little SCOPE and presto! One picture is worth a thousand words. Years ago there was talk about attaching a SCOPE of some sort to the telephone. It would be nice to see the person one says "Hello!" to. Would that be called a PHONOSCOPE?

1. baroscope   baro SCOPE (bar' o skope) n.
     Instrument showing changes in atmospheric pressure.

2. autoscope   auto SCOPE (au' to skope) n.
     An instrument for seeing one's own organs.

3. bioscope   bio SCOPE (bie' o skope) n.
     Instrument which projects motion pictures.

4. chronoscope   chrono SCOPE (kro' no skope) n.
     Instrument for measuring time.

5. endoscope   endo SCOPE (en' do skope) n.
     Instrument for showing the internal organs.

6. gyroscope   gyro SCOPE (jie' ro skope) n.
     A wheel mounted on an axis capable of spinning rapidly.

7. helioscope   helio SCOPE (hee' li o skope) n.
     Instrument to view the sun without eye injury.

8. horoscope   horo SCOPE (hor' o skope) n.
     A chart used by an astrologer to tell fortunes.

9. hydroscope   hydro SCOPE (hie' dro skope) n.
     A device to view the depths of the sea.

10. kaleidoscope   kaleido SCOPE (ka lide' o skope) n.
     An instrument showing various scenes.

11. periscope   peri SCOPE (per' i skope) n.
     An instrument for viewing on all sides.

12. photoscope   photo SCOPE (foe' to skope) n.
     Instrument for taking photos of lip movements in rapid succession.

13. seismoscope seismo SCOPE (size' mo skope) n.
   Instrument to record occurrence and time of earthquakes.
14. spectroscope spectro SCOPE (spek' tro skope) n.
   Instrument for viewing the sun's spectrum.
15. telescope tele SCOPE (tel' e skope) n.
   Instrument for viewing distant objects.
16. radioscope radio SCOPE (ray' di o skope) n.
   Instrument for detecting the presence of radio-active substances.
17. stethoscope stetho SCOPE (steth' o skope) n.
   Instrument for hearing sounds produced within the body; as, heartbeats and murmurs.
18. thermoscope thermo SCOPE (ther' mo skope) n.
   Instrument used to measure changes of temperature.
19. microscope micro SCOPE (mie' kro skope) n.
   Instrument to view organisms too small to be seen by the naked eye.
20. fluoroscope fluoro SCOPE (flur' o skope) n.
   Instrument used to observe the interior of something opaque; as, the human body.

word analysis

PERISCOPE—No. 11
   PERI—Prefix =around
   SCOPE (scopos)—Greek Root =see

practical exercises

1. Supply the missing word:
   In indicating temperatures the .... differs from the ordinary thermometer in that it does not accurately measure the change by degrees.

2. Analyze No. 7.

3. Choose the word which best expresses the italicized word:
   a. *luminescence* (1) chaos (2) ambition (3) gravity (4) economy (5) brightness ....
   b. *economical* (1) thrifty (2) extravagant (3) boastful (4) beautiful (5) lavish ....
   c. *crater* (1) manhole (2) ditch (3) crevice (4) fissure (5) mouth of a volcano ....

KEY NO. 186

DEM · DEMO

people

is the Root *DEM, DEMO* from the Greek *demos* meaning people. With this key we are right at home, and the vocabulary is more or less familiar. For example, we all know that there is a constant struggle between DEMOcratic and ANTIDEMOcratic forces.

1. demarch   DEM arch (dee' mark) n.
     Mayor in modern Greece.

2. demagogue   DEM agogue (dem' a gog) n.
     A rabble-rouser; a leader who rouses the prejudices of mobs.

3. demagogism   DEM agogism (dem' a gog iz um) n.
     The creed of the demagogue.

4. democracy   DEMO cracy (de mok' ra see) n.
     Government of the people, by the people.

5. democrat   DEMO crat (dem' o krat) n.
     One who believes in democracy.

6. democratian   DEMO cratian (dem o kray' shan) adj.
     Democratic.

7. democratically   DEMO cratically (dem o krat' i ka lee) adj.
     In the manner of a democracy.

8. democratifiable   DEMO cratifiable (dem o krat' i fie a b'l) adj.
     Able to be made into a democrat.

9. democratism   DEMO cratism (dem ok' rat izm) n.
     Theory or system of democracy.

10. democratize   DEMO cratize (de mok' ra tize) v.
     Shape into a democracy.

11. demogenic   DEMO genic (dee mo jen' ik) adj.
     Relating to a society based on citizenship, not on kinship or tribe.

12. demography   DEMO graphy (de mog' ra fee) n.
     Study of populations, births, deaths, etc.

13. demographist   DEMO graphist (de mog' ra fist) n.
     One who studies demography.

14. demophile   DEMO phile (dem' o file) n.
     A friend of the people.

15. demophobe   DEMO phobe (dem' o fobe) n.
     One who has an aversion to people.

16. demos   DEMO s (dee' mos) n.
     The people; the members of a community in ancient Greece.

17. demotic   DEMO tic (de mot′ ik) adj.
                       Of or relating to the language of the Greek
                       people.

18. demotics   DEMO tics (de mot′ iks) n.
                       Knowledge relative to welfare and culture
                       of people; sociology.

19. demotist   DEMO tist (de mot′ ist) n.
                       A student of sociological writings.

20. antidemocratic   anti DEMO cratic (an ti dem o krat′ ik) adj.
                       Opposed to the principles of democracy.

word analysis

DEMOCRATIFIABLE—No. 8
    DEMO (demos)—Greek Root =people
    CRAT (kratos)—Greek Root =authority
    FI (facere)—Latin Root =make
    ABLE—Suffix =can do; able

practical exercise

Read the following excerpt underlining all those words that contain keys you have already learned.

     Michael Faraday was born of poor and humble parents. When he became a great and famous scientist he still remained poor and humble. At the age of fifteen he found a job he loved—as a janitor in the laboratory of the Royal Institute. He loved and observed the phenomena of nature—sunset, which he called the daily "resurrection"; "the luminescence of the sea at night"; the crater of Vesuvius, which he called "that bottomless gulf that belches forth wreaths of smoke and showers of flaming rocks." He refused honors and money and preferred to stay in the laboratory, and for very little pay.

     One day a young man came to the laboratory to perform an experiment for the mint. He noticed the old, shabby man watching him.

     "You're sort of interested," said the young man.

     "Sort of," answered Faraday.

     "Are you the janitor here?"

     "I'm a sort of janitor."

     "I hope they pay you well."

     "I could do with a little more money."

     "What's your name, my good man?"

     "Michael Faraday."

KEY NO. *187*

O━━x

PORTION

**part
share**

is the Root *PORTION* which means PART; SHARE. That part is simple enough. We all know what a *POR-TION* of pie is. But in the variations of the word there is often a bit of trouble. Read the list carefully; notice the change in meaning as each key is added. Read the meanings carefully. Then you will be able to use this word correctly. It is a fine word when understood and carefully used.

1. portion   PORTION (por' shun) n.
         A part; a share; as, a portion of pie.

2. portion   PORTION (por' shun) v.
         To divide into parts; as, portion off a piece of land.

3. portionable   PORTION able (por' shun a b'l) adj.
         Can be divided.

4. portioner   PORTION er (por' shun er) n.
         The one who divides.

5. portionless   PORTION less (por' shun les) adj.
         Without a portion; without a dowry.

6. apportion   ap PORTION (ap por' shun) v.
         To give out a portion to each one.

7. apportionable   ap PORTION able (a por' shun a b'l) adj.
         Can be apportioned; as, the estate is apportionable.

8. apportionment   ap PORTION ment (ap por' shun ment) n.
         The act of the division; the act of giving to each one his portion.

9. proportion   pro PORTION (pro por' shun) n.
         The relation of one share to others.

10. proportionate   pro PORTION ate (pro por' shu nate) adj.
         Being in proportion; as results proportionate to efforts.

11. proportionately   pro PORTION ately (pro por' shu nate lee) adv.
         Being in proper measure.

12. proportionateness   pro PORTION ateness (pro por' shu nat nes) n.
         State of proper portion.

13. proportional   pro PORTION al (pro por' shun al) adj.
         Divided into the right proportions.

14. proportionalism   pro PORTION alism
                     (pro por' shun al iz um) n.
                     The principle of electing officers in proportion to population.

15. proportionality   pro PORTION ality
                     (pro por shu nal' it ee) n.
                     Quality of being proportional.

16. disproportion   dispro PORTION (dis pro por' shun) adj.
                     Not in proportion; not suitable.

17. disproportionate   dispro PORTION ate
                     (dis pro por' shu nat) adj.
                     Not fairly apportioned.

18. disproportionately dispro PORTION ately
                     (dis pro por' shu nat lee) adv.
                     Not fairly divided.

19. proportioned   pro PORTION ed (pro por' shund) adj.
                     Divided fairly; suitable; as, the punishment was proportioned to the crime.

word analysis

PROPORTIONALISM—No. 14
   PRO—Prefix = for
   PORTION—Root = part; share
   AL—Suffix = relating to
   ISM—Suffix = rule; principle

practical exercises

1. Supply the missing words:
   In a perfect human body none of the limbs is dis................
   The arms are in .... as well as legs, shoulders
   and head. Nature does a good job of ....(ing)
   the many parts of the human body.

2. Analyze No. 9.

3. Key review. Match keys with their meanings:
   a. sion   1. condition
   b. tude   2. share   ....
   c. sume   3. people   ....
   d. tend   4. state of   ....
   e. portion   5. watch   ....
   f. dem   6. waste   ....
   g. scope   7. stretch   ....

KEY NO. 188

0—x

**VEN · VENI
VENT**

come

is the Root *VEN, VENI, VENT,* which comes from the Latin, *venire, ventus* which means to COME. The famous message which Julius Caesar sent to the Senate in Rome announcing his victory in Asia over 2,000 years ago is a marvel of brevity and action: "I came, I saw, I conquered" —*"Veni, vidi, vici."* Of the many keys which you have accumulated so far, sixteen are reviewed with the new key, *VEN, VENI, VENT.* Every key is important and will appear somewhere in a new word.

1. venture   VENT ure (ven' chur) n.
              Entering a project which implies a risk.
2. venturesome VENT uresome (ven' chur som) adj.
              Bold; daring; unafraid.
3. convention con VENT ion (kon' vent shun) n.
              A coming together; a congress.
4. advene   ad VEN e (ad vene') v.
              To come to; to reach to.
5. Advent   Ad VENT (ad' vent) n.
              The Coming.
6. adventure   ad VENT ure (ad ven' chur) n.
              A remarkable experience.
7. adventurer ad VENT urer (ad ven' chur er) n.
              One who undertakes risky experiences.
8. adventuress ad VENT uress (ad vench' u res) n.
              A woman who makes a living by dangerous and doubtful means.
9. adventitious ad VENT itious (ad ven tish' us) adj.
              Not usual; accidental; as, adventitious *buds.*
10. adventurous ad VENT urous (ad vench' u rus) adj.
              Venturesome.
11. event   e VENT (e vent') n.
              A happening; a result; an occurrence; as, a blessed event.
12. eventful   e VENT ful (e vent' ful) adj.
              Full of excitement and importance.
13. eventually e VENT ually (e vench' u al ee) adv.
              Finally; as, eventually *we shall know.*
14. convene   con VENE (kon vene') v.
              Come together; to assemble for a purpose.

376

15. convenient   con VEN ient (kon vee' nyent) adj.
         Accommodating; as, at a convenient time.
16. convenience   con VENI ence (kon vee' nyens) n.
         Personal comfort; as, at your convenience.
17. conventional con VENT ional (kon ven' chun al) adj.
         The usual thing; not original.
18. intervention   inter VENT ion (int er ven' shun) n.
         A coming between; an interruption.
19. prevention   pre VENT ion (pre ven' chun) n.
         Coming before to stop something.
20. preventive   pre VENT ive (pre vent' iv) adj.
         Tending to stop the coming; as preventive
         medicine.

word analysis

INTERVENTION—No. 18
    INTER—Prefix =between
    VEN (venire)—Latin Root =to come
    TION—Suffix =act of

practical exercises

1. Supply the missing words:
    "An ounce of .... is worth a pound of cure."
    Sometimes, in the late fall, when the weather is springlike,
    we may find .... buds on flower stalks.

2. Analyze No. 14.

3. Use one word to express each phrase:
    a. the usual thing, not original   ....
    b. finally comes to be   ....
    c. a coming between   ....
    d. keeping something from happening   ....
    e. unsuitably divided   ....
    f. one skilled in rousing the mob   ....

KEY NO. *189*

0—🗝

LOC · LOCO

place

is *LOC, LOCO* a Root which means PLACE. We use it all the time because we are constantly on the move from place to place. Note well the spelling of this key, and its derivation. It comes from the Latin word *locus.* You will soon have another key with a similar spelling which does not mean PLACE. Watch out!

1. locomotion   LOCO motion (lo ko mo' shun) n.
   Act of moving from place to place.

2. locality   LOC ality (lo kal' it ee) n.
   Locale; neighborhood; district.

3. locomobile   LOCO mobile (lo ko moe' bil) n.
   A self-propelling vehicle.

4. locomotive   LOCO motive (lo ko mote' iv) n.
   A self-propelled engine or vehicle.

5. locomotor   LOCO motor (lo ko mote' or) adj.
   Of or relating to movement and locomotion.

6. loculus   LOC ulus (lok' yu lus) n.
   A little place; a room; a cavity.

7. locus   LOCUS (lo' kus) n.
   Place; locality.

8. locate   LOC ate (lo' kate) v.
   Assign a place to; to find the place of.

9. locative   LOC ative (lok' at iv) n.
   A grammatical case that expresses the place where.

10. locomotivity   LOC omotivity (lo ko mo tiv' i ti) n.
    The power to move from place to place.

11. dislocate   dis LOC ate (dis' lo kate) v.
    To move away from its place.

12. dislocator   dis LOC ator (dis' lo kay tor) n.
    One who or that which dislocates.

13. dislocation   dis LOC ation (dis lo kay' shun) n.
    State of being dislocated.

14. dislocatory   dis LOC atory (dis' lo kay to ri) adj.
    Causing dislocation.

15. dislocable   dis LOC able (dis' lo ka b'l) adj.
    Can be dislocated.

16. dislocated   dis LOC ated (dis' lo ka ted) adj.
    Removed from their homes; as, the refugees were dislocated.

378

17. relocated   re LOC ated (re loe' kate ed) adj.
                     Put into place again.
18. relocate   re LOC ate (re loe' kate) v.
                     To put back into their homes.
19. relocation   re LOC ation (re lo kay' shun) n.
                     Act of replacing something or someone.
20. allocate   al LOC ate (al' o kate) v.
                     To assign; to allot; apportion.

word analysis

LOCOMOTOR—No. 5
     LOCO (locus)—Latin Root =place
     MOT (motus)—Latin Root =move
     OR—Suffix =that which

practical exercises

1. Supply the missing words:
     The first two rows in the auditorium were ....(d)
     to the Boy Scouts. The accident caused a bad ....
     of the shoulder. Who will help me to .... my
     glasses?

2. Analyze No. 18.

3. Add a key and complete the word needed:
     a. the .... came shrieking into the station— ....motive
     b. a great crowd came to the ....— con..........tion
     c. known for his ....— ....turesomeness
     d. recognized by her ...., not by her face— ....ature
     e. a .... number of ladies— dis..........ate

KEY NO. *190*

0—✶

VER · VERI

true
genuine

is the Root *VER, VERI* which comes from the Latin *verus,* which means TRUE; GENUINE. To complete the meaning of VERism (No. 14)—the VERist (No. 15) who believes in VERism, calls it realism, impressionism. Ugliness does exist in life and so do vulgarity and other evils. Therefore they belong in the picture, the true picture of life. In one of Frank Stockton's stories he has a character who is called the *Very Imp* (See No. 19). Not once in the story is he called Imp. Always *Very* Imp.

1. veracious   VER acious (ve ray′ shus) adj.
   Truthful; accurate.
2. veracity   VER acity (ve ras′ it ee) n.
   Truth; accuracy.
3. verdict   VER dict (ver′ dikt) n.
   The opinion of the jury in a court of law.
4. verify   VER ify (ver′ i fie) v.
   To prove to be true; confirm.
5. verificate   VERI ficate (ver′ i fi kate) v.
   To confirm; to verify.
6. verifiable   VERI fiable (ver i fie′ a b'l) adj.
   Can be verified.
7. verily   VERI ly (ver′ i lee) adv.
   It is truly the truth; certainly.
8. verification   VERI fication (ver i fi kay′ shun) n.
   Proof; the act of proving to be true.
9. verisimilar   VERI similar (ver i sim′ i lar) adj.
   Having the appearance of truth.
10. verisimilitude   VERI similitude (ver i si mil′ i tude) n.
    The likeness of truth; probability.
11. veridical   VERI dical (ve rid′ i k'l) adj.
    Truthful; veracious; as, a veridical statement.
12. veridity   VERI dity (ve rid′ i ti) n.
    Genuineness; truth.
13. veridicality   VERI dicality (ve rid i kal′ i ti) n.
    Quality of being veridical.
14. verism   VERI sm (ver′ iz um) n.
    The doctrine that the ordinary is preferable to the heroic in artistic terms.

15. verist	VERI st (ver' ist) n.
	One who believes in verism.
16. veritable	VERI table (ver' it a b'l) adj.
	True.
17. veritability	VERI tability (ver i ta bil' i ti) n.
	The quality of truthfulness.
18. veritas	VERI tas (ver' i tas) n.
	Latin word for truth.
19. very	VER y (ver' ee) adj.
	Exact and absolute; as, real and very justice.
20. verifier	VERI fier (ver' i fie er) n.
	One who verifies the truth.

word analysis

VERISIMILITUDE—No. 10
    VERI (verus)—Latin Root =truth
    SIMILI (similis)—Latin Root =likeness
    TUDE—Suffix =state of

practical exercises

1. Supply the missing words:
    You must .... your statements with illustra-
    tions and examples. There was a .... landslide
    in favor of the old candidate.

2. Analyze No. 6.

3. Choose the word which best expresses the italicized word:
    a. *veritable* (1) actual (2) essential
        (3) serious (4) scornful (5) cheap   ....
    b. *venturesome* (1) saucy (2) timid
        (3) impatient (4) forceful (5) daring   ....
    c. *assume* (1) locate (2) convene (3) volcanize
        (4) take for granted (5) replace   ....
    d. *photogenic* (1) literate (2) idiotic
        (3) microscopic (4) photographs well
        (5) disturbed   ....
    e. *defamation* (1) debt (2) infection (3) slander
        (4) adventure (5) abbreviation   ....

KEY NO. *191*

O—⚷

LOQUI · LOC

speak

is the Root *LOQUI, LOC* which means SPEAK. It comes from the Latin *loquor, locutus*. This is the key I spoke of when we had KEY *LOCO, LOCUS*, meaning PLACE. I have mentioned before this that the Latin verb changes its spelling and pronunciation. Since the English word is based on the Latin, the English also changes. When you see *LOC* in a word, stop for a moment and think whether it is PLACE or SPEAK.

1. loquacious — LOQU acious (lo kway' shus) adj.
   Garrulous; talkative.

2. loquacity — LOQU acity (lo kwas' it ee) n.
   Garrulity; talkativeness.

3. circumlocution — circum LOC ution (sir kum lo kyue' shun) n.
   Indirect roundabout way of speech.

4. elocute — e LOC ute (el' o kute) v.
   Speak out in public; declaim.

5. elocution — e LOC ution (el o kyue' shun) n.
   Declamation; oratory; public speaking.

6. elocutionist — e LOC utionist (el o kyue' shu nist) n.
   A professional speaker.

7. eloquence — e LOQU ence (el' o kwens) n.
   Speech marked by fluent diction and imaginative fervor.

8. eloquent — e LOQU ent (el' o kwent) adj.
   Expressing oneself with fluency and force.

9. obloquy — ob LOQU y (ob' lo kwee) n.
   Blame; abuse.

10. obloquious — ob LOQU ious (ob loe' kwi us) adj.
    Characterized by obloquy.

11. soliloquy — soli LOQU y (so lil' o kwee) n.
    A long speech to oneself; a monologue.

12. soliloquize — soli LOQU ize (so lil' o kwize) v.
    To talk to oneself earnestly.

13. soliloquist — soli LOQU ist (so lil' o kwist) n.
    One who soliloquizes.

14. soliloquacious — soli LOQU acious (so lil o kway' shus) adj.
    Having a tendency to soliloquize.

15. loquent — LOQU ent (loe' kwent) adj.
    Inclined to speak; articulate.

382

16. loquitur   LOQU itur (lok' wi tur) v.
                 (*Latin stage direction*) *The actor will speak.*
17. interlocution   inter LOC ution (int er lo kyue' shun) n.
                 Interchange of speech; conversation.
18. interlocutor   inter LOC utor (int er lok' yut or) n.
                 One who takes part in a conversation.
19. interlocutory   inter LOC utory (int er lok' yu tor ee) adj.
                 Relating to an interlocution.
20. interlocutress   inter LOC utress (in ter lok' yu tres) n.
                 A female interlocutor.

word analysis

ELOCUTION—No. 5
    E (ex)—Prefix =out
    LOC (loquor)—Latin Root =to speak
    TION—Suffix =act of

practical exercise

Read the following excerpt underlining all those words that contain keys that you have already learned.

    This lonely and eccentric artist did his best work in New York, during the last twenty-five years of the 1800's. He lived in a studio heaped with odds and ends, and was indifferent to everything but painting. He often worked on a picture for years, returning to it again and again, and leaving it unsigned and undated. Many of his pictures were damaged because he did not understand the chemistry of the paints he used.

    Ryder's work stands out as an exception to the detailed realism which was fashionable in his time. He takes us into a dream world of symbolic ghostly riders, serpents, nymphs and lonely sailors under strange, unearthly, moonlit skies. He pays little attention to the drawing, but roughly blocks out areas and streaks of color thick and heavy with paint. His figures are often reduced to broad silhouettes or vague mysterious images, half obscured by darkness.

    (A description of the painting "Toilers of the Sea" and a note about the artist, Albert P. Ryder. The painting is in the Addison Gallery of American Art, Phillips Academy, Andover, Mass. This excerpt is reprinted by permission of Field Enterprises from the World Book Encyclopedia.)

KEY NO. 192

o—➤

NUNCI · NOUNC

declare
warn

is the Root *NUNCI, NOUNC* which comes from the Latin verb *nuntiare* which means to SPEAK, to DECLARE, WARN. This Latin root gives us a clue to the Italian pronunciation. In Italian the *ci* is pronounced like *ch* in English—*nunchio*. In English the *ci* is usually pronounced like *si*, although in the word deli*ci*ous we say deli*sh*us. So it is sometimes difficult to know how to pronounce a *ci* word without the help of a dictionary.

1. nuncio   NUNCI o (nun' see o) n.
                 Messenger; a papal representative.
2. nunciative   NUNCI ative (nun' shi ay tiv) adj.
                 Conveying messages.
3. nunciature   NUNCI ature (nun' see a chur) n.
                 The office of the nuncio.
4. nuncupate   NUNC upate (nun' kyu pate) v.
                 To declare orally; to proclaim.
5. nuncupative   NUNC upative (nun' kyu pate iv) adj.
                 Oral; not written.
6. nunciate   NUNC iate (nun' shi ate) n.
                 A messenger; announcer.
7. announce   an NOUNC e (a nouns') v.
                 To make knowledge public.
8. announcer   an NOUNC er (a noun' ser) n.
                 One who makes announcements publicly.
9. announcement an NOUNC ement (a noun' sment) n.
                 Information given to the public.
10. denounce   de NOUNC e (de nouns') v.
                 Accuse; inform against.
11. denunciation de NUNCI ation (de nun see ay' shun) n.
                 Act of informing against.
12. denunciable de NUNCI able (de nun shi a b'l) adj.
                 May or should be informed against.
13. denunciatory de NUNCI atory (de nun' see a tor ee) adj.
                 Characterized by denunciation.
14. enunciate   e NUNCI ate (ee nun' see ate) v.
                 To pronounce carefully.
15. enunciation e NUNCI ation (ee nun see ay' shun) n.
                 Pronunciation; articulation.
16. pronounce   pro NOUNC e (pro nouns') v.
                 Declare; articulate.

384

17. pronouncement   pro NOUNC ement (pro noun' sment) n.
                 Declaration; formal announcement.
18. pronunciation   pro NUNCI ation (pro nun se ay' shun) n.
                 Articulation; utterance.
19. renounce   re NOUNC e (re nouns') v.
                 Retract; revoke; abdicate.
20. renunciation   re NUNCI ation (re nun see ay' shun) n.
                 Abdication; the act of giving up.

word analysis

DENUNCIATION—No. 11
     DE—Prefix =away; intensive
     NUNCI (nuntiare)—Latin Root =to declare; warn
     TION—Suffix =act of

practical exercises

1. Supply the missing words:
     When your e............................ of words is exact, your
     pro............ .... is usually good, too. There was great
     applause when the .... made a formal ....
     of the noted star's appearance.

2. Analyze No. 19.

3. Use one word to express each phrase:
     a. informing against   ....
     b. information made known to the public   ....
     c. characterized by blame for disgrace   ....
     d. one who asks questions in a conversation   ....
     e. an act of confirming the truth   ....

KEY NO. 193

LITERA · LITER
LIT · LETTER

letters

is the Root *LITERA, LITER, LIT,* *LETTER* meaning LETTERS. As is natural to the key, the list is full of LITERary words. And so easy to learn from the key! Is there any reason in the world why anyone should be *ILLITER*ate when an aid like this is available? *IL* (in =not) and *AL* (ad =to) are both assimilates before a word with *l. Ob* means against. Soon you will be able to tackle the best in literature, unsimplified.

1. litany   LIT any (lit' an ee) n.
   A prayer consisting of invocations and responses.

2. literal   LITER al (lit' e ral) adj.
   Relating to the exact letter; as, a literal translation.

3. literacy   LITER acy (lit' e ra see) n.
   The state of being educated.

4. literalism   LITER alism (lit' e ra liz um) n.
   The doctrine of keeping to the exact meaning of a word.

5. literalist   LITER alist (lit' e ra list) n.
   One who believes in literalism.

6. literatus   LITER atus (lit e ray' tus) n.
   A well-educated person. (Plural, literati.)

7. literary   LITER ary (lit' e rare ee) adj.
   Concerned with books and writing; well-read.

8. literatist   LITER atist (lit' er a tist) n.
   An author; a writer.

9. literation   LITERA tion (lit er ay' shun) n.
   The act of representing something by letters.

10. literature   LITERA ture (lit' e ra chur) n.
    The best works written during the centuries.

11. letter   LETTER (let' er) n.
    One of the written symbols of the alphabet; also an epistle.

12. alliterate   al LITER ate (a lit' e rate) v.
    To repeat the same consonant sound in word after word; as, Peter picked a peck. . . .

13. alliteration   al LITERA tion (a lit e ray' shun) n.
    The recurrence of the same letter sound.

14. alliterative al LITERA tive (a lit' e rate iv) adj.
      Characterized by alliteration.
15. alliterator al LITER ator (a lit' er ay tor) n.
      One who uses alliteration.
16. obliterate ob LITER ate (o blit' e rate) v.
      To efface the letters; as, obliterate *the name.*
17. obliterative ob LITERA tive (o blit' e rate iv) adj.
      Causing to be obliterated.
18. obliteration ob LITERA tion (o blit e ray' shun) n.
      The effacement of a name.
19. transliterate trans LITER ate (tranz lit' e rate) v.
      To spell in the letters of another alphabet.
20. transliteration trans LITERA tion (tranz lit e ray' shun) n.
      The act of transliterating.

word analysis

TRANSLITERATION—No. 20
    TRANS—Prefix =across
    LITERA—Latin Root =letters
    TION—Suffix =act of

practical exercises

1. Supply the missing words:
    An example of .... is, Peter picked a peck
    of pickled peppers. An example of .... poetry
    is "Slow and silent the sun sank steadily." .... is
    necessary when one first studies Russian.

2. Analyze No. 4.

3. Syllabicate and indicate which syllable is most greatly stressed
    by placing the accent ('):
        reputable   repute
        contemplate   contemplative
        interlocutory   totalitarianism
        transliteration   illiteracy

KEY NO. 194

**PLU · PLUR
PLUS**

more

is the Root *PLU, PLUR, PLUS* meaning MORE. They come from the Latin *plus, pluris*. There is an odd collection of interests represented in our list—mathematics, languages, plants, votes, grammar, patriotism and even gentlemen's sports clothes. These last were loose, long, baggy knickerbockers which the golfers wore on the golf course. They were called Plus Fours, because they were four inches longer than the regular knickerbockers!

1. plupatriotic   PLU patriotic (plue pay tri ot' ik) adj.
       Showily patriotic.
2. pluperfect   PLU perfect (plu per' fekt) n.
       The past perfect tense.
3. plural   PLUR al (plur' al) adj.
       More than one.
4. pluralism   PLUR alism (plur' a liz um) n.
       The state of one person holding two or more jobs at once.
5. pluralist   PLUR alist (plur' a list) n.
       One who holds two or more jobs.
6. plurality   PLUR ality (plu ral' it ee) n.
       The state of being more numerous; majority.
7. pluralize   PLUR al ize (plur' a lize) v.
       To make singular nouns plural.
8. plurative   PLUR ative (plur' a tiv) adj.
       More than half but less than all.
9. plurennial   PLUR ennial (plu ren' i al) n.
       A plant living many years.
10. plurilingual PLUR ilingual (plur i lin' gwal) adj.
       Speaking several languages.
11. plurilateral PLUR ilateral (plur i lat' er al) adj.
       Having more than two sides.
12. plurinomial PLUR inomial (plur i nom' i al) adj.
       Having more than one name.
13. plurisyllable PLUR isyllable (plur i sil' a b'l) n.
       A word having more than one syllable.
14. plus   PLUS (plus) adj.
       Indicating that something is to be added; as, her age is forty plus.

15. plurivorous PLUR ivorous (plu riv' o rus) adj.
     Living on more than one host; as, fungi.
16. plurisyllabic PLUR isyllabic (plur i si lab' ik) adj.
     Having more than one syllable.

word analysis

PLURENNIAL—No. 9
   PLUR (pluris)—Latin Root =more
   ENNI (annum)—Latin Root =year
   AL—Suffix =relating to

practical exercises

1. Supply the missing words:
     He won the election by a .... of many hun-
     dred thousand votes. Fungi are parasitic organisms which
     live on more than one host at a time, and that is why they
     are called ....

2. Analyze No. 7.

3. Add key to complete each word, the meaning of which is
   given:
   a. state of being more numerous— ....ality
   b. having more than two sides— ....lateral
   c. a word with more than one syllable— pluri..........
   d. relating to many years— plur..........
   e. having to do with books and writing— ....ary
   f. making up a story beforehand— ....text

KEY NO. 195

PUT

think

is the Root *PUT* which comes from the Latin *putare*, to THINK. Here is a fine instance of the value of knowing many keys to combine and recombine with a Root. *PUT* means THINK, a very limited picture. With the addition of 13 prefixes and suffixes, handy little keys, a wealth of languages has surrounded this bare little Root. These keys have opened to us the world of I.B.M., a delegation, a debate, arguments, accusation and public opinion. The keys are priceless!

1. putation   PUT ation (pyue tay' shun) n.
   Act of thinking.
2. putative   PUT ative (pyute' a tiv) adj.
   Commonly thought; as, a putative millionaire.
3. compute   com PUT e (kom pyute') v.
   Calculate.
4. computable   com PUT able (kom pyute' a b'l) adj.
   Can be thought out.
5. computation   com PUT ation (kom pyue tay' shun) n.
   Calculation.
6. computer   com PUT er (kom pyute' er) n.
   A computing machine.
7. depute   de PUT e (de pyute') v.
   To appoint as deputy or agent; to delegate.
8. deputation   de PUT ation (dep yu tay' shun) n.
   Appointment to office of deputy; delegation.
9. deputy   de PUT y (dep' yut ee) n.
   One appointed to substitute for another; as, a deputy hostess.
10. deputize   de PUT ize (dep' yu tize) v.
    To appoint as deputy.
11. dispute   dis PUT e (dis pyute') v.
    To disagree about a matter; argue; quarrel.
12. disputation   dis PUT ation (dis pyue tay' shun) n.
    A formal debate.
13. disputants   dis PUT ants (dis pyute' ants) n.
    The debaters.
14. disputatious   dis PUT atious (dis pyu tay' shus) adj.
    Argumentative; quarrelsome.

15. disputable   dis PUT able (dis pyute′ a b′l) adj.
             Debatable.
16. impute   im PUT e (im pyute′) v.
             Ascribe to; charge with; accuse.
17. imputation im PUT ation (im pyu tay′ shun) n.
             Accusation; insinuation; as, imputation *of bribery.*
18. repute   re PUT e (re pyute′) n.
             Esteem; as, held in good repute.
19. reputable   re PUT able (rep′ yut a b′l) adj.
             Honorable; estimable.
20. reputation re PUT ation (rep yu tay′ shun) n.
             Public opinion.

word analysis

IMPUTATION—No. 17
   IM (in)—Prefix =into
   PUT (putare)—Latin Root =to think
   ION—Suffix =act of

practical exercises

1. Supply the missing words:
   He was well known for his .... character, and he always welcomed an argument at the drop of a hat. He had an excellent .... and no one would .... base motives to him.

2. Analyze No. 13.

3. Use a word for the phrase:
   a. inclined to be quarrelsome   ....
   b. the image of your character to people   ....
   c. in the nature of a conference   ....
   d. bitter, quarrelsome and nagging   ....
   e. causing to overthrow the government ....
   f. in the manner of an analysis   ....
   g. government by dictatorship   ....

0—🗝

GREG

herd
flock
mob
group
troop
crowd

is the Root *GREG* which comes from the Latin *grex, gregis* meaning HERD, FLOCK, MOB. From that rather sour meaning we have developed the better words, GROUP, TROOP, CROWD. The burning word in the list is No. 15, seGREGation, and it is good to be able to know just why it means what it means. No. 19 is the opposite of No. 18. What we need is peaceful conGREGation of all peoples and races so that we can have a peaceful world to live in. *Live and let live* is a maxim for all.

1. gregarian
    GREG arian (gre gar' i an) adj.
    Belonging to a herd.

2. gregarious
    GREG arious (gre gar' ee us) adj.
    Living with and moving with the herd.

3. aggregate
    ag GREG ate (ag' re gate) v.
    To collect; to unite.

4. aggregable
    ag GREG able (ag' re ga b'l) adj.
    Can be collected; can be united.

5. aggregation
    ag GREG ation (ag re gay' shun) n.
    A collection; a union into a mass.

6. aggregant
    ag GREG ant (ag' re gant) n.
    A proposition entering into an aggregate.

7. aggregative
    ag GREG ative (ag' re gate iv) adj.
    Tending to form a crowd; collective.

8. aggregatory
    ag GREG atory (ag' re ga to ri) adj.
    Assembled; of the nature of an assembly.

9. congregate
    con GREG ate (kon' gre gate) v.
    To flock together.

10. congregation
    con GREG ation (kon gre gay' shun) n.
    A group functioning together; as, church or synagogue.

11. congregational
    con GREG ational (kon gre gay' shun al) adj.
    Relating to a congregation.

12. congregative
    con GREG ative (kon' gre gay tiv) adj.
    Tending to come together.

13. egregious
    e GREG ious (e gree' jus) adj.
    Standing out from the group in an unfavorable sense; as, an egregious boor.

14. segregate   se GREG ate (seg' re gate) v.
                    To separate from the crowd; set apart.
15. segregation   se GREG ation (seg re gay' shun) n.
                    The act of separating; setting apart.
16. segregative   se GREG ative (seg' re gate iv) adj.
                    Tending to separate, to set apart.
17. segregational   se GREG ational (seg re gay' shun al) adj.
                    Relating to segregation.
18. segregationist   se GREG ationist (seg re gay' shun ist) n.
                    One who believes in segregation.
19. antisegregationist antise GREG ationist
                    (an ti se gre gay' shun ist) n.
                    One against segregation.
20. desegregate   dese GREG ate (dee seg' re gate) v.
                    To do away with segregation.

word analysis

CONGREGATIONAL—No. 11
    CON—Prefix =together
    GREG (gregis)—Latin Root =herd
    TION—Suffix =act of
    AL—Suffix =relating to

practical exercises

1. Supply the missing words:
    Some people .... themselves and others have
    .... thrust upon them. The students ....
    every Friday at the soda parlor where they eat huge
    ....(s) of ice cream.
2. Analyze No. 14.
3. Choose the number which best expresses the meaning of the
italicized word:
    a. *pretext*   (1) excuse   (2) sample   (3) book
        (4) program   (5) journey   ....
    b. *contemplate*   (1) watch   (2) meditate
        (3) answer   (4) imagine   (5) know   ....
    c. *conscience*   (1) furniture   (2) money
        (3) congregation   (4) righteousness   (5) duty   ....
    d. *pestiferous*   (1) entertaining   (2) annoying
        (3) tall   (4) delightful   (5) sad   ....
    e. *abode*   (1) street   (2) enemy   (3) home
        (4) road   (5) mountain   ....

KEY NO. 197

O—➤

JAC · JEC · JECT

throw
lie

is a Root, *JAC, JEC, JECT* meaning THROW; LIE. An oddity about this Root is that it never stands alone, as other Roots do. Standing alone it has no meaning. It is entirely dependent on prefixes and suffixes to be meaningful.

1. dejected   de JECT ed (de jekt' ed) adj.
      Low in spirits; cast down.

2. dejection   de JECT ion (de jek' shun) n.
      A condition of despair; depression.

3. adjacent   ad JAC ent (ad jas' ent) adj.
      Next to; as, the adjacent *house.*

4. adject   ad JECT (a jekt') v.
      To add to; to annex.

5. adjective   ad JECT ive (aj' ek tiv) n.
      Not standing alone; a word which modifies a noun.

6. adjectival   ad JECT ival (aj ek tie' val) adj.
      Using many adjectives; as, an adjectival *style.*

7. conject   con JECT (kon jekt') v.
      To plan; to surmise.

8. conjecture   con JECT ure (kon jek' chur) v.
      To form an opinion; to surmise.

9. ejaculate   e JAC ulate (e jak' yu late) v.
      To throw out; cry out.

10. eject   e JECT (e jekt) v.
      To throw out; as, eject *him from the hall.*

11. ejection   e JECT ion (e jek' shun) n.
      The throwing out; expulsion.

12. inject   in JECT (in jekt') v.
      To insert; as, inject *a syringe.*

13. injection   in JECT ion (in jek' shun) n.
      The throwing in of liquid by a syringe.

14. interjection   inter JECT ion (int er jek' shun) n.
      A word thrown between others; as, He went, alas! to die.

15. introjection   intro JECT ion (in tro jek' shun) n.
      The act of throwing oneself into a cause.

16. objection   ob JECT ion (ob jek' shun) n.
      Disapproval; refusal to accept.

17. projection   pro JECT ion (pro jek' shun) n.
                  A throwing forward; as, a projection *of the
                  voice.*
18. rejection   re JECT ion (re jek' shun) n.
                  Refusal; denial; as, a rejection *of his proposal.*
19. abject   ab JECT (ab' jekt) adj.
                  Degraded; debased.
20. abjection   ab JECT ion (ab jek' shun) n.
                  Abasement; degradation.

word analysis

REJECTION—No. 18
    RE—Prefix =back
    JEC (jacere)—Latin Root =to throw
    TION—Suffix =act of

practical exercise

Read the following excerpt underlining all those words that contain keys you have already learned.

It was in the early days of April; Bernard Longueville had been spending the winter in Rome. He had travelled northward with the consciousness of several social duties that appealed to him from the further side of the Alps, but he was under the charm of the Italian spring and he made a pretext for lingering. He had spent five days at Siena, where he had intended to spend two, and still it was impossible to continue his journey. He was a young man of a contemplative and speculative turn, and this was his first visit to Italy, so that if he dallied by the way he should not be harshly judged. He had a fancy for sketching, and it was on his conscience to make a few pictorial notes. There were two old inns at Siena, both of them very shabby and dirty. The one at which Longueville had taken up his abode was entered by a dark, pestiferous archway, surmounted by a sign which at a distance might have been read by the travellers as a Dantean injunction to renounce all hope.

(From *Confidence* by Henry James.)

KEY NO. 198

O—⚷

PATER · PATR

father

is the Root *PATER, PATR,* which is the Latin word for FATHER. Many young people, especially those who study Latin, call their fathers PATER and it is certainly preferable to *Governor* or *old man.* This key gives us a glimpse into Russian name calling, No. 4; to the early Dutch settlement system, No. 16; a Latin phrase, No. 10; the difference between the PATRiot and the PATRioteer.

1. Pater	PATER (pa′ ter) n.	*Word for father taken directly from the Latin.*
2. patriarch	PATR iarch (pay′ tree ark) n.	*The head of the tribe, family.*
3. patrimony	PATR imony (pa′ tri mo nee) n.	*The estate handed down from father to son.*
4. patronymic	PATR onymic (pa tro nim′ ik) n.	*The father's name added to the child's.*
5. patron	PATR on (pay′ tron) n.	*A wealthy person who supports a cause or an artist.*
6. patronize	PATR onize (pay′ tro nize) v.	*To act like a patron of; protect, support.*
7. paternity	PATER nity (pa ter′ nit ee) n.	*Fatherhood; responsibility of fatherhood.*
8. paternal	PATER nal (pa tern′ al) adj.	*Relating to the father; as, the* paternal *side of the family.*
9. paternalism	PATER nalism (pa tern′ al iz um) n.	*A government which acts as a father to the citizens; a father-child rather than a state-citizen relationship.*
10. paternoster	PATER noster (pat′ er nos ter) n.	*Lord's Prayer.*
11. patrician	PATR ician (pa trish′ an) n.	*One nobly born; aristocrat.*
12. patricide	PATR icide (pa′ tri side) n.	*The murder or murderer of one's father.*
13. patriot	PATR iot (pay′ tree ot) n.	*One who loves and serves his country.*
14. patriotism	PATR iotism (pay′ tree o tiz um) n.	*Love for one's fatherland.*

15. patrioteer   PATR ioteer (pay tri o teer') n.
                   One who waves the flag selfishly.

16. patroon   PATR oon (pa troon') n.
                   A feudal lordship under the Dutch in New York.

17. patruity   PATR uity (pa true' i ti) n.
                   The relationship of the father's brother.

18. patriotic   PATR iotic (pay tree ot' ik) adj.
                   Like a patriot.

19. unpatriotic   un PATR iotic (un pay tree ot' ik) adj.
                   Not loving one's country.

20. expatriate   ex PATR iate (ek spay' tree ate) n.
                   One who leaves his country and lives abroad.

word analysis

PATRICIDE—No. 12
    PATR (pater)—Latin Root =father
    CIDE (caedere)—Root =kill

practical exercises

1. Supply the missing words:
     In eighteenth-century England a writer could barely exist without a .... to help him. The Dutch .... system failed because people would not come to America to be serfs.

2. Analyze No. 8.

3. Three suffixes compounded, OR+AL+LY, gives you at once the idea of one who, relating to, and in the manner of. Note *i* after *or*!
    Example: Pictor. . . . pictorially (adv.), in the manner of what relates to a picture. Add this suffix to the following words:
    a. memory (change *y* to *i*)   ....
    b. dictator   ....
    c. professor   ....
    d. peremptory (change the *y* to *i*)   ....
    e. interlocutory   ....

KEY NO. *199*

CUB · CUMB

**lean back
lie down**

is the Root *CUB, CUMB* (It comes from the Latin *cubare* and *cumbere*.) which means LEAN back; LIE down. We get a glimpse of the manners of eating in ancient Rome. We become modern again with the inCUBator for eggs and babies. Don't look at the answer to the MISSING WORDS department till you've tried it. Have fun!

1. accubation   ac CUB ation (ak yue bay' shun) n.
   Posture of lying down; leaning.

2. accubitus   ac CUB itus (a kue' bi tus) n.
   A bishop's private office; a couch.

3. accubitum   ac CUB itum (a kue' bi tum) n.
   A couch, crescent-shaped, at which five people could recline.

4. accumbent   ac CUMB ent (a kum' bent) adj.
   Lying back; as, at meals in ancient Rome.

5. incumbent   in CUMB ent (in kum' bent) n.
   One who is the official holder of an office.

6. incumbency   in CUMB ency (in kum' ben see) n.
   Sphere of action of an office holder.

7. encumber   en CUMB er (en kum' ber) v.
   To place a burden upon; hamper; overload.

8. encumbrance   en CUMB rance (en kum' brans) n.
   A burden.

9. incubate   in CUB ate (in' kyu bate) v.
   To hatch by keeping warm.

10. incubator   in CUB ator (in' kyu bate or) n.
    An apparatus for hatching artificially.

11. incubation   in CUB ation (in kyu bay' shun) n.
    The process of incubating.

12. incubational   in CUB ational (in kyu bay' shun al) adj.
    Relating to incubation.

13. incubative   in CUB ative (in' kyu bay tiv) adj.
    Characteristic of incubation.

14. incubatorium   in CUB atorium (in kyu ba to' ri um) n.
    A structure used for incubation.

15. incubatory   in CUB atory (in' kyu ba to ri) adj.
    Serving for incubation.

16. incubus   in CUB us (in' kyu bus) n.
    Nightmare.

17. recumbent   re CUMB ent (re kum' bent) adj.
                    Leaning back; lying down.
18. recumbency re CUMB ency (re kum' ben see) n.
                    The state of lying down.
19. succumb   suc CUMB (su kum') v.
                    To sink under a burden or pressure.
20. succumber   suc CUMB er (su kum' er) n.
                    One who succumbs.

word analysis

RECUMBENT—No. 17
    RE—Prefix =back
    CUMB (cubo)—Latin Root =lie down
    ENT—Suffix =one who

practical exercises

1. Supply the missing words:
    The mayor, having ....(ed) to the ....(s)
    of the campaign to secure his ...., was found
    .... on the .... in his ....,
    peacefully snoring.

2. Analyze No. 19.

3. Use a word for each phrase:
    a. official holder of an office   ....
    b. sink down under pressure or burden ....
    c. burdens which hamper one   ....
    d. official sphere of action   ....
    e. the position of leaning backward   ....
    f. a crescent-shaped couch used by the
       Romans   ....
    g. private office or rest room   ....

VIC · VICIS

change
substitute
deputy

is the Root *VIC, VICIS* which means CHANGE; SUBSTITUTE; DEPUTY. Words Nos. 1 through 14 should not be difficult to pronounce because you have learned all the keys. No. 15 to No. 18 will not be difficult if you look at the key *VICIS* and then add the other syllables. In Latin the *VIC IS* sounds like *VIK IS*, but in English we pronounce *VIS IS*. Language study requires adaptability.

1. vicar
   VIC ar (vik′ ar) n.
   One who serves as assistant, substitute, or deputy to a rector.

2. vicarly
   VIC arly (vik′ ar li) adv.
   In the manner of a vicar.

3. vicarage
   VIC arage (vik′ a rij) n.
   The residence of a vicar.

4. vicaress
   VIC aress (vik′ ar es) n.
   A female vicar or the wife of a vicar.

5. vicarate
   VIC arate (vik′ a rat) n.
   The authority and office of vicar.

6. vicariate
   VIC ariate (vie kare′ ee at) n.
   The same as No. 5.

7. vicarial
   VIC arial (vie kare′ ee al) adj.
   Relating to a vicar; delegated.

8. vicarship
   VIC arship (vik′ ar ship) n.
   The state and dignity of the office of a vicar.

9. vicarianism
   VIC arianism (vie kar′ i an iz um) n.
   The belief that one man can substitute for another in the performance of religious duties.

10. vicarian
    VIC arian (vie kar′ i an) n.
    One who believes in vicarianism.

11. vicariate
    VIC ariate (vie kar′ i ate) v.
    To assume the duties and to serve in the place of another.

12. vicarious
    VIC arious (vie kare′ ee us) adj.
    Being substituted; as, a vicarious pleasure.

13. vicariously
    VIC ariously (vie kare′ ee us lee) adv.
    Substituting for another; experiencing through another's experience.

14. vicariousness
    VIC ariousness (vie kare′ ee us ness) n.
    The state of substitution for another.

15. vicissitude   VIC issitude (vi sis′ i tude) n.
                Change in fortune.
16. vicissitous   VIC issitous (vi sis′ i tus) adj.
                Experiencing changes in fortune.
17. vicissitudinous VIC issitudinous (vi sis i tude′ in us) adj.
                Filled with the changes of fortune, difficulties.
18. vicissitudinary VIC issitudinary (vi sis′ i tue di nar i) adj.
                Characterized by changes of fortune.

word analysis

VICISSITUDINOUS—No. 17
    VICISSITUDIN (vicissitudo)—Latin Root =change and in-
                      terchange
    OUS—Suffix =full of

practical exercises

1. Supply the missing words:
    In his poem "The Deserted Village," Oliver Goldsmith de-
    scribes the .... of the church and the ....
    where he lived. After many .... he enjoyed a
    prosperous old age, not .... but actually.

2. Analyze No. 1.

3. Key review. Match keys with their meanings:
    a. vic   1. crowd   ....
    b. cub, cumb 2. throw   ....
    c. patr   3. more   ....
    d. ject   4. think   ....
    e. greg   5. lie down   ....
    f. plu, plur   6. father   ....
    g. litera   7. substitute   ....
    h. put   8. letters   ....

BENE · BON

well
good

is the Root *BENE, BON* which means WELL; GOOD. As you see, the list is composed of ten words with each Root. Words No. 14, 15, 16 come from the French, are really French, but the Root *BON* comes from the Latin, to the French.

1. benefit   BENE fit (ben' e fit) n.
               An advantage; as, the job has fringe benefits.
2. benefiter   BENE fiter (ben' e fit er) n.
               One who benefits; as the employee is the benefiter.
3. beneficial   BENE ficial (ben e fish' al) adj.
               Wholesome; as, bathing is beneficial.
4. benefactor   BENE factor (ben' e fak tor) n.
               One who benefits others.
5. benefaction BENE faction (ben e fak' shun) n.
               A gift; a donation.
6. benefactress BENE factress (ben' e fak tres) n.
               A female benefactor.
7. Benedict   BENE dict (ben' e dikt) n.
               A male name which means "Blessed."
8. benediction BENE diction (ben e dik' shun) n.
               A blessing.
9. benefice   BENE fice (ben' e fis) n.
               The gift of an income to a priest of a church.
10. benevolent BENE volent (be nev' o lent) adj.
               Being good hearted; a well-wisher.
11. bonny   BON ny (bon' y) adj.
               Sweet and attractive; as, a bonny child.
12. bonus   BON us (boe' nus) n.
               An extra benefit, usually extra pay.
13. bonanza   BON anza (bo nan' za) n.
               An unusually rich vein of gold or silver in a mine.
14. bonbon   BON bon (bon' bon) n.
               A small candy.
15. bonbonnière BON bonnière (bon bo nyar') n.
               A fancy dish or box for bonbons.
16. bon mot   BON mot (bone moe') n.
               A witty remark or repartee.
17. bonify   BON ify (bon' i fie) n.
               To convert into good.

18. bounty   BOUN ty (bount' ee) n.
                 A reward; a gift; generosity.
19. bountiful   BOUN tiful (bount' i ful) adj.
                 Generous; munificent.
20. bountifully   BOUN tifully (bount' i fu lee) adv.
                 Generously.

word analysis

BENEFACTION—No. 5
     BENE—Root = well; good
     FAC (facere)—Latin Root = to make
     TION—Suffix = act of

practical exercises

1. Supply the missing words:
     He was a .... man, and when he died he
     left his fortune for housing projects for the poor. They
     spoke his name with a .... The ....
     she received was almost half her salary.

2. Analyze No. 17.

3. Choose the number of the word which best expresses the
     italicized word:
     a. *abdicate*   (1) achieve   (2) protest   (3) renounce
         (4) demand   (5) steal   ....
     b. *agility*   (1) wisdom   (2) nimbleness
         (3) agreeable   (4) simplicity   (5) excitement   ....
     c. *benevolent*   (1) malicious   (2) cautious
         (3) loquacious   (4) generous   (5) gregarious   ....
     d. *derision*   (1) disgust   (2) incubus   (3) ridicule
         (4) anger   (5) heredity   ....
     e. *injunction*   (1) order   (2) error   (3) attack
         (4) injustice   (5) suggestion   ....

KEY NO. 202

O━━☀

EE

one who receives the action

is the Suffix *EE* which means ONE WHO. But this ONE WHO is different from the ONE WHO of *ER* or *OR*. *EE* means ONE WHO RECEIVES THE ACTION. You will notice that every one of the words in the list is a verb plus *EE*. The *EE* is a suffix which makes a noun of these verbs. The newly created noun receives the action, either directly or indirectly. For example: No. 13. The legatEE is the *ONE WHO RECEIVES* the legacy; No. 15: The nominEE is the *ONE WHO RECEIVES* the nomination.

1. alienee   alien EE (ay lee e nee') n.
   One who receives property through a transfer.
2. donee   don EE (doe nee') n.
   One who receives a gift.
3. appellee   appell EE (ap e lee') n.
   A person who has an appeal made against him.
4. assessee   assess EE (as e see') n.
   One whose property is assessed.
5. assignee   assign EE (a sie nee') n.
   One to whom a duty is assigned.
6. biographee   biograph EE (bie og ra fee') n.
   One whose life is written about.
7. collatee   collat EE (ko late ee') n.
   One on whom a benefice is bestowed.
8. devotee   devot EE (dev o tee') n.
   One who is devoted to a cause.
9. deportee   deport EE (dee port ee') n.
   One who is deported.
10. employee   employ EE (em ploy ee') n.
    One who is employed.
11. fiancée   fianc EE (fee an say') n.
    One who is engaged; affianced.
12. gagee   gag EE (gay jee') n.
    One to whom security is pledged.
13. legatee   legat EE (leg a tee') n.
    One who has a legacy bequeathed to him.
14. mortgagee   mortgag EE (mor ga jee') n.
    A person to whom a property is mortgaged.

15. nominee	nomin EE (nom i nee') n.
	One who is nominated; a candidate.
16. refugee	refug EE (ref yu jee') n.
	One who flees for safety.
17. referee	refer EE (ref e ree') n.
	One who calls the game.
18. trustee	trust EE (trus tee') n.
	One who holds a position of trust.
19. expellee	expell EE (ek spel ee') n.
	One who is expelled.

word analysis

EXPELLEE—No. 19

    EX—Prefix =out

    PELL (pellere)—Root =throw

    EE—Suffix =one who receives

practical exercise

Read the following excerpt, underlining all those words that contain keys you have already learned.

    The need to know—the need for news and documentation on what's going on in the world—it is a need common to all people everywhere. Group W is in a unique position to help fill this need. The group has the creative, financial, and managerial resources to program with the authority of a network, yet it retains its flexibility and viewpoint of a local station. The group is a vital third force in broadcasting today.

    For our eleven radio and television stations we go to Haiti for a documentary on that troubled island. To Africa for a new perspective on the Peace Corps. To South America for fifty vignettes of the volatile continent . . . we service the eight Group W communities directly.

(From a travel advertisement.)

KEY NO. 203

OB

**against
facing**

is the Prefix *OB* which means AGAINST; FACING. You will notice that the *OB* can change to *OF*, to *OC*, or even to *OP*. You guessed it—assimilation. *OF* before words with *f*, *OC* before words with *c*, and *OP* before words with *p*. The words with *OB* are very interesting. In practically every one of them the thought is opposed to the action.

1. obese
OB ese (o bese') adj.
Excessively fat.

2. obituary
OB ituary (o bich' u ar ee) n.
A death notice.

3. object
OB ject (ob jekt') v.
Oppose; refuse.

4. oppressive
OP pressive (o pres' ive) adj.
Harsh pressures.

5. offend
OF fend (o fend') v.
To strike against moral law; to cause pain.

6. objurgate
OB jurgate (ob' jur gate) v.
To denounce harshly.

7. obligee
OB ligee (ob li jee') n.
The one who must carry out the duty.

8. obligate
OB ligate (ob' li gate) v.
To bind by duty; constrain.

9. obligatory
OB ligatory (o blig' a tore ee) adj.
Binding; required.

10. oblige
OB lige (o blije') v.
To bind by a favor or service; force.

11. oblique
OB lique (o bleke') adj.
Not straight; having a slanting position.

12. obliquity
OB liquity (o blik' wit ee) n.
Deviation from moral rectitude.

13. obliterate
OB literate (o blit' e rate) v.
Blot out.

14. oblivious
OB livious (o bliv' ee us) adj.
Unaware; forgetful.

15. obloquy
OB loquy (ob' lo kwee) n.
Condemnatory speech.

16. obscene
OB scene (ob sene') adj.
Against decency; disgusting to the senses; tasteless.

17. oppose   OP pose (o poze') v.
              Place oneself against; stand up against.
18. occlusion   OC clusion (o klu' zhun) n.
              State of being shut out of; as, of a passage.
19. occult   OC cult (o kult') adj.
              Kept hidden; dealing with mysterious knowl-edge.

word analysis

OCCLUSION—No. 18
    OC (ob)—Prefix =against
    CLUS (clud)—Latin Root =shut
    SION—Suffix =act of; state of

practical exercises

1. Supply the missing words:
      He did not .... to the hard work, but the
      .... restrictions were intolerable, and he was
      ....(d) to them.

2. Analyze No. 3.

3. Use one word for each phrase:
    a. a notice of death in the papers   ....
    b. blot out from word or thought   ....
    c. in a good and abundant manner   ....
    d. yield to burden and pressure   ....
    e. in the manner of a substitution   ....

KEY NO. 204

FUM

smoke

is the Root *FUM*, which comes from the Latin *fumus*, SMOKE, and *fumigare*, to smoke out. It is interesting to see how SMOKE has come to mean anger, see Nos. 5, 7. It is also associated with the gamy smell of old meats. Of course, fumed oak (No. 14) furniture is beautiful. Fumigation is necessary to health.

1. fume   FUM e (fyume) n.
     Smoke; odor; exhalation; state of excitement.

2. fume   FUM e (fyume) v.
     To rage in an emotional outburst.

3. fumigatory   FUM igatory (fyue' mi ga to ri) adj.
     Having the quality of fumigating by smoke.

4. fumy   FUM y (fyue' mee) adj.
     Smokelike; as, a fumy smell.

5. fumish   FUM ish (fyume' ish) adj.
     Smoky; easily angered.

6. fumet   FUM et (fyue' met) n.
     Odor of meat which has been kept too long; a gamy smell.

7. fumous   FUM ous (fyue' mus) adj.
     Letting off fumes; easily angered.

8. fumiduct   FUM iduct (fyue' mi dukt) n.
     An outlet for smoke; a chimney.

9. fumatory   FUM atory (fyue' ma to ri) adj.
     Concerned with smoking.

10. fumatorium   FUM atorium (fyue ma to' ri um) n.
     An airtight chamber for smoking out insect pests.

11. fumatory   FUM atory (fyue' ma to ri) n.
     The same as No. 10.

12. fumacious   FUM acious (fyue may' shus) adj.
     Addicted to smoking of tobacco.

13. fumiferous   FUM iferous (fyue mif' er us) adj.
     Producing smoke; as incinerators are fumiferous machines.

14. fumed oak   FUM ed oak (fyumed oke) n.
     Oak which has been exposed to smoke to give it a weathered look.

15. fumigate   FUM igate (fyue' mi gate) v.
                 Destroy germs by smoking them out; disinfect.
16. fumigation   FUM igation (fyue mi gay' shun) n.
                 The act of disinfecting.
17. fumigant   FUM igant (fyue' mi gant) n.
                 Any chemical used for fumigation.
18. fumigator   FUM igator (fyue' mi gate or) n.
                 One who or that which fumigates.

word analysis

FUMIFEROUS—No. 13
    FUM (fumus)—Latin Root =smoke
    FER (ferre)—Latin Root =bear; bring
    OUS—Suffix =full of; nature of

practical exercises

1. Supply the missing words:
       After a contagious disease, the room in which the patient lay goes through the process of .... He
       was a .... old gentleman who ....
       at every provocation.

2. Analyze No. 8.

3. Compound suffix: CIOUS+LY: in the manner of being full of.
   EXAMPLE: saga+ciously = sagaciously, meaning wisely.
   a. fuma + ... = ...   meaning ....
   b. viva + ... = ...   "   ....
   c. gra   + ... = ...   "   ....
   d. menda + ... = ...   "   ....
   e. spa   + ... = ...   "   ....

409

O—

GRAT

pleasing

is the Root *GRAT* which means PLEASING. Very PLEASING, indeed, are the words on the list, giving pleasure all around. Except one—No. 6. That is a tricky word to use. Actually it means giving something not asked for. That is implicit in the word because it means unearned, for nothing.

1. grateful	GRAT eful (grate' ful) adj.
	Thankful; appreciative.
2. gratis	GRAT is (grat' is) adv.
	As a favor; without payment; as, you may have it gratis.
3. gratify	GRAT ify (grat' i fie) v.
	To please; to satisfy.
4. gratification	GRAT ification (grat i fi kay' shun) n.
	State of being pleased.
5. gratuity	GRAT uity (gra tue' it ee) n.
	Extra money not earned; as, a tip.
6. gratuitous	GRAT uitous (gra tue' it us) adj.
	Not called for; as, a gratuitous insult.
7. gratuitant	GRAT uitant (gra tue' i tant) n.
	One who receives a favor.
8. gratulatory	GRAT ulatory (grach' u la tore ee) adj.
	Having the quality of pleasing.
9. Gratia	GRAT ia (gray' shi a) n.
	Feminine name meaning grace, favor.
10. gratitude	GRAT itude (grat' i tude) n.
	Thankfulness; appreciation.
11. gratulant	GRAT ulant (grach' u lant) adj.
	Showing satisfaction, gratification.
12. Gratiano	GRAT iano (gra shi a' no) n.
	A character in Shakespeare's "The Merchant of Venice."
13. ingrate	in GRAT e (in' grate) n.
	One who is ungrateful.
14. ingratitude	in GRAT itude (in grat' i tude) n.
	Thanklessness; failure to appreciate.
15. ingratiate	in GRAT iate (in gray' shee ate) v.
	Worm oneself into favor; be a sycophant.
16. gratulate	GRAT ulate (grach' u late) v.
	Congratulate; express joy.

17. congratulate   con GRAT ulate (kon grach' u late) v.
                    Rejoice together with the one who has been
                    honored.
18. con grazia   con GRAZ ia (kon gra' tzy a) n.
                    (*An Italian phrase used about music*) *With*
                    grace.
19. congratulation con GRAT ulation (kon grach u lay' shun) n.
                    Act of congratulating a person.
20. de gratia   de GRAT ia (dee gray' shi a)
                    (*A Latin phrase used in law*) *By favor.*

word analysis

CONGRATULATORY—No. 17+ORY
    CON—Prefix =with
    GRATULAT (gratulatus)—Latin Root =rejoice
    ORY—Suffix =relating to

practical exercises

1. Supply the missing words:
    He was ....(ied) to receive the prize. Man is
    showered with .... blessings. He resented the
    .... insult.

2. Analyze Ungrateful.

3. Key review. Match keys with their meanings:

a. un	1. one	....
b. ure	2. stand	....
c. uni	3. state	....
d. sta	4. wisdom	....
e. spons	5. not	....
f. scrib	6. take; waste	....
g. sume, sump	7. pledge	....
h. simil	8. look	....
i. soph	9. write	....
j. spect	10. like, resemble	....

KEY NO. 206

○━⚡

INTRA

within

is the Prefix *INTRA* which means WITHIN. Notice how similar it is to INTER. Notice how careless pronunciation makes them sound almost exactly alike. The meaning is very different. In ancient days every city had a protective wall around it. Within the wall meant within the city. That is why sports or events within one city are still called INTRAmural.

1. intracollegiate   INTRA collegiate (in tra ko lee' ji at) adj.
   Within the college.
2. intraschool   INTRA school (in tra skule') adj.
   Within the school.
3. intramural   INTRA mural (in tra myur' al) adj.
   Within the community or institution; as intramural *sports.*
4. intragroup   INTRA group (in tra grupe') adj.
   Within the group.
5. intracoastal   INTRA coastal (in tra kose' tal) adj.
   Within coastal waters.
6. intracontinental   INTRA continental
   (in tra kon ti nen' tal) adj.
   Within the continent.
7. intradepartmental   INTRA departmental
   (in tra de part ment' al) adj.
   Within the department.
8. intradistrict   INTRA district (in tra dis' trikt) adj.
   Within the district.
9. intra-European   INTRA European
   (in tra yur o pee' an) adj.
   Within the boundaries of Europe.
10. intramarginal   INTRA marginal (in tra mar' ji nal) adj.
    Within the margins.
11. intranuclear   INTRA nuclear (in tra nyu' klee ar) adj.
    Within a nucleus.
12. intrabred   INTRA bred (in tra bred') adj.
    Matings within tribe or race.
13. intraglacial   INTRA glacial (in tra glay' shal) adj.
    Within a glacier.
14. intramolecular   INTRA molecular
    (in tra mo lek' yu lar) adj.
    Within the molecule.

412

15. intramontane	INTRA montane (in tra mon' tane) adj.
	Within a mountainous region.
16. intramundane	INTRA mundane (in tra mun' dane) adj.
	Within the material world.
17. intranational	INTRA national (in tra nash' un al) adj.
	Within the nation.
18. intraneural	INTRA neural (in tra nyur' al) adj.
	Within the nerve.
19. intraoral	INTRA oral (in tra or' al) adj.
	Within the mouth.
20. intravenous	INTRA venous (in tra vee' nus) adj.
	Within the veins.

word analysis

INTRAMURAL—No. 3
    INTRA—Prefix =within
    MUR (murus)—Latin Root =city wall
    AL—Suffix =relating to

practical exercises

1. Supply the missing words:
    All the city schools participated in the ....
    sports. In the hospital she was given .... in-
    jections. The .... affair was just a small dance.

2. Analyze No. 17.

3. Choose the word which most nearly expresses the italicized word:
    a. *ingratitude* (1) thanklessness (2) friendship
        (3) pride (4) money (5) mercy   ....
    b. *intraoral* (1) in the mouth (2) in the city
        (3) in the room (4) in the garden
        (5) in the attic   ....
    c. *de gratia* (1) of doing (2) of the law
        (3) of pleasing (4) financial (5) of sadness   ....
    d. *obstinate* (1) willing (2) with work
        (3) playful (4) dejected (5) standing against   ....
    e. *fumous* (1) delighted (2) objectionable
        (3) devoid (4) furious (5) intradepartmental   ....

is the Suffix *INE*. It is used in giving names in chemistry (chlorine) and in Botany (columbine). It makes adjectives giving the NATURE OF: feminine, masculine. There are two ways of pronouncing *INE*, either *INE* to rhyme with *wine*, or *IN* to rhyme with *win*. Be careful!

1. columbine   columb INE (kol' um bine) n.
                 A plant.
2. divine   div INE (di vine') adj.
                 Godly; of the nature of God.
3. elephantine   elephant INE (el e fan' teen) adj.
                 Of the nature of an elephant; ponderous.
4. feminine   femin INE (fem' i nin) adj.
                 Of the nature of a woman.
5. genuine   genu INE (jen' yu in) adj.
                 Natural; free from artificiality.
6. masculine   mascul INE (mas' kyu lin) adj.
                 Of the nature of a man.
7. medicine   medic INE (med' i sin) n.
                 The science and art dealing with cure of disease.
8. pristine   prist INE (pris' teen) adj.
                 The first; primary; new.
9. calcine   calc INE (kal sine) v.
                 Reduce to a powder.
10. routine   rout INE (ru teen') adj.
                 According to the regular schedule of work.
11. saccharine   sacchar INE (sak' a rin) adj.
                 Of the nature of sugar; as, a saccharine taste.
12. saline   sal INE (say' leen) adj.
                 Consisting of salt; as, a saline solution.
13. saturnine   saturn INE (sat' ur nine) adj.
                 Of the nature of the planet Saturn; gloomy; grave; melancholy.
14. serpentine   serpent INE (ser' pen teen) adj.
                 Winding sinuously, like a snake.
15. calcarine   calcar INE (kal' kar in) adj.
                 Shaped like a spur.
16. chlorine   chlor INE (klore' een) n.
                 A greenish yellow gas of a suffocating odor.
17. turbine   turb INE (tur' bin) n.
                 A powerful rotary engine.

18. turpentine   turpent INE (tur' pen tine) n.
                  A resinous fluid; sap from the terebinth tree.
19. wolverine   wolver INE (wol' ver een) adj.
                  Wolfish.
20. supine   sup INE (sue pine') adj.
                  Lying on the back; recumbent.

word analysis

MEDICINE—No. 7
    MED (mederi)—Latin Root =to heal
    IC—Suffix =like
    INE—Suffix =nature of

practical exercise

Read the following excerpt underlining all those words that contain keys you have already learned.

Brooklyn Heights, bounded by the East River, Fulton St., Atlantic Ave. and Court St., is an old middle-class residential community that retains many of the refinements of past decades. A number of artists and writers reside in its brownstones, converted Victorian-era mansions, and modern apartment buildings. A plan has been proposed for 100,000 square feet of recreational space, 95 dwelling units, a 200-car garage, and a new public school. It is believed that the cultural advantages of Brooklyn Heights make the community an ideal residential locale for older people. It proposes an out-lay of 13 million dollars to redevelop the area. The plan of garden apartments for the older residents would supersede other plans which had been proposed. The rental of the garden apartments would be as low as possible and there would be no discrimination of any kind.

(From *The New York Times.*)

KEY NO. 208

○━★

MATRI · MATRIC MATRO

mother

is the Root *MATRI, MATRIC, MATRO*. It comes from the Latin word *mater*, MOTHER. It may come as a surprise to have words like No. 9 and No. 17 and No. 3 because we are accustomed to hear them in the male form. With the key *PATER*, father, you met many of these words with *PATER* instead of *MATER*.

1. mater   MATER (mate' er) n.
Word for mother taken directly from the Latin.

2. matrix   MATRI x (may' triks) n.
The womb; the material in which a gem, fossil, metal is embodied.

3. matriarch   MATRI arch (may' tree ark) n.
The head of the mothers in a group, tribe.

4. matriculate   MATRIC ulate (ma trik' yu late) v.
To enroll or register in a college.

5. matriculation   MATRIC ulation (ma trik yu lay' shun) n.
Enrollment in a college.

6. matriculant   MATRI culant (ma trik' yu lant) n.
One who registers in a college.

7. matrimony   MATRI mony (ma' tri moe nee) n.
State of wedlock; marriage.

8. matrimonial   MATRI monial (ma tri moe' nee al) adj.
Relating to marriage.

9. matriotism   MATRI otism (may' tri ot iz um) n.
Love of mother country or alma mater.

10. matripotestal   MATRI potestal (may tri po tes' tal) adj.
Relating to the power exercised by the mother.

11. matrilineal   MATRI lineal (ma tri lin' ee al) adj.
Relating to the mother's side of the family.

12. maternal   MATER nal (ma tern' al) adj.
Relating to the mother; motherly.

13. matris   MATRIS (ma' triz) n.
The mother goddess of the Hindu deities.

14. matricide   MATRI cide (ma' tri side) n.
The murder of one's mother.

15. matron   MATRO n (may' tron) n.
A woman who has a supervisory role in an institution for women or children.

416

16. **matroclinous**   MATRO clinous (mat ro klie' nus) adj.
          Inheriting characteristics from the mother.

17. **matronymic**   MATRO nymic (ma tro nim' ik) n.
          Name derived from the name of the mother or other female ancestor.

18. **maternity**   MATER nity (ma ter' nit ee) n.
          The state or quality of being a mother.

19. **matriarchate** MATRI archate (may' tree ark at) n.
          The rulership of a woman.

20. **metropolis**   METRO polis (me trop' o lis) n.
          The mother city; the chief city of a designated area.

word analysis

MATRIPOTESTAL—No. 10
    MATRI (mater)—Latin Root =mother
    POTEST (potesse)—Latin Root =to be powerful
    AL—Suffix =relating to

practical exercises

1. Supply the missing words:
    Rip Van Winkle did not enjoy the blessings of ....
    Every race has in its history the lives of famous women who were honored with the title of ....

2. Analyze No. 19.

3. Use one word for each phrase:
    a. inclined to the character of the mother   ....
    b. enrollment in a college   ....
    c. powerful, rotary engine   ....
    d. smoke out the germs of disease   ....
    e. takes a good picture   ....
    f. words having practically the same meaning   ....

KEY NO. 209

MULTUS · MULTI

many
much

is the Root *MULTUS, MULTI* which comes from the Latin *multus* and means MANY; MUCH. This KEY has mathematical significance, being completely involved with the process of *MULTI*plication. The very minute you see this key you know MUCH. No. 10 might be inconvenient, if four babies appeared at once, but no one minds the state of being a *MULTI*-millionaire, or seeing a *MULTI*tude of stars.

1. multifold
MULTI fold (mul' ti fold) adj.
Folded many times.

2. multifarious
MULTI farious (mul ti far' ee us) adj.
Varied; diversified.

3. multigraph
MULTI graph (mul' ti graf) n.
A machine which prints many copies.

4. multilateral
MULTI lateral (mul ti lat' e ral) adj.
Many sided; as, a multilateral treaty.

5. multilingual
MULTI lingual (mul ti lin' gwal) adj.
Relating to many languages.

6. multilinguist
MULTI linguist (mul ti lin' gwist) n.
One who speaks many languages.

7. multilocation
MULTI location (mul ti lo kay' shun) n.
Present in many places simultaneously.

8. multiloquent
MULTI loquent (mul til' o kwent) adj.
Speaking much; loquacious.

9. multimillionaire
MULTI millionaire (mul ti mil yu nair') n.
One who has many millions.

10. multiparous
MULTI parous (mul tip' a rus) adj.
Giving birth to more than one child at a time.

11. multiped
MULTI ped (mul' ti ped) n.
An organism with many feet; as, a centipede.

12. multiple
MULTI ple (mul' ti p'l) adj.
Consisting of more than one; manifold.

13. multiplicand
MULTI plicand (mul ti pli kand') n.
That number in an example which is to be multiplied.

14. multiplication
MULTI plication (mul ti pli kay' shun) n.
An arithmetical process for increasing a number quickly.

15. multiplicity   MULTI plicity (mul ti plis' it ee) n.
                           The quality of being multiple; as, a multi-
                           plicity of thoughts.

16. multiply   MULTI ply (mul' ti plie) v.
                           To increase a number quickly by multipli-
                           cation.

17. multitude   MULTI tude (mul' ti tyude) n.
                           A great number; cannot be counted.

18. multiplex   MULTI plex (mul' ti pleks) adj.
                           Manifold; multiple.

19. multiplier   MULTI plier (mul' ti plie er) n.
                           One who or that which multiplies.

word analysis

MULTILATERAL—No. 4
     MULTI (multus)—Latin Root =many
     LATER (latus)—Latin Root =side
     AL—Suffix =relating to

practical exercises

1. Supply the missing words:
     Because he lived in Switzerland where four languages are
     spoken, he became .... Due to the ....
     of available jobs she was unable to make a choice. He
     made fifty copies of the program by using a ....

2. Analyze No. 8.

3. Give a synonym for each of the following words from the
    list in this key:
    Example: indistinct—obscure
    a. garrulous   ....
    b. centipede   ....
    c. polyhedron   ....
    d. diversified   ....
    e. innumerable   ....

MEDI

half
middle
between
half-way

is the Root *MEDI* which comes from *medare*, to HALVE, make HALVES. If a knife is to cut a loaf into halves, the knife must get into the middle, and so we get the idea of MIDDLE, BETWEEN, HALFWAY. In considering No. 20 there is a question why so important a person as one who has this remarkable faculty should be called a medium. In this case the medium means *agency* through which the supernatural is attracted.

1. medial   MEDI al (mede' ee al) adj.
              Relating to the middle; situated in the middle.
2. median   MEDI an (mede' ee an) adj.
              Intermediate.
3. mediate   MEDI ate (mede' ee ate) v.
              Come between; intervene.
4. mediation   MEDI ation (mede ee ay' shun) n.
              Intervention between opposing parties.
5. mediator   MEDI ator (mede' ee ate or) n.
              One who comes between opposing parties.
6. mediacy   MEDI acy (mede' ee a see) n.
              The state of coming between.
7. mediatorial MEDI atorial (mee di a to' ri al) adj.
              Characteristic of mediation or a mediator.
8. mediatory   MEDI atory (me' di a tor y) adj.
              Of the nature of mediation.
9. mediatress MEDI atress (mede' ee ay tres) n.
              A female mediator; mediatrix.
10. mediety   MEDI ety (me die' e ti) n.
              The half; moderation; temperance.
11. medieval   MEDI eval (mede ee ee' val) n.
              Pertaining to the middle ages.
12. medievalism MEDI evalism (mede ee ee' val iz um) n.
              The method and spirit of the middle ages.
13. medievalist MEDI evalist (mede ee eve' a list) n.
              One versed in the history and arts of the middle ages.
14. medifixed MEDI fixed (mee' di fiksd) adj.
              Attached by the middle.
15. mediglacial MEDI glacial (mee di glay' shal) adj.
              Situated between or amidst glaciers.

16. mediocre   MEDI ocre (mede ee o' ker) adj.
                       Of middle quality.

17. mediocrity   MEDI ocrity (mede ee ok' rit ee) n.
                       Average capacity; middle quality.

18. mediterranean   MEDI terranean (med i te ray' nee an) adj.
                       Lying between lands; having land on all sides.

19. immediacy   im MEDI acy (im ede' ee a see) n.
                       Need for immediate attention; urgency.

20. medium   MEDI um (mede' ee um) n.
                       A person having the faculty to make contact with the supernatural.

word analysis

MEDITERRANEAN—No. 18
     MED (medare)—Latin Root =between
     TERRA—Root =land
     EAN—Suffix =belonging

practical exercises

1. Supply the missing words:
     .... minds soon settle for ....
     He had an excellent reputation as a .... between unions and industry.

2. Analyze No. 3.

3. Complete the following words by adding the missing keys:
     a. between low and high grades— inter..........iate
     b. that which turns many ways— ....versant
     c. relating to motherhood— ....nal
     d. within the city limits— ....mural
     e. the act of leading right in— ....duction

KEY NO. 211

○━✖

PUNCT

point
dot

is the Root *PUNCT* which comes from the Latin *punctum*, meaning POINT; DOT. Every word on the list is important, and you will find many more to recognize yourself. It takes you from the PUNCTuation of a sentence to the PUNCTure of a tire; to the PUNCT of a discussion; to the PUNCTographic printing for the blind and to the marvelous quality of PUNCTuality.

1. punct   PUNCT (punkt) n.
       A point; an element in discussion.

2. punctal   PUNCT al (punk′ tal) adj.
       Relating to a point.

3. punctuate   PUNCT uate (punk′ chu ate) v.
       To place a point at the end of a sentence.

4. punctuation   PUNCT uation (punk chu ay′ shun) n.
       The act of punctuating.

5. punctuative   PUNCT uative (punk′ tue ay tiv) adj.
       Relating to punctuation.

6. punctuator   PUNCT uator (punk′ chu ate or) n.
       One who punctuates a text.

7. punctiform   PUNCT iform (punk′ ti form) adj.
       Having the form of a point or a dot.

8. punctilio   PUNCT ilio (punkt il′ i o) n.
       Exactness; precision in form.

9. punctilious   PUNCT ilious (punk til′ ee us) adj.
       Most particular; very precise.

10. compunction   com PUNCT ion (kom punk′ shun) n.
       Remorse; twinges of guilt.

11. punctographic   PUNCT ographic (punk to graf′ ik) adj.
       Like the point writing and printing for the blind; Braille.

12. punctual   PUNCT ual (punk′ chu al) adj.
       Being exactly on time.

13. punctuality   PUNCT uality (punk chu al′ it ee) n.
       The quality of being exactly on time.

14. punctualness   PUNCT ualness (punk′ chu al nes) n.
       The same as No. 13.

15. punctator   PUNCT ator (punk′ tay tor) n.
       One who marks with points; as, the vowel points in Hebrew texts.

16. punctum   PUNCT um (punk′ tum) n.
                A dot; a point.

17. puncture   PUNCT ure (punk′ chur) v.
                To pierce with a pointed instrument.

18. punctate   PUNCT ate (punk′ tate) adj.
                Ending in a point.

19. unpunctuated un PUNCT uated (un punk′ tue ate ed) adj.
                Not punctuated; as, an unpunctuated *sentence.*

word analysis

PUNCTOGRAPHIC—No. 11
     PUNCT (punctum)—Latin Root =point; dot
     GRAPH (graphein)—Greek Root =to write
     IC—Suffix =like

practical exercises

1. Supply the missing words:
     Correct .... of a sentence is necessary to
comprehend it. The .... sentences are not always easy to understand. John is always ....
when he makes an appointment, and he is ....
about details.

2. Analyze No. 3.

3. Choose the word which most clearly expresses the italicized
word:
    a. *punctilio*   (1) freedom   (2) imagination
           (3) doldrums   (4) exactness   (5) disease   ....
    b. *mediocrity*   (1) average capacity   (2) punctuation
           (3) mediator   (4) multitude   (5) bounty   ....
    c. *matriculate*   (1) get married   (2) have a baby
           (3) register in a college (4) rule the family
           (5) run for president   ....
    d. *obnoxious*   (1) dreamy   (2) visible   (3) daring
           (4) angry   (5) objectionable   ....
    e. *theoretical*   (1) magical   (2) visual
           (3) two-faced   (4) excitable   (5) hypothetical   ....

o—🔑

LAV · LUT
LAUT · LOT

wash

is the Root *LAV, LUT, LAUT, LOT* meaning WASH. They come from *lavare,* to wash. The *LAUT* has become the LAUN that is in LAUNdry. Louis XV, the French king, said, "After me the deluge," and this French expression brought the French word for flood into English. Thus instead of a *v* we have the *j* sound.

1. lavabo   LAV abo (la vab′ bo) n.
           A wash basin fastened to a wall.

2. lavadero   LAV adero (la va de′ ro) n.
           Part of a stream used to wash gold from placers.

3. lavage   LAV age (la vazh′) n.
           Washing out of an organ.

4. lavandera   LAV andera (la van day′ ra) n.
           Washerwoman; laundress.

5. lavatory   LAV atory (lav′ a tore ee) n.
           A place where one can wash.

6. lavish   LAV ish (lav′ ish) adj.
           Flowing like water; luxurious.

7. lavisher   LAV isher (lav′ ish er) n.
           One who spends money and gives gifts freely.

8. laundry   LAU ndry (laun′ dree) n.
           Clothes to be washed; a place were washing is done.

9. laundress   LAU ndress (laun′ dres) n.
           A woman who washes clothes.

10. launder   LAU nder (laun′ der) v.
           To wash and iron clothes.

11. lotion   LOT ion (lo′ shun) n.
           A soothing fluid; emollient; as, hand lotion.

12. lotic   LOT ic (lote′ ik) adj.
           Living in rapidly moving waves' and currents.

13. deluge   de LUG e (del′ yuje) n.
           An uncontrolled mass of flowing water; a flood.

14. diluvial   di LUV ial (di lue′ vee al) adj.
           Relating to a flood.

15. diluvium   di LUV ium (di lue′ vi um) n.
           A drift; supposed to be the result of flood.

16. dilute   di LUT e (die′ lute) v.
           To make a liquid thinner and weaker.

17. dilutent   di LUT ent (di lute' ent) n.
                       A thinning agent; that which dilutes.

18. dilution   di LUT ion (die lue' shun) n.
                       State of being diluted.

19. diluter   di LUT er (die lute' er) n.
                       One who or that which dilutes.

20. ablution   ab LUT ion (a blue' shun) n.
                       A washing away; a cleansing.

21. ablutionary ab LUT ionary (a blue' shu nar ee) adj.
                       Relating to ablution.

word analysis

ABLUTIONARY—No. 21
    AB—Prefix =away; from
    LUT (lavare)—Latin Root =to wash
    TION—Suffix =act of
    ARY—Suffix =that which

practical exercise

Read the following excerpt underlining all those words that contain keys you have already learned.

    There are all degrees of proficiency in knowledge of the world. It is sufficient to our present purpose to indicate three. One class live to the utility of the symbol, esteeming health and wealth a final good. Another class live above this mark to the beauty of the symbol, as the poet and artist and the naturalist and man of science. A third class live above the beauty of the symbol to the beauty of the thing signified; these are wise men. The first class have common sense; the second, taste; and the third, spiritual perception. Once in a long while, a man traverses the whole scale, and sees and enjoys the symbol solidly, then also has a clear eye for its beauty, and lastly, while he pitches his tent on this sacred volcanic isle of nature, does not offer to build houses and barns thereon—reverencing the splendor of God which he sees bursting through each chink and cranny.

                  (From Emerson's discourse on "Prudence.")

0——⚷

POTEN · POTES
POSSE

power

is the Root *POTEN, POTES, POSSE*
meaning POWER. The Root comes
from the Latin *posse, potesse, pos-
sessus.* The word POSSE (No. 12)
has been adopted entirely; the others
we have manipulated and suited to
our uses. A very special word is No.
5. The most important qualities of a
person are his potentialities. Very few
people take the trouble to explore
their real potential.

1. potent   POTEN t (pote' ent) adj.
                   Powerful; capable.
2. potence   POTEN ce (pote' ens) n.
                   Degree of power; potency.
3. potentate   POTEN tate (pote' en tate) n.
                   A monarch; a ruler.
4. potential   POTEN tial (po ten' chal) adj.
                   Having the possibility of development.
5. potentiality   POTEN tiality (po ten chee al' it ee) n.
                   The ability to develop; possibility of power.
6. potentiate   POTEN tiate (po ten' chee ate) v.
                   To endow with power; with potentiality.
7. potentialize   POTEN tialize (po ten' shal ize) v.
                   To make capable; to make potential.
8. potentiometer   POTEN tiometer (po ten chee om' et er) n.
                   An instrument to measure electromotive forces.
9. potentize   POTEN tize (poe' ten tize) v.
                   To render potent; to make capable.
10. potestative   POTES tative (poe' tes tay tiv) adj.
                   Having authority or power.
11. omnipotent   omni POTEN t (om nip' ot ent) adj.
                   All powerful.
12. posse   POSSE (pos' ee) n.
                   An armed band; a force with legal authority.
13. possess   POSSE ss (po zes') v.
                   To have and to hold as legal property.
14. possessed   POSSE ssed (po zesd') adj.
                   Controlled and influenced as by evil ideas.
15. possessor   POSSE ssor (po zes' or) n.
                   *One who possesses property; as, a proud pos-
                   sessor of a large estate.*
16. possible   POSS ible (pos' i b'l) adj.
                   Able to be; it may chance; as, it is possible.

17. possibilitate   POSS ibilitate (pos i bil' i tate) v.
                     To make possible.
18. possibility   POSS ibility (pos i bil' it ee) n.
                     *The state of being possible; as, a possibility of
                     failure.*
19. impotent   im POTEN t (im' pot ent) adj.
                     Incapable; lacking power.

word analysis

POTENTIALITY—No. 5
     POTENT (potesse)—Latin Root =powerful
     IAL—Suffix =relating to
     ITY—Suffix =quality of

practical exercises

1. Supply the missing words:
     The horse thief awoke to find himself surrounded by a
     .... sent out to catch him. The ....
     of the drug creates the .... of prescribing an
     overdose.

2. Analyze No. 19.

3. Write a synonym for each of the following words:
     Example: Possible—   ....practicable....
     a. impotent—   ....
     b. potency—   ....
     c. owner—   ....
     d. mediocre—   ....
     e. punctilio—   ....
     f. saturnine—   ....

KEY NO. 214

O—⚷

END · ENDO

within

is the Root *END, ENDO* which means WITHIN. And what a formidable list of words! Fortunately I do not ask you to learn them. I ask only that you learn *ENDO*—WITHIN. Oh, you want to learn the words, too? Well, just grasp your key and go on. Remember the keys that are now within you and hold on tight to the key, *ENDO.*

1. endobronchial   ENDO bronchial (en do bron′ ki al) adj.
   Within the cavity of a bronchus.
2. endocardial   ENDO cardial (en do kard′ ee al) adj.
   Within the heart.
3. endochrome   ENDO chrome (en′ do krome) n.
   Coloring matter within the cell.
4. endocrine   ENDO crine (en′ do krin) n.
   Any internal secretion.
5. endocrinology   ENDO crinology (en do kri nol′ o jee) n.
   Science of the endocrine glands.
6. endocrinopathy   ENDO crinopathy (en do kri nop′ a thi) n.
   Disorder of the endocrine glands.
7. endogamy   ENDO gamy (en dog′ a mee) n.
   Marriage within a legally designated group.
8. endoparasite   ENDO parasite (en do par′ a site) n.
   A parasite living within the body; as, a tapeworm.
9. endogeny   ENDO geny (en doj′ e nee) n.
   Growth from within.
10. endogastric   ENDO gastric (en do gas′ trik) adj.
    Relating to the inside of the stomach.
11. endopsychic   ENDO psychic (en do sie′ kik) adj.
    Developing within the psyche.
12. endorachis   ENDO rachis (en do ray′ kis) n.
    The membrane lining in the spinal canal.
13. endoral   END oral (en do′ ral) adj.
    Within the mouth.
14. endoscope   ENDO scope (en′ do skope) n.
    Instrument to see the interior of a hollow organ.
15. endosepsis   ENDO sepsis (en do sep′ sis) n.
    Internal rotting away of figs.
16. endosteal   END osteal (en dos′ tee al) adj.
    Within the bone.

17. endothermy	ENDO thermy (en do ther' mee) n.
	Surgical production of heat within the tissues.
18. endotoxin	ENDO toxin (en do tok' sin) n.
	A toxin of internal origin.
19. endotrophic	ENDO trophic (en do trof' ik) adj.
	Nourished from within.
20. endophagy	ENDO phagy (en dof' a ji) n.
	Cannibalism within the family or tribe.

word analysis

ENDOGASTRIC—No. 10
ENDO (endon)—Root =within
GAST (gastros)—Greek Root =stomach
IC—Suffix =like; relating to

practical exercises

1. Supply the missing words:
It would be rewarding to the layman if, occasionally, he had access to an .... and could get a glimpse of his .... interior. He might see one or two .... living there in comfort.

2. Analyze No. 14.

3. Syllabicate and indicate which syllable is most greatly stressed by placing accent ('):

potentiality	impotent
endocrinology	endocrine
disputants	punctilio

KEY NO. 215

O———

DORM

sleep

is the Root *DORM* which comes from the Latin *dormire, dormitum,* to SLEEP. Many words are combined with *DORM.* The *dormer window* in the attic bedroom; the *dormant partner* in a business; *dormant buds* on spring blooming plants—all these and more.

1. dorm   DORM (dorm) n.
   A dormitory.

2. dormitory   DORM itory (dor' mi tore ee) n.
   A building of sleeping rooms or a room that sleeps many.

3. dormancy   DORM ancy (dor' man see) n.
   State of being static; motionless.

4. dormant   DORM ant (dor' mant) adj.
   Being in a state of suspended animation; as, a dormant animal.

5. dormouse   DORM ouse (dor' mous) n.
   A small kind of rodent resembling a squirrel.

6. dormitive   DORM itive (dor' mi tiv) adj.
   Causing sleep; as, a drug or sleeping potion.

7. dormition   DORM ition (dor mish' un) n.
   State of falling asleep; figuratively, death.

8. dormilona   DORM ilona (dor mi loe' na) n.
   A sensitive plant.

9. dormient   DORM ient (dor' mi ent) adj.
   Sleeping.

10. dormeuse   DORM euse (dor muz') n.
    A carriage arranged for sleeping while traveling.

11. dormer   DORM er (dor' mer) n.
    A small window in a bedroom under the roof.

word analysis

DORMITIVE—No. 6
    DORMI (dormire)—Latin Root = to sleep
    IVE—Suffix = tending to

practical exercise

Read the following excerpt, underlining all those words that contain keys you have already learned.

430

"REPUBLIC STEEL TO REACTIVATE
OHIO PLANT SHUT SINCE '60."

The Republic Steel Corporation announced yesterday plans to resume production at its Massillon, Ohio plant. The plant which includes a blast furnace and an open-hearth furnace shop has been shut down since July 1, 1960. R. H. H. manager of the central alloy district, which includes the Canton-Massillon operations would recall about 400 employees to man the plant. "Plans already are underway to put the plant and blast furnace back into operation," Mr. H. said. "We also will start up with several open-hearth furnaces, depending on our backlog of orders, the 34-inch billet mill and 24-inch billet mill," he added.

The blast furnace at the mill has a rated capacity of 800 tons a day, while the open-hearth shop consists of nine furnaces.

(From *The New York Times*.)

KEY NO. 216

NOV

new

is a Root *NOV* which means NEW. It comes from the Latin *nova, novus, novare*, all meaning NEW. An interesting phenomenon is the nova, No. 1. A nova is usually too faint to be seen with the naked eye, but it may suddenly burst out into tremendous light, ten thousand times its usual brightness. It may stay that way for a day or two, then fade again to its former faint light. Astronomers don't know why they act like that. Some novae (plural) have repeated outbursts, some only one.

1. nova	NOV a (no′ va) n.	*A star which suddenly increases in light.*
2. novalia	NOV alia (no vay′ li a) n.	*Newly plowed fields.*
3. novanglian	NOV anglian (no van gli′ an) n.	*A New Englander.*
4. novantique	NOV antique (no van teke′) adj.	*New, yet old.*
5. Nova Scotian	NOV a Scotian (no va skoe′ shan) adj.	*A native of Nova Scotia.*
6. novation	NOV ation (no vay′ shun) n.	*State of being renewed; the assumption of a new legal obligation for an old one.*
7. novative	NOV ative (no vay′ tiv) adj.	*Of the nature of a renewal.*
8. novator	NOV ator (no vay′ tor) n.	*One who renews or innovates.*
9. novatrix	NOV atrix (no vay′ triks) n.	*A female innovator.*
10. innovate	in NOV ate (in′ nov ate) v.	*To bring in something new.*
11. novel	NOV el (nov′ el) adj.	*New; strange; not formerly known.*
12. novel	NOV el (nov′ el) n.	*A story of book length; a work of fiction.*
13. novella	NOV ella (no vel′ a) n.	*A shorter book; a short work of fiction.*
14. novelette	NOV elette (nov e let′) n.	*A long story.*

432

15. novelist	NOV elist (nov' e list) n.
	One who writes a novel; the author.
16. novelistic	NOV elistic (nov e lis' tik) adj.
	Relating to the characteristics of a novel.
17. novelty	NOV elty (nov' el tee) n.
	Something new, unusual.
18. nouveau riche	(nue vo reesh') n.
	One who has suddenly become very rich.
19. novice	NOV ice (nov' is) n.
	One who is new at an enterprise.
20. renovate	re NOV ate (ren' o vate) v.
	To make like new again.

word analysis

NOVELISTIC—No. 16
    NOVEL (nova)—Latin Root =new
    IST—Suffix =that which
    IC—Suffix =like; character of

practical exercises

1. Supply the missing words:
    He was a .... at selling ....(d)
    furniture but he soon learned and introduced a few
    (in)............................(s) into the business. He discovered that
    people liked the ....(s) more than the ultra-
    modern.

2. Analyze No. 20.

3. Use one word for each phrase:
    a. has the characteristics of a novel ....
    b. introduce something new ....
    c. act of making things like new again ....
    d. willing to live and let others live ....
    e. does not hang on others ....
    f. a mistaken idea ....

KEY NO. 217

PAC · PLAIS

please

is the Root *PLAC*, *PLAIS* from the Latin *placere* meaning to PLEASE. Both mean the same thing. Why are they spelled differently? *Plais* shows the French influence on the Latin word. As a result, in English, even though the forms are pronounced similarly, they are spelled differently.

1. placebo
   PLAC ebo (play chay' bo) n.
   A useless but soothing medication; something intended to soothe; gratify; conciliate.

2. placet
   PLAC et (play' set) n.
   Expression of assent.

3. placid
   PLAC id (plas' id) adj.
   Calm, unruffled; as, a placid nature.

4. placidity
   PLAC idity (pla sid' it ee) n.
   Quality of calmness; serenity.

5. placidness
   PLAC idness (plas' id nes) n.
   State of being calm.

6. placidly
   PLAC idly (plas' id lee) adv.
   Calmly.

7. placidamente
   PLAC idamente (pla chee da men' ta) adv.
   Evenly; calmly, in musical direction.

8. placate
   PLAC ate (play' kate) v.
   To pacify; appease; conciliate.

9. placation
   PLAC ation (play kay' shun) n.
   Act of appeasement; a conciliatory gift.

10. placative
    PLAC ative (play' kate iv) adj.
    Placatory; soothing.

11. placable
    PLAC able (plak' a b'l) adj.
    Able to be appeased, soothed.

12. implacable
    im PLAC able (im plak' a b'l) adj.
    Cannot be appeased, soothed.

13. placatory
    PLAC atory (play' ka tor ee) adj.
    Appeasing; soothing.

14. complacent
    com PLAC ent (kom plase' ent) adj.
    Self-satisfied.

15. complacence
    com PLAC ence (kom plase' ens) n.
    Self-satisfaction.

16. complacently
    com PLAC ently (kom plase' ent lee) adv.
    In a satisfied manner.

17. complacency
    com PLAC ency (kom plase' en see) n.
    Self-satisfaction.

18. complaisant   com PLAIS ant (kom plase' ent) adj.
                    Affable; gracious; disposed to please.
19. complaisance   com PLAIS ance (kom plase' ens) n.
                    Courtesy; civility; affability.
20. complaisantly com PLAIS antly (kom plase' ent lee) adv.
                    Obligingly; affably.

word analysis

IMPLACABLE—No. 12
    IM (in) Prefix =not
    PLAC (placere)—Latin Root =to make calm
    ABLE—Suffix =can do

practical exercises

1. Supply the missing words:
   People who are .... give no heed to the worries
   of others. The greatest flaw in an individual's character is
   .... because it leads to neglect of many social
   ills.

2. Analyze No. 15.

3. Syllabicate and indicate which syllable is most greatly stressed
   by placing the accent ('):

distraught	amphitheater	macrology
potential	macrobiosis	mortician
gesticulation	evacuee	evacuator

KEY NO. 218

0—⚷

FLUC · FLU
FLUV · FLUX

flowing

is a Root, *FLUC, FLU, FLUV, FLUX* meaning FLOWING. It comes from *fluvio*, river, and *fluere*, flow. The words with this Root are beautiful to say and hear, and even to think about. The sound is rhythmical, easy, flowing, melodious or, to use a word which contains this key but is not on the list, the sound is melli*FLU*ous. One word, No. 18, is much used today in describing our society.

1. fluctuant   FLUC tuant (fluk' chu ant) adj.
         Moving like a wave; unstable.

2. fluctuate   FLUC tuate (fluk' chu ate) v.
         To wave in an unsteady motion; shift from one to another.

3. flue   FLU e (flue) n.
         A passageway for a flow of air.

4. flush   FLU sh (flush) v.
         To flow and spread suddenly and freely.

5. fluid   FLU id (flue' id) n.
         A flowing substance; a liquid.

6. fluent   FLU ent (flue' ent) adj.
         Flowing easily; facility in speech.

7. fluency   FLU ency (flue' en see) n.
         The quality of being fluent; smoothness; readiness; as, the fluency of language.

8. fluidity   FLU idity (flue id' it ee) n.
         The quality of a fluid; free flowing.

9. fluidimeter   FLU idimeter (flue id im' e ter) n.
         An instrument to measure fluidity.

10. fluidism   FLU idism (flue' id iz um) n.
         Theory that disease comes from change of fluids in the body.

11. fluidize   FLU idize (flue' i dize) v.
         Render fluid.

12. flume   FLU me (flume) n.
         An inclined channel with a stream running through.

13. fluminose   FLU minose (flue' mi nose) adj.
         Relating to rivers.

14. fluviose   FLU viose (flue' vi ose) adj.
         Flowing freely.

15. fluviograph   FLU viograph (flue' vi o graf) n.
                     Instrument for measuring rise and fall of rivers.

16. fluviology   FLU viology (flue vi ol' o ji) n.
                     Scientific study of watercourses, rivers, streams.

17. fluidal   FLU idal (flue' id al) adj.
                     Relating to a fluid or to its flowing motion.

18. affluent   af FLU ent (af' lue ent) adj.
                     Flowing freely; prosperous; as, an affluent *society.*

19. effluent   ef FLU ent (ef' lue ent) adj.
                     Flowing out; as, an effluent *branch of a main stream.*

20. influence   in FLU ence (in' flue ens) v.
                     To flow in; as, influence *for good.*

word analysis

FLUVIOLOGY—No. 16
    FLUVIO—Latin Root =river
    LOG (logos)—Greek Root =word
    Y—Suffix =tending to

practical exercises

1. Supply the missing words:
    Only by practice can one acquire .... in language. The science of .... is of the greatest importance in areas where there are large rivers.

2. Analyze No. 18.

3. Complete the following words by adding the missing KEY:
    a. take up again— re..........
    b. stocks go up and down— ....uate
    c. easy flow of language— ....ency
    d. flowing from— ....fluent
    e. science of rivers— ....ology

KEY NO. 219

O—⚡

**VALE · VALI
VALU**

strength
worth
valor

is the Root *VALE, VALI, VALU* meaning STRENGTH; WORTH; VALOR—all good things. The Latin *valeo, valere* means all these fine things, and the English words have retained and sustained the values inherent in the originals. Only a negative Prefix can abate the splendid quality this Root describes.

1. valetude   VALE tude (val' e tude) n.
      Health; strength; state of health.

2. valetudinarian   VALE tudinarian (val e tude in ar' ee an) n.
      A sickly person worried constantly about his health.

3. valedictory   VALE dictory (val e dik' to ree) n.
      A farewell address at graduation.

4. valedictorian   VALE dictorian (val e dik tor' ee an) n.
      The one who gives the valedictory.

5. valediction   VALE diction (val e dik' shun) n.
      A farewell.

6. valiant   VAL iant (val' yant) n.
      A person who is brave; honorable.

7. equivalent   equi VAL ent (e kwiv' a lent) adj.
      Of equal value; as, a dime is the equivalent *of ten pennies.*

8. valiancy   VALI ancy (val' yan see) n.
      The quality of bravery; valor.

9. valid   VALI d (val' id) adj.
      Strong; legally correct.

10. validity   VALI dity (va lid' it ee) n.
      Truth; legal strength.

11. validate   VALI date (val' i date) v.
      Make valid; approve legally; declare.

12. validation   VALI dation (val i day' shun) n.
      The act of declaring validity.

13. validatory   VALI datory (val i day' to ri) adj.
      Relating to a validation.

14. valor   VAL or (val' or) n.
      Value; worth; as, a woman of valor.

15. valorous   VAL orous (val' o rus) adj.
      Having the quality of valor; brave.

438

16. valorization VAL orization (val o ri zay' shun) n.
       Government subsidy for support of the prices
       of a commodity.

17. ad valorem ad VAL orem (ad va lore' em)
       Latin; according to market value.

18. value   VAL ue (val' yue) n.
       Purchasing price; actual worth.

19. evaluate e VAL uate (e val' yu ate) v.
       Find out the value; appraise actual worth.

word analysis

VALEDICTORY—No. 3
 VALE (valere)—Latin Root =fare well; be well
 DICT (dictus)—Latin Root =say
 ORY—Suffix =that which; one who

practical exercise

Read the following excerpt underlining those words that contain keys you have already learned.

 "Good day!" said Monsieur Defarge, looking down at the white head that bent low over the shoemaking.

 It was raised for a moment, and a very faint voice responded to the salutation, as if it were at a distance. "Good day!"

 "You are still hard at work, I see?"

 After a long silence, the head was lifted for another moment, and the voice replied, "Yes—I am working." This time, a pair of haggard eyes had looked at the questioner, before the face dropped again. The faintness of the voice was pitiable and dreadful. It was not the faintness of physical weakness, though confinement and hard fare no doubt had their part in it. Its deplorable peculiarity was, that it was the faintness of solitude and disuse. It was like the last feeble echo of a sound made long and long ago. So entirely had it lost the life and resonance of the human voice that it affected the senses like a once beautiful color faded away into a poor stain. So sunken and suppressed it was, that it was like a voice underground. So expressive it was of a hopeless and lost creature, that a famished traveller, wearied out by lonely wandering in a wilderness, would have remembered home and friends in such a tone before lying down to die.

   (From *A Tale of Two Cities* by Charles Dickens.)

O—⚡

CORPOR · CORP

is the Root *CORPOR, CORP* which comes from the Latin *corpus*, meaning BODY. The word flies from the important detective story prop, the CORPse—to the big business, the CORPORation.

body

1. corporal   CORPOR al (kor' po ral) adj.
       Relating to the body.

2. corporality   CORPOR ality (kor po ral' it ee) n.
       The state of being a body, or of having a body.

3. corporate   CORPOR ate (kor' po rat) adj.
       Combined into one body; united by legal enactment.

4. corporately   CORPOR ately (kor' po rat lee) adv.
       In the manner of being a corporation.

5. corporateness   CORPOR ateness (kor' po rate nes) n.
       The quality of being corporate.

6. incorporate   in CORPOR ate (in kor' po rate) v.
       To make into an association of persons by legal enactment.

7. corporation   CORPOR ation (kor po ray' shun) n.
       A body of men who have been incorporated.

8. corporational   CORPOR ational (kor po ray' shun al) adj.
       Relating to a corporation.

9. corpuscle   CORP uscle (kor' pus el) n.
       A cell that floats in the blood.

10. corporationer   CORPOR ationer (kor po ray' shun er) n.
       A member of a corporation.

11. corporeal   CORPOR eal (kor pore' ee al) adj.
       Having a material body.

12. corporealist   CORPOR ealist (kor po' re al ist) n.
       A materialist; one who is interested only in material things.

13. corporeality   CORPOR eality (kor pore ee al' it ee) n.
       The state of corporeal existence.

14. corporosity   CORPOR osity (kor po ros' i ti) n.
       Bulky; large bodied.

15. corporify   CORPOR ify (kor por' i fie) v.
       To embody; to incorporate.

16. corps   CORP s (kore) n.
       A group of people organized for a common service; as, Peace Corps.

17. corpse   CORP se (korps) n.
          A dead body.

18. corpulence   CORP ulence (kor′ pyu lens) n.
          Excessive fatness; obesity.

19. corpulent   CORP ulent (kor′ pyu lent) adj.
          Being excessively fat; obese.

word analysis

INCORPORATE—No. 6
    IN—Prefix =into
    CORPOR (corpus)—Latin Root =body
    ATE—Suffix =make

practical exercises

1. Supply the missing words:
    The .... on the bed was of such .... that there was a pardonable smile on every face, in spite of the fact that the unfortunate victim had been given the maximum in .... punishment.

2. Analyze No. 15.

3. Use one word for each of the following phrases:
    a. a body of associated persons   ....
    b. a body of persons engaged in activities
       for peace   ....
    c. having many brave qualities   ....
    d. claims on funds never made   ....

KEY NO. 221

O—⚡

SAT · SATIS

enough

is the Root *SAT, SATIS* meaning ENOUGH. It comes from the Latin *sat*, enough and *satio*, more than enough, overfill. It is a simple, uncomplicated key and says just what it means. Today nutritionists are interested in the SATurated fats, and unSATurated fats, finding the latter more healthful. *SAT*, ENOUGH, is good. SATurated is not good. SATiated is worse.

1. sate
   SAT e (sate') v.
   To satisfy; as, sate with food.
2. satiate
   SAT iate (say' shee ate) v.
   Satisfy fully.
3. satiable
   SAT iable (say' sha b'l) adj.
   Can be fully satisfied.
4. insatiable
   in SAT iable (in say' sha b'l) adj.
   Cannot be satisfied.
5. satiability
   SAT iability (say shi a bil' i ti) n.
   The quality of being able to be satisfied.
6. insatiability
   in SAT iability (in say shi a bil' i ty) n.
   The quality of not being able to be fully satisfied.
7. satisfy
   SAT isfy (sat' is fie) v.
   To give pleasure to; to give as much as is needed.
8. satisfier
   SATIS fier (sat' is fie er) n.
   One who or that which satisfies.
9. satisfactory
   SATIS factory (sat is fak' to ree) adj.
   Giving what is wanted.
10. satisfaction
    SATIS faction (sat is fak' shun) n.
    Pleasure; gratification.
11. unsatisfactory
    un SATIS factory (un sat is fak' to ree) adj.
    Not giving what is wanted.
12. dissatisfaction
    dis SATIS faction (dis sat is fak' shun) n.
    The state of not being pleased.
13. unsatisfactorily
    un SATIS factorily (un sat is fak' to ri li) adv.
    In a manner which does not satisfy.
14. insatiably
    in SAT iably (in say' sha blee) adv.
    Never able to be satisfied.
15. satient
    SAT ient (say' shi ent) adj.
    Giving pleasure; satisfying.

442

16. saturate   SAT urate (sach' u rate) v.
                         Soak thoroughly; fill completely.

17. saturation   SAT uration (sach u ray' shun) n.
                         State of being thoroughly filled.

18. saturant   SAT urant (sach' u rant) n.
                         A substance used to cause saturation.

19. unsaturated   un SAT urated (un sach' u rate ed) adj.
                         Not completely filled.

word analysis

SATIABILITY—No. 5
    SATI (satio)—Latin Root =more than enough
    ABIL (able)—Suffix =can do
    ITY—Suffix =quality of

practical exercises

1. Supply the missing words:
    Nutritionists have decided that .... fats are
    the most healthful. She had an (in)........................... craving
    for sweets. His frustration was at the ....,................... point.

2. Analyze No. 7.

3. How many of the keys and words can you recognize in this
    scramble?

    a. photographs   j. embellishment
    b. convention   k. cementing
    c. coronation   l. congressional
    d. preconvention   m. proceedings
    e. typically   n. preamble
    f. despite   o. administrations
    g. candidate   p. unprecedented
    h. political   q. achievement
    i. nonpolitical

is the Root *VAC* which comes from the Latin *vacare* and means to EMPTY. There seems to be a difference between our ideas of VACancy and the continental idea of the same word. To us VACant means EMPTY, exactly as the Latin Root says. To the French and British it means freedom from the job, time off from the job.

1. vacate   VAC ate (vay' kate) v.
  To make empty; to leave.

2. vacant   VAC ant (vay' kant) adj.
  Empty; not occupied.

3. vacancy   VAC ancy (vay' kan see) n.
  The state of being empty.

4. evacuant   e VAC uant (e vak' yu ant) n.
  A purgative.

5. vacation   VAC ation (vay kay' shun) n.
  A rest from work; a holiday.

6. vacational   VAC ational (vay kay' shun al) adj.
  Relating to a vacation.

7. vacationist   VAC ationist (vay kay' shu nist) n.
  One who is on vacation.

8. vacuum   VAC uum (vak' yu um) n.
  A space entirely devoid of matter; an emptiness; as, nature abhors a vacuum.

9. vacual   VAC ual (vak' yu al) adj.
  Relating to a vacuum.

10. vacuous   VAC uous (vak' yu us) adj.
  Empty of thought or activity; inane.

11. vacuole   VAC uole (vak' yu wole) n.
  A small cavity in space or tissue which contains air or fluid.

12. vacuolar   VAC uolar (vak yu woe' lar) adj.
  Relating to a vacuole.

13. vacuist   VAC uist (vak' yu ist) n.
  One who believes that a vacuum can exist.

14. vacuometer   VAC uometer (vak yu om' e ter) n.
  An instrument to measure low pressures.

15. evacuee   e VAC uee (e vak' yu ee) n.
  One who has been withdrawn from a bombing zone.

16. evacuate   e VAC uate (e vak' yu ate) v.
                  To remove troops or people; to make empty.
17. evacuation   e VAC uation (e vak yu ay' shun) n.
                  The act of removing troops or people.
18. evacuator   e VAC uator (e vak' yu ay tor) n.
                  One who removes people from the danger
                  zone.
19. vacantly   VAC antly (vay' kant lee) adv.
                  Emptily; idly; inanely; as, staring vacantly.

word analysis

EVACUATION—No. 17
    E (ex)—Prefix =out
    VAC (vacare)—Latin Root =to empty
    TION—Suffix =act of; state of

practical exercises

1. Supply the missing words:
      It has been accepted that "nature abhors a ...."
    The ...., however, maintains that there are
    ....(s) in nature.
2. Analyze No. 6.
3. Complete the following words:
    a. act of putting beauty in— ....bellish..........
    b. act of being crowned— corona..........
    c. act of being of service to— ....ministra..........
    d. in the manner of a certain type— typ..........
    e. to bear witness— testi..........

KEY NO. 223

GEST

carry bear

is the Root *GEST* which means CARRY, BEAR. It comes from the Latin *gerere, gestus*. This Root will enable you to *digest* such words as *gestative, gestatorial, gesticulate* and all other words with the key GEST.

1. gestant   GEST ant (jes' tant) adj.
         Pregnant.
2. gestate   GEST ate (jes' tate) v.
         To carry during pregnancy.
3. gestation   GEST ation (je stay' shun) n.
         The period of pregnancy.
4. gestational   GEST ational (je stay' shun al) adj.
         Relating to gestation.
5. gestative   GEST ative (jes' ta tiv) adj.
         The same as No. 4.
6. gestatory   GEST atory (jes' ta to ri) adj.
         Pertaining to carrying as a form of exercise.
7. gestatorial   GEST atorial (jes ta toe' ri al) adj.
         Relating to the chair on which the Pope is carried on ceremonial occasions.
8. gestatorium   GEST atorium (jes ta toe' ri um) n.
         A portable shrine.
9. gested   GEST ed (jes' ted) adj.
         Embellished with gestures and bodily movements.
10. gestic   GEST ic (jes' tik) adj.
         Consisting of gestures or bodily movements.
11. gesticulate   GEST iculate (je stik' yu late) v.
         Indicate by gestures when speaking.
12. gesticular   GEST icular (jes tik' yu lar) adj.
         Full of sudden motion.
13. gesticulation   GEST iculation (jes tik yu lay' shun) n.
         The act of making gestures.
14. gesture   GEST ure (jes' chur) n.
         The use of motions of the body as a mode of expression.
15. congest   con GEST (kon jest') v.
         To overcrowd; clog.
16. congestion   con GEST ion (kon jes' chun) n.
         An overcrowded state; as, congestion of traffic.

17. congestive   con GEST ive (kon jes' tiv) adj.
                     Causing congestion.

18. digest   di GEST (die jest') v.
                     To think over and arrange methodically in the
                     mind.

19. digestion   di GEST ion (die jes' chun) n.
                     The process by which food is made useful to
                     the body.

20. suggestion   sug GEST ion (su jes' chun) n.
                     The mental process by which one thought
                     leads to another.

word analysis

SUGGESTION—No. 20
    SUG (sub)—Prefix =under
    GEST (gerere)—Latin Root =to carry
    TION—Suffix =act of

practical exercises

1. Supply the missing words:
     The success of *Waverley* led friends to .... to
     Sir Walter Scott that he continue writing novels.
       "Now good .... wait on appetite
        And health on both." (Shakespeare)

2. Analyze No. 1.

3. Choose the number which most nearly expresses the italicized
    word:
    a. *melancholy*   (1) sadness   (2) despair   (3) ripple
        (4) twilight   (5) tenderness   ....
    b. *profile*   (1) mountains   (2) outline   (3) emotion
        (4) spirit   (5) side   ....
    c. *limitation*   (1) succession   (2) memories
        (3) unions   (4) interest   (5) boundary   ....
    d. *ardent*   (1) cold   (2) distant   (3) fiery
        (4) distinguished   (5) list   ....
    e. *profound*   (1) laughing   (2) mysterious
        (3) deep   (4) troubled   (5) hovering   ....

KEY NO. 224

**MORS · MORI
MORT**

death

is the Root MORS, MORI, MORT which comes from the Latin, *mors, mortis,* meaning DEATH. While No. 2 and No. 6 do not actually mean death, the humiliation suffered is a death to pride. No. 1 and No. 17 also mean a type of suffering, rather than death. Words have not only letters, but overtones of meaning; connotations.

1. remorse   re MORS e (re mors') n.
       Torture of conscience.

2. mortal   MORT al (mort' al) n.
       One who is subject to death; as, human beings are mortal.

3. mortality   MORT ality (mor tal' it ee) n.
       Subjection to death; death rate.

4. mortally   MORT ally (mort' al ee) adv.
       Bringing death; fatally.

5. immortable   im MORT able (i mor' ta b'l) adj.
       Can be made immortal.

6. mortify   MORT ify (mort' i fie) v.
       Hurt; embarrass; humiliate.

7. mortification   MORT ification (mort i fi kay' shun) n.
       Embarrassment; humiliation.

8. mortician   MORT ician (mor tish' an) n.
       Undertaker; funeral director.

9. mortuary   MORT uary (mor' chu wer ee) adj.
       Relating to the burial of the dead.

10. mortuous   MORT uous (mor' tyu us) adj.
       Deathlike.

11. moribund   MORI bund (mor' i bund) adj.
       Dying.

12. immortal   im MORT al (im ort' al) adj.
       Not subject to death; deathless.

13. immortality   im MORT ality (im or tal' it ee) n.
       Deathlessness.

14. immortalize   im MORT alize (im ort' al ize) v.
       To make deathless.

15. immortalism   im MORT alism (i mor' tal iz um) n.
       The doctrine of the soul's immortality.

16. immortelle   im MORT elle (im or tel') n.
       Everlasting.

17. remorseful   re MORS eful (re mors' ful) adj.
    Tortured by remorse.

word analysis

REMORSEFULLY—No. 17+ly
 RE—Prefix =back; again
 MORSE (mors)—Latin Root =death
 FUL—Suffix =full of
 LY—adverbial suffix =in the manner of

practical exercises

1. Supply the missing words:
    The wound was .... and he died. The statis-
    tics of infant .... are not as alarming as they
    were. He was tortured by .... for his deed.

2. Analyze No. 12.

3. Read the following excerpt underlining all those words that
   contain keys you have already learned.
    "Each House of Congress shall determine the rules of
    its proceedings, punish the members for disorderly behavior,
    and, with the concurrence of two-thirds, expel a member."
    Last week, the conviction of a member of the federal court
    was set aside on the ground that only Congress has the
    authority to punish him, under the Constitution. In vacating
    the conviction the judge said the Constitutional provision
    for Congressional privilege is to be interpreted liberally. The
    duty falls upon each House of Congress to punish its of-
    fending members.
        (From *The New York Times,* Sept. 30, 1964.)

KEY NO. 225

○━➤

MACRO

**large
excessive**

is the Prefix *MACRO* which means LARGE; EXCESSIVE development. It is the opposite of the Prefix *MICRO*, small. This list of words with its abnormalities and manias would be good for writing a science fiction story or opening a circus. There is another zoological oddity I had no room for—MACRObiotus—a strange, bearlike, little animal whose naked body is transparent, and has globules of fat which look like huge red corpuscles.

1. macron   MACRO n (make' ron) n.
A line over a vowel to show that it is long; as, ā, long a, in place.

2. macrometer   MACRO meter (ma krom' e ter) n.
Instrument to measure size and distance of objects.

3. macrotous   MACRO tous (ma kroe' tus) adj.
Having large ears.

4. macrodont   MACRO dont (mak' ro dont) adj.
Having large teeth.

5. macrocosm   MACRO cosm (mak' ro koz um) n.
The great world; universe.

6. macrocosmic   MACRO cosmic (mak ro koz' mik) adj.
Relating to the great world.

7. macrocosmology   MACRO cosmology
(mak ro koz mol' o ji) n.
A description of the macrocosm.

8. macromania   MACRO mania (mak ro may' ni a) n.
A delusion that parts of the patient's body are bigger than they really are.

9. macrograph   MACRO graph (mak' ro graf) n.
A photograph of an object magnified.

10. macrology   MACRO logy (ma krol' o ji) n.
A great deal of talking.

11. macrography   MACRO graphy (ma krog' ra fi) n.
Large size writing which shows a nervous disorder.

12. macrocyte   MACRO cyte (mak' ro site) n.
Large red corpuscles that appear in anemias.

13. macrophage	MACRO phage (mak' ro faje) n.
	A large white cell.
14. macrophotograph	MACRO photograph
	(mak ro foe' to graf) n.
	The production of enlarged photographs.
15. macrochemistry	MACRO chemistry (mak ro kem' is tri) n.
	Chemistry which does not require a micro-scope.
16. macrocephalous	MACRO cephalous (mak ro sef' a lus) adj.
	Having a larger head than normal.
17. macrobiote	MACRO biote (mak ro bie' ote) n.
	One that lives a long time.
18. macrobiosis	MACRO biosis (mak ro bie o' sis) n.
	Length of life; longevity.
19. macrobian	MACRO bian (ma kroe' bi an) adj.
	Having lived a long time.
20. macrobiotics	MACRO biotics (mak ro bie ot' iks) n.
	The science of prolonging life.

word analysis

MACROCOSMIC—No. 6
 MACRO—Prefix =large
 COSM (cosmos)—Greek Root =world
 IC—Suffix =like

practical exercises

1. Supply the missing words:
  Today, due to a great interest in ...., the life span is much increased. The unhappy man's .... caused him to think that he was .... The line over a vowel, which makes us call it a long vowel, is called a ....

2. Analyze No. 2.

3. Use one word for each phrase:
  a. having enormous teeth   ....
  b. too much talk   ....
  c. a long line over a vowel   ....
  d. a quality of deathlessness   ....
  e. a state of being embarrassed to death ....

O—⚹

MAGNA · MAGNI

great

is the Root *MAGNA, MAGNI* meaning GREAT. At first glance you may think this Root means the same as *MACRO*, which also means GREAT, LARGE. But it is not so. *MACRO* usually refers to abnormal size or cosmic matters. A few words do use *MAGNA* for big money, whiskey, boasting and such matters. But mostly the greatness of MAGNA is spiritual in quality—praise, excellence, religion, law, generosity and kindness.

1. Magna Charta   MAGNA Charta (mag na kart' a) n.
   The great charter of 1215 that gave liberties to the English.

2. magnanimously   MAGNA nimously (mag nan' i mus lee) adv.
   Generously; greatly.

3. magnate   MAGNA te (mag' nate) n.
   A man of great wealth.

4. magnify   MAGNI fy (mag' ni fie) v.
   Make great; intensify.

5. magnific   MAGNI fic (mag nif' ik) adj.
   Magnificent; made great.

6. magnificence   MAGNI ficence (mag nif' i sens) n.
   Splendor; richness; greatness.

7. magnitude   MAGNI tude (mag' ni tyude) n.
   Physical greatness; bigness; quality.

8. magnifico   MAGNI fico (mag nif' i koe) n.
   A person of high rank.

9. magnificative   MAGNI ficative (mag nif' i kay tiv) adj.
   Tending to magnify; to make great.

10. magnum   MAGN um (mag' num) n.
    Great, in size; a large bottle for wine.

11. magnascopic   MAGNA scopic (mag na skop' ik) adj.
    Using a magnascope.

12. magniloquent   MAGNI loquent (mag nil' o kwent) adj.
    High-flown, bombastic talk.

13. magnification   MAGNI fication (mag ni fi kay' shun) n.
    Enlargement, as seen through a magnifying glass.

14. magnificat   MAGNI ficat (mag nif' i kat) n.
    A song of praise.

15. magnanimous   MAGNA nimous (mag nan' i mus) adj.
    Great-hearted; generous.

16. magnanimity   MAGNA nimity (mag na nim' it ee) n.
                  Quality of generosity and kindness.
17. magnascope   MAGNA scope (mag' na skope) n.
                  A lens to enlarge the projected pictures.

word analysis

MAGNILOQUENT—No. 12
    MAGNI (magnus)—Latin Root =big
    LOQ (loqui)—Latin Root =to speak
    ENT—Suffix =one who

practical exercises

1. Supply the missing words:
    He was known to all for his .... contribu-
tions to charity and the .... of his palatial
home.

2. Analyze No. 7.

3. Recognize words and keys in the following:

a. accomplishments	k. promote
b. heritage	l. potential
c. depressed	m. facilities
d. defense	n. expand
e. redevelopment	o. popular
f. suitable	p. financed
g. economic	q. oriental
h. gratified	r. intelligence
i. disappointed	s. detachment
j. project	t. indigestion

MEGA · MEGALO

large

is the Root *MEGA*, *MEGALO*, which means very LARGE. We now have three keys with the meaning LARGE and every one of them means something different. *MACRO*, you remember, means large in size, physical largeness; *MAGNA* means large, great, principally in the spiritual sense; *MEGA* means huge in the abnormal, diseased sense, diseased both in mind and in body. Be aware of the idea, the unique personality of each key.

1. megadont   MEGA dont (meg′ a dont) adj.
Having large teeth.

2. megadynamics   MEGA dynamics (meg a die nam′ iks) n.
Mechanics of the major earth movements.

3. megapod   MEGA pod (meg′ a pod) adj.
Large footed.

4. megafog   MEGA fog (meg′ a fog) n.
Instrument to give directions to befogged ships.

5. megalith   MEGA lith (meg′ a lith) n.
Prehistoric stone monument.

6. megaphone   MEGA phone (meg′ a fone) n.
A device for magnifying sound.

7. megameter   MEGA meter (meg am′ e ter) n.
Instrument for observing the stars in order to determine longitude.

8. megascopic   MEGA scopic (meg′ a skop ik) adj.
Enlarged; visible to the naked eye.

9. megatherm   MEGA therm (meg′ a therm) n.
Any plant which requires great heat and abundant moisture for growth.

10. megalethoscope   MEGA lethoscope (meg a leth′ o skope) n.
A stereoscope with a magnifying lens.

11. megalomania   MEGALO mania (meg a lo may′ nee a) n.
Delusions of grandeur.

12. megalophonous   MEGALO phonous (meg al o fon′ us) adj.
Having a loud voice.

13. megalophthalmus   MEGALO phthalmus (meg al of thal′ mus) adj.
Having large eyes.

14. megalopolis   MEGALO polis (meg a lop' o lis) n.
   A very large city.
15. Megalosaurus   MEGALO saurus (meg a lo so' rus) n.
   A carnivorous dinosaur.
16. megaloscope   MEGALO scope (meg' a lo skope) n.
   An endoscope with an apparatus for magnifying.
17. acromegaly   acro MEGA ly (ak ro meg' a lee) n.
   Disease marked by the enlargement of the face and extremities.
18. megaprosopous   MEGA prosopous (meg a pros' o pus) n.
   Disease characterized by a large face.
19. Megaptera   MEGA ptera (me gap' ter a) n.
   Humpbacked whales.
20. Megapodiidae   MEGA podiidae (meg a po die' i dee) n.
   A genus of large-footed birds.

word analysis

MEGALOPHONOUS—No. 12
    MEGALO (megas)—Greek Root =huge
    PHON (phonon)—Greek Root =sound
    OUS—Suffix =full of; having

practical exercises

1. Supply the missing words:
   The voice of the .... is very welcome to the captain of a ship lost in a fog. Dictators are subject to a vicious .... which wants to make them master the world.

2. Analyze No. 9.

3. Give a synonym for each of the following words:
   a. macrology   ....
   b. sadness   ....
   c. macrodont   ....
   d. macrobiosis   ....
   e. limitations   ....

KEY NO. 228

O—➤

PSEUDO

false
untrue

is the Prefix *PSEUDO* which means
FALSE, UNTRUE. Here we have illusion, falsity, and falsehood. Try No.
14 on a liar. Unless he has read this
book, he may think it a compliment.

1. pseudoism
PSEUDO ism (sue' doe iz um) n.
A tendency to that which is false.

2. pseudonym
PSEUDO nym (sude' on im) n.
*A name adopted by an author for his
writings; a pen name.*

3. pseudonymal
PSEUDO nymal (sue don' i mal) adj.
Relating to a pen name.

4. pseudonymity
PSEUDO nymity (sue do nim' i ti) n.
The use of a pen name by an author.

5. pseudonymous
PSEUDO nymous (sue don' i mus) adj.
Using a fictitious name.

6. pseudodox
PSEUDO dox (sue' do doks) n.
A false opinion.

7. pseudogyny
PSEUDO gyny (su doj' i ni) n.
*The use of a feminine name by a male
author.*

8. pseudolatry
PSEUDO latry (sue dol' a tri) n.
False worship.

9. pseudograph
PSEUDO graph (sue' doe graf) n.
A false document.

10. pseudomorph
PSEUDO morph (sude' o morf) n.
An irregular or deceptive form.

11. pseudomania
PSEUDO mania (sue do may' ni a) n.
*A mania for making false statements; al-
so exaggerations.*

12. pseudology
PSEUDO logy (sue dol' o ji) n.
Lying; falsehood.

13. pseudological
PSEUDO logical (sue do loj' i kal) adj.
Falsified.

14. pseudologist
PSEUDO logist (sue dol' o jist) n.
A liar.

15. pseudoptics
PSEUDO ptics (su dop' tiks) n.
*The branch of psychology which treats
optical illusions.*

16. pseudopsia
PSEUDO psia (sue dop' si a) n.
False vision; optical illusion.

17. pseudoclassic	PSEUDO classic (sude o klas' ik) adj.
	Pretending to be a classic.
18. pseudosmia	PSEUDO smia (sue doz' mi a) n.
	A false sense of smell.
19. pseudographize	PSEUDO graphize (sue' doe gra fize) v.
	Write or print incorrectly.
20. pseudoacromegaly	PSEUDO acromegaly
	(sue do ak ro meg' a li) adj.
	Resembling, but not, acromegaly.

word analysis

PSEUDONYMAL—No. 3
    PSEUDO—Prefix =false
    NYM—Root =name
    AL—Suffix =relating to

practical exercises

1. Supply the missing words:

    Authors who turn out a great many stories often use more than one .... Sometimes .... complications arise for the critics. One critic said the style of A reminded him of the style of B, only to find that they were one and the same author.

2. Analyze No. 2.

3. Choose the number which most nearly expresses the italicized word:

  a. *illicit* (1) doubtful (2) grateful (3) unlawful
    (4) deceitful (5) playful ....

  b. *imprisonment* (1) confinement (2) solitude
    (3) famished (4) senses (5) stain ....

  c. *deplorable* (1) peculiar (2) pitiable
    (3) physical (4) resounding (5) personal ....

  d. *resonance* (1) dullness (2) hardness
    (3) echoing back (4) light (5) action ....

  e. *suppressed* (1) kept back (2) traveled
    (3) faint (4) dreadful (5) human ....

KEY NO. 229

O━➤

ULTRA

**beyond
exceeding
ulterior**

is the Prefix *ULTRA* which means
BEYOND, EXCEEDING, ULTERI-
OR. You can go as far as you like
with *ULTRA*. It's the most remote,
the farthest away. It's on the other
side of beyond. We are most certainly getting on with our keys. The
word analyzed today is the longest
you have had so far but it is not the
longest word you will meet by any
means. The 16 letters make one
third of the longest known word and
you will get it soon.

1. ultra
ULTRA (ul' tra) adj.
Going beyond the range or limits.

2. ultraism
ULTRA ism (ul' tra iz um) n.
The principles of advocates of extremism.

3. ultraist
ULTRA ist (ul' tra ist) n.
An extremist; a radical.

4. ultramarine
ULTRA marine (ul tra ma reen') adj.
Beyond the sea; a blue pigment.

5. ultramontane
ULTRA montane (ul tra mon' tane) adj.
Countries lying beyond the mountains.

6. ultramicrometer
ULTRA micrometer
(ul tra mie krom' e ter) n.
*Instrument which can measure even less
than 1/1,000,000 of an inch.*

7. ultramicroscope
ULTRA microscope
(ul tra mie' kro skope) n.
*An instrument which renders visible par-
ticles not seen with an ordinary microscope.*

8. ultramodern
ULTRA modern (ul tra mod' ern) adj.
Extremely modern in ideas.

9. ultramundane
ULTRA mundane (ul tra mun' dane) adj.
Beyond the known world.

10. ultrasonic
ULTRA sonic (ul tra son' ik) adj.
Supersonic; beyond sound.

11. ultrastellar
ULTRA stellar (ul tra stel' ar) adj.
Beyond the stars.

12. ultrafidian
ULTRA fidian (ul tra fid' i an) adj.
Going beyond faith.

13. ultravalorem
ULTRA valorem (ul tra va lo' rem) adj.
Beyond the value.

14. ultraviolet   ULTRA violet (ul tra vie' o let) adj.
                             Outside the violet end of the visible spectrum.

15. ultra vires   ULTRA vires (ul tra vie' reze) adv.
                             Beyond power; transcending authority.

16. ultraornate   ULTRA ornate (ul tra or nate') adj.
                             Too fancy.

17. ultraluxurious   ULTRA luxurious
                             (ul tra luk shu' ri us) adj.
                             Extremely luxurious.

18. ultraliberal   ULTRA liberal (ul tra lib' er al) adj.
                             Very liberal.

19. ultrafashionable ULTRA fashionable
                             (ul tra fash' u na b'l) adj.
                             Very fashionable.

word analysis

ULTRAMICROSCOPIC—No. 7+IC
    ULTRA—Prefix =beyond
    MICRO—Prefix =small
    SCOPE—Root =watch
    IC—Suffix =like

practical exercises

1. Supply the missing words:
    I read in the paper today that while ....
houses win prizes they do not win customers. Lapis lazuli
is supposed to have the pure blue called ....,
brought from Asia, beyond the sea.   ....

2. Analyze No. 2.

3. Choose the number of the word which most nearly expresses
the meaning of the italicized word:
    a. *hydrophobia* (1) headache (2) arthritis
        (3) neuralgia (4) heartburn (5) fear of water ....
    b. *microbes* (1) furniture (2) china
        (3) upholstery (4) germs (5) oriental rugs ....
    c. *spontaneous* (1) from sudden impulse
        (2) thoughtful (3) impatient
        (4) plodding along (5) careless ....
    d. *generation* (1) design (2) signal
        (3) production (4) destruction (5) result ....

KEY NO. 230

O—x

LOGO · LOG

word

is the Root *LOGO, LOG* which comes from the Greek meaning WORD. Several of the words on the list tend to show the extremes to which people go when using words, but these extremes need not worry you if you know your keys.

1. logic LOG ic (loj′ ik) n.
Science that deals with speech and reason.

2. logical LOG ical (loj′ i kal) adj.
Relating to logic; reasonable.

3. logicaster LOG icaster (loj′ ik as ter) n.
One who dabbles in logic and does not really know it.

4. logician LOG ician (lo jish′ an) n.
One skilled in logic.

5. logicize LOG icize (loj′ i size) v.
To use logic; to reason.

6. logistics LOG istics (lo jis′ tiks) n.
That branch of military art which deals with details of transport, etc.

7. logicity LOG icity (lo jis′ i ti) n.
Logical character.

8. logolatry LOGO latry (lo gol′ a tri) n.
The worship of logic.

9. logomania LOGO mania (log a may′ ni a) n.
A mania for talking.

10. logodaedaly LOGO daedaly (log o ded′ a li) n.
Playing with words; verbal legerdemain.

11. logogogue LOGO gogue (log′ o gog) n.
One who legislates about words.

12. logogram LOGO gram (log′ o gram) n.
A word letter that for the sake of brevity represents a word.

13. Logos LOGOS (loe′ gos) n.
The word; the rational principle in the universe.

14. logogriph LOGO griph (log′ o grif) n.
A word puzzle; a logogram.

15. logomachy LOGO machy (lo gom′ a kee) n.
War of words.

16. logorrhea LOGO rrhea (log o ree′ a) n.
A flux of words; excessively wordy.

460

17. logometric   LOGO metric (log o met' rik) adj.
        Measuring chemical equivalents.
18. logopedics   LOGO pedics (log o pee' diks) n.
        Science of treating speech defects.
19. logographer LOGO grapher (lo gog' ra fer) n.
        A speech writer.

word analysis

ILLOGICAL—IL+No. 2
    IL (in)—Prefix =not
    LOGIC (logos)—Greek Root =science of speech and reason
    AL—Suffix =relating to

practical exercise

Read the following excerpt underlining all those words that contain keys you have already learned.

True genius carries with it the character to develop that genius. Early in his life Louis Pasteur recognized the three "w's" as the mainspring of his life—*will, work, wait.*

In his day it was the current belief that microbes increased by "spontaneous generation." Pasteur did not believe this. He said, "Microbes have parents. Microbes never rise by themselves inside of grapes, or silkworms, or any healthy animal. All microbes get in from the outside." He made innumerable experiments and finally proved his point. His persistence proved the fruitfulness of his theory. He fought the doctors who disagreed with him and he won all the battles—the battle of hydrophobia, the battle for pasteurization, of sterilization. He saved the beer and wine industry, the silkworm industry, and he prophesied that keeping microbes out will arrest the plagues of disease.

Dr. Joseph Lister, the great surgeon who believed in Pasteur's theory, began to keep microbes away from his patients in his hospital, and wrote to Pasteur of great success. Dr. Lister wrote: "Permit me to thank you for having shown me the truth of the theory of germs of putrefaction and for giving me the simple principle which has made antisepsis such a success. In a large measure humanity has profited from your work."

VEST

clothe
to dress

comes from the Root *VEST* which comes from the Latin *vestire, vestus* meaning CLOTHE, TO DRESS. While most of the words on the list concern garments and clothing to wear, there are a few words which have a different meaning. The idea is still that of clothing, but not with garments. Nos. 2, 3, 15, 16, refer to the clothing of power and authority.

1. vest   VEST (vest) n.
         An article of clothing; vestment.

2. vest   VEST (vest) v.
         To clothe with authority and power of law.

3. vested   VEST ed (ves′ ted) adj.
         Clothed with authority and power; as, vested interests.

4. vestee   VEST ee (ve stee′) n.
         A small jacket-like garment.

5. travesty   tra VEST y (trav′ e stee) n.
         A parody; a disguise to make a thing ridiculous.

6. vestiary   VEST iary (ves′ tee ar ee) n.
         A room, esp. in a church, for its vestments.

7. vestment   VEST ment (vest′ ment) n.
         An outer garment; clothing.

8. vesting   VEST ing (ves′ ting) n.
         Material for making vests.

9. vestry   VEST ry (vest′ ry) n.
         That part of the church building where the vestments of the clergy are kept.

10. investor   in VEST or (in vest′ or) n.
         One who has laid out money for profit.

11. vestmented   VEST mented (vest′ men ted) adj.
         Arrayed, dressed for the services.

12. vesture   VEST ure (ves′ chur) n.
         Clothing; a covering.

13. vestural   VEST ural (ves′ tyu ral) adj.
         Relating to clothing; to vestments.

14. investiture   in VEST iture (in ves′ ti chur) n.
         The act of presenting the official robes of office.

15. invest   in VEST (in vest') v.

To clothe with garments of authority and power; to put out money for profit.

16. investment   in VEST ment (in vest' ment) n.

The money laid out for profit.

word analysis

INVESTMENT—No. 16

    IN—Prefix =in; into

    VEST (vestire)—Latin Root =to clothe

    MENT—Suffix =act of; state of

practical exercises

1. Supply the missing words:

    Power of life or death is .... in the courts. "Not seldom, clothed in radiant ...., Deceitfully goes forth the morning." (Wordsworth) A capitalist .... his money in a business hoping to earn more money by doing so.

2. Analyze No. 8.

3. Use one word to express each phrase:

    a. ruling over everything   ....

    b. completely worn out   ....

    c. to make stupid with amazement   ....

    d. enjoying the luxury   ....

    e. being composed of ingredients   ....

KEY NO. 232

○━╾

SPHERE

ball
sphere

is the Root *SPHERE* which means
BALL; SPHERE. It comes from the
Greek *sphaira*. The effect of the word
list is surely to make one wish to be
an astronaut and get a chance to
realize some of these words. One feels
lifted out of the geosphere and pulled
up to the universe of spheres.

1. sphere	SPHERE (sfer) n.	*A planet; a globe.*
2. spherical	SPHER ical (sfer′ i kal) adj.	*Relating to a sphere; having the form of a sphere.*
3. spheration	SPHER ation (sfe ray′ shun) n.	*The process of forming a sphere.*
4. spheroid	SPHER oid (sfer′ oid) adj.	*Resembling a sphere; globular.*
5. spherics	SPHER ics (sfer′ iks) n.	*The details of the science of spheres.*
6. spheriform	SPHER iform (sfer′ i form) adj.	*Having the shape of a sphere.*
7. spherometer	SPHER ometer (sfer om′ et er) n.	*Instrument to measure the curvature of spherical surfaces.*
8. atmosphere	atmo SPHERE (at′ mo sfer) n.	*The mass of air surrounding the earth.*
9. stratosphere	strato SPHERE (strat′ o sfer) n.	*The upper portion of the atmosphere.*
10. troposphere	tropo SPHERE (troe′ po sfer) n.	*The portion of the atmosphere below the stratosphere.*
11. astrosphere	astro SPHERE (as′ tro sfer) n.	*A star except for its central portion.*
12. pyrosphere	pyro SPHERE (pie′ ro sfer) n.	*The hot central portion of the earth.*
13. photosphere	photo SPHERE (fote′ o sfer) n.	*The layer of light which surrounds the sun.*
14. lithosphere	litho SPHERE (lith′ o sfer) n.	*The solid part of the earth.*
15. leucosphere	leuco SPHERE (lue′ ko sfer) n.	*The inner corona.*
16. geosphere	geo SPHERE (jee′ o sfer) n.	*The solid earth.*

464

17. chromosphere chromo SPHERE (kroe' mo sfer) n.
    The ruddy, gaseous layer surrounding the sun.
18. hydrosphere hydro SPHERE (hie' dro sfer) n.
    All the water and the vapor in the atmosphere.
19. biosphere bio SPHERE (bie' o sfer) n.
    The area of a sphere in which there are living organisms.
20. hemisphere hemi SPHERE (hem' i sfer) n.
    Half of the earth.

word analysis

ATMOSPHERIC—No. 8+IC
    ATMO (atmos)—Greek Root =vapor; air
    SPHER (sphaira)—Greek Root =sphere; ball
    IC—Suffix =nature of; like

practical exercises

1. Supply the missing words:
    Man seems bent on getting out of the .... in which he finds himself. He strains through the ...., the .... and the ...., and he is determined to reach the .... and find new worlds.

2. Analyze No. 11.

3. Read the following excerpt underlining all those words that contain keys you have already learned.
    Regardless of the merits of these arguments, they do indicate investment bankers are willing to strive harder to get business in Europe's dollar-capital market. Put another way, the competition reflects a step toward development of efficient, large capital markets outside of the United States. . . . S—— spoke at a conference in international financial developments sponsored by N.I.C.B. of a basic, philosophical shift in governmental policy toward capital markets.
    (From *The New York Times,* Oct. 18, 1964.)

KEY NO. 233

MIGRA

wander

is the Root *MIGRA* which comes from the Latin *migrare*, meaning to leave one place and WANDER to another. There is a spelling problem attached to this Root, as you will see if you compare No. 9 and No. 16. Why has No. 9 only one *m* while No. 16 has two *m*'s? The answer lies in the keys. *E* (ex) meaning *OUT* has no *m* so we only need the *m* from MIGRA. The key *IM* meaning into has an *m* of its own which, added to *MIGRA*, makes two *m*'s.

1. migrant   MIGRA nt (mie' grant) n.
   One who wanders, traveling from place to place.

2. immigratory   im MIGRA tory (im' i gra to ri) adj.
   Of or relating to immigration.

3. migrate   MIGRA te (mie' grate) v.
   To wander; to move about from place to place.

4. migration   MIGRA tion (mie gray' shun) n.
   A large scale wandering of people or animals.

5. migratory   MIGRA tory (mie' gra tore ee) adj.
   Wandering; as, migratory birds.

6. migrative   MIGRA tive (mie' gra tiv) adj.
   Migratory; wandering.

7. migratorial   MIGRA torial (mie gra toe' ri al) adj.
   Relating to roving about.

8. migrator   MIGRA tor (mie' grate or) n.
   One who roves; a nomad.

9. emigrate   e MIGRA te (em' i grate) v.
   To leave a land; to go out of a country.

10. emigrant   e MIGRA nt (em' i grant) n.
    One who leaves a country.

11. emigration   e MIGRA tion (em i gray' shun) n.
    The act of leaving one's country.

12. emigrative   e MIGRA tive (em' i gray tiv) adj.
    Inclined to emigrate.

13. emigrational   e MIGRA tional (em i gray' shun al) adj.
    Relating to emigration; as, emigrational difficulties.

14. emigré   é MIGR é (em i gray') n.
    A fugitive from a country.

15. emigrée   e MIGR ée (em i gray') n.
           One forced to emigrate.
16. immigrate   im MIGRA te (im' i grate) v.
           To come into the land to settle.
17. immigrant   im MIGRA nt (im' i grant) n.
           A settler in a new land.
18. immigration im MIGRA tion (im i gray' shun) n.
           The act of coming into a land to settle.

word analysis

IMMIGRATORY—No. 2
   IM—Prefix =into
   MIGRAT (migratus)—Latin Root =wander; rove
   ORY—Suffix =relating to

practical exercises

1. Supply the missing words:
       When John Tyler was President he sent an invitation to
   the revolution-torn refugees of Europe and thousands of
   .... became American citizens. More recently
   Hitler's dictatorship drove thousands of .... out
   of Europe. There is a treaty between the United States and
   Great Britain to protect .... game birds.

2. Analyze No. 10.

3. Choose the word that most nearly expresses the meaning of
   the italicized word:
   a. *intense*   (1) strained   (2) easy   (3) calm
       (4) faint   (5) indifferent   ....
   b. *interval*   (1) process   (2) disturbance
       (3) lapse of time between   (4) trellis   (5) iron   ....
   c. *endeavor*   (1) idea   (2) possibility   (3) effort
       (4) confusion   (5) glare   ....
   d. *incalculable*   (1) can be seen
       (2) cannot be counted   (3) flashing
       (4) trembling   (5) dazzled   ....
   e. *absolutely*   (1) completely   (2) upward
       (3) contentedly   (4) slightly   (5) tensely   ....

MONSTR
MONSTRI · MUST
MUST

is the Root *MONSTR, MONSTRI, MUST*, which comes from the Latin verb *monstrare* which means to SHOW. Eventually the SHOWING began to be associated with the dreadful, the monstrous, the monster.

show

1. monster   MONS ter (mon' ster) n.
   A malformed creature.

2. monstrous   MONSTR ous (mon' strus) adj.
   Having the qualities of a monster; unnatural.

3. monstrosity   MONSTR osity (mon stros' it ee) n.
   A malformation; freak.

4. monstrify   MONSTRI fy (mons' tri fie) v.
   To make into a monster; disfigure.

5. monstrification   MONSTRI fication
   (mons tri fi kay' shun) n.
   The act of turning into a monster.

6. monstriferous   MONSTRI ferous (mon stri' fer us) adj.
   Bearing monsters.

7. muster   MUST er (mus' ter) v.
   To gather together; collect; put on display.

8. remonstrance   re MONSTR ance (re mon' strans) n.
   Protest; expostulation.

9. musterer   MUST erer (mus' ter er) n.
   The one who gathers all together for display.

10. remonstration   re MONSTR ation (re mon stray' shun) n.
    Expostulation; opposition.

11. undemonstrative   unde MONSTR ative
    (un de mon' strat iv) adj.
    Not showing affection.

12. demonstrate   de MONSTR ate (dem' on strate) v.
    To display; show.

13. demonstrator   de MONSTR ator (dem' on strate or) n.
    One who displays; exhibits.

14. demonstration   de MONSTR ation (dem on stray' shun) n.
    A display; an exhibition.

15. demonstrational   de MONSTR ational adj.
    Relating to a demonstration.

16. remonstrate   re MONSTR ate (re mon' strate) v.
                       To protest; reprove; find fault.
17. demonstrative   de MONSTR ative (de mon' strat iv) adj.
                       Showing to be real; showing affection.

word analysis

UNDEMONSTRATIVE—No. 11
    UN—Prefix =not
    DE—Prefix =out from
    MONSTR (monstrare)—Latin Root =to show
    IVE—Suffix =causing

practical exercise

Read the following excerpt underlining all those words that contain keys you have already learned.

     We now worked in earnest, and never did I pass ten minutes of more intense excitement. During this interval we had fairly unearthed an oblong chest of wood, which from its perfect preservation and wonderful hardness, had plainly been subjected to some mineralizing process—perhaps that of bichloride of mercury. This box was three and a half feet long, three feet broad, and two and a half feet deep. It was firmly secured by bands of wrought iron, riveted and forming a kind of open trellis work over the whole. On each side of the chest, near the top, were three rings of iron—six in all—by means of which a firm hold could be obtained by six persons. Our utmost united endeavors served only to disturb the coffer very slightly in its bed. We at once saw the impossibility of removing so great a weight. Luckily, the sole fastenings of the lid consisted of two sliding bolts. These we drew back—trembling and panting with anxiety. In an instant, a treasure of incalculable value lay gleaming before us. As the rays of the lanterns fell within the pit, there flashed upwards a glow and a glare, from a confused heap of gold and jewels, that absolutely dazzled our eyes.

              (From "The Gold Bug" by Edgar Allan Poe.)

0—🗝

CHROM

color

is the Root *CHROM*, from the Greek, *chroma*, meaning COLOR. You will find more use of this key in *CHROMO*photography and also in *CHROMO*therapy. No. 18 and No. 19 show beautifully how simple it is to understand words when you know keys *PHOB* meaning fear and *PHIL* meaning love.

1. chroma
CHROM a (kroe' ma) n.
Color.

2. chromascope
CHROM ascope (kroe' ma skope) n.
An instrument showing the effects of color.

3. chromatic
CHROM atic (kroe mat' ik) adj.
Color; relating to color.

4. chromatic scale
CHROM atic scale (kroe mat' ik scale)
A musical scale of many shades of tone.

5. chromatics
CHROM atics (kroe mat' iks) n.
Science of colors and hues of colors.

6. chromatist
CHROM atist (kroe' ma tist) n.
One expert in chromatics.

7. chromosome
CHROM osome (kroe' mo some) n.
A tiny body found in living cells which controls heredity.

8. chromatin
CHROM atin (kroe' ma tin) n.
A deeply staining material found in nucleus of cells.

9. chromatology
CHROM atology (kroe ma tol' o ji) n.
Science of colors.

10. chromatometer
CHROM atometer (kroe ma tom' e ter) n.
Instrument for measuring color perception.

11. chromatosis
CHROM atosis (kroe ma toe' sis) n.
Unnatural pigmentation of the skin.

12. chrome
CHROM e (krome) n.
A pigment; as, chrome yellow; chrome green, etc.

13. chromium
CHROM ium (kroe' mee um) n.
A rust-resisting metal.

14. chromidrosis
CHROM idrosis (kroe mi droe' sis) n.
An abnormally colored sweat.

15. chromatism
CHROM atism (kroe' ma tiz um) n.
Abnormal coloration of the green parts of plants.

16. chromoblast   CHROM oblast (kroe' mo blast) n.
                     An embryonic cell that becomes a pigment cell.

17. chromogenesis   CHROM ogenesis (kroe mo jen' e sis) n.
                     Color production.

18. chromophobic   CHROM ophobic (kroe mo foe' bik) adj.
                     Difficult to stain.

19. chromophilic   CHROM ophilic (kroe mo fil' ik) adj.
                     Easy to stain.

word analysis

CHROMOPHILIC—No. 19
    CHROM (chroma)—Greek Root =color
    PHIL (philos)—Greek Root =love
    IC—Suffix =like; nature of

practical exercises

1. Supply the missing words:
      The heredity of plant or animal is controlled by the tiny
.... (s) in its cells. Coating a metal with ....
keeps rust and tarnish away. A .... is sometimes called a color engineer.

2. Analyze No. 18.

3. Use one word for the phrase:
    a. very difficult to stain or color   ....
    b. the tiny cell which controls heredity   ....
    c. that which stands out high above others   ....
    d. entering a new land to settle there   ....
    e. refuse to give in   ....

KEY NO. 236

HYPN · HYPNO

sleep

is the Root *HYPN, HYPNO* which comes from the Greek *hypnos* meaning SLEEP. This key is the basis of the vocabulary of *HYPNO*tism. There is no magic in hypnotism. Rather it is psychological. An essential factor of hypnotism is suggestion. In the eighteenth century a doctor, Franz A. Mesmer, invented a technique which was called by his name, mesmerism. It was found to be a fraud. After that the term *hypnotism* was used.

1. hypnobate   HYPNO bate (hip′ no bate) n.
   A sleepwalker; somnambulist.
2. hypnogenesis   HYPNO genesis (hip noe jen′ e sis) n.
   Production of the hypnotic state.
3. hypnogenetic   HYPNO genetic (hip noe je net′ ik) adj.
   Inducing hypnotism.
4. hypnoidal   HYPN oidal (hip noid′ al) adj.
   Relating to hypnosis or sleep.
5. hypnoidize   HYPN oidize (hip′ noid ize) v.
   Induce into a hypnoidal state.
6. hypnology   HYPNO logy (hip nol′ o ji) n.
   Science which treats of hypnotic sleep.
7. hypnophobia   HYPNO phobia (hip no foe′ bi a) n.
   Fear of sleep.
8. hypnopompic   HYPNO pompic (hip no pom′ pik) adj.
   Dispelling sleep; waking.
9. Hypnos   HYPNOS (hip′ nos) n.
   The god of sleep.
10. hypnosis   HYPNO sis (hip noe′ sis) n.
    State resembling sleep induced by suggestion.
11. hypnotic   HYPNO tic (hip not′ ik) adj.
    Inducing sleep; soporific.
12. hypnotism   HYPNO tism (hip′ no tiz um) n.
    The study and practice of hypnosis.
13. hypnotist   HYPNO tist (hip′ no tist) n.
    One who practices hypnotism.
14. hypnotize   HYPNO tize (hip′ no tize) v.
    To induce sleep by hypnotism.
15. hypnotherapy   HYPNO therapy (hip noe ther′ a pee) n.
    Treatment of disease by hypnosis.
16. hypnotoid   HYPNO toid (hip′ no toid) adj.
    Resembling hypnotism.

17. hypnotizable   HYPNO tizable (hip' no tie za b'l) adj.
            Can be hypnotized.
18. hypnagogic   HYPN agogic (hip no goj' ik) adj.
            Bringing on sleep.
19. hypnophobic   HYPNO phobic (hip no foe' bik) adj.
            Having fear of sleep.
20. hypnesthesis   HYPN esthesis (hip nes thee' sis) n.
            Dulled sensibility.

word analysis

HYPNOPHOBIC—No. 19
    HYPNO (hypnos)—Greek Root =sleep
    PHOB (phobia)—Greek Root =fear
    IC—Suffix =like

practical exercises

1. Supply the missing words:
     Not everyone is suggestible enough to be ....
     The story of "Trilby" contains an amazing experience of
     .... The .... is Svengali and his
     power over Trilby is even super...........................

2. Analyze No. 7.

3. Give a synonym for each of the following words:
    a. deportee   ....
    b. artillery   ....
    c. slacken   ....
    d. imperial   ....
    e. hypnobate   ....

KEY NO. 237

0━━➤

SANGUI

blood

is the Root *SANG; SANGUI* from the Latin *sanguis*, BLOOD. With all these bloody words, this page is certainly a bloody business. There is only one word from the list that isn't dripping with blood—No. 1 SANGUIne.

1. sanguine   SANGUI ne (san' gwin) adj.
       Red, like blood; ardent; confident.

2. sanguinary   SANGUI nary (san' gwi nar ee) adj.
       Bloody; bloodthirsty.

3. sanguineless   SANGUI neless (san' gwin les) adj.
       Pale; lacking blood; anemic.

4. sanguineous   SANGUI neous (san gwin' ee us) adj.
       Abounding with bloodshed; as, "sanguineous histories of queens."

5. sanguinolent   SANGUI nolent (san gwin' ol ent) adj.
       Tinged with blood.

6. sanguinous   SANGUI nous (san' gwi nus) adj.
       Containing blood; bloodthirsty.

7. sanguisuge   SANGUI suge (san' gwi suje) n.
       A bloodsucker; leech.

8. sanguisugent   SANGUI sugent (san gwi sue' jent) adj.
       Bloodsucking.

9. sangfroid   SANG froid (sang frwa') n.
       Cold-bloodedness; calmness; nonchalance.

10. sanguify   SANGUI fy (san' gwi fie) v.
       To make blood; as using foods containing iron.

11. sanguifier   SANGUI fier (san' gwi fie er) n.
       That which makes blood; as iron, a restorer of blood.

12. sanguimotor   SANGUI motor (san gwi moe' tor) adj.
       Relating to the circulation of the blood.

13. sanguinaceous   SANGUI naceous (san gwi nay' shus) adj.
       Full-blooded; ardent; sanguine.

14. sanguinity   SANGUI nity (san gwin' it ee) n.
       The quality of full-bloodedness; ardor; enthusiasm.

15. consanguinity   con SANGUI nity (kon san gwin' it eee) n.
       Blood-relationship; having ancestors in common.

16. sanguinaria   SANGUI naria (san gwi nar' ee a) n.
            The blood-root; an herb which has reddish
            juice.

word analysis

SANGUISUGENT—No. 8
    SANGUI (sanguis)—Latin Root =blood
    SUG (sugere)—Latin Root =to suck
    ENT—Suffix =that which

practical exercises

1. Supply the missing words:
        Thackeray refers to the reign of Henry VIII, when so
    many queens were killed off, as the " .... history
    of Queens." When harsh laws inflict the death penalty for
    small offenses, those laws are as .... as war it-
    self.

2. Analyze No. 14.

3. Recognize words and keys in the words below. Place a star (*)
    next to those words which are completely recognizable.
    a. intellect
    b. demarch
    c. congregate
    d. intrigue
    e. corrupt
    f. prestige

O━x

PAN

all

is the Root *PAN* which means ALL. It is the most comprehensive ALL that can be used. No. 16 is the most inclusive of civil rights, even extending it to No. 9 where government is not only for all citizens but all citizens are the rulers. Wisely, the language has a word for that, too—No. 6. When all are rulers, PANdemonium cannot be far behind.

1. panacea PAN acea (pan a see' a) n.
   A cure for all ills.

2. panarchy PAN archy (pan' ar ki) n.
   Universal rule.

3. pancratic PAN cratic (pan krat' ik) adj.
   Knowing all subjects.

4. pancreas PAN creas (pan' kree as) n.
   A large gland in vertebrates.

5. pandemic PAN demic (pan dem' ik) adj.
   Relating to all people; universal.

6. pandemonium PAN demonium (pan de moe' nee um) n.
   Wild uproar as if all demons were let loose.

7. panegyric PAN egyric (pan e jir' ik) n.
   Exaggerated eulogy.

8. pangenesis PAN genesis (pan jen' e sis) n.
   A theory that claims that heredity is a result of all cells circulating freely in the body.

9. pantisocracy PAN tisocracy (pant i sok' ra si) n.
   A Utopia where all would rule equally.

10. panharmonic PAN harmonic (pan har mon' ik) adj.
    In universal accord.

11. panhuman PAN human (pan hyu' man) adj.
    Relating to all humanity.

12. panjandrum PAN jandrum (pan jan' drum) n.
    A burlesque title for a pretentious official.

13. panmnesia PAN mnesia (pan nee' zhi a) n.
    A theory that all mental impressions continue in the memory.

14. panopticon PAN opticon (pan op' ti kon) n.
    A combination of telescope and microscope.

15. panorama PAN orama (pan o ram' a) n.
    A picture unrolled, part by part, before the spectator.

16. panpolism   PAN polism (pan' po liz um) n.
                      Equality of civic rights.

17. pansophy   PAN sophy (pan' so fi) n.
                      Universal wisdom.

18. pantheism   PAN theism (pan' thee iz um) n.
                      The doctrine that the forces and laws of the universe are equal to God.

19. pantheon   PAN theon (pan' thee on) n.
                      A temple dedicated to all the gods.

word analysis

PANDEMIC—No. 5
     PAN (pas)—Root =all
     DEM (demos)—Greek Root =people
     IC—Suffix =nature of

practical exercises

1. Supply the missing words:
     .... and .... belong together. In viewing the scene I had the impression of a vast .... which had been unrolled before me. The .... is an important gland.

2. Analyze No. 11.

3. Choose the word which most nearly expresses the italicized word:
    a. *appropriate*   (1) suitable   (2) engaging
         (3) slackening   (4) imperial   (5) maintained   ....
    b. *artillery*   (1) bombs   (2) submarines
         (3) bayonets   (4) cannons   (5) mines   ....
    c. *crest*   (1) distance   (2) wave   (3) eminence
         (4) column   (5) enemy   ....
    d. *hurled*   (1) dislodged   (2) thrown   (3) fired
         (4) pursued   (5) seared   ....
    e. *panpolism*   (1) civil rights for all   (2) pantheism
         (3) pancreas   (4) universe   (5) anarchy   ....

KEY NO. 239

○━━➤

FILA · FILI

thread

is the Root *FILA, FILI* which means THREAD. We meet words with this Root in electricity and the electrically operated machines of modern invention. The word *filament* is as well known as *thread*. The silkworm culture is another fascinating industry where some of these words are used, as well as botany, anatomy and zoology. And in all these areas, the knowledge of the Root *FILUM*, (which comes from the Latin *filum* meaning thread), from which these words are made, immediately increases and intensifies vocabulary enrichment.

1. filament   FILA ment (fil' a ment) n.
         A threadlike conductor heated by electrical current.

2. filate   FILA te (fie' late) adj.
         Slender; threadlike.

3. filator   FILA tor (fie' lay tor) n.
         An organ connected with the silkworm's spinneret.

4. filature   FILA ture (fil' a chur) n.
         A reel for drawing the silk from a cocoon.

5. filet   FIL et (fi lay') n.
         Lace made of fine threads.

6. filigree   FILI gree (fil' i gree) n.
         Delicate ornamental work of gold and silver in intricate design.

7. filipendulous   FILI pendulous (fil i pen' due lus) adj.
         Suspended by thread or string.

8. filite   FILI te (fie' lite) n.
         A smokeless powder made in cords.

9. fillet   FIL let (fil' et) n.
         A little band to encircle the hair.

10. filum   FIL um (fie' lum) n.
         A thread.

11. filipendula   FILI pendula (fil i pen' due la) n.
         A small genus of herbs that blooms perennially.

12. filiform   FILI form (fil' i form) adj.
         Having the shape of a thread.

13. filiferous   FILI ferous (fie lif' er us) adj.
         Bearing threads.

14. filicauline   FILI cauline (fil i kau' lin) n.
           Having a threadlike stem.
15. filamentous   FILA mentous (fil a ment' us) adj.
           Full of threads; having threads.
16. filaceous   FILA ceous (fil lay' shus) adj.
           Composed of threads.

word analysis

FILIFEROUS—No. 13
    FIL (filum)—Latin Root =thread
    FER—Root =bear; yield
    OUS—Suffix =full of

practical exercises

1. Supply the missing words:
     The .... cocoons of the silkworm are un-
wound most carefully. Ornaments of .... work
are exquisitely beautiful and, of course, expensive.

2. Analyze No. 12.

3. KEY Review. Match keys with their meanings:
    a. pan   1. color   ....
    b. hypno   2. wander   ....
    c. chrom   3. ball   ....
    d. monstr   4. thread   ....
    e. sangui   5. clothe   ....
    f. migra   6. all   ....
    g. fili, fila   7. show   ....
    h. sphere   8. law   ....
    i. vest   9. blood   ....
    j. jus   10. sleep   ....

KEY NO. 240

DIA

through

is the Prefix *DIA* which means THROUGH. You will meet this key in geometry, music, medicine, chemistry and even in Communist *DIA*-lectics, so dear to the Russian soul in arguments which are more *DIA*-tribes against democracy than logical arguments.

1. diameter
DIA meter (die am' et er) n.
The length of a straight line drawn through the center of a circle.

2. diagram
DIA gram (die' a gram) n.
A combination of lines drawn to explain an idea.

3. diagonal
DIA gonal (die ag' on al) adj.
Passing through two opposite angles of a plane figure.

4. diagnose
DIA gnose (die ag nose') v.
Recognize a disease through symptoms.

5. diaglyph
DIA glyph (die' a glyf) n.
An engraving on metal; an intaglio.

6. dialyze
DIA lyze (die' a lize) v.
To separate into elements.

7. dialysis
DIA lysis (die al' a sis) n.
The separation into elements.

8. diagenesis
DIA genesis (die a jen' e sis) n.
A recombining of elements which results in a new product.

9. dialogue
DIA logue (die' a log) n.
Conversation between two or more persons.

10. diatribe
DIA tribe (die' a tribe) n.
A long and bitter discussion or lecture which is usually abusive.

11. diathermy
DIA thermy (die' a ther mee) n.
Treatment of disease by penetrating heat.

12. diadermic
DIA dermic (die a der' mik) adj.
Acting through the skin; as, a skin lotion.

13. diastema
DIA stema (die a stee' ma) n.
A vacant space or gap between teeth in the jaw.

14. diaspora
DIA spora (di as' po ra) n.
A scattering among the nations.

15. diapason
DIA pason (die a paze' on) n.
The whole scale of tones; range.

16. dialectic   DIA lectic (die a lek' tik) n.
                 Argument through critical discussion.

17. diacritical   DIA critical (die a krit' i kal) adj.
                 Serving to distinguish; as, diacritical marks on words aid pronunciation.

18. diadem   DIA dem (die' a dem) n.
                 Crown.

19. diascope   DIA scope (die' a skope) n.
                 Instrument to expel the blood from a part of the body and thus reveal changes in it.

20. diaeresis   DIA eresis (die er' e sis) n.
                 When two vowels appear together, a mark (··) is placed over the second vowel to show that it is pronounced as a separate syllable, as naïve.

word analysis

DIATHERMY—No. 11
    DIA—Prefix =through
    THERM (thermos)—Greek Root =heat
    Y—Suffix =tending to

practical exercises

1. Supply the missing words:
    In a .... two dots are placed over the second vowel to show separation. His notebook is full of .... to demonstrate his laboratory experiments.

2. Analyze No. 1.

3. Recognize words and keys in the following words, taken from the newspapers (many words contain more than one key):
    a. progressive   e. continued
    b. decide   f. conversation
    c. response   g. potential
    d. suggestion   h. potent

CALOR

heat

is the Root *CALOR* which means HEAT. Today the word is well known to us. *CALOR*ie (No. 3) is constantly on our minds. Words 17, 18, 19 and 20 are very different in appearance, but have close relations with the meaning. It is odd how words are like people, who completely change the color of their hair and face.

1. calor
CALOR (kal' or) n.
Heat.

2. caloric
CALOR ic (ka lor' ik) adj.
Like heat; giving off heat.

3. calorie
CALOR ie (kal' o ree) n.
A unit of heat.

4. caloricity
CALOR icity (kal o ris' i ti) n.
Ability to develop and maintain animal heat.

5. calorify
CALOR ify (ka lor' i fie) v.
To make hot; make heat producing.

6. calorific
CALOR ific (kal o rif' ik) adj.
Heat producing.

7. calorifacient
CALOR ifacient (ka lor i fay' shent) adj.
Same as No. 6.

8. calorifics
CALOR ifics (kal o rif' iks) n.
Study, phenomena, and details of heat.

9. calorigenic
CALOR igenic (kal lor i jen' ik) adj.
Generating heat.

10. calorimeter
CALOR imeter (kal o rim' et er) n.
Instrument for measuring the quantity of heat used.

11. calorimetry
CALOR imetry (kal o rim' e tree) n.
The science of measuring heat.

12. calorescence
CALOR escence (kal o res' ens) n.
Heat waves changed to light.

13. calorimotor
CALOR imotor (ka lor' i moe tor) n.
A battery of large plates producing heat effects.

14. calorist
CALOR ist (kal' o rist) n.
One who believed that heat is caloric.

15. Calorite
CALOR ite (kal' o rite) n.
A heat-resisting alloy, often used for electric wiring.

16. calorize   CALOR ize (kal' o rize) v.
                To treat by a process of coating metal to
                make it rust resisting under heat.

17. cauldron   CAUL dron (kaul' dron) n.
                A huge kettle for warming or boiling.

18. caudle   CAUD le (kaud' el) n.
                A warm, nutritious drink for an invalid.

19. scald   s CAL d (skald) v.
                To burn with boiling water.

20. nonchalant   non CHAL ant (non sha lant') adj.
                Unconcerned; indifferent.

word analysis

NONCHALANT—No. 20
    NON—Prefix = not
    CHAL (calere)—Latin Root = to be hot
    ANT—Suffix = one who; that which

practical exercises

1. Supply the missing words:
     Fat people do not count the .... they con-
sume. Medical students soon learn to recognize the signs of
inflammation—heat = ...; pain = dolor; redness
= rubor; swelling = tumor.

2. Analyze No. 9.

3. Give a synonym for each of the following words:
    a. suitable   ....
    b. pandemic   ....
    c. eulogy   ....
    d. thesis   ....
    e. mournful   ....

KEY NO. 242

CIV

citizen

is the Root *CIV* which comes from the Latin *civis*, CITIZEN. That is what you must think of when you see *CIV*, CITIZEN: No. 1, relating to a citizen; No. 2, science of citizenship, etc. Even the magnificent No. 11: what is it but training to be a good citizen, with all due rights and responsibilities? Please notice No. 3 and No. 8. They look very much alike, but they are not alike: No. 3—principles of government; No. 8—principles of citizenship.

1. civic
CIV ic (siv′ ik) adj.
Relating to a citizen; as, a civic *duty.*

2. civics
CIV ics (siv′ iks) n.
The science dealing with the rights and duties of the citizen.

3. civicism
CIV icism (siv′ i siz um) n.
Principles of civil government.

4. civil
CIV il (siv′ il) adj.
Trained; refined; relating to citizens.

5. civilian
CIV ilian (si vil′ yan) n.
One who is not in the armed forces but in a common society.

6. civility
CIV ility (si vil′ it ee) n.
Quality of being civilized; the manner of a civil person; politeness.

7. civilize
CIV ilize (siv′ i lize) v.
To bring up from barbarism; to train to live with others.

8. civism
CIV ism (siv′ iz um) n.
Principles of citizenship.

9. civvy
CIV vy (siv′ y) n.
A civilian.

10. civvies
CIV vies (siv′ eze) n.
Civilian clothes as opposed to military dress.

11. civilization
CIV ilization (siv i li zay′ shun) n.
The cultural development of man; the process of developing from barbarism.

12. civilizational
CIV ilizational (siv i li zay′ shun al) adj.
Relating to civilization.

13. civilizatory
CIV ilizatory (siv i lize′ a to ri) adj.
Contributing to civilization.

484

14. uncivil   un CIV il (un siv′ il) adj.
           Rude; untrained; disregarding the duties of citizenship.

15. uncivilized   un CIV ilized (un siv′ i lized) adj.
           Lacking the values of civilization.

16. decivilize   de CIV ilize (dee siv′ i lize) v.
           Make to act like a barbarian.

word analysis

DECIVILIZE—No. 16
     DE—Prefix =away; from
     CIVIL (civis)—Latin Root =citizen
     IZE—Suffix =make

practical exercises

1. Supply the missing words:
     When a soldier completes his military service, he is usually glad to get into .... again. The Nazi regime .... its followers.

2. Analyze No. 6.

3. Choose the number of the word most nearly suited to the italicized word:
     a. *tenderness*   (1) harshness   (2) establishment
        (3) ardor   (4) praise   (5) kindness   ....
     b. *limitation*   (1) boundary   (2) succession
        (3) treason   (4) accent   (5) affection   ....
     c. *tradition*   (1) twilight   (2) heritage   (3) wail
        (4) anxiety   (5) lanterns   ....
     d. *prophetic*   (1) indistinct   (2) disconsolate
        (3) patient   (4) foretelling   (5) ancient   ....
     e. *devotion*   (1) sorrow   (2) endurance   (3) love
        (4) memory   (5) pity   ....

KEY NO. 243

O━x

DYN · DYNAMO

power

is the Prefix *DYN, DYNAMO* which means POWER. It is really a DYNamo of a word. Wherever you see it there is POWER. Take a special minute for No. 13. It is one of the most wonderful words as an example for word building.

1. dyne   DYN e (dine) n.
       A unit of force.

2. dynagraph   DYNA graph (die′ na graf) n.
       Apparatus for recording the condition of a line of track.

3. dynameter   DYNA meter (die nam′ e ter) n.
       Instrument for determining a telescope's magnifying power.

4. dynamotor   DYNA motor (die′ na mote or) n.
       A special kind of electric generator.

5. dynamic   DYNAM ic (die nam′ ik) adj.
       Forceful; powerful.

6. dynamism   DYNAM ism (die′ na miz um) n.
       The quality of forcefulness.

7. dynamist   DYNAM ist (die′ na mist) n.
       One who believes in dynamism.

8. dynamistic   DYNAM istic (die na mist′ ik) adj.
       Of or relating to dynamism.

9. dynamite   DYNAM ite (die′ na mite) n.
       An explosive.

10. dynamitic   DYNAM itic (die na mit′ ik) adj.
       Like dynamite; having explosive force.

11. dynamo   DYNAMO (die′ na moe) n.
       A machine for converting mechanical energy to electrical energy.

12. dynamoelectric   DYNAMO electric
       (die′ na moe e lek′ trik) adj.
       Relating to the conversion of mechanical energy to electrical energy.

13. dynamogenesis   DYN amogenesis (die′ am o jen′ e sis) n.
       The production of power.

14. dynamometry   DYNAMO metry (die na mom′ e tree) n.
       The process of measuring forces doing work.

15. dynamis   DYNAM is (die′ na mis) n.
       The potential of power not yet realized.

16. dynamiter   DYNAM iter (die′ na mite er) n.
       One who uses dynamite.

17. dynast   **DYN** ast (die′ nast) n.
                        An especially powerful ruler.

18. dynasty   **DYN** asty (die′ na stee) n.
                        An especially powerful line of kings.

word analysis

DYNAMOGENESIS—No. 13
    DYNAMO (dynamics)—Greek Root =power
    GEN (genos)—Greek Root =race
    ESIS—Suffix =process of

practical exercise

Read the following excerpt underlining all those words that contain keys you have already learned.

> This is the forest primeval. The murmuring pines and the hemlocks,
> Bearded with moss, and in garments green, indistinct in the twilight,
> Stand like Druids of eld, with voices sad and prophetic,
> Stand like harpers hoar, with beards that rest on their bosoms.
> Loud from its rocky caverns, the deep-voiced neighboring ocean
> Speaks, and in accents disconsolate answers the wail of the forest
>
> . . . .
>
> Ye who believe in affection that hopes, and endures, and is patient,
> Ye who believe in the beauty and strength of woman's devotion,
> List to the mournful tradition still sung by the pines of the forest;
> List to a Tale of Love in Acadie, home of the happy.
>
>   (From *Evangeline* by Henry Wadsworth Longfellow.)

KEY NO. 244

0—x

ROGA · ROG

ask
beg

is the Root *ROGA, ROG* which comes from the Latin *rogare*, to ASK, BEG. The interesting thing is that as the words accumulate, the meanings change. No. 1 is distinctly prayer, No. 2 and No. 3 begin to claim selfishly, to presume. In No. 4 and No. 5 pride enters in. In Nos. 6, 7, and 8 the dictator annuls his treaties, breaks his word. In Nos. 9, 10, and 11 jealousy and ill will enter into the words, and they have a belittling effect.

1. rogation   ROGA tion (roe gay' shun) n.
   Petition; prayer.

2. arrogate   ar ROGA te (ar' o gate) v.
   Claim for oneself; presume.

3. arrogation   ar ROGA tion (ar o gay' shun) n.
   The act of claiming for oneself.

4. arrogant   ar ROGA nt (ar' o gant) adj.
   Proud; presuming.

5. arrogance   ar ROGA nce (ar' o gans) n.
   Pride; presumption.

6. abrogate   ab ROGA te (ab' ro gate) v.
   Do away with; annul; as, abrogate *a treaty.*

7. abrogative   ab ROGA tive (ab' ro gay tiv) adj.
   Causing annulment.

8. abrogation   ab ROGA tion (ab ro gay' shun) n.
   Annulment; cancellation.

9. derogate   de ROGA te (der' o gate) v.
   To lessen; to diminish; as, derogate *the importance of an event.*

10. derogative   de ROGA tive (de rog' at iv) adj.
    Tending to belittle; to derogate.

11. derogatory   de ROGA tory (de rog' a tor ee) adj.
    Making a thing appear to be less important.

12. interrogate   inter ROGA te (in ter' o gate) v.
    To question formally; ask the reason.

13. interrogation   inter ROGA tion (in ter o gay' shun) n.
    Questioning; the act of questioning.

14. prerogative   pre ROGA tive (pre rog' at iv) n.
    A privilege; superiority.

15. prorogate   pro ROGA te (pror' o gate) v.
    To delay; postpone.

16. supererogatory superer ROGA tory
                    (su pe re rog' a tor ee) adj.
                        More than needed; nonessential.

17. supererogative superer ROGA tive (su per e rog' a tiv) adj.
                        Supererogatory.

18. supererogation superer ROGA tion (su pe rer o gay' shun) n.
                        Act of performing the nonessential.

19. surrogate   sur ROGA te (sur' o gate) n.
                        A substitute; as, a surrogate *judge.*

word analysis

SURROGATE—No. 19
    SUR (sub)—Prefix =under
    ROGA (rogare)—Latin Root =to ask
    ATE—Suffix =make

practical exercises

1. Supply the missing words:

    People who consider themselves superior to others often .... to themselves .... to which they are not entitled. An .... dictator will not hesitate to .... a treaty if he finds it convenient to do so.

2. Analyze No. 12.

3. Use one word for each of the following phrases:
    a. an explosive invented by Alfred Nobel   ....
    b. a ruler with more than usual power   ....
    c. inclined to have a belittling effect   ....
    d. principles of civil government   ....
    e. a warm, nutritious drink for an invalid   ....

KEY NO. 245

o—x

**OSIS · ESIS
ASIS**

**action
process
condition**

is the Suffix *OSIS, ESIS, ASIS* used to express a course of ACTION, a PROCESS, or a CONDITION. The last is used much in medicine and means a diseased condition. About a dozen words on the list are of the medical kind. But No. 9 is a good, healthy condition and, after the rest, well worth aiming at. No. 1, Anab-ASIS, is the report of a military journey. That is Action. Note the key's spellings.

1. anabasis   anab ASIS (a nab′ a sis) n.
   A military advance.

2. thrombosis   thromb OSIS (throm boe′ sis) n.
   Formation of a clot in the blood vessels.

3. elephantiasis   elephanti ASIS (el e fan tie′ a sis) n.
   Disease in which the skin gets hard and dry like an elephant's.

4. exegesis   exeg ESIS (ek se jee′ sis) n.
   The act, explanation and interpretation of Scripture.

5. genesis   gen ESIS (jen′ e sis) n.
   The act of coming into being; the origin.

6. halitosis   halit OSIS (hal i toe′ sis) n.
   The condition in which the breath is offensive.

7. hypochondriasis   hypochondri ASIS (hie po kon drie′ a sis) n.
   Condition of anxiety about imagined ailments.

8. hypnosis   hypn OSIS (hip noe′ sis) n.
   State of being hypnotized.

9. orthobiosis   orthobi OSIS (or tho bie o′ sis) n.
   Right living according to the principles of good health and morals.

10. metamorphosis   metamorph OSIS (met a mor′ fo sis) n.
    Complete change of form and character.

11. neurosis   neur OSIS (nu roe′ sis) n.
    Condition of disordered nerves; emotional disorder.

12. osmosis   osm OSIS (o smoe′ sis) n.
    A mutual fusing of liquids which have been separated by a membrane.

13. osmidrosis   osmidr OSIS (oz mi droe' sis) n.
                             A fetid, sweaty secretion.

14. ostosis   ost OSIS (os toe' sis) n.
                             The hardening of tissue into bone.

15. psoriasis   psori ASIS (so rie' a sis) n.
                             A diseased condition of the skin.

16. psychosis   psych OSIS (sie koe' sis) n.
                             A serious mental disorder.

17. pyreticosis   pyretic OSIS (pie ret i koe' sis) n.
                             Fever.

18. symptosis   sympt OSIS (simp toe' sis) n.
                             Gradual wasting away of the body or of any part of it.

19. symbiosis   symbi OSIS (sim bie o' sis) n.
                             The living together of two dissimilar organisms.

word analysis

PYRETICOSIS—No. 17
     PYRE (pyros)—Greek Root =fire
     ETIC—Suffix =like
     OSIS—Suffix =condition

practical exercises

1. Supply the missing words:
     After all the "oses" and "ases" we've been reading about it is refreshing to think of .... The imaginary ailments of .... are the most difficult to cure. Many doctors are experimenting with .... in the treatment of illness.

2. Analyze No. 8.

3. Give a synonym for each of the following words:
     a. derogate   ....
     b. assume   ....
     c. dynamic   ....
     d. question   ....
     e. prerogative   ....
     f. explanation   ....

O━➤

OLOGY

study
science
theory

is the Suffix *OLOGY* which means STUDY, SCIENCE, THEORY. *OLOGY* is a compound Suffix: it is a combination of *O* which means OF and *LOGY* which means STUDY, SCIENCE, THEORY. If you wish to add to your *OLOGY* you will have no trouble in doing so. There seems to be an endless list of them. I doubt whether there is a single individual in the world who cannot find an OLOGY that relates to his interests.

1. embryology embry OLOGY (em bree ol' o jee) n.
   The study of the organism in the early stage of development.

2. bacteriology bacteri OLOGY (bak ter ee ol' o jee) n.
   The study of bacteria, microbes, germs.

3. biology bi OLOGY (bie ol' o jee) n.
   The study of living creatures.

4. anthropology anthrop OLOGY (an thro pol' o jee) n.
   The study of the development of man.

5. climatology climat OLOGY (klie ma tol' o jee) n.
   The study of climates.

6. criminology crimin OLOGY (krim i nol' o jee) n.
   The study of crime and its social implications.

7. demonology demon OLOGY (dee mo nol' o jee) n.
   The study of demons and belief in them.

8. ethnology ethn OLOGY (eth nol' o jee) n.
   The study of the races of mankind.

9. geology ge OLOGY (jee ol' o jee) n.
   The study of the earth as recorded in rock formations.

10. gynecology gynec OLOGY (jin e kol' o jee) n.
    The study of the diseases of women.

11. mineralogy mineral OGY (min e ral' o jee) n.
    Study of minerals.

12. neurology neur OLOGY (nu rol' o jee) n.
    The study of the nervous system.

13. ontology ont OLOGY (on tol' o jee) n.
    The study of things existing and being.

14. paleontology paleont OLOGY (pay lee on tol' o jee) n.
    The study of life in past geological periods.

15. pathology   path OLOGY (pa thol' o jee) n.
                The science of disease.
16. pharmacology pharmac OLOGY (far ma kol' o jee) n.
                The study of drugs.
17. philology   phil OLOGY (fi lol' o jee) n.
                The study of languages.
18. phrenology   phren OLOGY (fri nol' o jee) n.
                The study of the shape of the skull as in-
                dication of mental faculty.
19. psychology   psych OLOGY (sie kol' o jee) n.
                The study of the mind and its functions.
20. theology   the OLOGY (thee ol' o jee) n.
                The study of religions and God.

word analysis

ETHNOLOGY—No. 8
    ETHN (ethnos)—Greek Root = race
    OLOGY—Suffix = study of

practical exercise

Read the following excerpt underlining all those words that contain keys you have already learned.

At the time when he was concluding his very eloquent Preface, Johnson's mind appears to have been in such a state of depression, that we cannot contemplate without wonder, the vigorous and splendid thoughts which so highly distinguish that performance.

"I," says he, "may surely be contented without the praise of perfection, which if I could obtain in this gloom of solitude, what would it avail me? I have protracted my work till most of those whom I wished to please have sunk into the grave; and success and miscarriage are empty sounds. I therefore dismiss it with frigid tranquility, having little to fear or hope from censure or from praise."

That this indifference was rather a temporary than a habitual feeling, appears, I think, from his letters to Mr. Warton; and however he may have been affected for the moment, certain it is that the honors which his great work procured him at home and abroad, were very grateful to him.

(From James Boswell's *The Life of Samuel Johnson,* 1775; at the completion of the Dictionary.)

493

KEY NO. 247

0—🗝

NEUR

nerve

is the Root *NEUR* which comes from the Greek *neuron,* which means NERVE. The most subtle and evasive of diseases are the NEURological (No. 11) ones. If we studied NEURo-physiology, the physiology of the nervous system, we would know more about NEURism (No. 6) and know how to prevent NEURoses (plural of No. 15), and be better equipped to avoid NEURoticism (No. 17).

1. neural   NEUR al (nur' al) adj.
           Relating to a nerve.
2. neuralgia   NEUR algia (nu ral' ja) n.
           Acute pain extending along the nerve.
3. neuralgic   NEUR algic (nu' ral' jik) adj.
           Resembling neuralgia; as, a neuralgic pain.
4. neuric   NEUR ic (nue' rik) adj.
           Relating to the nervous system.
5. neurility   NEUR ility (nu ril' i ti) n.
           Function of the nerves.
6. neurism   NEUR ism (nu' riz um) n.
           Nerve force.
7. neuritis   NEUR itis (nu rite' is) n.
           Inflammation of a nerve.
8. neuroid   NEUR oid (nu' roid) adj.
           Similar to a nerve or nerve tissue.
9. neuronym   NEUR onym (nu' ro nim) n.
           The name of either a nerve or part of the nervous system, or both.
10. neurology   NEUR ology (nu rol' o jee) n.
           Branch of medicine which studies the nervous system.
11. neurological   NEUR ological (nur o loj' i kal) n.
           Relating to neurology.
12. neurologist   NEUR ologist (nu rol' o jist) n.
           One who practices neurology.
13. neurergic   NEUR ergic (nu rer' jik) adj.
           Relating to the action of the nerves.
14. neurography   NEUR ography (nu rog' ra fi) n.
           A description of the nervous system.
15. neurosis   NEUR osis (nu roe' sis) n.
           A nonphysical disorder of the nervous system.

16. neurotic   NEUR otic (nu rot' ik) adj.
                Acting on the nerves; instability.
17. neuroticism NEUR oticism (nu rot' i siz um) n.
                A neurotic condition.
18. neuropathic NEUR opathic (nur o path' ik) adj.
                Having a nerve disease.
19. neurasthenia NEUR asthenia (nur as thee' nee a) n.
                A nervous condition of extreme fatigue.
20. neurexairesis NEUR exairesis (nur eks i' ree sis) n.
                The removal of a nerve to obtain relief from
                such diseases as neuralgia.

word analysis

NEURITIS—No. 7
    NEUR (neuron)—Greek Root =nerve
    ITIS—Suffix =disease

practical exercises

1. Supply the missing words:
    Chronic fatigue may be a symptom of .... If
    the doctors would teach the layman more about ....
    and .... many .... ills might be
    prevented.

2. Analyze No. 12.

3. Add the missing key to complete word and comprehension:
    a. subject to nerve disease— ....path..........
    b. tearing out a nerve as a cure— ....exair..........
    c. a disease from inhaling dust— coni..........
    d. causing one to take a privilege— pre..........tive
    e. a study of the mind and its functions— psych..........

0—

NEO

**new
recent**

is the Root *NEO* which comes from the Greek word *neos*, meaning NEW; RECENT. Many old things become of interest again; people often will believe in something, come to accept it as everyday, and then a new interest awakens and it is revived.

1. neoblastic   NEO blastic (nee o blas' tik) adj.
     Having the nature of new growth.

2. Neocene   NEO cene (nee' o sene) adj.
     Belonging to the tertiary period.

3. neocosmic   NEO cosmic (nee o koz' mik) adj.
     Relating to the present known world and races.

4. neocracy   NEO cracy (nee ok' ra si) n.
     Government by new, inexperienced officials.

5. neocriticism   NEO criticism (nee o krit' i siz um) n.
     The new philosophy, rejecting Kant.

6. neo-Darwinism   NEO Darwinism (nee o dar' wi niz um) n.
     A new form of Darwin's theory.

7. neofetus   NEO fetus (nee o fee' tus) n.
     The embryo in the very early stages of development.

8. neogenesis   NEO genesis (nee o jen' e sis) n.
     A new formation or regeneration of tissue.

9. neo-Gothic   NEO Gothic (nee o goth' ik) adj.
     Art based on study of medieval Gothic.

10. neogrammarian   NEO grammarian (nee o gra mar' i an) n.
     A new, scientific direction to linguistics.

11. neo-Hellenism   NEO Hellenism (nee o hel' en iz um) n.
     The practice of ancient Greek ideals in modern life and art.

12. neolatry   NEO latry (nee ol' a tri) n.
     The worship of the new, the novelty.

13. neolithic   NEO lithic (nee o lith' ik) adj.
     Relating to the era when polished stone implements were used.

14. neology   NEO logy (nee ol' o jee) n.
     The use of new words in the language.

15. neomenia   NEO menia (nee o mee' ni a) n.
     The festival of the new moon.

16. neomorph   NEO morph (nee' o morf) n.
     A new form not derived from an ancestor.

17. neon   NEO n (nee' on) n.
                   A gaseous element used in neon lights.

19. neophrastic   NEO phrastic (nee o fras' tik) adj.
                   Relating to neology (No. 14).

20. neophyte   NEO phyte (nee' o fite) n.
                   A new convert; a novice; a beginner.

word analysis

NEOLITHIC—No. 13
     NEO (neos)—Greek Root =new
     LITH (lithos)—Greek Root =stone
     IC—Suffix =nature of; like

practical exercise

Read the following excerpt underlining all those words that contain keys you have already learned.

    Is not a Patron, my Lord, one who looks with unconcern on a man struggling for life in the water, and when he has reached ground, encumbers him with help? The notice which you have been pleased to take of my labours, had it been early, had been kind. But it has been delayed till I am indifferent, and cannot enjoy it; till I am solitary and cannot impart it; till I am known and do not want it. I hope it is no very cynical asperity not to confess obligation where no benefit has been received, or to be unwilling that the Publick should consider me as owing that to a Patron, which Providence has enabled me to do for myself.

    Having carried on my work thus far with so little obligation to any favourer of learning, I shall not be disappointed though I should conclude it, if less be possible, with less; for I have been long wakened from that dream of hope, in which I once boasted myself with so much exultation, my Lord, your Lordship's most humble, most obedient servant,

                                 Sam. Johnson

(From Samuel Johnson's letter to Lord Chesterfield.)

KEY NO. 249

o—➤

OSS · OSTEO

bone

is the Root *OSS, OSTEO*, meaning BONE. It comes from the Greek and Latin. *Ossa* is the plural of *os*. The average person knows very little about his bones, even after he breaks one, but there is much to know about them, and the list gives a glimpse here and there.

1. osseous   OSS eous (os' e us) adj.
                 Bony.

2. ossicle   OSS icle (os' i k'l) n.
                 A small bone.

3. ossiculectomy OSS iculectomy (os i ku lek' to mi) n.
                 Removal of a small bone in the ear.

4. ossify   OSS ify (os' i fie) v.
                 To make into bone.

5. ossification OSS ification (os i fi kay' shun) n.
                 The process of making into bone.

6. ossifluent   OSS ifluent (o sif' lue ent) adj.
                 Having a discharge from an abscessed bone.

7. ossifrage   OSS ifrage (os' i fraj) n.
                 "Breakbones" is the name given to the osprey, a large fish hawk.

8. ossuary   OSS uary (osh' u ar ree) adj.
                 A depository for bones; cemetery; urn.

9. osteal   OSTE al (os' tee al) adj.
                 Relating to bone.

10. osteitis   OSTE itis (os tee ite' is) n.
                 Inflammation of the bone.

11. osteopathy   OSTEO pathy (os tee op' a thee) n.
                 Treatment of diseases by manipulation of bones.

12. osteodentine OSTEO dentine (os te o den' tene) n.
                 Bone found in the teeth of fishes.

13. osteogen   OSTEO gen (os' te o jen) n.
                 Soft tissue which ossifies to form bone.

14. osteology   OSTEO logy (os tee ol' o jee) n.
                 Science which treats of the bones of vertebrates.

15. osteomancy   OSTEO mancy (os' te o man si) n.
                 Divination by bones.

16. osteometry   OSTEO metry (os te om' e tri) n.
                 The measuring of bones.

17. osteopath   OSTEO path (os' tee o path) n.
One who practices osteopathy; as, Dr. X is an osteopath.

18. osteophagia   OSTEO phagia (os te o fay' ji a) n.
The chewing of bones by cattle to get phosphorus.

19. osteophone   OSTEO phone (os' te o fone) n.
A hearing-aid device.

20. osteoporosis   OSTEO porosis (os te o po roe' sis) n.
A condition in old age when bones become porous and fragile.

word analysis

OSSIFICATION—No. 5
    OSSI (ossa)—Greek Root =bone
    FIC (facere)—Latin Root =to make
    TION—Suffix =act of

practical exercises

1. Supply the missing words:
    An old superstition that bones held the secrets of the future led to the practice of .... Many modern ....(s) are almost invisible. "Breakbones" is a literal translation of ...., a nickname for the osprey.

2. Analyze No. 9.

3. Use one word for each phrase:
    a. inflammation of the bone   ....
    b. condition when bones are porous and fragile   ....
    c. a regeneration of old tissues   ....
    d. worship of novelty   ....
    e. a pleasing sound   ....

KEY NO. 250

0—🗝

ANTHROP

man

is the Root *ANTHROP* which comes from the Greek *anthropos,* meaning MAN. This key opens the door to a much debated subject—is man an ape or an angel? Disraeli said, "I repudiate with abhorrence and indignation these new-fangled theories." Darwin thought differently. Here is some vocabulary relating to the subject.

1. anthropic

ANTHROP ic (an throp' ik) adj.
Of or pertaining to mankind.

2. anthropocentric

ANTHROP ocentric
(an thro po sen' trik) adj.
Assuming that man is the center of all.

3. anthropogeography

ANTHROP ogeography
(an thro po je og' ra fi) n.
Study of distribution of man in the world.

4. anthropogenesis

ANTHROP ogenesis
(an thro po jen' e sis) n.
Study of the development and origin of man.

5. anthropoglot

ANTHROP oglot (an throe' po glot) n.
Animal with a tongue like man.

6. anthropography

ANTHROP ography
(an thro pog' ra fee) n.
Study of the distribution of the language, customs, institutions of man.

7. anthropoid

ANTHROP oid (an' thro poid) adj.
Resembling man; as, the anthropoid *ape.*

8. anthropology

ANTHROP ology (an thro pol' o jee) n.
The science of man.

9. anthropolatry

ANTHROP olatry (an thro pol' a tri) n.
The worship of man as God.

10. anthropolith

ANTHROP olith (an throe' po lith) n.
The petrified body or part of a body of a man.

11. anthropological

ANTHROP ological
(an thro po loj' i kal) adj.
Relating to anthropology.

12. anthropologist

ANTHROP ologist (an thro pol' o jist) n.
One who is versed in anthropology.

500

13. anthropometer   ANTHROP ometer (an thro pom' e ter) n.
An instrument to measure the parts of the human body.

14. anthropomorphism ANTHROP omorphism
(an thro po mor' fiz um) n.
      Attributing human form to the non-human.

15. anthropopathy   ANTHROP opathy (an thro pop' a thi) n.
      Attributing human feeling to God.

16. anthroponomy   ANTHROP onomy (an thro pon' o mi) n.
      The science of human behavior.

17. anthropophagy   ANTHROP ophagy (an thro pof' a jee) n.
      Cannibalism.

18. anthropophagus   ANTHROP ophagus
(an thro pof' a gus) n.
      Cannibal.

19. philanthropy   phil ANTHROP y (fi lan' thro pee) n.
      Love of mankind.

20. misanthropy   mis ANTHROP y (mis an' thro pee) n.
      Hatred of mankind.

word analysis

PHILANTHROPY—No. 19
    PHIL (philos)—Greek Root =love
    ANTHROP (anthropos)—Greek Root =man
    Y—Suffix =tend to; incline to

practical exercises

1. Supply the missing words:
    The science of .... calls certain apes which
    resemble man .... apes.

2. Analyze No. 20.

3. Complete words by supplying necessary keys for understanding:
    a. enough— suf..........ent
    b. a job one takes on— ....cupa..........
    c. a state of keeping apart from others— ....clusion
    d. stick together— ....here
    e. take up again— re..........
    f. inflammation of the eye— ophthalm..........

o—⚷

GE · GEO

earth
soil
ground

is the Root *GE, GEO* meaning EARTH, SOIL, GROUND. This invaluable key opens doors to the land and water, both on the surface and below, and to every living creature in every nook and corner of our planet. There are many words you will want to know that are not on the list.

1. geobios GEO bios (jee o bie' os) n.
   Life on earth.

2. geocarpic GEO carpic (jee o kar' pik) adj.
   Producing fruit under the surface of the ground; as the potato.

3. geocentric GEO centric (jee o sen' trik) adj.
   Measuring from the center of the earth.

4. geochemistry GEO chemistry (jee o kem' i stree) n.
   Science of the chemical composition of the earth's crust.

5. geochronic GEO chronic (jee o kron' ik) adj.
   Relating to geological time divisions.

6. geocratic GEO cratic (jee o krat' ik) adj.
   Concerning the predominance of land areas in relation to ocean areas.

7. geocyclic GEO cyclic (jee o sie' klik) adj.
   Relating to the rotation of the earth.

8. geode GEO de (jee' ode) n.
   A cavity lined with minerals or crystal in a nodule of stone.

9. geodesy GEO desy (jee od' e see) n.
   Concern with measurements of size and position of earth.

10. geodynamics GEO dynamics (jee o die nam' iks) n.
    Study of forces and processes within the earth.

11. geogenous GEO genous (jee oj' e nus) adj.
    Growing in or on the ground.

12. geoglyphic GEO glyphic (jee o glif' ik) adj.
    Relating to marks in rocks that reveal the geologic past.

13. geognosy GEO gnosy (jee og' no si) n.
    Knowledge of the materials of the earth.

14. geography GEO graphy (jee og' ra fee) n.
    The science of the earth and its life.

15. geohydrology   GEO hydrology (jee o hie drol' o ji) n.
    Science treating of underground waters.
16. geoid   GEO id (jee' oid) n.
    The surface of the earth.
17. geology   GEO logy (jee ol' o jee) n.
    History of the earth as recorded in the rocks.
18. geophagia   GEO phagia (jee o fay' ji a) n.
    Study of nutrition of primitive tribes who eat clay.
19. geomorphic   GEO morphic (jee o mor' fik) adj.
    Relating to the form of the earth.
20. geophilous   GEO philous (jee of' i lus) adj.
    Growing or living on or under the ground.

word analysis

GEOHYDROLOGY—No. 15
    GEO—Root =earth
    HYDRO (hydros)—Greek Root =water
    LOG (logos)—Greek Root =word; study
    Y—Suffix =result of action

practical exercises

1. Supply the missing words:
    Insects which live underground are said to be ....
    Scientists who wish to know why certain primitive tribes eat
    clay, study ....

2. Analyze No. 12.

3. Choose the word which most nearly expresses the italicized word:
    a. *invalid* (1) imaginings (2) occupation
       (3) substance (4) despair
       (5) a sick person   ....
    b. *coherence* (1) stickiness (2) seclusion
       (3) exclusion (4) impatience (5) surgeon   ....
    c. *philosophically* (1) angrily (2) wisely
       (3) loudly (4) softly (5) bitterly   ....
    d. *distinct* (1) clear (2) blurred (3) ambiguous
       (4) congenial (5) conducive   ....

KEY NO. 252

HYPER

over
above
excessive

is the Prefix *HYPER* meaning OVER, ABOVE, EXCESSIVE. The key to the use of this Prefix is best shown in the figure of speech—HYPERbole (No. 4), exaggeration. We are very quick to use *HYPER* the minute a person criticizes more than we like, is too easily irritated, or is too sensitive.

1. hyperacusia   HYPER acusia (hie per a kue′ zhi a) n.
   Abnormally acute hearing.

2. hyperalgesia   HYPER algesia (hie per al jee′ zi a) n.
   Excessive sensitivity to pain.

3. hyperaphia   HYPER aphia (hie per ay′ fi a) n.
   Abnormally sensitive sense of touch.

4. hyperbole   HYPER bole (hie per′ bo lee) n.
   A figure of speech; exaggeration.

5. hyperbolize   HYPER bolize (hie per′ bo lize) v.
   To state, speak, or write to a hyperbolic degree.

6. hypercritical   HYPER critical (hie per krit′ i kal) adj.
   Too demanding; finding too much to criticize.

7. hyperdiapason   HYPER diapason
   (hie per die a pay′ zon) n.
   An octave that is measured upward.

8. Hyperion   HYPER ion (hie per′ ee on) n.
   A Greek god, identified with Apollo, the ideal of manly character and beauty.

9. hyperdimensional HYPER dimensional
   (hie per di men′ shun al) adj.
   Relating to the space of more than three dimensions.

10. hyperirritability   HYPER irritability
    (hie pe rir it a bil′ it ee) n.
    Excessive irritability.

11. hyperkinesis   HYPER kinesis (hie per ki nee′ sis) n.
    Abnormal muscular movement.

12. hypermeter   HYPER meter (hie per′ met er) n.
    Verse which exceeds the common measure.

13. hyperodontogeny HYPER odontogeny
    (hie per o don toj′ e ni) n.
    An abnormal number of teeth.

14. hypernephroma   HYPER nephroma (hie per nef roe' ma) n.
                    A tumor of the kidneys.

15. hyperosmia   HYPER osmia (hie per oz' mi a) n.
                    Excessive acuteness of the sense of smell.

16. hyperostosis   HYPER ostosis (hie pe ros toe' sis) n.
                    Marked thickening of bony tissue.

17. hypersensitive HYPER sensitive (hie per sen' sit iv) adj.
                    Too sensitive.

18. hypervitaminosis HYPER vitaminosis
                    (hie per vite a mi noe' sis) n.
                    *Condition resulting from excessive use of
                    vitamins.*

19. hyperpnea   HYPER pnea (hie per nee' a) n.
                    Too rapid breathing.

word analysis

HYPERODONTOGENY—No. 13
    HYPERO (Hyper)—Prefix =beyond; excessive
    DONTO (dont)—Latin Root =tooth
    GEN (Gene)—Latin Root =develop; produce
    Y—Suffix =the result of the action

practical exercises

1. Supply the missing words:
        Paul Bunyan's tall tales make abundant use of ....
    In Shakespeare's *Hamlet* the murdered King is likened to
    .... and his brother to a satyr. People with
    asthma often suffer from ....

2. Analyze No. 12.

3. Recognize words and keys in the following lists:
    a. increased   k. architect
    b. radioactive   l. commissioned
    c. experience   m. reinforced
    d. content   n. accommodation
    e. pasturage   o. cooperative
    f. exposed   p. available
    g. equivalent   q. residence
    h. acceptable   r. commercial
    i. industry   s. motel
    j. transient   t. assessed

505

O⟶

TUI · TUIT · TUT

**guard
teach**

is the Root *TUT, TUIT, TUI,* which comes from the Latin *tueri, tuitus* which means to protect, to GUARD, and from that comes the meaning to TEACH. With the addition of the Prefix *IN* which, as you know, means NOT, a new concept comes into the word, INTUITion, learning without instruction. How wonderful it would be to get all knowledge by INTUI-Tion! If the multiplication tables were inTUITable? If . . . ?

1. tutor	TUTOR (tute′ or) n.
	One who teaches a pupil and supervises his progress.
2. tutoress	TUT oress (tute′ o res) n.
	A woman who teaches and supervises a pupil.
3. tutorly	TUT orly (tue′ tor li) adv.
	Relating to a tutor.
4. tutorage	TUT orage (tute′ o rij) n.
	Office of being a tutor.
5. tutorial	TUT orial (tue tore′ ee al) adj.
	Relating to a tutor; as, tutorial *duties.*
6. tutoriate	TUT oriate (tue toe′ ri at) n.
	A body of tutors; as, the tutoriate *of a college.*
7. tuition	TUI tion (tu ish′ un) n.
	Act of teaching; payment for instruction, as tuition *fees.*
8. intuit	in TUIT (in tue′ it) v.
	To know directly, by intuition.
9. tuitional	TUIT ional (tu ish′ un al) adj.
	Relating to teaching or to the payment for it.
10. intuition	in TUIT ion (in tu ish′ un) n.
	Knowledge obtained without instruction; insight.
11. intuent	in TU ent (in′ tue ent) adj.
	Knowing by intuition.
12. intuitable	in TUIT able (in tue′ it a b′l) adj.
	Able to be known without instruction.
13. intuicity	in TUI city (in tu is′ i ti) n.
	The quality of intuition.
14. intuitive	in TUIT ive (in tue′ it iv) adj.
	Having the quality of insight.

15. intuitively   in TUIT ively (in tue' it iv lee) adv.
>   *In the manner of intuition; as, we understood his fear intuitively.*

16. intuitionism in TUIT ionism (in tue ish' u niz um) n.
>   *The doctrine that basic truths are understood intuitively.*

17. intuitionist in TUIT ionist (in tue ish' u nist) n.
>   *One who believes in intuitionism.*

18. intuitivism in TUIT ivism (in tue' i tiv iz um) n.
>   *Intuitive power.*

word analysis

INTUITIONISM—No. 16
>   IN—Prefix = not
>   TUIT (tuitio)—Latin Root = to guard; to teach
>   TION—Suffix = act of
>   ISM—Suffix = doctrine

practical exercises

1. Supply the missing words:

    He had not only the wisdom but a nameless something more—let us call it .... The .... believes that moral and ethical values come to man .... and that man is .... and can receive them.

2. Analyze No. 9.

3. Give a synonym for each of the following words:
    a. exaggeration   ....
    b. curse   ....
    c. substitute   ....
    d. insight   ....
    e. powerless   ....

KEY NO. 254

○━╼

**TECHNI · TECHNY
TECHNIC**

skill
art

is the ROOT *TECHNI, TECHNY, TECHNIC,* meaning SKILL, ART. The words on the list give you some idea of the formidable vocabulary of the technicologist. Thanks to our key we can follow along with the words. A better acquaintance with technocracy itself is needed if you want to feel at home in a conversation with the experts. As mentioned in the sentence below, the arts are mechanical and the mechanics are artistic and artist and technician are impressively combined.

1. technical — TECHNIC al (tek′ ni kal) adj.
Relating to the mechanical arts.
2. technician — TECHNI cian (tek nish′ an) n.
One who is skilled in the mechanical arts.
3. technicalist — TECHNIC alist (tek′ ni kal ist) n.
One who is interested in technical matters.
4. technicality — TECHNIC ality (tek ni kal′ it ee) n.
A detail of skill and procedure.
5. technicist — TECHNIC ist (tek′ ni sist) n.
A technician.
6. technicon — TECHNIC on (tek′ nik on) n.
An exercising device for developing the hands.
7. technics — TECHNIC s (tek′ niks) n.
The science of mechanical skills and arts.
8. electrotechnics — electro TECHNIC s (e lek tro tek′ niks) n.
The science of electro-mechanical skills.
9. psychotechnics — psycho TECHNIC s (sie ko tek′ niks) n.
Psychology applicable to industry.
10. techniphone — TECHNI phone (tek′ ni fone) n.
A dummy keyboard for finger practice.
11. pyrotechnics — pyro TECHNIC s (py ro tek′ niks) n.
Display of fireworks.
12. technique — TECHNI que (tek neke′) n.
Expert method in executing technical details, especially in the arts.
13. technocracy — TECHN ocracy (tek nok′ ra see) n.
Management of a society by technical experts.

14. technocrat TECHN ocrat (tek' no krat) n.
An expert technician.

15. technology TECHN ology (tek nol' o jee) n.
Science of the industrial arts.

16. technonomy TECHN onomy (tek non' o mi) n.
The laws of the industrial arts.

17. technologist TECHN ologist (tek nol' o jist) n.
One versed in the science of the industrial arts.

18. hydrotechny hydro TECHNY (hie' dro tek ni) n.
One versed in the use of water in industry.

word analysis

TECHNICALITY—No. 4
  TECHNIC—Greek Root =skill
  AL—Suffix =relating to
  ITY—Suffix =quality of

practical exercises

1. Supply the missing words:
    The skills of the modern .... have been
raised to the level of art because of the delicacy and precision which modern .... demands in every
.... He is no longer a ...., but
an artist.

2. Analyze No. 18.

3. Add the keys which will complete the words expressed by
the phrases:
    a. cannot be measured— ....mense
    b. of the first— ....ary
    c. different from— di..........
    d. the service of a teacher— ....tion
    e. untaught knowledge— in..........
    f. coming forth of itself— spon..........
    g. set apart with understanding— ....cern

KEY NO. 255

ULTIMA

last

is the root *ULTIMA* which means LAST. It comes from the Latin *ultimus, ultimare* which means to come to the end. There are some very interesting Latin phrases in our list and it would be very nice to recognize them in your reading, in a law book, and, certainly, thrilling to use them in the right place. No. 16 is a very poetic conception of the end of the world, the end of all goals, the end of the end.

1. ultima   ULTIMA (ul' ti ma) adj.
        Last; final; most remote.

2. ultimacy   ULTIMA cy (ul' ti ma see) n.
        Quality of being last.

3. ultima ratio   ULTIMA ratio (ul ti ma rate' ee o) n.
        (Latin) The last and final argument.

4. ultimate   ULTIMA te (ul' ti mat) adj.
        Last; as, man's ultimate destiny.

5. ultimately   ULTIMA tely (ul' ti mat lee) adv.
        At the last.

6. ultimation   ULTIMA tion (ul ti may' shun) n.
        State of being ultimate, last.

7. ultimatum   ULTIMA tum (ul ti mate' um) n.
        The final offer that can be made.

8. ultimo   ULTIM o (ul' ti moe) adv.
        Last month; the month preceding the present.

9. ultimo geniture   ULTIM ogeniture (ul ti moe jen' i chur) n.
        A law by which the youngest son, the last born, inherits the estate.

10. ultimo genitary   ULTIM o genitary (ul ti moe jen' i tar i) adj.
        Relating to the last born.

11. penult   pen ULT (pee' nult) n.
        Next to the last syllable of a word.

12. penultimate   pen ULTIMA te (pe nul' ti mat) adj.
        Next to the last.

13. penultimatum   pen ULTIMA tum (pe nul ti may' tum) n.
        Nearly the final offer.

14. antepenult   antepen ULT (ant e pee' nult) n.
        The syllable before the last two.

15. antepenultimate antepen ULTIMA te
    (ant e pe nul' ti mat) adj.
    Relating to the antepenult.

16. Ultima Thule ULTIMA Thule (ul ti ma thue' lee) n.
    (Latin) *The last inhabitable place; a remote goal.*

word analysis

PENULTIMATE—No. 12
    PEN (paene)—Greek Root =almost
    ULTIMA (ultimus)—Latin Root =last
    ATE—Suffix =to make; cause

practical exercises

1. Supply the missing words:
    The law of ...., by which the last born child
    becomes the heir, is the direct opposite of ....,
    by which the first son becomes heir. In the word ul ti ma tum
    the accent is on the ....

2. Analyze No. 4.

3. Give a synonym for each of the following words:
    a. prorogate   ....
    b. adjoining   ....
    c. supererogatory   ....
    d. question   ....

KEY NO. 256

PNEUMON
PNEUMA

breath

is the Root *PNEUMON, PNEUMA* which come from the Greek *pnea*, sometimes spelled *pnoea* and *pnein*, and is concerned with BREATH which is air through the lungs. There is no life without BREATH.

1. pneumatic   PNEUMA tic (nue mat' ik) adj.
Pertaining to air, wind, or other gases.

2. pneumatics   PNEUMA tics (nue mat' iks) n.
That branch of physics which treats of air and other gases.

3. pneumatogram   PNEUMA togram (nue' ma to gram) n.
Tracing of respiratory movements.

4. pneumatometer   PNEUMA tometer (nue ma tom' et er) n.
An instrument for measuring the force exerted by the lungs in breathing.

5. pneumatoscope   PNEUMA toscope (nue ma' ta skope) n.
An instrument for finding abnormal matter in the mastoid.

6. pneumatosis   PNEUMA tosis (nue ma toe' sis) n.
An abnormal amount of gas or air in the body; flatulence.

7. pneumectomy   PNEUM ectomy (nue mek' to mee) n.
The removal of part of a lung.

8. pneumonia   PNEUMON ia (nue moe' nya) n.
A disease of the lungs.

9. pneumatology   PNEUMA tology (nue ma tol' o jee) n.
The study of pneumatics.

10. pneumoconiosis   PNEUMO coniosis (nue mo ko ni o' sis) n.
A disease of the lungs due to inhaling mineral dust.

word analysis

PNEUMOCONIOSIS—No. 10
     PNEUMO (pneumon)—Root =lung
     CONI (konis)—Root =dust
     OSIS—Suffix =disease

practical exercises

1. Supply the missing words:

   called .... It comes from inhaling dust. All diseases which affect breathing can be helped by ....

2. Analyze No. 1.

3. Choose the number of the word which best expresses the italicized word:

   a. *depression* (1) complication (2) discouragement
      (3) cheer (4) caution (5) plan   ....
   b. *distinguished* (1) frightened (2) forgotten
      (3) eminent (4) unnoticed (5) punished   ....
   c. *protracted* (1) copied (2) blamed (3) wanted
      (4) extended (5) ignored   ....
   d. *censure* (1) praise (2) applaud (3) derogate
      (4) report (5) fame   ....
   e. *solitude* (1) loneliness (2) company
      (3) sunstroke (4) bias (5) crowd   ....

KEY NO. 257

○━━►

SESQUI

one and a half

is the Prefix *SESQUI* which comes from the Latin *sesqui* which means ONE AND A HALF. It is not advisable to form the habit of *SESQUI*pedality, but it is good not to be afraid of *SESQUI*pedalian words. They are simple to analyze. In the next pages you will find a genuine *SESQUI*pedalian.

1. sesquialteral   SESQUI alteral (ses kwi al' ter al) adj.
   Having the ratio of 1½ to 1; 1½ times as great as the other.

2. sesquicentennial   SESQUI centennial
   (ses kwi sen ten' ee al) adj.
   Relating to a century and a half.

3. sesquiduplicate   SESQUI duplicate (ses kwi due' pli kat) adj.
   Having the ratio of 5 to 2.

4. sesquipedalia   SESQUI pedalia
   (ses kwi pe day' li a) n. pl.
   Very long words; (Humorous) Words a foot and a half long.

5. sesquipedalian   SESQUI pedalian (ses kwi pe dale' yen) adj.
   Said of a very long word.

6. sesquipedality   SESQUI pedality (ses kwi pe dal' i ti) n.
   The quality of a style which uses very long words.

7. sesquipedalianism   SESQUI pedalianism
   (ses kwi pe day' li an iz um) n.
   Sesquipedality.

8. sesquisulphide   SESQUI sulphide (ses kwi sul' fide) n.
   A sulphide containing 3 atoms of sulphur to 2 of the other ingredients.

word analysis

SESQUIPEDALIAN—No. 5
    SESQUI—Latin Root = one and a half
    PED—Root = foot
    AL—Suffix = relating to
    IAN—Suffix = belonging to

practical exercise

1. Supply the missing words:

Samuel Johnson, the great .... was much given to .... in speech and in writing.

KEY NO. 258

○━━ㄨ

SILIC

flint

is the Root *SILIC* which comes from the Latin *silex, silicis* meaning FLINT. Silica, silicam, silicon—all mean practically the same thing. To the chemist there are distinctions to be sure, but to the layman they all mean that flinty combination. No. 10 is the disease which is caused by breathing into the lungs air which contains dust particles from stone-cutting and mining. You have seen drilling in the streets. Dangerous work.

1. silicon   SILIC on (sil' i kon) n.
             A nonmetallic element found in the earth's crust.

2. silica   SILIC a (sil' i ka) n.
             Silicon dioxide.

3. silicam   SILIC am (sil' i kam) n.
             A compound of silicon.

4. silicate   SILIC ate (sil' i kate) v.
             To combine with silica.

5. siliceous SILIC eous (si lish' us) adj.
             Containing silica.

6. silicic   SILIC ic (si lis' ik) adj.
             Designating a compound of silica.

7. siliciferous SILIC iferous (sil i sif' e rus) adj.
             Producing, containing, or uniting with silica.

8. silicify   SILIC ify (si lis' i fie) v.
             To impregnate with silica.

9. silicification SILIC ification (si lis i fi kay' shun) n.
             The process of silicifying.

10. silicosis SILIC osis (sil i koe' sis) n.
             A disease prevalent among miners and stone cutters who breathe much dust.

word analysis

SILICOSIS—No. 10
    SILIC (silicis)—Root =flint
    OSIS—Suffix =disease

practical exercises

1. Supply the missing words:

   ...., ..., ... and
   .... are all .... compounds, in one
   proportion or another. All of them, when inhaled, are
   causes of ....

2. Analyze No. 7.

3. Indicate the pronunciation by placing the accent ('):

   pharmacology   arrogant
   pneumatomorphic   dynamogenesis
   plagiarist   dynast
   supererogatory   caloric
   civilize   fulminate

KEY NO. 259

O—🗝

CONI · KONI

dust

is *CONI, KONI* from the Greek word *konia, konis*, which means DUST. There are not so many words with this KEY, but the ones listed are important to know, related to your health.

1. coniosis

CONI osis (koe ni o' sis) n.
Disease which comes from inhaling dust particles.

2. pneumonoconiosis

pneumono CONI osis
(nue mo no koe ni o' sis) n.
A disease of the lungs caused by inhaling dust; as, Stone-cutters and miners are often subject to pneumonoconiosis.

3. koniscope

KONI scope (kon' i skope) n.
An instrument for estimating the dust in the atmosphere.

4. konimeter

KONI meter (koe' ni mee ter) n.
A device for estimating the dust content of the air.

5. koniology

KONI ology (koe ni ol' o ji) n.
The science of atmospheric and floating germs.

6. conium

CONI um (koe nie' um) n.
A genus of poisonous herbs, as poison hemlock.

7. coniophora

CONI ophora (koe ni of' o ra) n.
A genus of fungus which causes dry rot in the timber of buildings.

8. coniothyrium

CONI othyrium (koe ni o thir' i um) n.
The cause of white rot in grapes.

9. otoconia

oto CONI a (a to' ko neea) n.
Ear dust.

word analysis

KONISCOPE—No. 3
    KONI (konis)—Greek Root =dust
    SCOPE (scopus)—Latin Root =watch

practical exercise

1. Supply the missing words:

Stone-cutters and miners often suffer from ....

A .... estimates the amount of dust in the air.

.... will help to eliminate ....

SELF TEST

In the very beginning of this book I promised to give you the longest word in the English language. According to the new third edition of Webster's International Unabridged Dictionary, this is it:

PNEUMONOULTRAMICROSCOPICSILICOVOLCANO-
CONIOSIS

You will not gasp at the length. You will not count letters. In this book we count KEYS, not letters. In this sesquipedalian word there are nine KEYS. If you remember your KEYS you will have no trouble with the word.

Break the word up into KEYS as we always do in Word
  Analysis.
List your KEYS, one under the other.
Give the meaning of each KEY.
Do not look at the answer page until you have finished the
  test.
Rate yourself 10% for each KEY remembered.
Rate yourself 10% extra for knowing the meaning of the word.

ANSWER TO SELF TEST

pneumonoultramicroscopicsilicovolcanoconiosis

WORD ANALYSIS

1. PNEUMONO (pneumon)—Root =lung; breathe
2. ULTRA—Prefix =beyond; exceeding
3. MICRO (mikros)—Root=minute; small by comparison
4. SCOP (scopos)—Root =watch; see
5. IC—Suffix =like; nature of
6. SILICO (silicis)—Root =flint
7. VOLCANO (volcan, vulcan)—Root =volcano
8. CONI (konis)—Root =dust
9. OSIS—Suffix =disease

The first brief interpretation is:

A lung(1) disease(9) caused by inhaling dust(8).

A complete interpretation is:

A lung(1) disease(9) caused by inhaling dust(8) like(5) silicon(6) and volcanic(7) ash particles so exceedingly(2) minute(3) as to be seen(4) only with a microscope.

A second complete interpretation would be:

A lung(1) disease(9) caused by inhaling dust(8) like(5) silicon(6) and volcanic(7) ash particles so minute(3) that in order to see(4) them a microscope which exceeds(2) the ordinary is needed.

ANSWER TO THE PRACTICAL EXERCISES

KEY NO. 1

1. arty—wary—dirty
2. CRAFTY: CRAFT—Root = cunning; Y—Suffix = inclined to
3. a. slinky b. faulty c. catty d. rosy

KEY NO. 2

1. wrecker—tractor—doctor—sufferer
2. PAINTER: PAINT—Root = apply paint; ER—Suffix = one who
3. a. 4 b. 5 c. 4

KEY NO. 3

1. rejoin—return
2. RECALL: RE—Prefix = again, back; CALL—Root = summon
3. pret*ty*   scan*ty*   *re*pay
   danc*er*   peculi*ar*   *re*side
   tract*or*   mov*er*   me*ter*

KEY NO. 4

1. unspoken—unread—uneducated
2. UNWELCOME: UN—Prefix = not; WELCOME—Root = welcome
3. a. 2 b. 4 c. 1 d. 3

KEY NO. 5

1. sleepless—weightless
2. ARTLESS: ART—Root = art; LESS—Suffix = without
3. tire' less   re write'   weight' less
   un hur' ried   voice' less   ex hib' it or
   use' less   un touch' able   hair' y

KEY NO. *6*

1. fearlessly—breathlessly—noiselessly
2. VOICELESSLY: VOICE—Root =voice; LESS—Suffix = without; LY—Suffix =manner of
3. a. faultless b. graceless c. hopeless d. noiseless

KEY NO. *7*

1. weightlessness—hopelessness
2. CARELESSNESS: CARE—Root =care; LESS—Suffix = without; NESS—Suffix =state of
3. a. helplessness b. hopelessness c. lifelessness d. joylessness
   e. carelessness

KEY NO. *8*

1. tactful—grateful—careful
2. PITIFUL: PITI (pietas)—Latin Root =pity; FUL— Suffix =full of
3. a. 2 b. 4 c. 3

KEY NO. *9*

1. Cuban—Australians
2. AMERICAN: AMERICA (Americus)—Latin Root = America; AN—Suffix =native of
3. a. dutiFUL b. sleepY c. blindNESS d. daintiLY
   e. merciLESS

KEY NO. *10*

1. reliable—capable—forcible—acceptable
2. BEARABLE: BEAR—Root =endure; ABLE—Suffix = can do
3. a. accept*able* b. hope*lessness* c. tact*fully* d. beauti*fully*
   e. *un*re*mark*able f. *un*accept*able*

KEY NO. *11*

1. transportation—Transit—transfer
2. TRANSFER: TRANS—Prefix =across; FER (ferre)— Latin Root =bear; carry
3. a. 5 b. 1 c. 3 d. 2

KEY NO. 12

1. reporter—supported—support
2. REPORTER: RE—Prefix =back, again; PORT (portare)—
   Latin Root =carry; ER—Suffix =one who
3. a. 8 b. 6 c. 4 d. 2 e. 7 f. 5 g. 3 h. 1

KEY NO. 13

1. implacable—immaturity
2. IMMORAL: IM—Prefix =not; MORAL—Root =moral
3. in a bil' i ty   in ar tic' u late   im ma ture'
   in ad' e quate   in ac ces' si ble   im mor' tal
   im pla' ca ble   im per' fect   im mod' er ate

KEY NO. 14

1. environment—embarked
2. ENDANGER: EN—Prefix =into; DANGER—Root =
   danger
3. a. encourage b. embrace c. employ d. implacable
   e. inarticulate

KEY NO. 15

1. aggressive—affianced—advance
2. ADHERE: AD—Prefix =to; HERE (haerere)—Latin
   Root =stick
3. a. 4 b. 3 c. 4

KEY NO. 16

1. irrevocable—irreparable—irreproachable—irresistible
2. ILLEGAL: IL—Prefix =not; LEGAL (legis)—Latin Root =
   legal
3. il leg' i ble   il lit' er ate   ir rev' er ent
   il le' gal   ir re spon' si ble   ir res' o lute
   il lu' sion   ir ra' tion al   ir rev' o ca ble

KEY NO. 17

1. dynamite—stalactites—stalagmites
2. ISRAELITE: ISRAEL—Root =Israel; ITE—Suffix =
   native of
3. a. plebiscite b. favorite c. illogical d. impatient e. adjacent

525

KEY NO. *18*

1. optional—moral—spiritual
2. SPIRITUAL: SPIRIT—Root =spirit; AL—Suffix = relating to
3. a. 8 b. 5 c. 6 d. 2 e. 1 f. 3 g. 4 h. 7

KEY NO. *19*

1. dilemma—diphthong
2. PORTER: PORT—Latin Root =carry; ER—Suffix = one who
3. a. 3 b. 2 c. 4 d. 2 e. 5

KEY NO. *20*

1. coniferous—interference—preference
2. TRANSFER: TRANS—Prefix =across; FER—Root = bear; carry
3. a. conference b. preference c. dilemma
   d. deportment e. transact

KEY NO. *21*

1. oaken—whiten—brighten—heighten
2. LIGHTEN: LIGHT—Root =easy, not heavy; EN—Suffix =make
3. a. toughen b. euphony c. adjacent d. announce
   e. irreclaimable

KEY NO. *22*

1. immigrant—imbued—important
2. IMPLANT: IM (in)—Prefix =into; PLANT—Root = plant
3. 1. AD (at)—to 2. IM (in)—not 3. Same as 2 4. DI—two 5. UN—not 6. ER—that which 7. LY—adverbial 8. TRANS—across 9. FER—bear

KEY NO. *23*

1. Expectations—excellence
2. EXCLAIM: EX—prefix =out; CLAIM (clamare)—Root =cry out
3. a. transplant b. agreeable c. unendurable
   c. unapproachable e. dilemma

526

KEY NO. 24

1. eccentric—effusive—effect
2. EXPRESS: EX—Prefix =out; PRESS—Root =press
3. a. *as*sure b. *ap*proach c. *ar*range d. *at*tract
   e. *an*nounce

KEY NO. 25

1. reflection—limitation—expulsion
2. ENSLAVE: EN—Prefix =into; SLAVE—Root =slavery
3. vit ri fi ca′ tion   ver si fi ca′ tion   ver i fi ca′ tion
   sus pen′ sion   pur i fi ca′ tion   cel e bra′ tion

KEY NO. 26

1. nativism—naturalized
2. NATIONAL: NATION (natio)—Latin Root =nation;
   AL—Suffix =relating to
3. a. innate b. naïveté c. nationality d. natural(ist)
   e. national

KEY NO. 27

1. strategic—patriotic—heroic
2. POETIC: POET—Root =poet; IC—Suffix =nature of
3. a. poetically b. heroically c. drastically d. patriotically
   e. tragically f. emphatically

KEY NO. 28

1. audition—audible—auditorium
2. INAUDIBLE: IN—Prefix =not; AUD (audire)—Latin
   Root =to hear; IBLE—Suffix =able
3. a. 5 b. 2 c. 5 d. 4

KEY NO. 29

1. visile—visualize—provide(r)—provisions
2. VISION: VIS (visus)—Latin Root =see; SION—Suffix =
   act of; state of
3. aus cul ta′ tion   stra te′ gi cal ly   prac′ ti cal ly
   au di to′ ri um   pa thet′ i cal ly   vis′ it ant
   dras′ ti cal ly   tel′ e vi sion

527

KEY NO. 30

1. forage—outrageous—adage
2. COURAGE: COUR—Root =heart, spirit; AGE—
   Suffix =state of
3. a. 6 b. 3 c. 1 d. 5 e. 4 f. 2

KEY NO. 31

1. disapproved—disinherited—disloyal—distrust—
   discredit(ed)
2. DISBAR: DIS—Prefix =away, from; BAR—Root =bar
3. a. *disreputable* b. *dis*credited c. *dis*inheriting
   d. *dis*dain*ful*

KEY NO. 32

1. appointment—achievement—resentment—excitement—
   statement
2. DISGRACEFUL: DIS—Prefix =away; GRACE—
   Root =grace; FUL—Suffix =full of
3. a. nourishment b. achievement c. postponement
   d. compliment e. disreputable

KEY NO. 33

1. facility—facile—facetious
2. FACTOR: FACT (facere)—Latin Root =make; OR—
   Suffix =one who
3. a. 4 b. 3 c. 4 d. 1 e. 2

KEY NO. 34

1. beneficiary—defective
2. MAGNIFICENT: MAGN—Latin Root =great; FIC
   (facere)—Latin Root =to make; ENT—Suffix =one who,
   that which
3. a cid i fi ca' tion   cer tif' i cate   ef' fi ca cy
   bene fic' i ar y   ef fec' tu al   dis in fect'

KEY NO. 35

1. non compos mentis—nonpartisan
2. NONSENSE: NON—Prefix =not; SENSE—Root =sense
3. a. 4 b. 4 c. 1 d. 2

KEY NO. 36

1. dietary—bribery—memory
2. FACTORY: FACT (facere)—Latin Root = a thing made;
   ORY—Suffix = place where
3. a. repertory b. depository c. dormitory d. certificate
   e. deficiency

KEY NO. 37

1. dedicate—consecrate—dedicate(d)—infiltrate
2. LIQUIDATE: LIQUID—Root = liquid; ATE—Suffix =
   make, cause
3. a. 8 b. 1 c. 7 d. 5 e. 3 f. 4 g. 6 h. 2

KEY NO. 38

1. Liberty—Fraternity—Equality—absurdity
2. ACIDITY: ACID (acidus)—Latin Root = sour; ITY—
   Suffix = state, quality
3. chas' ti ty   de bil' i ty   lu mi nos' i ty
   e ter' ni ty   a cu' i ty   a cer' bi ty
   am bi gu' i ty   gar ru' li ty   au thor' i ty

KEY NO. 39

1. oblivious—obsequious—spacious—gracious
2. NERVOUS: NERV—Root = nerve; OUS—Suffix = full of
3. a. mysterious b. vivacious c. approbrious d. spacious
   e. malicious

KEY NO. 40

1. abdicate—absolve—abscond
2. ABNORMAL: AB—Prefix = away; NORM—Root = the
   usual, the average; AL—Suffix = relating to
3. a. rapacity b. luminosity c. acuity d. clarity
   e. dignity

KEY NO. 41

1. citizenship—dictatorship—authorship—craftsmanship—
   scholarship
2. LADYSHIP: LADY—Root = lady; SHIP—Suffix = rank
3. a. 4 b. 3 c. 2 d. 5 e. 3

KEY NO. 42

1. vigilance—assailant—defiance—attendance
2. RESISTANCE: RE—Prefix =against; SIST (sistere)—
   Latin Root =take a stand; ANCE—Suffix =state of
3. a. 10 b. 6 c. 1 d. 9 e. 2 f. 7 g. 3 h. 4 i. 5 j. 8

KEY NO. 43

1. competence—fluency—difference—deficiency—conference
2. FLUENCY: FLU (fluere)—Latin Root =flow; ENCY—
   Suffix =quality
3. a. complacency b. influence c. politically
   d. proficiency e. efficiency or competence

KEY NO. 44

1. Courtship—encouraged
2. CORDIALITY: CORD—Root =heart; AL—Suffix =
   relating to; ITY—Suffix =quality
3. a. EXistence b. EFfluent c. ECcentric d. EFfect
   e. Eclipse f. EXcellent g. EXit h. EXplain
   i. EXamine j. Education k. Emanate l. EXaggerate
   m. Enervate

KEY NO. 45

1. bestride—beguiled—behooves
2. BESMIRCH: BE—Prefix =intensity; SMIRCH—Root =
   make dirty
3. a. 5 b. 5 c. 2 d. 4 e. 1

KEY NO. 46

1. liberalize(d)—scrutinize(d)
2. SLENDERIZE: SLENDER—Root =slim; IZE—Suffix =
   make
3. a. penalize b. ostracize c. pauperize or impoverish
   d. emphasize e. scrutinize

KEY NO. 47

1. correlated—cooperation—Congress
2. CONGRESS: CON—Prefix =together; GRESS
   (gressus, to step)—Root =walk
3. a. CONnection   f. CORrelate
   b. COMmand   g. CORrect
   c. COMplaint   h. COMpound
   d. COOperate   i. COMpany
   e. COLlect   j. COLlide

530

KEY NO. 48

1. Proclamation—progressive—producer—provide—
   production
2. PRODUCE: PRO—Prefix =forward;—DUCE (ducere)—
   Latin Root =lead
3. a. progress b. promotion c. procedure d. professor
   e. proclaim

KEY NO. 49

1. anniversary—centennial anniversary—
   sesquicentennial
2. ANNUALLY: ANNU (annus)—Latin Root =year; AL—
   Prefix =relating; LY—Suffix =manner of
3. a. 2 b. 1 c. 2 d. 3

KEY NO. 50

This is a self-test.

KEY NO. 51

1. Brigade—myriad(s)—serenade
2. LEMONADE: LEMON—Root =lemon; ADE—Suffix =
   result of action
3. a. decade b. hebdomad c. monad d. serenade

KEY NO. 52

1. proclaim—proclamation—proclamatory—exclamatory—
   exclamation
2. EXCLAIM: EX—Prefix =out; CLAIM (clamare)—
   Latin Root =cry out
3. a. 4 b. 1 c. 7 d. 9 e. 2 f. 3 g. 5 h. 6 i. 8

KEY NO. 53

1. decay—delude
2. DEFORM: DE—Prefix =away, from; FORM—Root =
   form
3. de pend' ent   trans por ta' tion   de prive'
   dec' a dence   de lu' sion   de ri' sion
   de form'   re for' ma to ry

531

KEY NO. 54

1. immemorial—memory—Memoriam—memory
2. MEMORABLE: MEM (meminisse)—Latin Root =
   to remember; OR—Suffix =one who, that which; ABLE—
   Suffix =can do
3. *UN*told; *UN*sold   UN— not
   *RE*gard; *RE*member; *RE*late;   RE— back; again
   *RE*tard
   re*MEM*ber; com*MEM*orate;   MEM— remember
   *MEM*orial
   rememb*ER*   ER— one who; that which
   craft*Y*; war*Y*; lump*Y*   Y— inclined to
   memori*AL*   AL— relating to
   *DE*prive; *DE*rision; *DE*spair;   DE— away; from
   *DE*sperate; *DE*lude
   *CON*nection; *COM*memorate;   COM— with
   *COM*mit
   *IM*memorial   IM— not
   suf*FER*   FER— bear

KEY NO. 55

1. contentment—continually—untenanted
2. UNTENABLE: UN—Prefix =not; TEN (teneo)—
   Latin Root =hold; ABLE—Suffix =can do
3. a. 3 b. 5 c. 4 d. 1 e. 2

KEY NO. 56

1. conclusively—exclusive
2. EXCLUDE: EX—Prefix =out; CLUDE (claudere)—
   Latin Root =to shut
3. a. TINU b. IN c. CLUS d. DE e. MEM f. TINU
   g. CLUS h. FER

KEY NO. 57

This is a self-test.

KEY NO. 58

1. vicissitude(s)—solicitude—gratitude
2. SERVITUDE: SERV (servus)—Latin Root =serve;
   TUDE—Suffix =condition of
3. dis con cert' ed   re cov' er   in vin' ci ble
   at' ti tude   tri' umph   bat' ter ing
   rec' ti tude   ver i si mil' i tude so lic' i tude
   vi cis' si tude   tur' pi tude   ser' vi tude

KEY NO. 59

1. bifocal—bipartisan—bilabial
2. BIENNIAL: BI—Prefix =two; ENNI (annus)—
   Latin Root =year; AL—Suffix =relating to
3. a. 3 b. 1 c. 6 d. 8 e. 10 f. 2 g. 5 h. 9 i. 7
   j. 4

KEY NO. 60

1. convince—victor—vanquish(ed)
2. EVICT: E (ex)—Prefix =out; VICT (victus)—
   Latin Root =conquer
3. a. 2 b. 5 c. 4 d. 1 e. 4

KEY NO. 61

1. dentigerous—dentifrice—denticate—dentin
2. DENTAL: DENT—Root =tooth; AL—Suffix =
   relating to
3. a. DENT b. DENT c. DENT d. DENT e. VICT
   f. VINC IBLE g. VINCIBIL h. CONCERT

KEY NO. 62

This is a self-test.

KEY NO. 63

1. anecdote—anomaly—anemic
2. ANONYMITY: AN—Prefix =not; NYM—Root =name;
   ITY—Suffix =state of; quality of
3. a. ILlegal b. IRrational c. IMperfect
   d. ANesthetic e. UNseen f. NONsense g. INadequate
   h. ANemia i. UNreasonable j. IRregular

KEY NO. 64

1. manuscript—emancipation
2. MANUAL: MANU (manu)—Latin Root =hand; AL—
   Suffix =relating to
3. a. animality b. criminality c. mentality d. fatality
   e. abnormality f. totality

KEY NO. 65

1. credit—creditable—incredibly—credulous—credulously
2. CREDITOR: CRED (credere)—Latin Root =to believe;
   IT (itus)—Latin Root =goes; OR—Suffix =one who
3. a. 4 b. 1 c. 5 d. 4 e. 4

KEY NO. 66

1. antipodes—antipathy—antitoxin
2. ANTIBODY: ANTI—Prefix =against; BODY—
   Root=body
3.

clam' or	ad' mi ra ble	fac' ile
bi en' ni al	in ter' po late	an tip' o des
an tiq' ui ty	an ti tox' in	al' ka line
dis cred' it a ble	in cred i bil' i ty	cer' ti tude

KEY NO. 67

1. unison—union—universal
2. UNIMANUAL: UNI (unis)—Latin Root =one; MANU—
   Latin Root =hand; AL—Suffix =relating to

KEY NO. 68

1. confidence—perfidy—confidential
2. CONFIDE: CON—Prefix =with; FIDE (fidere)—
   Latin Root =trust
3. a. 2 b. 4 c. 1 d. 4 e. 5 f. 4

KEY NO. 69

1. cooperation—operator
2. OPERATE: OPER (opus)—Latin Root =work; ATE—
   Suffix =make, cause
3. a. credulous b. confidential c. anecdote d. operettist
   e. dun f. guinea g. accident h. manufacture i. debt
   j. confidence

KEY NO. 70

1. expletive
2. ADOPTIVE: ADOPT—Root =adopt; IVE—Suffix =cause
3. a. 10 b. 1 c. 9 d. 3 e. 6 f. 8 g. 4 h. 7 i. 5
   j. 2

KEY NO. 71

1. princeling(s)—underling(s)
2. ANIMALCULE: ANIMAL—Root =animal; CULE—
   Suffix =very small, tiny
3.

in duct'	dis course' (verb)	dis' course (noun)
an ti knock'	re cede'	dis solve'
re place'	an' ti quat ed	rem i nisce'
an i mal' cule	fledg' ling	mol' e cule

534

KEY NO. 72

1. exposure—pressure—tenure—signature
2. PROCEDURE: PRO—Prefix =forward; CEDE (cedere)—Latin Root =to go; URE—Suffix =state of

KEY NO. 73

1. affixed—fixity—transfixed
2. FIXITY: FIX (figere)—Latin Root =fix; ITY—Suffix = quality
3. a. recreational—recreationally
   b. sensational—sensationally
   c. educational—educationally
   d. emotional—emotionally
   e. promotional—promotionally
   f. functional—functionally
   g. optional—optionally

KEY NO. 74

1. amateurish—waspish—flourish
2. FOOLISH: FOOL—Root =fool; ISH—Suffix =nature of
3. a. antipodes b. antagonism c. molecule d. distinctive
   e. cooperate f. confidante g. unanimous

KEY NO. 75

1. incognito—recognizable
2. COGNIZE: COGN (cognoscere)—Latin Root =know; IZE—Suffix =make
3. a. RE b. IN c. ING d. AF—ER e. OR f. ABLE

KEY NO. 76

1. reckoning—director—directive—direction
2. RECTIFY: RECTI—Root =right; FY—Suffix =make
3. a. 4 b. 1 c. 4 d. 5 e. 4 f. 3

KEY NO. 77

1. biologist—biographer—biostatics—biostatistics—biology
2. BIOLOGY: BIO (bios)—Greek Root =life; LOGY (logos)—Greek Suffix =study of

KEY NO. 78

1. expelled—propel(led)
2. COMPEL: COM—Prefix =with, together; PEL (pellere)—
   Latin Root =to push
3. a. impulse b. rectificator c. prognosis d. biographee
   e. primogeniture

KEY NO. 79

1. response—sponsor—responsibility
2. RESPOND: RE—Prefix =again; SPOND (spondere)—
   Latin Root =answer
3. a. 5 b. 5 c. 4 d. 3 e. 4 f. 1

KEY NO. 80

1. intercede—precedent
2. PRECEDE: PRE—Prefix =before; CEDE (cedere)—
   Latin Root =to go
3. in dif' fer ent ly   prec' e dent (noun)
   dis fig u ra' tion   con' flict (noun)
   sin cere'   mix' ture
   bach' e lor   pre par' a to ry
   re gret'   spon ta ne' i ty

KEY NO. 81

1. polyglot (n.)—polyglot (adj.)
2. POLYARCHY: POLY—Prefix =many; ARCH (archos)—
   Greek Root =rule; Y—Suffix =tending to
3. a. *poly*dontia b. *poly*ethnic c. pro*cede*ure d. *expul*sion
   e. re*gret* f. corre*spond*ence

KEY NO. 82

This is a self-test.

KEY NO. 83

1. perennial—perforate(d)
2. PERCEIVE: PER—Prefix =through; CEIVE (cept)—
   Latin Root =take
3. a. 4 b. 6 c. 1 d. 7 e. 2 f. 8 g. 3 h. 5

KEY NO. 84

1. accusation—causeless—inexcusable—excusator—excuse
2. ACCUSER: AC (ad)—Prefix =to, toward; CUS (cause)—
   Latin Root =motive; ER—Suffix =one who
3. a. accusatory b. inexcusable c. peradventure
   d. peremptory e. apocryphal f. polygon
   g. confidently h. antiquity

KEY NO. 85

1. humanities—inhumanity
2. HUMANITY: HUMAN (humanus)—Latin Root =man;
   ITY—Suffix =quality
3. a. 4 b. 5 c. 1 d. 3 e. 4

KEY NO. 86

1. motions—motorcade
2. DEMOTE: DE—Prefix =down, away; MOTE (movere)—
   Latin Root =to move
3. a.d.g. all mean 3–6–9 b.c.f. all mean 1–4–10
   i.j. mean 2–8 e. 5 h. 7

KEY NO. 87

1. prejudice—prevent—precaution
2. PRECEDE: PRE—Prefix =before; CEDE (cedere)—
   Latin Root =to go

KEY NO. 88

1. miscarriage—miscast
2. MISCAST: MIS—Root =wrong, bad; CAST—Root =
   chosen
3. a. misanthrope b. misogynist c. misopedia
   d. humiliation e. automobile f. preview g. precaution

KEY NO. 89

1. license—licensee—licensor—license—licensor—licensee
2. ILLICIT: IL (in)—Prefix =not; LICIT (licere)—
   Latin Root =to permit
3. li' cense   pred' e ces sor
   li cen' tious   pre cede'
   mis' an thrope   hu mil' i at ing
   mi sog' y nist   hum' ble
   pre em' i nence   mo bi li za' tion

537

KEY NO. 90

1. capitulate—decapitate(d)
2. CAPITALIZE: CAPIT (caput)—Latin Root =head;
   AL—Suffix =relating to; IZE—Suffix =make
3. a. 5 b. 2 c. 4 d. 1 e. 4

KEY NO. 91

1. stamina—circumstance—standard—resist—obstacle(s)
2. PERSIST: PER—Prefix =through; SIST (sistere)—
   Latin Root =stand
3. a. 5 b. 6 c. 10 d. 7 e. 2 f. 3 g. 8 h. 9 i. 4
   j. 1

KEY NO. 92

1. reduce—production
2. SEDUCE: SE—Prefix =apart, astray; DUCE (ducere)—
   Latin Root =to lead

KEY NO. 93

1. omnipotent—omnivorous
2. OMNIBUS: OMNIBUS (dative plural of omnis)—
   Latin Root =all
3. a. omnibus b. omniscient c. omnipotent
   d. omnimeter e. omnivorous f. omnigenous
   g. aqueduct h. traduce i. stamina

KEY NO. 94

1. fortitude—forçat
2. ENFORCE: EN—Prefix =into; FORCE (fortis)—
   Latin Root =strength
3. a. urb*anity* b. virtuos*ity* c. veloc*ity* d. verbos*ity*
   e. prolix*ity*

KEY NO. 95

1. chronology—chronologist
2. CHRONOLOGIZE: CHRONO (chronos)—Greek Root =
   time; LOG (logos)—Greek Root =word; IZE—Suffix =
   make
3. a. chronicle b. fortitude c. omnivorous d. chronologize
   e. stamina f. recapitulate g. licentiousness
   h. misunderstand

KEY NO. 96

1. reflection—flexor—inflection
2. DEFLECT: DE—Prefix =away, from; FLECT (flectere)—Latin Root =to bend
3. a. genuflection b. chronologically c. anomaly
   d. misanthrope e. abolish f. reduction g. trifling

KEY NO. 97

1. meter(s)—seismometer
2. CHRONOMETER: CHRONO (chronos)—Greek Root = time; METER—Root =measure
3. a. reflection b. fortitude c. chronometer
   d. inexcusable e. resistance f. omniscient g. reductions
   h. decapitation

KEY NO. 98

1. peripatetic—perigee
2. PERIHELION: PERI—Prefix =around; HELION— Root =sun
3. a. 1 b. 1 c. 4 d. 2 e. 3

KEY NO. 99

1. supreme—supremacy—superimposes—insuperable— supercilious
2. SUPERABLE: SUPER—Prefix =over, beyond; ABLE— Suffix =can do
3. a. 8 b. 6 c. 2 d. 1 e. 7 f. 3 g. 4 h. 5

KEY NO. 100

1. parody—paralysis—parabiosis
2. Parallel: PARA—Latin Root =side by side; LLEL (allos) —Greek Root =other
3. a. 5, paralysis b. 3, parallel c. 2, periodically
   d. 6, supremacy e. 4, thermometer f. 1, superlative

KEY NO. 101

1. gradually—graduation—progress—ingredients
2. EGRESS: E (ex)—Prefix =out; GRESS (gressus)— Latin Root =walk
3. ag gres' sive   prog' ress   gra di om' e ter
   pa ral' y sis   in cre du' li ty pe' ri od
   au thor' i ties   in sist' ed   su per' la tive
   com par' i son   crys' tal   pre serves'
   om' ni bus   om nis' cient   om nip' o tent

KEY NO. 102

This is a self-test.

KEY NO. 103

1. patrician—physician
2. BEAUTICIAN: BEAUTI—ROOT =beauty; CIAN—Suffix =one who has skill
3. a. beautician b. electrician c. statistician d. logician
   e. optician f. technician g. musician h. dietitian

KEY NO. 104

1. innumerability—supernumerary—numberless
2. SUPERNUMERARY: SUPER—Prefix =beyond, above; NUMER—Root =number; ARY—Suffix =that which
3. a. numerably b. numerologically c. numerously
   d. numerically e. numeratively f. innumerably
   g. supernumerarily h. numberlessly

KEY NO. 105

1. Extraction—contractual—abstract(ed)
2. ABSTRACT: ABS (ab)—Prefix =away; TRACT (trahere)—Latin Root =to draw
3. a. dis*tract*ion b. re*tract*—accu*sation c. ex*tract*ion
   d. *de*tract e. *sub*tractions

KEY NO. 106

1. suspended—independence—appendage
2. PENDANT: PEND (pendere)—Latin Root =to hang; ANT—Suffix =that which
3. a. 2 b. 3 c. 3 d. 3 e. 5

KEY NO. 107

1. Astronomy—astrology—astronaut—astrophysics
2. ASTROMETER: ASTRO (astron) Greek Root =star; METER—Root =measure

KEY NO. 108

1. monarchists—accompanist—violinist—pianist
2. DENTIST: DENT (dentis)—Latin Root =tooth; IST—Suffix =one who
3. a. artistic b. artistically c. humanist—humanistic—humanistically d. legalistically e. terroristic

540

KEY NO. *109*

1. automotive—Autocrat—autograph
2. AUTARCH: AUT (auto)—Prefix =self; ARCH (archos)
   Greek Root =ruler
3. a. automation b. autoinfection or autointoxication
   c. automaton d. omnivorous e. autonomy

KEY NO. *110*

1. prehensile—juvenile—agile—fragile
2. FERTILE: FER (ferre)—Latin Root =to bear, yield; ILE
   —Suffix =suitable for
3. a. volatile b. infantile c. juvenile d. sterile e. fragile
   f. imbecile g. puerile

KEY NO. *111*

1. posture—deponent('s)—positive—exposure(s)
2. EXPOSE: EX—Prefix =out; POSE (positus)—Latin
   Root =place
3. a. 2 b. 3 c. 4 d. 5 e. 5

KEY NO. *112*

1. mission—transmitted—intermission
2. REMIT: RE—Prefix =back, again; MIT (mittere)—Latin
   Root =to send
3. a. re*miss* b. *dismiss*al c. *emiss*ary d. trans*miss*ible
   e. *commit*ment

KEY NO. *113*

1. popularity—popularist—populace
2. POPULOUS: POPUL (populi)—Latin Root =people;
   OUS—Suffix =having, full of
3. a. 6 b. 4 c. 7 d. 5 e. 1 f. 3 g. 2

KEY NO. *114*

1. legacy—legatee—legislative—illegal
2. ILLEGAL: IL (in)—Prefix =not; LEG (lex)—Latin
   Root =law; AL—Suffix =relating to
3. a. illegal b. legitimate c. legacy d. legislature
   e. legalize f. depopulate

1. heliotrope(s)—heliophilous—heliofugal
2. HELIOPHOBIC: HELIO (helios)—Greek Root =sun; PHOB (phobia)—Greek Root =fear; IC—Suffix =nature of, like
3. as' tro naut   ran' dom   su per nu' mer ar y
   as tro nau' tics   py ro tech ni' cian   sub' tra hend
   as' ter oid   in nu' mer a ble   per pen dic' u lar
                       pre hen' sile

1. ambles—ambition—ambiguously
2. AMBIENT: AMBI—Root =moving around; ENT—Suffix =that which
3. a. *unin*spired b. *unin*vited c. *unin*tentional
   d. *unin*telligent e. *unin*formed f. *unim*portant
   g. *unin*quiring

1. ridiculously—derided
2. RIDICULE: RIDI—Root =laugh; CULE—Suffix =very small
3. a. 5 b. 6 c. 7 d. 3 e. 1 f. 4 g. 2

1. evoked—provocation—invoke(d)
2. INVOKE: IN—Prefix =into; VOKE (vocare)—Latin Root =call
3. a. 5 b. 4 c. 5 d. 1 e. 4

This is a self-test.

1. calligraphy—orthography—holograph
2. HOMOGRAPH: HOMO—Root =same; GRAPH (graphein)—Greek Root =write
3. cal lig' ra phy   graph o ma' ni a   lex i cog' ra pher
   mon' o graph   te leg' ra phy   hom' o graph
   in qui si' tion   rid' i cule   pop' u lace
                        or thog' ra phy

KEY NO. 121

1. precise—precision—excision—decidedly
2. DECIDE: DE—Prefix =away, from; CIDE (caedere)—
   Latin Root =to cut
3. a. 9 b. 7 c. 6 d. 3 e. 4 f. 8 g. 2 h. 5 i. 1

KEY NO. 122

1. contested—testimony—attest(ed)—testament
2. TESTIFY: TESTI (testare)—Latin Root =a witness; FY
   —Suffix =make
3. a. *inadvisably* b. *inaccessibly* c. *inapproachably*
   d. *inadvertently* e. *inattentively*

KEY NO. 123

1. unintentionally—intensive
2. DISTEND: DIS—Prefix =away; TEND (tendo)—
   Latin Root =stretch
3. a. 1 b. 4 c. 3 d. 3 e. 4

KEY NO. 124

1. submission—subversive—subpoena
2. SUBMISSION: SUB—Prefix =under; MISS (missus)—
   Latin Root =sent; SION—Suffix =state of, act of
3. a. *sub*cutane*ous* b. *sub*merge c. *sub*ject d. *sub*poena
   e. subs*titute* f. *sub*versive

KEY NO. 125

This is a self-test.

KEY NO. 126

1. posthumously—postmortal—postlude
2. POSTNATAL: POST—Prefix =after; NAT (natus)—Latin
   Root =born; AL—Suffix =relating to
3. a. *post*humous b. *post*script c. *post*graduate
   d. insecti*cide* e. *sub*scrip*tion*

KEY NO. 127

1. monodrama—monogamy—monandry
2. MONOCHORD: MONO (monos)—Greek Prefix =one;
   CHORD—Root =string
3. a. monodrama b. monologue c. monody
   d. monocycle e. monocracy f. monochord

KEY NO. *128*

1. malpractice—malady—malignant—mal de mer
2. MALADROIT: MAL—Prefix =bad; ADROIT—Root = skillful
3. a. 5 b. 4 c. 2 d. 1 e. 3

KEY NO. *129*

This is a self-test.

KEY NO. *130*

1. tabloid(s)—typhoid
2. HELIOID: HELI (helios)—Greek Root =sun; OID—Suffix =like
3. a. 7 b. 1 c. 5 d. 10 e. 3 f. 9 g. 2 h. 6 i. 4
   j. 8

KEY NO. *131*

1. creation—creative—creative(ly)
2. UNCREATIVE: UN—Prefix =not; CREAT (creare)—Latin Root =to create; IVE—Suffix =cause
3. a. creative b. creatures c. recreate d. creator
   e. procreation f. malpractice g. postorbital

KEY NO. *132*

1. misanthrope—philanthropist—philogynist—philadelphy
2. PHILOMUSE: PHILO (philos)—Greek Root =love; MUSE—Root =arts
3. a. 4 b. 7 c. 1 d. 10 e. 9 f. 3 g. 6 h. 8 i. 2
   j. 5

KEY NO. *133*

1. Sophist—philosophy—sophisticate—philosophism
2. PHILOSOPHER: PHIL (philos) Greek Root =love; SOPH (sophos)—Greek Root =wisdom; ER—Suffix =one who
3. soph' o more   Soph' ist   soph i ol' o gist
   so phis ti ca' tion phi lat' e list   phil o den' dron
   cre a' tion al   pro' cre a tor y   an' thro poid.

KEY NO. *134*

1. hypocrisy—hypochondria(c)—hypothesis
2. HYPOMANIA: HYPO—Prefix =less; MANIA—Root =manic excitement
3. a. 2 b. 4 c. 2 d. 3

544

1. synthesis—symphony
2. SYMMETRY: SYM—Prefix =together, with; METR (meter)—Latin Root =measure; Y—Suffix =tending to
3. a. synchronize b. system c. theologian or theologist
   d. hypothesis e. synthesis f. gravitation

1. atheist—theologian—theological—theody
2. THEARCHY: THE (theos)—Greek Root =God; ARCH (archos)—Greek Root =ruler; Y—Suffix =tends to
3. a. 2 b. 3 c. 3 d. 5 e. 1 f. 3 g. 1

This is a self-test.

1. terrorism—totalitarianism—colloquialism(s)
2. ROMANTICISM: ROMANT (romance)—Latin Root = romance; IC—Suffix =like; ISM—Suffix =doctrine
3. a. system b. Stoicism c. totalitarianism
   d. colloquialism

1. subversive—universal—invert
2. OBVERSE: OB—Prefix =against; VERSE (versare)— Latin Root =to turn
3. a. 5 b. 7 c. 1 d. 6 e. 8 f. 2 g. 3 h. 9 i. 10
   j. 4

1. pedestrian—pedal(ing)—pedomotor
2. PEDAL: PED—Prefix =foot; AL—Suffix =relating to
3. a. 1 b. 5 c. 4 d. 3 e. 4

1. tangled—contingency
2. TANGENT: TANG (tangere) Latin Root =to touch; ENT —Suffix =that which

KEY NO. *142*

1. jurisprudence—jurisdiction—justification
2. ADJURE: AD—Prefix =to; JURE (juris)—Latin Root = swear by oath
3. a. *en*throne b. mighti*est* c. *un*restrained d. *be*coming e. *mon*archy f. juris*diction* g. *jur*or

KEY NO. *143*

1. temporary—pro tem—extempore or extemporaneous
2. TEMPORAL: TEMPOR—Root =time; AL—Suffix = relating to
3. a. 5 b. 4 c. 5 d. 5 e. 1

KEY NO. *144*

1. attribute—contributory—tributar(ies)—redistribution
2. DISTRIBUTOR: DIS—Prefix =away; TRIBUT (tributare)—Latin Root =to pay out; OR—Suffix =one who, that which

KEY NO. *145*

1. anarchy—architect
2. ANARCHY: AN—Prefix =not; ARCH (archos)—Greek Root =ruler; Y—Suffix =tending to
3. at' tri bute (n.)   at trib' ute (v.)   ret ri bu' tion
   dis trib' u tor   tac ti' cian   tem' po ral
   en throned'   sea' sons   tem po ra' ne ous
   con tem' po ra ry   ab jur' a to ry   jus ti fi ca' tion
   ad' ju tant   con' jur or   suf fice'

KEY NO. *146*

1. dromedary—hippodrome—hydrodrome
2. HIPPODROME: HIPPO (hippos)—Greek Root =horse; DROME (dromos)—Greek Root =running
3. a. dromedary b. motordrome c. syndrome d. tributary e. attribute f. retribution

KEY NO. *147*

1. alienist—alteration
2. ALTERATION: ALTER—Root =other; TION—Suffix = state of
3. a. *allo*nym b. *ali*bi c. *alter*ation d. *alter*nate e. *in*alien*able* f. *alter*cate

KEY NO. *148*

1. epigrams—epizeuxis
2. ARCHANGEL: ARCH (archos)—Greek Root =rule;
   ANGEL—Root =angel
3. a. 1 b. 1 c. 2 d. 5

KEY NO. *149*

1. *Mariner*—Mare
2. MARINER: MAR (mare)—Latin Root =sea; INE—Suffix
   =relating to; ER—Suffix =one who

KEY NO. *150*

1. dissimilarity—simulated—similize
2. SIMILITUDE: SIMILI (similis)—Latin Root =like;
   TUDE—Suffix =state of
3. a. 9 b. 7 c. 5 d. 1 e. 3 f. 8 g. 2 h. 10
   i. 4 j. 6

KEY NO. *151*

1. seclusion—sequestration—secret
2. SEDUCTIVE: SE—Prefix =aside, apart; DUC (ducere)—
   Latin Root =to lead; IVE—Suffix =cause, make
3. a. mariner b. distinguished c. undistinguished
   d. simultaneously e. engrossed f. utterance

KEY NO. *152*

1. catachresis—catalepsy
2. CATALOGUE: CATA—Prefix =down; LOGUE (logos)
   —Greek Root =word
3. a. 2 b. 3 c. 4 d. 4 e. 5 f. 5

KEY NO. *153*

This is a self-test.

KEY NO. *154*

1. acerbity—acidosis—acidiferous
2. ACIDITY: ACID—Root =sour; ITY—Suffix =quality of
3. a. *acri*monious b. acidi*ferous* c. genu*flection*
   d. *chrono*logically e. a*nomal*y f. miso*gyn*ist g. tra*duce*

547

KEY NO. 155

1. microscope—microaudiphone—micromania
2. MICRODONT: MICRO—Root =very small; DONT—
   Root =tooth
3. sub stan' ti ate   si mul ta' ne ous   sub cu ta' ne ous
   mi crom' e ter   si mul ta' ne ous ly   sim u la' crum
   mar' i time   ma rine'   se ques tra' tion
      mi crol' o gy

KEY NO. 156

1. hydrangea—hydraulic—dehydrate
2. DEHYDRATE: DE—Prefix =away; HYDR (hydros)—
   Greek Root =water; ATE—Suffix =make, cause
3. a. *hydra*ulics b. *hydro*therapy c. *hydro*phobia
   d. *environ*ment e. *psychology* f. *micro*phone
   g. *micro*lith

KEY NO. 157

1. germ—germule—germination—germinative
2. GERMULE: GERM—Root =germ; ULE—
   Suffix =small
3. a. 8 b. 7 c. 5 d. 2 e. 3 f. 1 g. 9 h. 4 i. 10
   j. 6

KEY NO. 158

1. genealogist—generation—genetics
2. GENERAL: GEN (genus)—Latin Root =kind; ER—
   Suffix =that which; AL—Suffix =relating to
3. a. 4 b. 4 c. 5 d. 3 e. 3

KEY NO. 159

1. specimen—spectacular
2. SPECTROMETRY: SPECTRO (spectare)—Latin Root =
   observe; METR (meter)—Root =measure; Y—Suffix =
   tending to

KEY NO. 160

1. stereoscope—stereoscopic
2. STEREOTYPE: STEREO—Greek Root =solid; TYPE—
   Root =fix
3. a. 3 b. 7 c. 10 d. 1 e. 4 f. 8 g. 2 h. 5 i. 6
   j. 9

1. semicivilized—demitone
2. SEMICIRCLE: SEMI—Prefix =half; CIRCLE—Root = circle
3. a. demitone b. resist c. maintain d. semimonthly
   e. dislodge f. pursuing

1. contradicted—indictment—diction—dictator—dictatorial
2. DICTIONARY: DIC (dicere)—Latin Root =to say; TION—Suffix =act of, state of; ARY—Suffix =that which
3. a. contra*dict*ed b. in*dict*er c. in*dict*ment d. *hemi*algia
   e. *hemi*plegia f. *speci*men

1. agitate(d)—agility—demagogue
2. AGENT: AG (agere)—Latin Root =move, go; ENT—Suffix =one who
3. a. 4 b. 5 c. 1 d. 4 e. 5

1. injunction—adjunct—conjunction
2. JUNCTIVE: JUNCT—Root =join; IVE—Suffix =cause to
3. a. to b. with c. away from d. not e. between
   f. under

1. picture—picturedom—picturesque
2. PICTORIAL: PICT (pingere)—Latin Root =to paint; OR—Suffix =one who, that which; AL—Suffix =relating to
3. a. *enjoy*ment b. *endear*ment c. *endow*ment
   d. *enforce*ment e. *enact*ment f. *employ*ment
   g. *em*barrass*ment*

1. liberality—libertinage—liberticide
2. LIBERATE: LIBER (libertas)—Latin Root =free; ATE—Suffix =make
3. a. 4 b. 5 c. 4 d. 1 e. 2 f. 5

KEY NO. 167

This is a self-test.

KEY NO. 168

1. infinite—definitive—finite
2. DEFINE: DE—Prefix =from, away; FIN (finis)—
   Latin Root =end
3. a. *finis* b. in*finit*esimal c. *fin*ite d. de*finit*e e. af*fin*ity
   f. de*fin*e

KEY NO. 169

1. judge—injudicious—judgment—prejudice
2. JUDGMENT: JUDG (judex)—Latin Root =judge;
   MENT—Suffix =state of
3. a. judicate b. judicable c. judicious d. prejudicial
   e. judicative

KEY NO. 170

1. primeval—primitive
2. PRIMARY: PRIM (primus)—Latin Root =first; ARY—
   Suffix =that which
3. a. primo*genit*ure b. *pre*judice c. con*junct*ion d. *fin*ally
   e. de*liver*ed f. dis*simil*arity g. *semi*starva*tion*

KEY NO. 171

1. survival—surveyor—surmise
2. SURFACE: SUR—Prefix =over; FACE—Root =face, top

KEY NO. 172

1. viviparous—vivisepulture—vivisect(ion)
2. VIVEUR: VIV—Latin Root =life; EUR (er)—Suffix =
   one who
3. a. 1 b. 4 c. 5 d. 3 e. 1

KEY NO. 173

1. encyclopedia—cyclic
2. CYCLOID: CYCL (cyclos)—Greek Root =circle, wheel;
   OID—Suffix =like
3. a. 6 b. 9 c. 10 d. 1 e. 7 f. 2 g. 3 h. 4 i. 5
   j. 8

550

KEY NO. *174*

1. intromit(s)—introspection—introvert
2. INTROMIT: INTRO—Prefix =inward; MIT (mitto)—
   Latin Root =send, permit to pass
3. a. introject b. introspection c. introflex
   d. introduction e. introversion f. cycloid

KEY NO. *175*

1. signal—insignificant—signature—signatory
2. SIGNALIZE: SIGN—Root =call attention to; AL—
   Suffix =relating to; IZE—Suffix =make
3. a. esteem b. utility c. reverence d. chink e. cranny
   f. perception g. prudence

KEY NO. *176*

This is a self-test.

KEY NO. *177*

1. lucid—pellucid—luminescent—luminist—elucidate
2. LUCENT: LUC (lucis)—Latin Root =light; ENT—
   Suffix =that which
3. a. lunambulism b. elucidate c. illuminate
   d. translucent e. intelligibility

KEY NO. *178*

1. amphora—amphitheater
2. AMPHITHEATER: AMPHI (amphi)—Greek Prefix =
   both; THEATER (theatron)—Greek Root =theater
3. a. *amphi*bolic b. *amphi*rhina c. *amph*ora
   d. *amphi*logism e. *amphi*vorous f. *amphi*bian

KEY NO. *179*

1. ratify—putrefy—verified
2. TESTIFY: TEST (testis)—Latin Root =bear witness;
   FY—Suffix =make
3. a. 10 b. 7 c. 5 d. 9 e. 2 f. 4 g. 3 h. 1 i. 6
   j. 8

KEY NO. *180*

1. photomicroscope—photograph
2. PHOTOGENIC: PHOTO (photos)—Greek Root =light;
   GEN—Root =suitable for; IC—Suffix =like
3. a. 5 b. 1 c. 2 d. 5

KEY NO. *181*

1. Vulcan—volcano—vulcanist—volcanic
2. VOLCANIST: VOLCAN (Vulcan)—Latin Root =fire; volcano; IST—Suffix =one who
3. e lu' ci date   phot top' a thy
   e lu ci da' tion   am' phi the a ter
   pho to gram' me try   am phib' i an

KEY NO. *182*

1. assumption—presumably—sumptuosity
2. PRESUMPTION: PRE—Suffix =before; SUMP (sumptus)—Latin Root =take; TION—Suffix =act of

KEY NO. *183*

1. euphemism—Eumenides—eugenics
2. EUPHONY: EU—Prefix =pleasing; PHON (phone)— Greek Root =sound; Y—Suffix =inclined to
3. a. euphonious b. eurhythmics c. euharmonic
   d. Eureka! e. eugenics f. photogenic

KEY NO. *184*

1. hemorrhage—hemospasia
2. HEMOID: HEM (haima)—Greek Root =blood; OID— Suffix =resembling
3. a. documentation b. ornamentation c. argumentation
   d. fragmentation e. implementation f. regimentation
   g. supplementation h. segmentation

KEY NO. *185*

1. thermoscope—photoscope
2. HELIOSCOPE: HELIO (helios)—Greek Root =sun; SCOPE (scopos)—Greek Root =watch
3. a. 5 b. 1 c. 5 d. 4 e. 2

KEY NO. *186*

This is a self-test.

KEY NO. *187*

1. proportionate—proportion—apportion(ing)
2. PROPORTION: PRO—Prefix =for; PORTION— Latin Root =part, share
3. a. 4 b. 1 c. 6 d. 7 e. 2 f. 3 g. 5

KEY NO. 188

1. prevention—adventitious
2. CONVENE: CON—Prefix =together; with; VENE
   (venire)—Latin Root =to come
3. a. conventional b. eventually c. intervention
   d. prevention e. disproportionately f. demagogue

KEY NO. 189

1. allocate(d)—dislocation—locate
2. RELOCATE: RE—Prefix =again; LOC (locus)—Latin
   Root =place; ATE—Suffix =make, cause
3. a. *loco*motive b. con*ven*tion c. *ven*turesomeness
   d. *sign*ature e. dis*proportion*ate

KEY NO. 190

1. verify—veritable
2. VERIFIABLE: VERI (verus)—Latin Root =true; FI
   (fy)—Suffix =make; ABLE—Suffix =can do
3. a. 1 b. 5 c. 4 d. 4 e. 3

KEY NO. 191

This is a self-test.

KEY NO. 192

1. enunciation—pronunciation—announcer—announcement
2. RENOUNCE: RE—Prefix =back; NOUNCE
   (nuntiare)—Latin Root =to warn
3. a. denouncing b. announcement c. obloquious
   d. interlocutor e. verification

KEY NO. 193

1. alliteration—alliterative—Transliteration
2. LITERALISM: LITER—Root =letter; word; AL—
   Suffix =relating to; ISM—Suffix =doctrine
3. rep' u ta ble   rep ute'
   con' tem plate   con tem' pla tive
   in ter loc' u to ry   to tal i tar' i an ism
   trans lit er a' tion   il lit' er a cy

553

KEY NO. 194

1. plurality—plurivorous
2. PLURALIZE: PLUR (pluris)—Latin Root =more; AL—
   Suffix =relating to; IZE—Suffix =make
3. a. *plur*ality b. *pluri*lateral c. pluri*syllabic*
   d. plur*ennial* e. *liter*ary f. *pre*text

KEY NO. 195

1. disputatious—reputation—impute
2. DISPUTANTS: DIS—Prefix =away; PUT (putare)—
   Latin Root =to think; ANTS—Suffix =those who
3. a. disputatious b. reputation c. interlocutory
   d. acrimonious e. subversive f. analytically
   g. totalitarianism

KEY NO. 196

1. segregate—segregation—congregate—aggregate
2. SEGREGATE: SE—Prefix =apart; GREG (gregis)—
   Latin Root =crowd; ATE—Suffix =make
3. a. 1 b. 2 c. 4 d. 2 e. 3

KEY NO. 197

This is a self-test.

KEY NO. 198

1. patron—patroon
2. PATERNAL: PATER—Latin Root =father; AL—Suffix =
   relating to
3. a. memorially b. dictatorially c. professorially
   d. peremptorily e. interlocutorily

KEY NO. 199

1. succumb(ed)—encumbrance(s)—incumbency—
   recumbent—accubitum—accubitus
2. SUCCUMB: SUC (sub)—Prefix =under; CUMB
   (cumbere)—Latin Root =lie down
3. The same as the *missing words*, in modern English: The
   Governor, having *succumbed* to the *burdens* of the cam-
   paign to secure his re-election to office, was found *lying
   down on the couch* in his *private office*, peacefully snoring.

KEY NO. 200

1. vicar—vicarage—vicissitudes—vicariously
2. VICAR: VIC (vicis)—Latin Root =substitute; AR—Suffix =one who
3. a. 7 b. 5 c. 6 d. 2 e. 1 f. 3 g. 8 h. 4

KEY NO. 201

1. benevolent—benediction—bonus
2. BONIFY: BON—Root =good; FY—Suffix =make
3. a. 3 b. 2 c. 4 d. 3 e. 1

KEY NO. 202

This is a self-test.

KEY NO. 203

1. object—oppressive—oppose(d)
2. OBJECT: OB—Prefix =against; JECT (jacere)—Latin Root =to throw
3. a. obituary b. obliterate c. bountifully d. succumb
   e. vicariously

KEY NO. 204

1. fumigation—fumish or fumous—fumed
2. FUMIDUCT: FUM (fumus)—Latin Root =smoke; DUCT (ductus)—Latin Root =lead
3. a. fumaciously—furiously b. vivaciously—lively
   c. graciously—with grace d. mendaciously—untruthfully
   e. spaciously—with plenty of space

KEY NO. 205

1. gratified—gratuitous—gratuitous
2. UNGRATEFUL: UN—Prefix =not; GRAT—Root = pleasing; FUL—Suffix =full of
3. a. 5 b. 3 c. 1 d. 2 e. 7 f. 9 g. 6 h. 10 i. 4
   j. 8

KEY NO. 206

1. intramural—intravenous—intracollegiate
2. INTRANATIONAL: INTRA—Prefix =within; NATION—Root =nation; AL—Suffix =relating to
3. a. 1 b. 1 c. 3 d. 5 e. 4

KEY NO. 207

This is a self-test.

KEY NO. 208

1. matrimony—matriarch
2. MATRIARCHATE: MATRI (mater)—Latin Root = mother; ARCH—Root = chief; ATE—Suffix = make
3. a. matroclinous b. matriculation c. turbine
   d. fumigate e. photogenic f. synonyms

KEY NO. 209

1. multiloquent—multiplicity—multigraph
2. MULTILOQUENT: MULTI—Prefix = much; LOQU (loquor)—Latin Root = to speak; ENT—Suffix = one who
3. a. multiloquent b. multiped c. multilateral
   d. multifarious e. multitude

KEY NO. 210

1. Mediocre—mediocrity—mediator
2. MEDIATE: MED (medare)—Latin Root = middle; ATE—Suffix = make, cause
3. a. interMEDiate b. MULTIversant c. MATERnal
   d. INTRAmural e. INTROduction

KEY NO. 211

1. punctuation—unpunctuated—punctual—punctilious
2. PUNCTUATE: PUNCT (punctum)—Latin Root = point, dot; ATE—Suffix = make
3. a. 4 b. 1 c. 3 d. 5 e. 5

KEY NO. 212

This is a self-test.

KEY NO. 213

1. posse—potency—possibility
2. IMPOTENT: IM—Prefix = not; POT (potesse)—Latin Root = have power; ENT—Suffix = one who
3. a. powerless b. efficiency c. possessor d. average
   e. exactness f. melancholy

KEY NO. 214

1. endoscope—endogastric—endoparasite(s)
2. ENDOSCOPE: ENDO (endon)—Root =within;
   SCOPE (scopos)—Root =watch
3. po ten ti al' i ty   im' po tent
   en do cri nol' o gy   en' do crine
   dis' put ants   punc til' i o

KEY NO. 215

This is a self-test.

KEY NO. 216

1. novice—renovated—(in)novation(s)—novantique(s)
2. RENOVATE: RE—Prefix =again; NOV (nova)—Latin
   Root =new; ATE—Suffix =make
3. a. novelistic   b. innovate   c. renovation   d. tolerant
   e. independent   f. misconception

KEY NO. 217

1. complacent—complacency
2. COMPLACENCE: COM (con)—Prefix =with; PLAC
   (placere)—Latin Root =to please; ENCE—Suffix =state
   of
3. dis traught'   am' phi the a ter   mac rol' o gy
   po ten' tial   mac ro bi o' sis   mor ti' cian
   ges tic u la' tion   e vac u ee'   e vac' u a tor

KEY NO. 218

1. fluency—fluviology
2. AFFLUENT: AF (ad) Prefix =to; FLU (fluere)—
   Latin Root =flow; ENT—Suffix =that which
3. a. re*sume*   b. *fluct*uate   c. *flu*ency   d. *ef*fluent
   e. *fluvi*ology

KEY NO. 219

This is a self-test.

KEY NO. 220

1. corpse—corporosity—corporal
2. CORPORIFY: CORPOR (corpus)—Latin Root =body;
   FY—Suffix =make
3. a. corporation   b. (Peace) Corps   c. valorous
   d. dormant

KEY NO. *221*

1. unsaturated—insatiable—saturation
2. SATISFY: SATIS (satio)—Latin Root =enough; FY—Suffix =make
3. Words Recognized: a, b, d, f, l, m, n, p, q
   KEYS recognized: photo, graph, tion, con, ven, ically, de, ate, non, em, ish, ment, pro, ceed, ing, pre, gres

KEY NO. 222

1. vacuum—vacuist—vacuum(s)
2. VACATIONAL: VAC (vacare)—Latin Root =empty; TION—Suffix =act of; AL—Suffix =relating to
3. a. *em*bellish*ment* b. corona*tion* c. *ad*ministra*tion*
   d. typ*ically* e. testi*fy*

KEY NO. 223

1. suggest—digestion
2. GESTANT: GEST (gerere)—Latin Root =to bear, to carry; ANT—Suffix =that which
3. a. 1 b. 2 c. 5 d. 3 e. 3

KEY NO. 224

1. mortal—mortality—remorse
2. IMMORTAL: IM (in)—Prefix =not; MORT (mors)—Latin Root =death; AL—Suffix =relating to

KEY NO. 225

1. macrobiosis—macromania—macrotous—macron
2. MACROMETER: MACRO—Prefix =large; METER—Root =measure
3. a. macrodont b. macrology c. macron d. immortality
   e. mortification

KEY NO. 226

1. magnanimous—magnificence
2. MAGNITUDE: MAGNI (magnus)—Latin Root =great; TUDE—Suffix =condition of
3. a. *ac*complish*ments* b. *age* c. *de*pressed d. *de*fense
   e. *re*development f. suit*able* g. economi*c* h. *grat*ified
   i. *dis*appointed j. *pro*ject k. *pro*mote l. *pot*ential
   m. *fac*ilities n. *ex*pand o. *popul*ar p. *fin*anced
   q. orient*al* r. *intelli*gence s. *de*tachment t. *in*digestion

558

KEY NO. 227

1. megafog—megalomania
2. MEGATHERM: MEGA (megas)—Greek Root =big;
   THERM (thermos)—Greek Root =heat
3. a. loquacity b. melancholy c. megadont d. longevity
   e. boundaries

KEY NO. 228

1. pseudonym—pseudonymal
2. PSEUDONYM: PSEUDO—Prefix =false; NYM—
   Root =name
3. a. 3 b. 1 c. 2 d. 3 e. 1

KEY NO. 229

1. ultramodern—ultramarine
2. ULTRAISM: ULTRA—Prefix =beyond; ISM—Suffix =
   doctrine
3. a. 5 b. 4 c. 1 d. 3

KEY NO. 230

This is a self-test.

KEY NO. 231

1. vested—vest—invests
2. VESTING: VEST (vestire)—Latin Root =an article of
   clothing, material; ING—Suffix =being what it is
3. a. predominant b. exhausted c. stupefy d. luxuriate
   e. consist

KEY NO. 232

1. geosphere—atmosphere—troposphere—stratosphere—
   astrosphere
2. ASTROSPHERE: ASTRO (astra)—Latin Root =star;
   SPHERE (sphaira)—Greek Root =sphere, ball

KEY NO. 233

1. immigrants—emigrants—migratory
2. EMIGRANT: E (ex)—Prefix =out; MIGRA (migrare)—
   Latin Root =to wander; ANT—Suffix =one who
3. a. 1 b. 3 c. 3 d. 2 e. 1

This is a self-test.

1. chromosome(s)—chromium—chromatist
2. CHROMOPHOBIC: CHROMO (chromos)—Greek Root = color; PHOBE (phobia)—Greek Root =fear; IC— Suffix =like
3. a. chromophobic b. chromosome c. eminence
   d. immigrate e. resist

1. hypnotizable—hypnotism—hypnotist—hypnotic
2. HYPNOPHOBIA: HYPNO (hypnos)—Greek Root = sleep; PHOBIA (phobia)—Greek Root =fear
3. a. emigrée b. guns or cannon c. weaken d. royal
   e. somnambulist

1. sanguineous—sanguinaceous or sanguinary
2. SANGUINITY: SANGUIN (sanguis)—Latin Root = bloody; ITY—Suffix =quality of
3. a. * b. * c. * d. *in* e. *cor* f. *pre*

1. Pandemonium—panarchy—panorama—pancreas
2. PANHUMAN: PAN—Root =all; HUM (humus)— Latin Root =earth; AN—Suffix =belonging to
3. a. 1 b. 4 c. 3 d. 2 e. 1

1. filiferous—filigree
2. FILIFORM: FILI (filum)—Latin Root =thread; FORM—Root =form
3. a. 6 b. 10 c. 1 d. 7 e. 9 f. 2 g. 4 h. 3 i. 5
   j. 8

1. diaeresis (··)—diagrams
2. DIAMETER: DIA—Prefix =through; METER—Root = measure

KEY NO. 241

1. calories—calor
2. CALORIGENIC: CALOR—Root =heat; GEN—Root = produce; IC—Suffix =like
3. a. appropriate b. universal c. panegyric d. theory
   e. melancholy, sad, sorrowful

KEY NO. 242

1. civvies—decivilized
2. CIVILITY: CIV (civis)—Latin Root =citizen; IL (al)—Suffix =relating to; ITY—Suffix =quality of
3. a. 5 b. 1 c. 2 d. 4 e. 2

KEY NO. 243

This is a self-test.

KEY NO. 244

1. arrogate—prerogatives—arrogant—abrogate
2. INTERROGATE: INTER—Prefix =between; ROG (rogare)—Latin Root =to ask; ATE—Suffix =make
3. a. dynamite b. dynast c. derogatory d. civicism
   e. caudle

KEY NO. 245

1. orthobiosis—hypochondriasis—hypnosis
2. HYPNOSIS: HYPNO (hypnos)—Greek Root =sleep; OSIS—Suffix =condition
3. a. diminish b. arrogate c. forceful d. interrogate
   e. privilege f. exegesis

KEY NO. 246

This is a self-test.

KEY NO. 247

1. neurasthenia—neurility—neurism—neurological
2. NEUROLOGIST: NEUR (neuron)—Greek Root = nerve; LOG (logos)—Greek Root =word; IST—Suffix = one who
3. a. *neuro*pathic b. *neuro*exairesis c. con*iosis*
   d. pre*rog*ative e. psych*ology*

KEY NO. 248

This is a self-test.

KEY NO. 249

1. osteomancy—osteophone(s)—ossifrage
2. OSTEAL: OSTE (osteo)—Greek Root =bone; AL—
   Suffix =relating to
3. a. osteitis b. osteoporosis c. neogenesis d. neolatry
   e. euphony

KEY NO. 250

1. Anthropology—anthropoid
2. MISANTHROPY: MIS—Prefix =wrong; ANTHROP—
   Greek Root =man; Y—Suffix =tend to
3. a. suf*fic*ient b. *occupa*tion c. *se*clusion d. *co*here
   e. re*sume* f. ophthalm*ia*

KEY NO. 251

1. geophilous—geophagia
2. GEOGLYPHIC: GEO—Root =earth; GLYPH—Root =
   engrave; IC—Suffix =like
3. a. 5 b. 1 c. 2 d. 1

KEY NO. 252

1. hyperbole—Hyperion—hyperpnea
2. HYPERMETER: HYPER—Prefix =beyond; METER—
   Root =measure

KEY NO. 253

1. intuition—intuitionist—intuitively—intuitent
2. TUITIONAL: TUIT (tuitio)—Latin Root =protection,
   teaching; TION—Suffix =act of, state of; AL—Suffix =
   relating to
3. a. hyperbole b. malediction c. surrogate d. intuition
   e. impotent

KEY NO. 254

1. technologist—technocracy—technicality—technocrat
2. HYDROTECHNY: HYDRO (hydros)—Greek Root =
   water; TECHNY (technos)—Greek Root =skill
3. a. *im*mense b. *pri*mary c. di*verse* d. *tuition*
   e. in*stinct* or in*tuition* f. spon*taneous* g. *discern*

562

KEY NO. 255

1. ultimogeniture—primogeniture—penult
2. ULTIMATELY: ULTIM (ultima)—Latin Root =last;
   ATE—Suffix =to make; LY—Suffix =in the manner of
3. a. postpone b. adjacent c. nonessential
   d. interrogation or interrogate

KEY NO. 256

1. pneumoconiosis—pneumatology
2. PNEUMATIC: PNEUMA—Root =breath; IZE—Suffix =
   make
3. a. 2 b. 3 c. 4 d. 3 e. 1

KEY NO. 257

1. lexicographer—sesquipedality

KEY NO. 258

1. Silica—silicam—silicon—silicosis
2. SILICIFEROUS: SILIC—Root =flint; FER (ferre) Root
   =to bear; OUS—Suffix =full of; having
3. phar ma col' o gy   ar' ro gant
   pneu mat o mor' phic   dy nam o gen' e sis
   pla' gi a rist   dy' nast
   su per e rog' a to ry   ca lor' ic
   civ' i lize   ful' mi nate

KEY NO. 259

1. pneumonoconiosis—konimeter—koniology—coniosis

563

INDEX

The number following each key refers to the number of the key. The letter in italics indicates the type of key: *p* =prefix; *s* = suffix; *r* =root.

566